Insolvency Law and Multinational Groups

The insolvency of multinational corporate groups creates a compelling challenge to the commercial world.

As many medium- and large-sized companies are multinational companies with operations in different countries, it is important to provide appropriate solutions for the insolvency of these key market players. This book provides a comprehensive overview of the cross-border insolvency theories, and practical and regulatory solutions for the insolvency of multinational corporate groups. Whilst the book recognizes certain merits of these solutions, it also reveals the limitations and uncertainty that they cause. An analysis of the provisions and tools relating to cross-border insolvency of multinational corporate groups in the new EU Regulation on insolvency proceedings 2015, the UNCITRAL Model Law on cross-border insolvency, the Directive on preventive restructuring frameworks and the Bank Recovery and Resolution Directive 2014, along with a study of directors' duties, are included in this book. It focusses on the insolvency and rescue of non-financial corporate groups. However, it is also important to recognize the similarities and differences between corporate insolvency regimes and bank resolution regimes. In particular, lessons learned from bank resolution practices may be useful for non-financial corporate groups.

This book aims to provide an in-depth examination of the existing solutions for the insolvency of multinational corporate groups. It also aims to view cross-border insolvency of corporate groups within a broad context where all relevant regimes and theories interact with each other. Therefore, directors' duties in the vicinity of insolvency, preventive insolvency proceedings, procedural consolidation, international cooperative frameworks and bank resolution regimes are considered together. This book may appeal to academics, students and practitioners within the areas of corporate law, cross-border insolvency law and financial law.

Daoning Zhang is a lecturer in law at Canterbury Christ Church University, UK; he obtained his PhD in law from the University of Manchester.

Routledge Research in Corporate Law

Available titles in this series include:

Indonesian Company Law
Soonpeel Edgar Chang

Regulation and Inequality at Work
Isolation and Inequality Beyond the Regulation of Labour
Vanisha Sukdeo

Regulation and the Credit Rating Agencies
Restraining Ancillary Services
Daniel Cash

Law and Responsible Supply Chain Management
Contract and Tort Interplay and Overlap
Edited by Vibe Ulfbeck, Alexandra Andhov and Kateřina Mitkidis

Shareholder Primacy and Global Business
Re-clothing the EU Corporate Law
Lela Mélon

Corporate Law, Codes of Conduct and Workers' Rights
Vanisha Sukdeo

Insolvency Law and Multinational Groups
Theories, Solutions and Recommendations for Business Failure
Daoning Zhang

For more information about this series, please visit: https://www.routledge.com

Insolvency Law and Multinational Groups

Theories, Solutions and Recommendations for Business Failure

Daoning Zhang

LONDON AND NEW YORK

First published 2020
by Routledge
2 Park Square, Milton Park, Abingdon, Oxon OX14 4RN

and by Routledge
605 Third Avenue, New York, NY 10017

Routledge is an imprint of the Taylor & Francis Group, an informa business

First issued in paperback 2021

© 2020 Daoning Zhang

The right of Daoning Zhang to be identified as author of this work has been asserted by him in accordance with sections 77 and 78 of the Copyright, Designs and Patents Act 1988.

All rights reserved. No part of this book may be reprinted or reproduced or utilised in any form or by any electronic, mechanical, or other means, now known or hereafter invented, including photocopying and recording, or in any information storage or retrieval system, without permission in writing from the publishers.

Trademark notice: Product or corporate names may be trademarks or registered trademarks, and are used only for identification and explanation without intent to infringe.

Publisher's Note
The publisher has gone to great lengths to ensure the quality of this reprint but points out that some imperfections in the original copies may be apparent.

British Library Cataloguing-in-Publication Data
A catalogue record for this book is available from the British Library

Library of Congress Cataloging-in-Publication Data
Names: Zhang, Daoning, author.
Title: Insolvency law and multinational groups : theories, solutions and recommendations for business failure / Daoning Zhang.
Description: Abingdon, Oxon ; New York, NY : Routledge, 2020. |
Series: Routledge research in corporate law | Based on author's
thesis (doctoral - University of Manchester, 2017) issued under title:
Multinational corporate groups rescue in the EU : theories, solutions and recommendations. | Includes bibliographical references.
Identifiers: LCCN 2019017384 (print) | LCCN 2019018264 (ebook) |
ISBN 9780429288487 (ebk) | ISBN 9780367222017 (hbk)
Subjects: LCSH: Bankruptcy. | International business enterprises—
Law and legislation. | Conglomerate corporations—Law and legislation.
Classification: LCC K1370 (ebook) | LCC K1370 .Z43 2020 (print) |
DDC 346.07/8—dc23
LC record available at https://lccn.loc.gov/2019017384

ISBN 13: 978-0-367-22201-7 (hbk)
ISBN 13: 978-1-03-224073-2 (pbk)
ISBN 13: 978-0-429-28848-7 (ebk)

Typeset in Galliard
by codeMantra

For Xiao Liu

Contents

List of abbreviations	ix
Table of cases	xi
Table of legislation	xiii
Abstract	xvii
Acknowledgement	xix

1	Introduction	1
2	Theoretical basis of corporate rescue and implications on rescue of multinational groups of companies	12
3	Cross-border insolvency theories and procedural consolidation	44
4	Market/hybrid approaches to cross-border insolvency of MCGs in the EU	105
5	Group coordination and planning proceedings	133
6	Directors' duties of corporate groups	165
7	Lessons from financial institution resolutions	171
8	A way forward	197

Bibliography	203
Index	227

List of abbreviations

CoMI	Centre of main interest
EIR	Council regulation (EC) No 1346/2000 of 29 May 2000 on insolvency proceedings
EIR recast	Regulation (EU) 2015/848 of the European Parliament and of the Council of 20 May 2015 on insolvency proceedings (recast)
MCGs	Multinational corporate groups
BRRD	Bank recovery and resolution directive
SRM	Single resolution mechanism
FDIC	Federal Deposit Insurance Corporation
SIFIs	Systemic important financial institutions
OLA	Orderly Liquidation Authority

Table of cases

Apcoa Parking (UK) Ltd, Re [2014] EWHC 997 (Ch).

Barclays Bank Plc v HHY Luxembourg Sàrl [2011] 1 B.C.L.C. 336.

Bray v Ford [1896] AC 44 (HL).

C-339/07 Seagon v Dekomarty Belgium NV 2009.

C-81/87 Daily Mail 1988 ECR 5483.

Cambridge Gas Transportation Corpn v Official Committee of Unsecured Creditors of Navigator Holdings plc and others [2007] 1 A.C. 508.

Case C-167/01 Kamer van Koophandelen Fabriekenvoor Amsterdam v Inspire Art Ltd [2003] ECR I-10155.

Case C-208/00 Überseering BV v Nordic Construction Company Baumanagement GmbH [2002] ECR I-9919.

Case C-210/06 Cartesio Oktato′ Szola′ltato′ bt [2008] ECR I-9641.

Case C-210/06 CartesioOktatóésSzolgáltatóbt [2008] ECR I-9614.

Case C-212/97 Centros Ltd v Erhvervs- ogSelskabsstyrelsen [1999] ECR I-1459.

Charterbridge Corporation Ltd v Lloyds Bank Ltd [1970] Ch 62 (Ch).

Eurofood [2006] Ch.508.

Facia Footwear Ltd, Wisebird Limited (Both in Administration) v Stephen 1997 WL 1102751.

Gebhard v. Consiglio di Milano Case C-55/94 [1995] E.C.R. 4165.

Hans Brochier Holdings Ltd v Exner [2006] EWHC 2594 (Ch) Warren J.

Hellard v Carvalho [2014] B.C.C. 337.

HHY Luxembourg S.A.R.L & Anr v Barclays Bank PLC & Ors [2010] EWHC 2406.

HHY Luxembourg S.A.R.L &Anr v Barclays Bank PLC & Ors [2010] EWHC 2406.

In re Bluebrook [2009] EWHC 2114 (Ch).

In re Eurofood IFSC Ltd [2006] Ch. 508.

In re HIH Casualty and General Insurance Ltd [2008] 1 W.L.R.852.

In re MyTravel Group [2004] EWHC 2741 (Ch).

In re Nortel Networks, Inc, 532 BR 494 (Bankr D Del 2015).

In re Nortel Networks, Inc, 532 BR 494 (Bankr D Del 2015).

In re Stanford International Bank Ltd and another [2010] Bus. L.R. 1270.

In the Matter of Christophorus 3 Limited [2014] EWHC 1162 (Ch).

xii *Table of cases*

In the Matters of Collins & Aikman Europe SA and Others [2006] EWHC 1343 (Ch).

Interedil Srl (in liquidation) v Fallimen to InteredilSrl and another [2012] Bus. L.R. 1582.

La seda de Barcelona SA, re [2010] EWHC 1364 (CH).

Liquidator of West Mercia Safetywear Ltd v Dodd & Anor. (1988) 4 B.C.C. 30.

MPOTEC GmbH [2006] B.C.C. 681.

Percival v Wright [1902] Ch 421 (Ch).

Polly Peck International Plc (In Administration) (No. 4), Re [1996] 1 B.C.L.C. 428.

Primacom Holding GmbH v A Group of the Senior Lenders & Credit Agricole [2011] EWHC 3746 (Ch) [2013] B.C.C. 201.

Public Prosecutor v Segard [2006] (As Administrator for Rover France SAS) I.L.Pr. 32.

Re Bluebrook Ltd [2010] B.C.C. 209.

Re Daisytek-ISA Ltd [2004] B.P.I.R. 30.

Re Hellas Telecommunications [2009] EWHC 3199 (Ch) p. 4.

Re HLC Environmental Projects Ltd (in liq.).

Re Magyar Telecom BV [2013] EWHC 3800 (Ch).

Re Marini Ltd Liquidator of Marini Ltd v Dickenson & Ors [2004] B.C.C. 172.

Re MG Rover Espana SA [2006] B.C.C. 599.

Re Nortel Networks SA [2009] EWHC 206 (Ch).

Re Pantone 485 Ltd [2002] 1 BCLC 266.

Re Rodenstock GmbH [2011] EWHC 1104 (Ch).

Re Southern Countries Fresh Foods Ltd [2008] EWHC 2810 (Ch).

Re Stanford [2010] EWCA Civ 137.

Re Transbus International Ltd [2004] EWHC 932 (Ch) Chancery Division.

Re Zlomrex International Finance SA [2013] EWHC 3866 (Ch).

Sequana S.A. v Bat Industries Plc, Windward Prospects Limited, Selarl C. Basse [2019] EWCA Civ 112.

Trustees of Olympic Airlines SA Pension & Life Assurance Scheme v Olympic Airlines SA [2013] EWCA Civ 643.

Trustees of the Olympic Airlines SA Pension & Life Assurance Scheme v Olympic Airlines SA [2015] UKSC 27.

Westpac Banking Corporation v Bell Group Ltd (in liq.) [No. 3] (2012) WASCA 157.

Table of legislation

Act for the Further Facilitation of the Restructuring of Companies ESUG 2012.
Banking Act 2009 Part 1.
Company Act 2006 s. 175(5) 171–177.
Council Regulation (EC) No. 1346/2000 of 29 May 2000 on insolvency proceedings.
Council Regulation (EC) No. 139/2004 of 20 January 2004 on the control of concentrations between undertakings (the EC Merger Regulation).
Directive 2000/12/EC of the European Parliament and of the Council of 20 March 2000 relating to the taking up and pursuit of the business of credit institutions Art.1(6).
Directive 2001/24/EC of the European Parliament and of the Council of 4 April 2001 on the reorganization and winding up of credit institutions. Art.3(1) Art.3(2).
Directive 2006/43/EC of the European Parliament and of the Council of 17 May 2006 on statutory audits of annual accounts and consolidated accounts, amending Council Directives 78/660/EEC and 83/349/EEC and repealing Council Directive 84/253/EEC.
Directive 2013/34/EU of the European Parliament and of the Council of 26 June 2013 on the annual financial statements, consolidated financial statements and related reports of certain types of undertakings, amending Directive 2006/43/EC of the European Parliament and of the Council and repealing Council Directives 78/660/EEC and 83/349/EEC.
Directive 2014/59/EU of the European Parliament and of the Council of 15 May 2014 establishing a framework for the recovery and resolution of credit institutions and investment firms and amending Council Directive 82/891/EEC, and Directives 2001/24/EC, 2002/47/EC, 2004/25/EC, 2005/56/EC, 2007/36/EC, 2011/35/EU, 2012/30/EU and 2013/36/EU, and Regulation (EU) Nos. 1093/2010 and 648/2012, of the European Parliament and of the Council Text with EEA relevance (BRRD) Art.38(1) 44(3).
Directive (2019) of the European Parliament and of the Council on preventive restructuring frameworks, on discharge of debt and disqualifications, and on measures to increase the efficiency of procedures concerning restructuring, insolvency and discharge of debt, and amending Directive (EU) 2017/1132 (Directive on restructuring and insolvency).

xiv *Table of legislation*

Directive 69/335/EEC of 17 July 1969.

Directors' obligations in the period approaching insolvency: enterprise groups, Working Group V, United Nations Commission on International Trade Law. A/CN.9/WG.V/WP.153.

European Parliament legislative resolution of 28 March 2019 on the proposal for a Directive of the European Parliament and of the Council on preventive restructuring frameworks, second chance and measures to increase the efficiency of restructuring, insolvency and discharge procedures and amending Directive 2012/30/EU (COM(2016)0723 – C8-0475/2016 – 2016/0359(COD)).

Enterprise Act 2002.

Environmental Protection Act 1990.

FDIA 11(n)(1)(A).

FSB Key Attributes of Effective Resolution Regimes for Financial Institutions (2014) para. 3.2–3.6.

Insolvency Act 1986, Art.213, 214, 246ZB.

Proposal for a Directive of the European Parliament and of the Council on preventive restructuring frameworks, second chance and measures to increase the efficiency of restructuring, insolvency and discharge procedures and amending Directive 2012/30/EU, 12536/18.

Recommendation 1 of Basel Committee on Banking Supervision Report and Recommendations of the Cross-Border Bank Resolution Group (2010).

Regulation (EU) 2015/848 of the European Parliament and the Council of 20 May 2015 on insolvency proceedings (recast).

Regulation (EU) No. 806/2014 of the European Parliament and of the Council of 15 July 2014 establishing uniform rules and a uniform procedure for the resolution of credit institutions and certain investment firms in the framework of a single resolution mechanism and a single resolution fund and amending Regulation (EU) No. 1093/2010(SRM) Art.24(1) 27(5) SRM Regulation.

Statement of practice 16 issued on 01 November 2015 by R3: Association of Business Recovery Professionals.

The CRD IV Directive (2013/36/EU) Directive 2013/36/EU of the European Parliament and of the Council of 26 June 2013 on access to the activity of credit institutions and the prudential supervision of credit institutions and investment firms, amending Directive 2002/87/EC and repealing Directives 2006/48/EC and 2006/49/EC. Art.28(2).

The MiFID II Directive (2014/65/EU).

The Securities Investor Protection Act of 1970.

The Solvency II Directive (2009/138/EC).

The Treaty on the Functioning of the European Union (2007).

Title 11 U.S. Code s. 541(a) s. 507 and s. 726. s. 1129.

UK Corporation Tax Act 2010 Part 5 Group Relief Chapter 1 section 152.

UNCITRAL Model Law on cross-border insolvency 1997.

United Nations Commission on International Trade Law Working Group V (Insolvency Law) Fifty-third session, Facilitating the cross-border insolvency of enterprise groups: draft legislative provisions A/CN.9/WG.V/WP.158 2018, Art 2.

US Code Title 11 Bankruptcy Chapter 11 1978.

Abstract

This book is a study on theories and solutions for the cross-border insolvency of multinational corporate groups, with particular reference to the EU regulation on insolvency proceedings recast 2015 (EIR recast). In this book, the author also briefly considers bank resolution regime for financial institutions as a special type of multinational corporate group on the basis of Bank Recovery and Resolution Directive. The book reveals the difficulties arising from separate corporate personality and unharmonized insolvency laws, and it argues that the classic aims of insolvency law – maximization of value for creditors and certainty of insolvency rules – are difficult to achieve. For financial corporate groups, uncooperative bank resolution may even give rise to systemic risks.

The aim of this book is to examine the existing solutions for the cross-border insolvency of multinational corporate groups on the basis of a combination of insolvency law/cross-border insolvency law theories and multinational enterprises theories. The existing solutions for non-financial corporate groups include substantive consolidation, procedural consolidation, market/hybrid legal solutions and the EIR recast which unprecedentedly provides 'group coordination proceedings' to respond to this issue. For financial corporate groups, the recent Bank Recovery and Resolution Directive which harmonized resolution tools in the EU for financial institutions and the US experience will be examined.

Acknowledgement

I would like to thank the following journals for allowing me to use my previous publications in this book:

Zhang, D. 'A Recommendation to Improve the Opt-Out Mechanism in the EU Regulation on Insolvency Proceedings Recast' (2017) *International Company and Commercial Law Review* 5 167–175.

Zhang, D. 'Preventive Restructuring Frameworks: A Possible Solution for Financially Distressed Multinational Corporate Groups in the EU' (2019) *European Business Organization Law Review.* doi:10.1007/s40804-018-0125-3; T.M.C. Asser Press.

Zhang, D. 'Reconsidering Procedural Consolidation for Multinational Corporate Groups in the Context of the Recast European Insolvency Regulation' (2017) *International Insolvency Review* 26 (3) 241–357.

1 Introduction

Background and the value of this study

European countries' slow economic growth rates and a record number of insolvency cases have made the EU Commission call for a reform of insolvency laws at both the national and the EU level, with an aim to mitigate further losses to creditors and stakeholders. The EU Commission's current political priority is to promote economic recovery and sustainable growth as well as a higher investment rate and the preservation of employment, as listed in the Europe 2020 strategy for jobs and growth. To achieve this task, the EU believes that a rescue-friendly culture of insolvency law will help to facilitate economic recovery.[1] As part of the new Europe 2020 strategies, a new EU Regulation on insolvency proceedings (EIR Recast),[2] focusing on the tasks of saving the economically healthy but financially distressed business, has come into force.[3] The European Commission believes that the benefits of business rescue include, among other things, maximization of assets, higher recovery rate to creditors and saved jobs.[4] Also, the EIR Recast unprecedentedly provides a new mechanism for the rescue of groups of companies: the group coordination proceedings.[5] This may be seen as a milestone, which reveals that the European Commission has acknowledged the necessity of rescuing cross-border groups of companies.

---

1 Commission staff working document executive summary of the impact assessment – accompanying the document-commission recommendation on a new approach to business failure and insolvency SWD (2014) 62 final, p. 2.

2 Regulation (EU) 2015/848 of the European Parliament and the Council of 20 May 2015 on insolvency proceedings (EIR Recast 2015).

3 Ibid., Recital 10.

4 The Commission has acknowledged that the benefits of business rescue, among other things, including maximization of assets, preservation of goodwill and know-how), higher recovery rates for creditors (e.g. average French liquidation proceedings recovery rate 31% vs rescue proceedings recovery rate 96%) and saving jobs. The main policy is aimed at encouraging economic growth. The commission staff working document impact assessment, accompanying the document Revision of Regulation (EC) No. 1346/2000 on insolvency proceedings SWD(2012) 416 final, p. 7, p. 11, are available at ec.europa.eu/justice/civil/files/insolvency-ia_en.pdf.

5 EIR Recast 2015, Chapter V, Section 2.

2 Introduction

The scope of new EU Regulation on insolvency proceedings has also been expanded; it now encompasses a variety of rescue-oriented proceedings of member states.[6] Many member states recently updated and reformed their insolvency law to facilitate corporate rescue. In the UK, the Cork Report first stressed the rescue culture and elucidated that the aim of rescue should consider a broader scope of interests.[7] The Enterprise Act 2002 placed corporate rescue as the foremost goal for administrators to fulfil. On 22 September 2011, the Spanish Congress passed the reform of insolvency law, which provides pre-insolvency solutions that aim to prevent insolvency.[8] Germany introduced its reformed insolvency procedures – 'ESUG' – on 1 March 2012 for the purpose of pursuing stable economic policy and preserving jobs, thus benefiting the public.[9] France also approved a deep reform to its insolvency law, which encompasses the pre-insolvency proceedings, accelerated financial safeguard proceedings, safeguard proceedings and restructuring proceedings.[10] All these examples imply that the EU has entered an era of corporate rescue at both the EU and the national level.

The 2007–2008 world financial crisis pushed many countries into recession. The collapse of financial corporate groups during the crisis included, but was not limited to, some big names: Lehman Brothers and Northern Rock. The most recent financial distress faced by many Italian banks also draws attention to the importance of financial corporate groups and the effectiveness of bank resolution regimes. Therefore, parallel to the development of non-financial corporate insolvency law in the EU, the recent Bank Recovery and Resolution Directive (BRRD),[11] together with Single Resolution Mechanism Regulation,[12] in response to the Financial Stability Board and Basel Committee's recommendations, set up financial resolution tools at the EU level. In particular, both legislations contain resolution rules for financial corporate groups.

---

6 EIR Recast 2015, Article 1.

7 Report of the Review Committee on Insolvency Law and Practice (1982) Cmnd 8558, p. 204.

8 Bernardino Muñiz, 'New restructuring regime in Spain' (2012) *Eurofenix Spring*, p. 1.

9 The new features, among other things, include a three-month cap on the time limit, which aims to urge that a viable restructuring plan of a financially distressed company could be submitted early by the debtor. Also, interim protection order may be made by the court to prevent creditors from interrupting the restructuring plan during such a period. Gerret Höher, 'ESUG: German for 'Modernising Bankruptcy Law' (2012) *Eurofenix Spring*, p. 19.

10 Jean-Luc Vallens, 'Reforms planned in France' (2014) *Eurofenix Spring*, p. 26.

11 Directive 2014/59/EU of the European Parliament and of the Council of 15 May 2014 establishing a framework for the recovery and resolution of credit institutions and investment firms, and amending Council Directive 82/891/EEC, and Directives 2001/24/EC, 2002/47/EC, 2004/25/EC, 2005/56/EC, 2007/36/EC, 2011/35/EU, 2012/30/EU and 2013/36/EU, and Regulations (EU) No. 1093/2010 and (EU) No. 648/2012, of the European Parliament and of the Council Text with EEA relevance.

12 Regulation (EU) No. 806/2014 of the European Parliament and of the Council of 15 July 2014, establishing uniform rules and a uniform procedure for the resolution of credit institutions and certain investment firms in the framework of a Single Resolution Mechanism and a Single Resolution Fund, and amending Regulation (EU) No. 1093/2010.

Introduction 3

Undoubtedly, both non-financial corporate groups and financial corporate groups play important roles in the commercial world. On the macro level, the insolvency of large corporate groups has a far-reaching impact on the European economy. Large corporate groups account for 30% of the jobs in the EU and 41% of the gross added value.[13] Financial groups, such as banks, directly supply money to the real economy and provide a payment system for everyone. On the micro level, large multinational European corporate groups typically operate through the network of subsidiaries[14]; thus, when parent companies or subsidiaries face financial difficulties, the other companies in the same group may also suffer.[15] This shows that it is important to have desirable group solutions. A classic example is the insolvency of KPNQwest N.V.,[16] which has subsidiaries in many member states. As a telecom company, the value of the whole business relies on the integration of its underground cables in different member states. Due to lack of cross-border insolvency solutions, in KPNQwest N.V., multiple insolvency proceedings were inevitable, and therefore the value of the whole business was dissipated. This shows that it is important to provide cross-border insolvency solutions for multinational corporate groups (MCGs).

This book sets the EU Regulation on insolvency proceedings (EIR Recast) as the main target of study.[17] One particular feature of this Regulation is that it introduced a new 'group coordination proceeding' that is the first type of proceeding concerning cross-border cooperation in the area of insolvency law of MCGs.[18] Resolution theories and tools for financial corporate groups will be examined at the end of this book. This study does not aim to provide a comprehensive analysis of all relevant bank resolution rules. It simply aims to provide a better understanding of both areas of rules through a comparison of theories and tools for corporate insolvency law and financial institution resolution.

The author is aware of the Brexit incidence, but how much impact it will have on the EU remains to be seen. If the UK leaves the EU, it may mean that EIR

---

13 Commission staff working document executive summary of the impact assessment – accompanying the document-commission recommendation on a new approach to business failure and insolvency SWD(2014) 61 final, p. 20.

14 Ibid., p. 20.

15 Commission staff working document executive summary of the impact assessment – accompanying the document-commission recommendation on a new approach to business failure and insolvency SWD(2014) 62 final, p. 2.

16 Different functions of operations and assets of KPNQwest group are located in different European member states. M. Natasha Labovitz and Jessica I. Basil, 'How Will New Chapter 15 Affect Multinational Restructurings?' (2005) *New York Law Journal*, p. 2; Robert Van Galen, 'The European Insolvency Regulation and Groups of Companies' (2003) INSOL Europe Annual Congress, Cork, Ireland, pp. 16–18.

17 The new EU regulation on insolvency proceedings, which was drafted in 2015 and came into effect in 2017, introduces a group coordination proceeding for group insolvency. EIR Recast embodies cross-border insolvency law in the EU, which is designed to allocate insolvency law jurisdiction and choice of law, and set recognition and enforcement rules among member states.

18 Gerard McCormack, 'Something Old, Something New: Recasting the European Insolvency Regulation' (2016) *The Modern Law Review* 79(1) 102–146.

4   *Introduction*

Recast will not be applicable to the UK unless there is a new agreement between the UK and the EU.[19] As the cross-border insolvency solutions of MCGs are important to both the UK and the EU, it would be desirable to see an agreement with similar functions being drafted.

This section has introduced the importance of cross-border corporate groups against a broad background. The next section will analyse the main issues and difficulties in liquidating or rescuing MCGs.

Issues and difficulties of MCG insolvency and resolution

Cross-border insolvency of MCGs[20] is a relatively new research topic, and it is the point where private international law, insolvency law, bank resolution and multinational enterprises theories meet. Academics and insolvency practitioners propose and design either theoretical solutions or pragmatic solutions for the insolvency or rescue of MCGs. It is argued that solutions for non-financial cross-border insolvency of MCGs may include private/hybrid legal solutions,[21] substantive consolidation, procedural consolidation and procedural cooperation.[22] For financial corporate groups whose collapse may lead to systemic risks, a separate set of rules, termed 'resolution rules', are applied.

Arguably, non-financial and financial corporate groups face similar difficulties when it comes to cross-border insolvency and rescue, which will be examined below.

The first difficulty is that most of the national and cross-border insolvency law regimes focus on individual entities rather than corporate groups. Without a well-developed framework for corporate groups, the success of rescue and insolvency of MCGs depends only on the effectiveness of ad hoc solutions provided by insolvency practitioners. The problem is that one cannot predict the result of

19 One main effect following Brexit may be that the insolvency proceedings that are opened in the UK will not enjoy automatic recognition by other courts of EU member states. Chris Birch and Victoria Procter, 'Brexit – implications for the UK restructuring and insolvency market' 2016, at www.eversheds.com/documents/services/commercial/Brexit-implications-for-UK-restructuring-and-insolvency-market.pdf, p. 4; Ken Baird *et al.*, 'Brexit: What Does It Mean for Restructuring and Insolvency?' 2016, at www.law.ox.ac.uk/business-law-blog/blog/2016/07/brexit-what-does-it-mean-restructuring-and-insolvency; another is that EIR Recast introduces a group coordination proceeding as a framework for MNCs. The UK may not be able to use this coordination framework after Brexit. All these may make the UK less popular as a restructuring and insolvency jurisdiction than before.

20 MCGs are the main research target in this thesis. It means a group of companies that conduct business in more than one member state in the EU. The thesis chose corporate groups as the target because companies have their independent legal status, which creates particular challenges in cases of cross-border insolvency law. Each member company may have its own creditors and assets; each subsidiary may be subject to a different insolvency jurisdiction. This thesis aims to deal with these issues.

21 Private solutions rely on contracts; creditors and debtors may renegotiate a new deal, such as a debt waiver, to avoid triggering insolvency proceedings. Hybrid legal solutions are a combination of private solutions and legal solutions, such as pre-pack sale of business.

22 Robert van Galen, 'Insolvent groups of companies in cross border cases and rescue plan' (2012) Report to the Netherlands Association for Comparative and International Insolvency Law.

Introduction 5

insolvency of a cross-border corporate group; neither can one be sure whether the value of a group can be preserved in non-financial corporate group cases nor whether a systemic risk can be controlled in financial corporate group cases.

The second difficulty comes from unharmonized insolvency law in different member states. This issue is twofold. First, different values and laws make it almost impossible for member states to cooperate with each other as one member state may not be happy with the treatment of other member states under a different set of rules.[23] Second, the insolvency law of some member states may not be effective in saving a failed corporate group. Therefore, they need to be equipped with effective insolvency law tools.

The third difficulty arises from a lack of effective international cooperative framework. Since MCGs operate across borders, it is almost inevitable that different national courts and private parties need to cooperate with each other. However, the question to dwell on is whether we have an effective cooperative framework. This third obstacle has been gradually resolved along with the most recent development in the cross-border insolvency law field. EIR Recast provides a group coordination proceeding. The UNCITRAL Model Law also provides a group planning proceeding. The BRRD provides a framework where national supervisory and resolution authorities need to cooperate. A single-point-of-entry mechanism is suggested to deal with cross-border insolvency of financial institutions.

Aims and structure of the book

Aims of the book

The aim of this book is to explore and examine effective solutions for the cross-border insolvency of groups of companies in the EU, with a focus on non-financial corporate groups. This main objective can be divided into three sub-objectives: (1) analysing theories of corporate rescue law, cross-border insolvency law and multinational enterprise theories; (2) analysing existing solutions of cross-border MCGs' rescue; and (3) seeking lessons from bank resolution regimes by offering a comparison between non-financial and financial corporate group insolvency regimes.

Three tasks will be conducted in order:

a   The first task is theoretical, and the aim is to examine what values we expect to embrace and how they should be balanced. Insolvency law and cross-border insolvency law aim to preserve values and provide predictable rules for creditors. This conclusion paves a theoretical ground for further analysis of different practical solutions for cross-border corporate rescue of MCGs.

---

23 For example, a MCG may consist of subsidiaries in more than one member state, and each member company may have its own assets and creditors subject to a different set of national insolvency rules. Creditors may not necessarily agree on a joint group rescue plan when the groups enter into insolvency in differing jurisdictions. Under these circumstance, how to maximize the group value and how to provide rules with certainty are issues that need to be resolved.

6   *Introduction*

The author would like to explore how insolvency law theories, groups of companies theories and cross-border insolvency law theories collectively respond to cross-border insolvency of MCGs. The book examines MCGs with reference to multinational enterprise theories. In particular, it considers MCGs from a new perspective: the business network perspective. This perspective sees MCGs as a network through which resources and information can be transferred. It argues that they may have group going concern value regarding the relationships among member companies. For the purpose of achieving the goals of insolvency law theories and cross-border insolvency law theories, it is desirable to preserve the relationships between member companies in MCGs.

However, the goal of value preservation needs to be balanced with the goal of certainty. For the purpose of gaining group going concern value in a given MCG, certain head office functions have to be allocated at the subsidiary level. This may have implications on the insolvency jurisdiction rule – centre of main interest (CoMI) – which is defined as the place where the head office functions are carried out. Therefore, one should respect not only the legal independent identity of group members (each has its own creditors and assets) but also each subsidiary's insolvency jurisdiction.

b   The second task is to examine the effectiveness of the existing solutions of cross-border insolvency for groups of companies – procedural consolidation, market/hybrid legal solutions and procedural cooperation and coordination – whereby the effectiveness will be measured by the aforementioned theories. In particular, the task is to examine whether the existing solutions can preserve group going concern value and provide certainty. With the insight gained from analysis of theories, this book first aims to contribute to the existing literature by considering whether the hotly debated procedural consolidation can be a reliable solution. The book argues that there is considerable uncertainty about allocating insolvency jurisdiction of the group members into one court, such as the group CoMI approach.[24] The goal of certainty may indicate that procedural consolidation can only be applied in limited cases.

Some market/hybrid legal solutions may avoid group-wide insolvency through a renegotiation of debt agreements or a pre-pack sale. If the capital structure of a given insolvent company and the terms of its debt instruments allow these solutions to be executed, then the solutions are desirable as they preserve the group going concern value, based on consensual agreement or clear cramdown tools. Nonetheless, the book also identifies the limitations of market/hybrid legal solutions. For example, the fragmented categories of debts and creditors cause significant challenges to private solutions. Also, where the debts

---

24 See Chapters 3 and 4.

are not arranged by holding companies, and the profiles of creditors in diverse subsidiaries are different, parties may not be able to avoid a group-wide insolvency by modifying their loan agreements. As in the latter cases, creditors of different profiles may not be subject to a joint inter-creditor agreement. Also, the drawbacks of a pre-pack sale may not always provide creditors with a high level of recovery.

In light of the drawbacks and limitations of the above-mentioned solutions, the book argues that the group coordination proceedings in the EIR Recast may play a role in filling this gap. However, the current EIR Recast group coordination proceeding has a notable weakness: namely, the opt-out mechanism. Such a rule could be invoked without limitation, allowing subsidiaries to be pulled out of a group plan, or without even considering the group plan. This is particularly true as senior creditors may control the subsidiaries by providing refinancing or buying debt from the debt market so that it is possible for them to control certain important subsidiaries and hold out or conduct a fire sale without cooperation from other group companies. The book considers the option of harmonization of insolvency law in the EU as a way to fix the drawbacks of national law and facilitate cooperation. However, due to the significant difficulties in doing so, the book opts for a modest option.

Based on the conclusion examined in the first task, the book also argues that it is difficult to achieve the goal of preservation of group going concern value in light of the opt-out mechanism. As a result, the book makes an original modest recommendation of group coordination proceedings by providing that EIR Recast provisions need to create an atmosphere that encourages parties to consider a group rescue plan. This can be done by interpreting Article 56 and Recital 58 in the EIR Recast as a limitation on the invocation of the opt-out mechanism. The requirement can be obtained as a purposive way of interpreting the existing provisions of EIR.

c   The third task is to draw lessons from financial corporate groups' resolution regimes. Traditional cross-border insolvency law does not apply to financial institutions as the latter deserve a separate regime to prevent systemic risks to the real economy. The author will examine the bank resolution theory and solutions in light of non-financial corporate group insolvency law. Differences and similarities between both regimes can be found. By determining these, a deep understanding of both regimes for financial and non-financial corporate groups can be achieved.

Structure of this book

Chapter 1 is the introductory chapter of this book, which explains the significance of the research question, aims and structure. The purpose of Chapter 2 is to explore the rationale of corporate rescue law and the theories of MCGs. It then examines the implications of corporate rescue law on the insolvency of MCGs. Without understanding the purposes of corporate rescue law, it is difficult to

8 Introduction

know the goals that a desirable solution for insolvency of MCGs should pursue. Chapter 2 introduces key concepts, such as financially distressed companies and going concern value. It also explores the raison d'être of corporate insolvency law – preservation of going concern value of the distressed business. Additionally, it engages in a discussion of theories of corporate rescue law and argues that its goals should be preservation of going concern value and certainty. The chapter finally examines the multinational enterprise theories and concludes that MCGs may have group going concern value in terms of the relationships between member companies; this value should be preserved. On the other hand, the independent legal personality of group member companies and their respective insolvency jurisdiction should be respected due to the certainty requirement.

Chapter 3 examines all cross-border insolvency law theories with a focus on an analysis of procedural consolidation. Among other solutions, procedural consolidation has attracted great attention as the potential solution for cross-border insolvency of MCGs.[25] Procedural consolidation is a solution proposed for cross-border insolvency of MCGs; it aims to allow the whole group to come to one court to resolve cross-border insolvency issues.

To examine the desirability of procedural consolidation, the chapter starts from a classic dichotomy of cross-border insolvency theories – territorialism and universalism. Universalism supporters believe that the insolvency of one company should be subject to only one court and one set of insolvency rules – the law of CoMI of the company. By comparison, territorialism supporters assert that any court where the assets of the distressed companies are located can exert insolvency jurisdiction. For the purpose of understanding which paradigm can offer better certainty, Chapter 3 discusses the issue of forum shopping and the vulnerability of the CoMI to forum shopping.

By analysing the abilities of the two paradigms along the lines of preservation of value and predictability, a conclusion can be drawn that universalism has advantages over territorialism. Universalism is increasingly gaining support. EIR Recast adopts the concept of CoMI as the insolvency jurisdiction rule of companies in the EU. According to the statutory and case definition, CoMI means the place where the head office functions of a company are carried out.

Procedural consolidation, based on universalism and the concept of group CoMI, allows the insolvency proceeding of all group members to open in a single jurisdiction. One contribution of the book is that, by using resource-based theory, knowledge-based theory, resource dependence theory and business network theory, the chapter analyses the relationships between the parent company

---

25 Irit Mevorach 'The "Home Country" of a Multinational Enterprise Group Facing Insolvency' (2008) *International & Comparative Law Quarterly* 57 427–448; Irit Mevorach, 'Cross-Border Insolvency Law of Enterprise Groups: The Choice of Law Challenge' (2014) *Brooklyn Journal of Corporate, Financial & Commercial Law* 9 107; Edward J. Janger, 'Universal Proceduralism' (2006–2007) *Brooklyn Journal of International Law* 32 819; Samuel L. Bufford, 'Coordination of Insolvency Cases for International Enterprise Groups: A Proposal' (2012) *American Bankruptcy Law Journal* 86 685.

Introduction 9

and its subsidiaries. The business network perspective particularly discusses the allocation of head office functions between subsidiaries and the parent company, which, in turn, affects the jurisdiction of insolvency proceedings of companies under the EU Regulation. The business network perspective[26] is relevant in that large European corporate groups typically operate through the network of subsidiaries.[27] It could lend itself to this question by analysing the control thereof. It is one thing if one subsidiary in the group is influenced by its parent company and other group members; it is another thing if such a subsidiary may also be delegated head office functions and have the ability to affect others. The implication is that group CoMI concept may be problematic due to its uncertainty and its inconsistency with the reality of the situation.

Other proposed cross-border insolvency theories for MCGs generally aim to achieve procedural consolidation by assigning jurisdiction to the court of group CoMI in an ex ante way. Cooperative territorialism (which argues that every court should have jurisdiction over all the assets in its territory), modified universalism (which enunciates that the court that possesses the CoMI of the group should have jurisdiction) and universal proceduralism (similar to modified universalism, arguing that insolvency jurisdiction should be allocated to the group CoMI; the substantive insolvency law of one group member should be the law where its individual CoMI is located, that is, to mitigate the contradiction between the court where the group CoMI is situated and the court where the individual CoMI is situated) are examined, in turn. The existing literature generally assumes it is desirable to centralize the insolvency proceedings of group member companies: for example, into one court. These solutions mainly focus on cross-border insolvency jurisdictional rules; it is generally believed that procedural consolidation can achieve a successful group reorganization result. However, the existing cross-border insolvency law literature may ignore the multinational enterprise theories regarding the value of MCGs and how they obtain such value. Without understanding the characteristics of MCGs, it is difficult to examine any proposed cross-border insolvency solutions for them. This

---

26 Mats Forsgren *et al.*, 'Managing the Embedded Multinational – A Business Network View' (Edward Elgar 2006); Jeffrey H. Dyer and Harbir Singh, 'The Relational View: Cooperative Strategy and Sources of Inter-organisational Competitive Advantage' (1998) *The Academy of Management Review* 23(4) 660–679; Bernard Surlemont, 'A Typology of Centres within Multinational Corporations: An Empirical Investigation', in J. Birkinshaw and N. Hood (eds.), *Multinational Corporate Evolution and Subsidiary Development* (Macmillan Press 1998); Mats Forsgren, *Theories of the Multinational Firm* (2nd edn, Edward Elgar 2013); Ulf Andersson, Mats Forsgren and Ulf Holm, 'Balancing Subsidiary Influence in the Federative MNC: A Business Network View' (2007) *Journal of International Business Studies* 38(5) 802–818; Håkansson and Ivan Snehota, *Developing Relationships in Business Networks*' (Routledge 1995); Kirsten Foss and others, 'MNC Organisational Form and Subsidiary Motivation Problems: Controlling Intervention Hazards in the Network of MNC' (2011) <available at: http://ssrn.com/abstract=1969402>.

27 Commission staff working document executive summary of the impact assessment – accompanying the document-commission recommendation on a new approach to business failure and insolvency SWD(2014) 61 final, p. 20.

10 *Introduction*

book tries to fill this gap. It examines the three main solutions for cross-border insolvency of MCGs in light of a combination of insolvency law theories, multinational enterprise theories and cross-border insolvency law theories. The result is that the proposed cross-border insolvency group theories invariably rely on a group CoMI approach which brings in too much uncertainty. The most viable solution may arguably be the modified universalism; meanwhile, cooperation and coordination between courts and insolvency practitioners should be enhanced. By contrast, certain ex post means of procedural consolidation by interpretation of CoMI or forum shopping are also discussed. The conclusion is that procedural consolidation may only be applied in limited cases.

Chapter 4 examines the market/hybrid legal solutions and protocols for cross-border insolvency of MCGs. The aim of this chapter is to assess whether the market/hybrid legal solutions have provided desirable solutions to the cross-border insolvency of groups of companies. It shows that market and contracts cannot completely replace insolvency rescue tools due to market failure and hold-out issues. Different from procedural consolidation which relies on insolvency jurisdiction rules, market/hybrid legal solutions focus on the renegotiation of debt agreements or the transfer of the whole business to senior creditors. This may provide the advantage of keeping the relationships within MCGs intact. Also, creditors will take actions by following the terms in the inter-creditor agreements to which they all agreed before. As a result, one may argue that market/hybrid legal solutions may have the potential to preserve group going concern value and certainty.

After acknowledging the merits of some market/hybrid solutions which can prevent group-wide insolvency and preserve group going concern value, the limitations of these solutions are identified. The conclusion is that the implementation of market solutions is increasingly difficult to solve cross-border insolvency of MCGs. The success of some market solutions, such as renegotiation of debts at the holding companies level, relies on the presence of concentrated debt instruments. Other private agreements between parties, such as protocols, are also vulnerable due to their contractual nature. It is therefore desirable to have a general framework to support cross-border insolvency for groups of companies.

Chapter 5 discusses the new group coordination proceedings and provides a recommendation to improve their low efficacy. It has been identified that though group coordination proceedings respect the entity law which provides more certainty, their efficacy may be dampened if every group member is free to opt out of group coordination proceedings. As certain creditors or investors with better information may have the ability to control the subsidiaries, they may use opt-out mechanisms to extract value from other creditors. So, this chapter considers the effectiveness of this proceeding and its possible improvement. It also analyses the possibility of harmonization of insolvency law. On the one hand, uniform insolvency law may help mitigate the potential for abuse by national insolvency tools; on the other hand, the harmonized rules may facilitate cooperation and coordination between courts and insolvency practitioners. However, insurmountable difficulties of harmonization of insolvency law in the EU have been revealed. Such a solution may be too radical to achieve now.

In Chapter 6, the author focusses on the role of directors in this broad cross-border insolvency setting. Directors have important roles to play, not only because they have day-to-day control of their own companies but also because of their access to the first-hand information relating to the financial conditions of companies. It is desirable if the current cooperative regimes encourage directors of member companies within the same group to communicate and coordinate with each other. Since they know their own companies better than anyone else, they are the people that creditors can rely on to take early actions in order to save a corporate group. Directors' duties in the vicinity of insolvency and their duty to cooperate will be examined in this chapter.

Chapter 7 provides an overview of resolution and insolvency regimes for financial corporate groups. The author provides a comparison between insolvency law theories and tools, and resolution theories and tools. Since other books have provided a full-fledged account of bank resolution, the purpose of this chapter is to understand both of these regimes by comparing and integrating them. The focus is again on corporate groups, so the main topics are what value financial corporate groups have in theory and how resolution tools and international co-operation can preserve such value in financial corporate groups.

Chapter 8 concludes the main arguments of this book and suggests direction for further development.

2 Theoretical basis of corporate rescue and implications on rescue of multinational groups of companies

In Chapter 2, this book aims to deal with the first sub-objective articulated in Chapter 1 – the examination of corporate rescue theories and MCGs theories. This chapter aims to answer the questions why do we need to provide special solutions for MCGs, and why is it desirable to rescue MCGs?[1] Also, what values can we expect to achieve from the rescue of MCGs? These values may then be used as benchmarks to analyse the drawbacks and merits of the existing cross-border insolvency law theories as well as practical solutions for the cross-border insolvency of MCGs.

The purpose of this exploration is to examine the theoretical basis underpinning the corporate rescue regime and its implications on the cross-border insolvency of MCGs.[2] By engaging in the debate on the significance of corporate rescue between economic school and traditional school insolvency theories, this chapter argues that the preservation of going concern value and certainty are the goals that corporate rescue law generally pursues. It further draws a connection between corporate rescue law theories and multinational enterprise theories: multinational enterprise theories shed light on the existence of group going concern value and how such value is formed in MCGs. As a result, to achieve the goals of corporate rescue law, one needs to consider the implications of multinational enterprise theories. The final implication will be further connected to the cross-border insolvency law theories in Chapter 3.

Theoretical views of corporate rescue

This section tries to explore the purpose of corporate rescue on the basis of insolvency law theories. Economic insolvency law theorists and traditional insolvency theorists hold different views regarding the value of corporate rescue. The aim of this section is to examine the values that corporate rescue law should

---

1 Compared to corporate rescue, liquidation may be a more straightforward solution in many cases. Through liquidation proceedings, subsidiaries of MCGs can simply be liquidated separately in their respective countries without the need to design any tools and mechanisms for them.
2 See Chapter 3.

Rescue of multinational groups of companies 13

pursue; these values are the benchmarks by which groups of companies' rescue practices and theories need to abide.

Corporate rescue and going concern value

Before entering the debate between schools of insolvency law regarding the goals of corporate rescue law, it is helpful to examine some key concepts.

It is generally believed that going concern value[3] may exist only when a company is kept intact and running.[4] In other words, an operating company may be worth more when it is intact than when it is broken up.[5] It is believed that the going concern value of a business is much larger than the piecemeal value in liquidation proceedings; therefore, releasing going concern value is in the interest of all the creditors and stakeholders.[6] Even though in many cases, certain categories of creditors, such as unsecured creditors, may be far from being fully compensated, the 'enlarged pie' available for distribution is a better deal for most of the creditors.

Resource-[7] and knowledge-based theories provide good insights into going concern value. In resource-based theory, if a company would like to achieve success in a market, it needs to obtain certain resources that are rare and idiosyncratic. An example of these resources is the relationships that the company has formed with its suppliers and customers.[8] Because of these relationships, the distress of one company may lead to distress of all the parties linked with this company, and legislators have long been aware of this effect on the wider world.[9]

However, it is possible that the company does not have the capacity to coordinate different resources and relationships. In knowledge-based theory,[10] the

---

3 See definition of going concern value: going concern value is the value of a company as an ongoing entity. This value differs from the value of a liquidated company's assets because an ongoing operation has the ability to continue to earn profit, while a liquidated company does not. At www.investopedia.com/terms/g/going_concern_value.asp.

4 Douglas G. Baird, 'Bankruptcy's Uncontested Axioms' (1998–1999) *The Yale Law Journal* 108 573, p. 577.

5 Douglas G. Baird and Robert K. Rasmussen, 'The End of Bankruptcy' (2002) *Stanford Law Review* 55 751 p. 758.

6 The rationale behind corporate rescue procedures, such as CVA or administration procedures in the UK insolvency act, is to release the going concern value of the potential business. London Department of Trade and Industry Review (2000) p. 5.

7 Jay Barney, 'Firm Resources and Sustained Competitive Advantage' (1991) *Journal of Management* 17 99–120. Kathleen Conner and C.K. Prahalad, 'A Resource-Based Theory of the Firm: Knowledge versus Opportunism.' (1996) *Organization Science* 7 477–501.

8 David Wheeler, Barry Colbert and R. Edward Freeman, 'Focusing on Value: Reconciling Corporate Social Responsibility, Sustain ability and a Stakeholder Approach in a Network World' (2003) *Journal of General Management* 28(3) 1–28, p. 3.

9 Peter Dahlin *et al.*, 'Netquakes – Describing Effects of Ending Business Relationships on Business Networks' (2005) Working Paper to be presented at IMP in Rotterdam, p. 5.

10 R. Grant, 'Toward a Knowledge-Based Theory of the Firm' (1996) *Strategic Management Journal* 17 109–122.

14 *Rescue of multinational groups of companies*

capacity of a given company to use the knowledge and its capacity to transfer and coordinate different knowledge are also important resources.[11] As these capacities are possessed by the people working at the companies, certain employees and managers in one company or group of companies are also key assets.[12]

The possession of rare resources and the companies' capacities to use the resources together allow one company to be more efficient than others as it can use its assets in the most productive way.[13] The companies that do not possess the rare resources or capacities will not be able to match their competitors which have those capacities to produce more profits in the market.[14] As a result, these inefficient companies may suffer negative cash flow and become insolvent in the future. Due to the rare resources and capacities, the additional value that the efficient company can gain can be considered the going concern value of that company.[15] Therefore, efficient companies generally have going concern value.[16]

When assets are held and used in an inefficient way in a company, the company cannot generate profit to cover its operating costs. This is because the market punishes inefficient companies and screens them out. The longer such companies are kept alive, the more costs they are going to incur.[17] This type of company is called an economically distressed company; in general it should not be rescued as it has no going concern value. Economic distress denotes that a company may not survive in the market, even if its temporary financial issues could be solved.

---

11 Bruce Kogut and Udo Zander, 'Knowledge of the Firm and the Evolutionary Theory of the Multinational Corporation' (1993) *Journal of International Business Studies*, Fourth Quarter 24 625–645, p. 625.

12 It makes more sense to consider firms as relationships between labours and commodities. R.H. Coase, 'The Nature of the Firm' (1937) *Economica*, New Series 4(16) 368–405, p. 403; a given distressed company might have an 'external' going concern value, which is the value of its relationships with other business or non-business parties. Richard V. Butler and Scott M. Gilpatric, 'A Re-Examination of the Purposes and Goals of Bankruptcy' (1994) *The American Bankruptcy Institute Law Review* 2 269, p. 283; Lynn M. LoPucki, 'The Nature of the Bankrupt Firm: A Response to Baird and Rasmussen's "The End of Bankruptcy"' (2003) *Stanford Law Review* 56(3) 645–671, p. 652; see also Cheryl Carleton Asher, *et al.* 'Towards a Property Rights Foundation for a Stakeholder Theory of the Firm' (2005) *Journal of Management and Governance* 9 5–32, p. 13.

13 Richard Makadok, 'Toward a Synthesis of the Resource-Based and Dynamic-Capability Views of Rent Creation' (2001) *Strategic Management Journal* 22 387–401, p. 1; Robert Rasmussen and David A. Skeel, Jr., 'The Economic Analysis of Corporate Bankruptcy Law' (1995) *American Bankruptcy Institute Law Review* 3 85, p. 86.

14 Michelle J. White, 'Does Chapter 11 Save Economically Inefficient Firms' (1994) *Wash. U. L. Q.* 72 1319.

15 Michelle M. Harner, 'The Value of Soft Variables in Corporate Reorganizations' (2015) *University of Illinois Law Review* 2015 509, p. 512.

16 Efficiency means the maximization of the wealth of society. In the insolvency context, ex post efficiency can be achieved if the value of distressed companies can be maximized. Ex ante efficiency can be achieved if insolvency law does not create incentives for stakeholders to engage in inefficient activities. Robert K. Rasmussen, 'The Efficiency of Chapter 11' (1991) *Emory Bankruptcy Developments Journal* 8 319, p. 323.

17 Robert Rasmussen and David A. Skeel, Jr., 'The Economic Analysis of Corporate Bankruptcy Law' (1995) *American Bankruptcy Institute Law Review* 3 85, p. 87.

Rescue of multinational groups of companies 15

In other words, the company's business plan is flawed. For example, it does not have competitive people on its staff, nor does it have information, resources, networks – or at least their combination does not work. Economically distressed companies should be sifted out by the market as even if they can overcome their financial difficulties, they will return to financial distress due to an inherent lack of competitiveness.[18] Keeping such companies operating will decrease, not increase, the value available to creditors in general.

By contrast, if companies can generate net profit but temporarily cannot satisfy their debt obligations, it is worth giving them the chance to restructure their capital structure.[19] This type of company is called a financially distressed company. These companies are those facing liquidity difficulties. The reasons behind financial distress are various and not always the fault of the companies; for example, distress could be due to a temporary downturn of the market or a currency fluctuation. Generally speaking, it is likely that the financially distressed companies are competitive and deserve a chance to overcome their temporary liquidity issues.[20] They have going concern value in that the longer they can be kept alive and operating, the more profit they could generate for creditors in general.

The key to preserving the going concern value is keeping the business intact and operating. Breaking up a company with going concern value may destroy the 'key resources' and capacities of that company. There are two possible ways of keeping the business intact: corporate rescue and business rescue. Corporate rescue involves a compromise between debtors and creditors so that the debtor per se is still alive with its capital structure issues sorted out. By contrast, business rescue may involve a sale of the business to third parties so that the shell of the distressed debtor is 'dead'. However, the viable business of the company may be bought as a whole by new owners. This can also save jobs and reduce externalities of insolvency.[21]

Business rescue focusses on preserving the business of the debtor rather than debtor itself. It embodies a sale to either the pre-insolvency stakeholders or a third party from the market.[22] Practically, a sale may be the only solution to rescue the business as the debtor might not be able to find alternative ways to get rid of debts.

One may argue that corporate rescue conducts a necessary major intervention to salvage the failure of companies[23] or businesses. The major intervention in-

---

18 Gerard McCormack, *Corporate Rescue Law – An Anglo-American Perspective* (Edward Elgar Publishing Limited 2008), p. 9.

19 Robert Rasmussen and David A. Skeel, Jr., 'The Economic Analysis of Corporate Bankruptcy Law' (1995) *American Bankruptcy Institute Law Review* 3 85, p. 88.

20 Gerard McCormack, *Corporate Rescue Law – An Anglo-American Perspective* (Edward Elgar Publishing Limited 2008), p. 9.

21 Vanessa Finch, *Corporate Insolvency Law Perspectives and Principles* (2nd edn, Cambridge University Press 2009), p. 244.

22 Bolanle Adebola, 'A Few Shades of Rescue: Towards an Understanding of the Corporate Rescue Concept in England and Wales' (2014) INSOL Europe Academics' Conference, p. 9 (available at: http://ssrn.com/abstract=2524488).

23 Alice Belcher, *Corporate Rescue* (Sweet & Maxwell 1997), p. 12.

16 *Rescue of multinational groups of companies*

dicates that the action is urgent, that is, it aims to prevent a significant decline in a business's fortunes.[24] The value of an insolvent company will quickly disappear, so quick decision-making is necessary to preserve the going concern value of the company. To conduct a company rescue, accurate information regarding the distressed company is necessary.[25] The difficulty is that administrators are rarely sure of all the details of the distressed company, so they choose business rescue as a fast solution; that is how business rescue became the prevalent type of rescue in practice.[26] Insolvency Law Schedule B1 para. 4 prescribes that 'The administrator of a company must perform his functions as quickly and efficiently as is reasonably practicable'.[27]

Company rescue requires that the identity of the company be preserved, though in practice it is very difficult as the company cannot pay back all it owes to stakeholders.[28] Company rescue is the purest form of rescue, and it has been put at the top of the hierarchy of goals for administrators in the Enterprise Act 2002.[29] It requires the administrator to first identify rescuing the company as a going concern.[30] However, this does not mean that corporate rescue is the ultimate aim that should be pursued at all costs.[31] The Insolvency Act articulates that if a business rescue could achieve a better result for creditors in general, it should be given priority.[32] Similar to the UK position, the US reorganization law chapter 11[33] also moves from corporate rescue to business rescue for the purpose of benefiting a broad range of stakeholders.[34]

In cases where a business has key relationships with suppliers or firm-specific human capital, other buyers may not easily acquire these values by purchasing the business.[35] For example, the replacement of directors may sacrifice key knowledge about supplier relationships, which can lead to a loss in business.[36] Therefore, in certain cases corporate rescue may be preferable to business rescue.

---

24 Ibid., p. 12.
25 Sandra Frisby, 'In Search of a Rescue Regime: The Enterprise Act 2002' (2004) *MLR* 67(2) 247–272, p. 261.
26 Vanessa Finch, 'Control and Co-Ordination Incorporate Rescue' (2005) *Legal Studies* 25 374, p. 396.
27 Insolvency Act 1986, B1, para. 4.
28 Alice Belcher, *Corporate Rescue* (Sweet & Maxwell 1997), p. 23.
29 Enterprise act 2002, Part 10, para. 3(1).
30 Mark Phillips and Jeremy Goldring, 'Rescue and Reconstruction' (2002) *Insolvency Intelligence* 15 75–76.
31 Vanessa Finch, 'Corporate Rescue: A Game of Three Halves' (2012) *Legal Studies* 32(2) 302, p. 303.
32 Insolvency Act 1986 B1 Administration Art. 3(3) b.
33 US Code Title 11 Bankruptcy Chapter 11, 1978.
34 Gerard McCormack, 'Something Old, Something New: Recasting the European Insolvency Regulation' (2016) *The Modern Law Review* 79(1) 102–146, p. 125.
35 Maria Brouwer, 'Reorganization in US and European Bankruptcy Law' *European Journal of Law and Economics* (2006) 22 5–20. Springer Science Business Media, LLC, p. 11.
36 Lynn M. LoPucki, 'The Nature of the Bankrupt Firm: A Response to Baird and Rasmussen's "The End of Bankruptcy"' (2003) *Stanford Law Review* 56(3) 645–671, p. 668.

Rescue of multinational groups of companies 17

However, both successful business rescues and successful company rescues can benefit many of the companies' creditors and stakeholders.

The concept of corporate rescue used in this book includes corporate rescue and business rescue; it refers to solutions which can preserve the going concern value of distressed businesses or companies.

The debate between the economic account and the traditional account of insolvency law

Debate on the preservation of going concern value

The economic account of insolvency law is of the opinion that insolvency law is designed to deal with common pool issues.[37] By setting up a scene in which the common pool issue is the unique problem that insolvency law needs to deal with, it asks what solution concerned creditors will come up with. The answer is a collective and compulsory insolvency proceeding imposed on parties' individual actions. Without an insolvency system, creditors with diverse interests have to monitor other creditors after lending money to the debtor as they know that they have to compete with others. Therefore, the loan contract may involve significant uncertainty, and the transaction cost may be high. Some creditors may also try to enforce their individual claims against distressed debtors, which will make an already gloomy situation worse.[38] Insolvency proceedings reduce considerable monitoring and dispute costs for all creditors; most importantly, they preserve the going concern value of distressed companies.

The economic account suggests that insolvency law may redistribute certain value to other stakeholders only if doing so can preserve the going concern value. In other words, redistribution itself is not the goal of insolvency law; its purpose is to facilitate the preservation of going concern value.[39] It is plausible to pay employees and suppliers over the course of reorganization as doing so can be the only way to keep the business intact. As the above section argues, going

---

37 Assume that the debtor runs a fish pool, and the value of the fishes is not enough to pay back creditors. What would happen if the creditors were privy to the financial distress of the debtor? They would probably compete with each other and grab as many of the assets (within the limit of what they are owed) of the debtor as possible to compensate their debts. Such a situation will happen without insolvency law. However, the chaotic situation may not help to preserve the going concern value as creditors tear the debtor into pieces such that they can no longer operate on behalf of the creditors. Insolvency law is an instrument to maximize the assets of the distressed companies and distribute them to the creditors. Thomas H. Jackson, *The Logic and Limits of Bankruptcy Law* (Harvard University Press 1986), p. 11.

38 Thomas H. Jackson, *The Logic and Limits of Bankruptcy Law* (Harvard University Press 1986), p. 10.

39 Ted Janger, 'Crystals and Mud in Bankruptcy Law: Judicial Competence and Statutory Design' (2001) *Arizona Law Review* 43 559, 566. Charles W. Mooney, Jr., 'A Normative Theory of Bankruptcy Law: Bankruptcy As (Is) Civil Procedure' (2004) *Washington and Lee Law Review* 61 931, p. 946.

18   Rescue of multinational groups of companies

concern value can be made up by the relationships between debtor companies and suppliers, skilled managers and employees. To keep these relationships and employees is to keep going concern value. A straightforward liquidation may not be the correct solution[40]; even though liquidation is also a collective insolvency law proceeding, it mainly aims to sell the components of the debtors and not to run the business.

Traditionalists adopt a multi-value approach by arguing that the economic interest is not the only value that insolvency law should pursue[41]; insolvency law should pursue other values: preserving jobs, protecting other stakeholders besides creditors and protecting the community's interests.[42] The traditional account of insolvency law argues that the task of insolvency law is to deal with the defaults between one debtor and various creditors; therefore insolvency law needs to decide how to distribute the loss incurred from such a default by considering creditors' respective abilities to bear loss and risks.[43] Conflicting interests among stakeholders give rise to a tough issue for bankruptcy law to resolve.[44] As a result, insolvency laws become vehicles to redistribute the loss and risks which the different stakeholders need to bear.

Advocates of the traditional account believe that the welfare of the community should also be considered in insolvency law.[45] From their point of view, insolvency should not focus only on the maximization of creditors' interests. Rather, it is justified to redistribute certain interests of a distressed company in favour of other affected stakeholders, such as the community that the company exists in.[46]

---

40 Going concern value exists in the operation of business; the corporate rescue procedures are hence necessary to fill in this gap. The corporate rescue procedures should respond to the common pool issues and preserve the value for creditors in general.

41 Donald R. Korobkin, 'Rehabilitating Values: A Jurisprudence of Bankruptcy' (1991) *Columbia Law Review* 91(4) 717–789, p. 764.

42 Douglas G. Baird, 'Bankruptcy's Uncontested Axioms' (1998–1999) *The Yale Law Journal* 108 573, p. 577.

43 For example, certain employees, not including managers, do not have access to the financial information of the companies they are working for, so they have difficulties predicting risks; they also suffer severe hardship when they lose their jobs and thus incomes. Furthermore, employees are not experts in shielding themselves from risks, and rarely do they have more than one job to spread the risk of layoff. Elizabeth Warren, 'Bankruptcy Policy' (1987) *University of Chicago Law Review* 54 775, p. 777, p. 790; Donald R. Korobkin, 'Employee Interests in Bankruptcy' (1996) *The American Bankruptcy Institute Law Review* 4 5, p. 12 arguing that the reason why a company internalizes employees is to reduce the cost as employees may accept lower than the market remuneration to conduct certain works. They may expect other informal benefits, such as promotion opportunities, from the company. When a company is wound up, the direct effect on the employees, among other things, is that they heavily rely on their owed income, and it is not easy for them to immediately find another job.

44 It is more practical and views bankruptcy as 'dirty complex elastic and interconnected policies', thereby it is difficult, if not impossible, to elucidate insolvency policies. See Elizabeth Warren, 'Bankruptcy Policy' (1987) *University of Chicago Law Review* 54 775, p. 811.

45 Vanessa Finch, *Corporate Insolvency Law Perspectives and Principles* (2nd edn, Cambridge University Press 2009), p. 40.

46 Ibid., p. 41.

Rescue of multinational groups of companies 19

However, advocates do not endow a superior status to the community.[47] The choices between rescue and liquidation still need to be judged in a business sense so as to sift out economically distressed businesses.[48] Granted, sometimes the interests of communities may be difficult to measure, but that does not mean that we should never make efforts to protect them, irrespective of their huge value.[49]

Thus far, the chapter has established that economic account advocates believe that preservation of going concern value is the goal of insolvency law.[50] By contrast, traditionalists aver that preservation of going concern value is not the only end; keeping distressed companies running on behalf of a broad range of stakeholders is the main purpose of insolvency law.[51]

The issue here is not whether other stakeholders are affected by the insolvency of a given company; nor is it whether those negatively affected parties are worth protecting. The issue is how to protect them in a reasonable way. The economic account advocates set one precondition on rescue: the businesses should be financially distressed rather than economically distressed. The sound business plan of a financially distressed business will show that it has going concern value, which may be formed by other stakeholders, such as employees and suppliers. Protecting their interests in the insolvency proceeding is in line with the goal of preservation of going concern value and is in line with the interests of creditors.

By contrast, though, traditionalists also recognize that stakeholders' support may be important to the preservation of business[52]; they do not set up clear rules on when to protect a distressed business and how to balance the different interests that they propose to protect. They insist that the continuance of distressed business per se is a good thing in itself.

Surely, the need to keep the going concern value gives rise to the necessity of running the business, while the reorganization plan or the sale plan is in the drafting stage. This is especially true when the market is thin, and the given distressed company cannot be sold immediately or when no fair price can be secured.[53] It is also possible that buyers may not want to buy the companies at fair value due to a lack of information. All these cases require insolvency rescue law to provide a platform allowing the companies to be run for a period of time so as to either recover or attract buyers.

---

47 Karen Gross, 'Taking Community Interests into Account in Bankruptcy: An Essay', (1994) *Washington University Law Quarterly* 72 1031.
48 Ibid., p. 1033.
49 Ibid., p. 1046.
50 Douglas G. Baird, 'Bankruptcy's Uncontested Axioms' (1998–1999) *The Yale Law Journal* 108 573, p. 577.
51 It argues that unlike other legal systems, bankruptcy law uniquely deals with the insolvency issues by providing a systematic structure and forum. Bankruptcy law considers and respects moral, political and social values. Donald R. Korobkin, 'Rehabilitating Values: A Jurisprudence of Bankruptcy' (1991) *Columbia Law Review* 91(4) 717–789, p. 766.
52 Donald R. Korobkin, 'Employee Interests in Bankruptcy' (1996) *The American Bankruptcy Institute Law Review* 4 5, p. 7.
53 Lucian AryeBebchuk, 'A New Approach to Corporate Reorganizations' (1988) *Harvard Law Review* 101 775–804, p. 776.

20 *Rescue of multinational groups of companies*

But the caveat of the above is that if the distressed business has no going concern value, and if the relationships between stakeholders and debtor companies contribute no going concern value, should the business still be kept alive? It is in this situation that the economic account advocates and the traditionalists hold different views.

If relationships between distressed companies and stakeholders do not form going concern value, the relationships should be cut off and allocated back to the market. The market will reallocate these resources to places where the resources can be better used.

Without the clear balance of multi-values that traditionalists propose to protect, traditionalists' bankruptcy law policies run the risk of preserving the distressed companies with no going concern value solely for the purpose of protecting jobs and communities.[54] Such a strategy may only offer short-term protection to employees and communities as the resources formed by these relationships do not constitute any going concern value that the companies could use to trade themselves out of difficulty. As a result, it is not only the creditors who will suffer from this strategy – due to the reduction of the value of the business, the employees and community will suffer as well due to inevitable insolvency in the near future.

Economically distressed companies which are destined to be screened out by the market should not be saved as doing so will not maximize either the creditors' value or the other stakeholders' value. In other words, protecting other stakeholders can only be worthwhile when their participation in the distressed companies generates going concern value. Since stakeholders' participation in the companies is part of the going concern value of the companies, protecting their interests protects the going concern value, which can maximize the value of insolvency estate for stakeholders in general in the long term.[55] By contrast, solely pursuing the goal of reducing the impact of insolvency to other stakeholders, irrespective of the existence of going concern value, will do more harm than good.

One should therefore not underestimate the importance of the concepts of financial distress and going concern value suggested by the economic school.

---

54 Donald R. Korobkin, 'Contractarianism and the Normative Foundations of Bankruptcy Law' (1992–1993) *Texas Law Review* 71 541, p. 575.

55 Michael C. Jensen, 'Value Maximization, Stakeholder Theory, and the Corporate Objective Function' October (2001) *Business Ethics Quarterly* 12(2), p. 17; see also Jill Solomon, *Corporate Governance and Accountability* (4th edn, John Wiley & Sons Ltd 2013), p. 20 (also see the third King Report on corporate governance in South Africa); also, consistent with company law, directors of companies consider a wider range of stakeholders' interests, such as employees, suppliers, customers and communities. Company Act 2006 bases such prescript on the enlightened shareholder value theory, which gives priority to the interests of shareholders while accepting that other stakeholders' interests should be respected as long as there is no conflict between shareholders' and stakeholders' interests – considering the stakeholders' interests will be the most effective way of maximizing them. Also, since the stakeholders' interests need to be considered outside of insolvency, considering these interests separate from creditors' interests is consistent with the non-insolvency requirements of the law. See Company Act 2006 UK Part 10, Chapter 2 s. 172; Christine A. Mall, *Corporate Governance* (4th edn, Oxford University Press 2012), p. 76.

Traditionalists ignore the fact that stakeholders' relationships with debtor companies may not form going concern value, which, in turn, explains that the debtor companies have neither enough resources nor capacities that are worth keeping intact. Saving such a company will cost creditors dearly, and the final fate of the company will be still insolvency. Preservation of such a business does not preserve going concern value for the purpose of insolvency law.

To sum up, the aim of insolvency rescue mechanisms is to preserve viable financially distressed businesses or companies (or parts of them).[56] It is the going concern value of financially distressed companies that makes corporate rescue, as opposed to liquidation, a desirable option. The rationale behind rescue procedures is that only those financially distressed companies that have a viable future, despite suffering temporary financial difficulties, should be saved.[57] By contrast, companies which have no viable business should be sifted out by the market so that the resources can be reallocated to better use. Giving too much sympathy to a business without going concern value could be considered an inefficient use of resources, which is harmful to the society.[58] It can be argued that such assets should be sold to buyers who can use them more efficiently.[59] That is to say that insolvency law should respect the sifting function of the market to filter out inefficient companies.

If corporate rescue law cannot effectively preserve the going concern value of financially distressed companies, their creditors will suffer more loss. As a result, it is very likely that creditors will increase the price of capital as a way of adjusting risks. This is a general cost to all companies, including efficient ones.[60] The rise in interest rates will discourage investment by creditors and reduce the wealth growth rate of society. This makes it clear that one cannot ignore the incentive created by corporate rescue law. The next section will discuss this.

Debate on certainty of insolvency law

The economic account values the ex ante influence[61] of insolvency law, while the traditional account does not.[62] The economic account believes that insolvency

---

56 Gerard McCormack, *Corporate Rescue Law – An Anglo-American Perspective* (Edward Elgar Publishing Limited 2008), p. 3.

57 Commission staff working document, impact assessment, accompanying the document Revision of Regulation (EC) No. 1346/2000 on insolvency proceedings SWD(2012) 416 final, p. 12 (available at ec.europa.eu/justice/civil/files/insolvency-ia_en.pdf).

58 Douglas G. Baird and Thomas H. Jackson, 'Corporate Reorganizations and the Treatment of Diverse Ownership Interests: A Comment on Adequate Protection of Secured Creditors in Bankruptcy' (1984) *University of Chicago Law Review* 51 97, p. 102.

59 Ibid., p. 102.

60 Frank H. Easterbrook, 'Is Corporate Bankruptcy Efficient' (1990) *Journal of Financial Economics* 27(2) 414.

61 According to this thesis efficiency means the maximization of the wealth of society. Therefore, it is equally important to check whether corporate rescue law provides the wrong incentives to people for conducting value-decreasing activities.

62 Douglas G. Baird, 'Bankruptcy's Uncontested Axioms' (1998–1999) *The Yale Law Journal* 108 573, p. 589.

22   Rescue of multinational groups of companies

law should respect non-insolvency law as a baseline as alteration of non-insolvency law inside insolvency proceedings will provide stakeholders with incentives to conduct strategic behaviour, thereby giving rise to the cost of insolvency[63] and the high cost of borrowing interest rate.[64]

Strategic behaviours exist as certain stakeholders may be treated better or worse in insolvency law proceedings. Assume that unsecured creditors are given the same priority inside the insolvency proceedings, while they are not so blessed outside the insolvency; unsecured creditors will have incentives to file for insolvency proceedings without considering whether doing so will cause loss to other stakeholders. Unsecured creditors know that without insolvency proceedings, they will not obtain the same priority; they will open insolvency proceedings to serve their own interests. Similarly, secured creditors may try to delay insolvency proceedings by using their power over the debtors, if any, or avoid insolvency proceeding by trying to foreclose their rights well before the appearance of insolvency risk.[65] All these strategic behaviours will lead to insolvency proceedings opening either too early or too late, which is harmful for the stakeholders in general. So, corporate rescue law should not provide stakeholders with the wrong incentives.[66] It is generally submitted that the timing of opening insolvency proceedings plays an important role in insolvency.[67] For example, opening insolvency too early may not be the optimal option as the possibility for a cheaper private restructuring may be available; opening insolvency too late may cause distressed businesses to lose much value, and it could become too late for them to be reorganized.

On a micro level, the costs of strategic behaviours are generally harmful as they reduce the going concern value. On a macro level, the uncertainty of such strategies leads to risks for creditors as they need to factor in the interest rate at the point of lending.

In addition to the problem of strategic behaviours, not respecting the non-insolvency law entitlements of creditors leads to a rise of interest rates. As mentioned before, if courts decide to save jobs and protect communities, even when the business in question is economically distressed, the uncertainty this causes

---

63 Thomas H. Jackson, *The Logic and Limits of Bankruptcy Law* (Harvard University Press 1986), p. 21; Douglas G. Baird, 'Loss Distribution, Forum Shopping, and Bankruptcy: A Reply to Warren' (1987) *University of Chicago Law Review* 54 815, p. 825.

64 See general Alan Schwartz, 'A Normative Theory of Business Bankruptcy' (2005) Faculty Scholarship Series Paper 303; Yaad Rotem, 'Pursuing Preservation of Pre-Bankruptcy Entitlements: Corporate Bankruptcy Law's Self-Executing Mechanisms' (2008) *Berkeley Business Law Journal* 5 79.

65 Yaad Rotem, 'Pursuing Preservation of Pre-Bankruptcy Entitlements: Corporate Bankruptcy Law's Self-Executing Mechanisms' (2008) *Berkeley Business Law Journal* 5 79, p. 107.

66 Without value-decreasing strategic behaviours, stakeholders may be more cooperative when considering corporate rescue. The going concern value of the distressed companies will remain largely intact; it may be a good time to consider corporate rescue.

67 Horst Eidenmüller, 'Comparative Corporate Insolvency Law' (2016) European Corporate Governance Institute (ECGI) – Law Working Paper No. 319, p. 9.

Rescue of multinational groups of companies 23

will lead to a higher borrowing interest rate.[68] This is because economically distressed companies cannot use resources efficiently, so they may have negative net cash flow. The loss incurred from operating inefficient companies will be borne by creditors, while the employees and the community will benefit. Saving economically distressed companies is tantamount to transferring value from creditors to communities, but creditors do not know when their support of the community will end. The unclear policies will dramatically raise interest rates.

As low interest rates can help borrowers keep more profits and engage in more investment,[69] it is desirable to reduce interest rates by respecting non-insolvency law in insolvency proceedings. In the business world, one thing that must be borne in mind is that most companies are solvent.[70] Therefore, certainty is a goal of insolvency law, and it is no less important than the preservation of going concern value. This is the reason insolvency law generally respects pre-insolvency rights (with some exceptions, which will be discussed later).[71]

However, it seems possible for a radical advocate of the economic account to argue that the reorganization procedure itself is wrong as it always involves methods to modify the pre-bankruptcy entitlements of creditors.[72] This is true as the opening of collective insolvency procedures may substitute individual creditors' actions under non-insolvency law; the 'stay' on individual creditors may constrain their ability to exert their entitlements under non-insolvency law. However, without such mechanism, insolvency law does not exist.[73]

If insolvency law strictly conforms to non-insolvency law, one may conclude that there is something we should not expect insolvency law to do.[74] That is, insolvency law should only consider the interests of contractual parties but does

---

68 For example the court may decide to rescue a distressed company, even though it is economically distressed, for the purpose of preserving jobs or benefitting certain stakeholders.

69 Alan Schwartz, 'A Normative Theory of Business Bankruptcy' (2005) Faculty Scholarship Series Paper 303, p. 1220.

70 Richard V. Butler and Scott M. Gilpatric, 'A Re-Examination of the Purposes and Goals of Bankruptcy' (1994) *The American* Bankruptcy Institute Law Review 2 269, p. 277.

71 Irit Mevorach, *Insolvency within Multinational Enterprise Groups* (Oxford University Press 2009), p. 111.

72 Thomas H. Jackson, 'Bankruptcy, Non-Bankruptcy Entitlements and the Creditors' (1982) Bargain', *Yale Law Journal* 91 857; Thomas H. Jackson, 'Avoiding Powers in Bankruptcy' (1984) *Stanford Law Review* 36 725; Thomas H. Jackson, 'Of Liquidation, Continuation, and Delay: An Analysis of Bankruptcy Policy and Non-Bankruptcy Rules' (1986) *American Bankruptcy Law Journal* 60 399; Robert E. Scott, 'Through Bankruptcy with the Creditors' Bargain Heuristic' (1986) *University of Chicago Law Review* 53 690; Douglas G. Baird, 'The Uneasy Case for Corporate Reorganizations' (1986) *The Journal of Legal Studies* 15 127; Douglas G. Baird, 'Loss Distribution, Forum Shopping, and Bankruptcy: A Reply to Warren' (1987) *University of Chicago Law Review* 54 815; Thomas H. Jackson and Robert E. Scott, 'On the Nature of Bankruptcy: An Essay on Bankruptcy Sharing and the Creditors' Bargain' (1989) *Virginia Law Review* 75 155.

73 Stephen Lubben, 'The Overstated Absolute Priority Rule' (2016) *The Fordham Journal of Corporate & Financial Law* 21 581, p. 585.

74 Thomas H. Jackson, *The Logic and Limits of Bankruptcy Law* (Harvard University Press 1986), p. 2.

24 Rescue of multinational groups of companies

not consider other non-contractual parties.[75] Such a radical economic account thus adopts a narrow path when considering insolvency law, which excludes the protection of other stakeholders, such as managers, employees and others, insomuch as they are not creditors.[76] There are two problems with this radical point of view. One is that insolvency itself is not an excuse to avoid non-contractual obligations. For instance, distressed companies still need to compensate the community for pollution clear-up fees[77] in the context of corporate insolvency.[78] Insolvency policies should not focus on the protection of contractual relationships just to overlook non-contractual relationships.[79]

Focussing only on creditors also jeopardizes relationships between debtor companies and those non-creditors who contribute to the going concern value that insolvency law aims to preserve. To ensure that suppliers and customers or other parties continue to support the business, it is important for the business to pay them cash immediately after receiving their goods or service, or provide lien superior to other pre-insolvency creditors.[80] A narrow focus on repaying money owed to managers and suppliers, without being concerned about maintaining these key relationships, may result in going concern value being lost.

Nevertheless, it does not mean that insolvency law should protect non-contractual parties at the expense of creditors. Even if these parties are worth protecting, the question of how these parties should be protected in a cost-effective way inside insolvency law must be answered.

If courts reorder non-insolvency law entitlements[81] for the purpose of protecting jobs and the community without differentiating between economic distress/ financial distress and without considering whether non-creditors contribute

---

75 Vanessa Finch, *Corporate Insolvency Law Perspectives and Principles* (2nd edn, Cambridge University Press 2009), p. 34.

76 For example, employees' interest can only be considered in insolvency law to the extent that they are owed wages, which qualifies them as creditors. Insolvency law may not consider any interest on the employees' behalf other than this.

77 Environmental Protection Act 1990 ss.26(1) and 82(2).

78 Roy Goode, *Principle of Corporate Insolvency Law* (4th edn, Sweet Maxwell London 2011), p. 86.

79 Elizabeth Warren, 'Bankruptcy Policymaking in an Imperfect World' (1993) *Michigan Law Review* 92(2) 336–387, p. 356.

80 Mark J. Roe and Frederick Tung, 'Breaking Bankruptcy Priority: How Rent-Seeking Upends the Creditors' Bargain (2013) *Virginia Law Review* 99 1236, p. 1245; for example, according to Chapter 11 U.S. Code § 503 it elevates the position of certain post-petition claims to the status of administrative expense, including 'wages, salaries, and commissions for services rendered after the commencement of the case', as a way to encourage these key parties to support the operation of business. 11 U.S. Code § 503 – allowance of administrative expenses.

81 From the traditionalists' point of view, the rehabilitation function of insolvency law plays an important and independent role. Redistribution is used to balance the conflicting interests of all the stakeholders; this is a tough job, equal to that of selecting values worth protecting. Elizabeth Warren, 'Bankruptcy Policy' (1987) *University of Chicago Law Review* 54 775, p. 786; Donald R. Korobkin, 'Rehabilitating Values: A Jurisprudence of Bankruptcy' (1991) *Columbia Law Review* 91(4) 717–789, p. 773.

Rescue of multinational groups of companies 25

to the going concern value,[82] they ignore the ex ante effect of insolvency law completely. This protection of jobs and community comes at a high cost due to the uncertainty caused by such practice.[83] Insolvency law may protect these non-creditor stakeholders if doing so is necessary for insolvency law to function and can maximize the going concern value of the companies. In other words, protecting non-creditors in such a case not only aligns with creditors' interests[84] but also causes the smallest alteration of non-insolvency law rights. By adopting the insolvency proceedings, every party will have a larger piece of the pie to share. Such added value derives from a going concern surplus of the aggregate assets.[85] Also, insolvency law replaces the first come, first served danger of a world without bankruptcy law, so it saves on the monitoring costs of the debtors' assets and guarantees the same portion of assets for the creditors who are similarly situated.[86]

Also, one needs to be aware that non-insolvency law does not explain how to resolve collective issues faced by insolvency law. Issues regarding how to offer protection to different stakeholders and how to distribute assets are of a collective nature which cannot be answered by non-insolvency law envisaged by the economic account's scholars.[87] Arguably, general laws are ill-equipped to deal with bankruptcy issues due to their collective nature; bankruptcy law is better positioned to tackle these issues.[88] Insolvency law should deal with the disputes

---

82 When insolvency laws try to rescue an economically inefficient company for the community, the creditors' interests will be harmed. This is because creditors have to keep supporting the distressed company, even if further operating will incur loss. The redistribution from creditors to those who will benefit in the community will increase the uncertainty for the creditors. Even though the community may not suffer disturbance immediately, the rise of the cost of credit arising from such uncertainty will lead to fewer economic activities, which, in turn, will lead to less investment and fewer jobs in the community. Robert Rasmussen and David A. Skeel, Jr., 'The Economic Analysis of Corporate Bankruptcy Law' (1995) *American Bankruptcy Institute Law Review* 3 85, p. 87.

83 John Armour, 'The Law and Economics of Corporate Insolvency: A Review' (2001) ESRC Center for Business Research University of Cambridge, Working Paper No. 197, p. 15.

84 An example would be the 'stay' mechanism under the insolvency law, which binds all the creditors from destroying the intact value of insolvency assets. Douglas G. Baird and Thomas H. Jackson, 'Corporate Reorganizations and the Treatment of Diverse Ownership Interests: A Comment on Adequate Protection of Secured Creditors in Bankruptcy' (1984) *University of Chicago Law Review* 51 97, p. 101.

85 Douglas G. Baird, 'The Uneasy Case for Corporate Reorganizations' (1986) *The Journal of Legal Studies* 15 127; Thomas H. Jackson, *The Logic and Limits of Bankruptcy Law* (Harvard University Press 1986), p. 14.

86 As a result, bankruptcy law effectively constrains the self-interest of individuals by forcing them to agree to collective and compulsive insolvency proceedings in order to achieve a better result. Thomas H. Jackson, *The Logic and Limits of Bankruptcy Law* (Harvard University Press 1986), p. 15.

87 Douglas G. Baird, 'Corporate Reorganizations and the Treatment of Diverse Ownership Interests: A Comment on Adequate Protection of Secured Creditors in Bankruptcy' (1984) *University of Chicago Law Review* 51 97, p. 103.

88 Nicholas L. Georgakopoulos, 'Bankruptcy Law for Productivity' (2002) *Wake Forest Law Review* 37 51, p. 92.

26 *Rescue of multinational groups of companies*

in a collective way; otherwise, bankruptcy courts cannot obtain the information needed to determine whether it will be beneficial to save the business because creditors go to different courts to resolve their general disputes.[89] The insolvency of debtors influences all the creditors together, so only insolvency law can collectively repay the debtors and make wise decisions on behalf of all creditors.

Therefore, insolvency mechanisms need to supplement non-insolvency laws in this regard.[90] For example, stay can be viewed as supplementary to non-insolvency law rather than as simply aiming to alter the non-insolvency entitlements of creditors.[91] The priority of stakeholders is supplemented by non-insolvency law to arrange redistribution of value in a collective way.[92]

The economic account is correct to value the ex ante influence while ignoring the fact that it may not be possible to sell businesses right away on the market.[93] The reality is that the insolvency law market may sometimes be very sparse, such that buyers are difficult to find, especially for large companies. Even when the companies can be sold at a good price, the sales may take some months due to market failures. For example, potential buyers may hesitate to buy as they lack information regarding the value of a distressed business. This indicates that the business still needs to be run in order to keep it functioning. Without the ability to pay certain employees and suppliers during reorganization, the going concern value made up by these parties will dramatically disappear.[94] Insolvency law creates an incentive for creditors to preserve the going concern value of insolvent companies during reorganization.

---

89 For example, tort law may offer victims entitlement to compensation; however, such rules does not indicate how much compensation a victim can expect when the company is insolvent. To regulate such issues, tort law may create a new section, titled compensation, where the debtor is insolvent. As a result, this section could also be seen as part of insolvency substantive law. It does not make too much difference whether the insolvency section of tort law appears under tort law or under insolvency law.

90 Therefore, insolvency laws exist to fill in a gap left by many non-bankruptcy laws in the sense that insolvency law provides a collective solution to all the stakeholders whose rights come from non-insolvency laws. For example, without insolvency law, creditors may not have incentive to rescue a business; debtors may distribute assets to third parties at prices below their actual value. G. Eric Brunstad, Jr., 'Bankruptcy and Problems of Economic Futility: A Theory on the Unique Role of Bankruptcy Law' (1999–2000) *Business Law* 55 499, p. 506; Charles W. Mooney, Jr., 'A Normative Theory of Bankruptcy Law: Bankruptcy As (Is) Civil Procedure' (2004) *Washington and Lee Law Review* 61 931, p. 1011.

91 Charles W. Mooney, Jr., 'A Normative Theory of Bankruptcy Law: Bankruptcy As (Is) Civil Procedure' (2004) *Washington and Lee Law Review* 61 931, p. 1011.

92 Without insolvency, for example, there is no need to promulgate rules to pay employees' wages first. Since the debtor company has the ability to pay all its debt, everyone's payment will be honoured. Roy Goode, *Principle of Corporate Insolvency Law* (4th edn, Sweet Maxwell London 2011), p. 74.

93 Some may argue that liquidation is enough to preserve the going concern value of a distressed business as nothing stops liquidation from selling the business as a whole. However, this point of view can only be true if the distressed companies can be sold at a fair market price immediately.

94 This is why it is beneficial to give administration fee priority and to give insolvency practitioners the ability to make direct payment as they think fit for the purpose of value preservation.

The goals of corporate rescue law are the preservation of going concern value and that of certainty. The two goals need to be balanced as strict conformity to the certainty requirement will render insolvency law unable to preserve going concern value.[95] A possible balance point could be found where non-insolvency law can only be altered in insolvency proceedings for the purpose of preserving going concern value. This can be seen as the supplementary tools provided by insolvency law to deal with specific collective insolvency issues.

Theories of MCGs in the light of corporate rescue theories

After arguing that the goal of corporate rescue law is the preservation of going concern value and certainty, this section will examine their implications on the cross-border insolvency of MCGs. The section will first examine the legal definition of MCGs. After concluding that control is the key factor used to define MCGs, the book moves to the task of examining the theoretical grounds of control and its relationship to the group going concern value. The discussion is conducted in light of theories of MCGs. The next section explores the relationship between the formation of the group going concern value and the allocation of head office functions inside the MCGs.[96] This not only provides a better understanding of group going concern value and MCGs but also has implications on cross-border insolvency jurisdiction rule. Finally, the section examines the implication of corporate rescue theories on the cross-border insolvency of MCGs and provides an analysis for three main solutions that can preserve group going concern value.

Legal definition of MCGs

As the name indicates, MCGs are multinational corporate groups which carry out business in two or more countries.[97] The member companies in an MCG may be situated in different EU member states and subject to different company laws and insolvency laws.

Multinational business can be conducted on a cross-border scale by many legal entities, including companies, partnerships and non-equity-based organizations,

---

95 Stephen Lubben, 'The Overstated Absolute Priority Rule' (2016) *The Fordham Journal of Corporate & Financial Law* 21 581, p. 585.
96 Relevant discussion of MCG theories and the relationship between group going concern value and the allocation of head office functions can be found in Daoning Zhang, 'Reconsidering Procedural Consolidation for Multinational Corporate Groups in the Context of the Recast European Insolvency Regulation' (2017) *International Insolvency Review* 26(3) 241–357. This section is built on it and updates it by adding more details of MCG theories.
97 Bruce Kogut, *Multinational Corporations* (International Encyclopaedia of the Social & Behavioural Sciences Elsevier Science Ltd 2001), p. 1.

28 Rescue of multinational groups of companies

such as franchise agreements.[98] Nonetheless, in the current business world, most large firms adopt the form of groups of companies with different group structures.[99] Among other things, a prevalent form is corporate groups formed by limited liability companies.[100] Most large companies are MCGs, and they play a very important role in the EU. Corporate groups should be taken as the research focus in this case because the insolvency of large corporate groups has a far-reaching impact on the European economy. Large corporate groups yield 30% of jobs in the EU and produce 41% of gross added value.[101] This book focusses on MCGs as the typical target to discuss cross-border insolvency issues.

The general method of defining a 'group', i.e. an internal environment, is by means of control, which can be exerted by ownership and contracts. Ownership is one typical way of determining control. It is a way to define the boundary of an MNC as it clearly shows that one subsidiary belongs to the group if the parent company owns majority of shares of the former.[102] There are many ways in which a parent can own subsidiaries directly or indirectly. Even when the parent company does not directly own the subsidiary, it can still exert control over it.

It is important to note the difference in two cases: that in which shares are held by the parent in subsidiaries as a means of transfer of resources and that in which shares are held as a simple means of investment.[103] In the corporate laws of many countries, once a parent company holds more than 51% of shares of its subsidiaries, it can establish control over them by ownership.[104] Sometimes, de jure control can be established by cross holdings whereby three companies mutually hold a certain amount of each other's shares and agree to operate in a uniform way.[105] Another form – circular holding in a chain structure – allows the top parent to control the subsidiaries way down the hierarchy when the parent company owns less than 51% shares. For example, the parent company may be able to directly control a subsidiary by owning 51% of shares of the latter,

---

98 Irit Mevorach, *Insolvency within Multinational Enterprise Groups* (Oxford University Press 2009), p. 20.

99 Irit Mevorach, 'The Road to a Suitable and Comprehensive Global Approach to Insolvencies within Multinational Corporate Groups' (2005) *JPLP* 15 5, p. 4.

100 Such a phenomenon arguably may be facilitated by the EU member states' removal of obstacles to setting up companies: for instance the removal of minimum capital requirements. Christoph Teichmann, 'Corporate Groups within the Legal Framework of the European Union: The Group-Related Aspects of the SUP Proposal and the EU Freedom of Establishment' (2015) *European Company and Financial Law Review* 12(2) 202–229, p. 2.

101 Commission staff working document executive summary of the impact assessment – accompanying the document-commission recommendation on a new approach to business failure and insolvency SWD(2014) 61 final, p. 20.

102 Virginia Harper Ho, 'Theories of Corporate Groups: Corporate Identity Reconceived' (2012) *Seton Hall Law Review* 42(3), p. 886.

103 Ibid., p. 889.

104 Klaus J. Hopt, 'Groups of Companies – A Comparative Study on the Economics, Law and Regulation of Corporate Groups' (2015), p. 2. http://ssrn.com/abstract=2560935.

105 Daniel D. Prentice, 'Some Aspects of the Law Relating to Corporate Groups in the United Kingdom' (1998–1999) *Connecticut Journal of International Law* 13 305, p. 313.

but it can also indirectly control the sub-subsidiary by owning less than 51% of shares of it.[106]

Control could also be obtained by means of contracts. In EU competition law, control is defined as:

> Means which confer the possibility of exercising decisive influence on an undertaking, in particular by rights or contracts which confer decisive influence on the composition, voting or decisions of the organs of an undertaking.[107]

Control could be used as a workable standard for the corporate groups which assign obligations to parent companies.[108] Also, the control of parent companies is sometimes expressed as the existence of the share ownership in subsidiaries and the determination of the board members of subsidiaries.[109]

Even though MCGs are the prevalent form of doing business in a cross-border context, the specific legal regimes needed to deal with corporate groups are rare.[110] Unlike the well-established concept of companies,, MCGs in many areas of law are seen not as whole entities but as a group of individual companies. In certain areas of law, MCGs have been treated as an economic integration while the issues of limited liabilities of individual companies are respected, such as accounting and tax areas.[111]

In the area of cross-border insolvency law, legislations for MCGs are rare. However, there is a new development in this area. The newly released EU regulation on insolvency proceedings provides a definition for groups of companies which corresponds to the Accounting Directive 2013/34/EU above. Its definition is as follows:

> *(13) 'group of companies' means a parent undertaking and all its subsidiary undertakings; (14) 'parent undertaking' means an undertaking which controls, either directly or indirectly, one or more subsidiary undertakings. An undertaking which prepares consolidated financial statements in accordance with Directive 2013/34/EU of the European Parliament and of the Council (1) shall be deemed to be a parent undertaking.*[112]

From the EIR recast, one can see that control is the key factor in defining MCGs. Control can be exerted by a certain percentage of shareholdings or votes, either

---

106 Ibid., p. 313.
107 Council Regulation (EC) No. 139/2004 of 20 January 2004 on the control of concentrations between undertakings (the EC Merger Regulation) Article 2(b).
108 See the following examples:*Texas International Law Journal*
    'For the purposes of this Part two companies are members of the same group of companies if—
109 Phillip I. Blumberg, 'The Corporate Entity in an Era of Multinational Corporations' (1990) *Delaware Journal of Corporate Law* 15(2) 283–374, p. 329.
110 Eva M.F. de Vette, 'Multinational Enterprise Groups in Insolvency: How Should the European Union Act?' (2011) *Utrechtlawreview.org* 7(1), p. 1.
111 UNCITRAL Legislative Guide on Insolvency Law – Part three, p. 14.
112 EIR recast 2015 Art. 2.

30 Rescue of multinational groups of companies

directly or indirectly, or a functional means of control formed by either owner-ship or contracts (de facto).[113] The essence is that control links member companies in MCGs together.

Theories of MCGs

As mentioned above, control is the key factor in defining MCGs in many areas of law. One may ask why 'control' is the best test of MCGs. To examine the control test, it is helpful to consider why MCGs exist in the first place.

Transaction cost and internalization theories of MCGs

In an imperfect market, doing business with a third party may give rise to mark-able transaction costs, which may be reduced if certain transactions or business activities are allowed to occur inside the group.[114] The transfer of knowledge to foreign agents may contain transaction costs. Transaction costs deriving from unbounded rationality[115] and opportunism[116] make the contracts of knowledge transfer costly.[117] For example, licensees have the incentive to know exactly what they are buying, while the seller company has the incentive to conceal information, so licensees cannot learn their trade secrets and compete with them later.[118] The information cost and the bargain cost will rise as a result. In terms of vertically integrated business where the intermediate product of one company is the raw material of another, the possibility of the withdrawal of any party from the cooperation will cause uncertainty. Contracting with new suppliers or customers requires original parties to acquire new information and adapt to new requirements.[119] The costs of uncertainty and contracting may be huge.

By contrast, if the licensees are replaced by internal subsidiaries, the group may send employees with relevant knowledge to educate subsidiaries at a low cost, and the group does not need to worry about knowledge leakage.[120] The bargaining cost and information cost of relevant contracts will be lower. Theoretically, the boundary of an MCG lies where the benefits of the further internalization of

---

113 UNCITRAL Legislative Guide on Insolvency Law – Part three, p. 15.
114 Michael Galanis, 'Vicious Spirals in Corporate Governance: Mandatory Rules for Systemic (Re) balance?' (2011) *Oxford Journal of Legal Studies* 31(2) 327–363, p. 331; see also Ronald Coase, 'The Nature of the Firm' (1937) *Economica*, New Series 4(16) 368–405.
115 The difficulty of absorbing and understanding complicated information.
116 The contractual parties may pursue self-interest.
117 Alan M. Rugman, 'New Theories of the Multinational Enterprise: An Assessment of Internalization Theory' (1986) *Bulletin of Economic Research* 38(2) 101–118, p. 109.
118 David J. Teece, 'Transactions Cost Economics and the Multinational Enterprise: An Assessment' (1986) *Journal of Economic Behavior and Organization* 7 21–45, p. 29.
119 Ibid., p. 32.
120 James R. Markusen, 'The Boundaries of Multinational Enterprises and the Theory of International Trade' (1995) *The Journal of Economic Perspectives* 9(2) 169–189, p. 184.

Rescue of multinational groups of companies 31

markets equals the costs.[121] Therefore, for the purposes of internalization and the reduction of transaction cost, it may be necessary for groups to be able to control their advantageous resources.[122] This demand justifies the control test.

Different from an arms-length market relationship, group members in a given MCG create an internal environment which may give the whole group certain advantages. In this regard, internalization theory[123] provides useful insights into the boundaries of MCGs. Nonetheless the cost of setting up foreign subsidiaries is high compared to licensing agents, forming alliances in foreign countries or exporting products; the corporate groups still choose to set up subsidiaries as the benefit of such internal relationships outweighs the cost.[124]

Resource- and knowledge-based theories of MCGs

Resource-based theory states that in order to succeed in the market, companies should possess rare valuable non-substitutable and inimitable resources.[125] These valuable resources include not only valuable physical assets but also the knowledge regarding the use of these resources as well as learning and accumulating knowledge and external opportunities.[126] In addition to other resources, knowledge-based theory argues that organizational structures may be formed in order to use knowledge in the most efficient way, especially with regard to tacit knowledge, which is only available to internal staff and environment.[127] Foreign subsidiaries have better access to information and country-specific advantages,

---

121 Peter J. Buckley and Mark C. Casson, 'The Internalization Theory of the Multinational Enterprise: A Review of Progress of a Research Agenda after 30 years' (2009) *Journal of International Business Studies* 40 1563–1580, p. 1564.

122 John H. Dunning, 'The Eclectic Paradigm as an Envelope for Economic and Business Theories of MNE Activity' (2000) *International Business Review* 9 163–190, p. 180.

123 Alan M. Rugman, 'Reconciling Internalization Theory and the Eclectic Paradigm' (2009) *The Multinational Business Review* 18(1) 1–12; Peter J. Buckley and Roger Strange, 'The Governance of the Multinational Enterprise: Insights from Internalization Theory' (2011) *Journal of Management Studies* 48(2) 460–470.

124 Alan M. Rugman, 'Reconciling Internalization Theory and the Eclectic Paradigm' (2009) *The Multinational Business Review* 18(1) 1–12, p. 2.

125 Examples of valued resources and capabilities include reputation, buyer-supplier relationships, tacit knowledge, R&D expertise and technological capabilities. Jay Barney, 'Firm Resources and Sustained Competitive Advantage' (1991) *Journal of Management* 17 99–120. Christine Oliver, 'Sustainable Competitive Advantage: Combining Institutional and Resource-Based Views' (1997) *Strategic Management Journal* 18(9) 697–713.

126 Sidney G. Winter, 'On Coase, Competence, and the Corporation' (1988) *Journal of Law, Economics, and Organization* 4, pp. 175–177; D.J. Teece, G. Pisano and A. Shuen, *Firm Capabilities, Resources, and the Concept of Strategy* (Mimeo, University of California at Berkeley, Haas School of Business 1990), p. 11; R.M. Cyert, P. Kumar and J.R. Williams (1993), 'Information, Market Imperfections and Strategy,' (1993) *Strategic Management Journal* 14 (Winter Special Issue) 47–58, p. 57; see generally, Kathleen R. Conner and C.K. Prahalad, 'A Resource-Based Theory of the Firm: Knowledge Versus Opportunism.' (1996) *Organization Science* 7 477–501.

127 Jeffrey A. Miles, *Management and Organization Theory* (Jossey-Bass, 2012), p. 153.

32   *Rescue of multinational groups of companies*

such as technology and low cost of labour. Business relationships allow other group members to understand the foreign environment and demand, and learn and share with each other.[128] The group can locate subsidiaries to gain local advantage, transform country-related advantages into firm-specific advantages and transfer these to other subsidiaries.[129] The knowledge possessed by groups of companies is invaluable, and the key for them is to transfer and coordinate knowledge to produce advantages.[130]

Group members in MCGs may rely on each other's advantages and resources. Companies are open systems as they interact with the outside environment.[131] The MCGs attract resources from foreign countries and coordinate between member companies internally in an efficient way, which in return allows them to generate huge profits.[132] In order to make products or service competitive, the value that one product or service could generate should be higher than the average level.[133] Resources themselves do not automatically generate value, but value is wielded through unique combinations of resources and capacities. To create value, MCGs have to combine their resources[134] and capacities[135] in a unique way, which may require certain cooperation between member companies. MCGs will consider expanding their business to other countries if they can gain more net benefits from managing the interdependent relationships between different subsidiaries than the market.[136] It is possible to assert that the relationships of group member companies in an MCG may be of great value. This is more likely to be true if the

128 Francesco Ciabuschi, Ulf Holm and Oscar Martin, 'Dual Embeddedness, Influence and Performance of Innovating Subsidiaries in the Multinational Corporation' (2014) *International Business Review* 23 897–909, p. 905.

129 Ulf Andersson, Henrik Dellestrand and Torben Pedersen, 'The Contribution of Local Environments to Competence Creation in Multinational Enterprises' (2014) *Long Range Planning* 47 87–99, p. 95.

130 Robert M. Gant, 'Toward a Knowledge-Based Theory of the Firm' (1996) *Strategic Management Journal* 17 109–122, p. 120.

131 Mats Forsgren *et al.*, *Managing the Embedded Multinational – A Business Network View* (Edward Elgar 2006), p. 92.

132 Ibid., p. 1.

133 Value is gauged by the products' performance attributes according to the customers who would like to purchase them. Resources can include financial resources, organizational resources (coordinating system), physical resources and technological resources, or intangible resources, such as knowledge capacities to innovate, goodwill, etc. See R. Duane Ireland *et al.*, *The Management of Strategies Concept and Cases* (9th International Edition, South-Western Cengage Learning 2012), p. 66.

134 'Capacities exist when resources have been purposely integrated to achieve a specific task or set of tasks, such as develop and transfer knowledge'. R. Duane Ireland *et al.*, *The Management of Strategies Concept and Cases* (9th International Edition, South-Western Cengage Learning 2012), p. 70.

135 Advantages gained from preceding combination conferring core competences to some corporate groups, such as Amazon, which combines its e-commerce team with its distribution resources. R. Duane Ireland *et al.*, *The Management of Strategies Concept and Cases* (9th International Edition, South-Western Cengage Learning 2012), p. 72.

136 Jean-Francois Hennart, 'Theories of the Multinational Enterprise', in A.M. Rugman (ed.), *The Oxford Handbook of International Business* (2nd edn, Oxford University Press 2009), p. 133.

Rescue of multinational groups of companies   33

member companies are functionally connected with each other. This possibility is supported by resource-based theory and knowledge-based theory as these indicate that relationships are valuable resources. MCGs need competitive advantages such as innovations to stay successful in the market. Nowadays, many important innovations are achieved at the subsidiaries' levels so that they become strategic resources of the MCGs.[137] As it is not enough to perform better than rivals in the global market by relying on the strength of the parent company, all the subsidiaries should contribute their knowledge of the local environment to the MCGs.[138]

The internalization theory and resource-based theory may therefore indicate that it is possible for certain MCGs to have group going concern value due to their relationships[139] that make them worth preserving for the purpose of insolvency law. Without corporate group insolvency rules, the mutual adaptation networks of business could break down, and relational rent would be lost.[140] It may be the case that certain companies cannot be rescued without returning to the network to cooperate with other member companies. This possibility has been recognized by the European Commission, which believes that an insolvent subsidiary may itself not be viable without the support of the other members of the group.[141] Without a group solution, the value of groups dissipates significantly.

A contingency theory and business network theory of MCGs

Since the above sections have touched on the 'relationships' and 'networks' of group members in an MCG, this section aims to further shed light on how group structure may be explained and researched.

Contingency theory and business network theory are both useful theories waiting to be examined. From the perspective of contingency theory, the characteristics of an organization should fit its own contingencies, including size, environment and strategies, so as to achieve desirable results.[142] One insight gained from contingency theory is that the operational structure and legal structure of

---

137 Francesco Ciabuschi, Ulf Holm and Oscar Martin, 'Dual Embeddedness, Influence and Performance of Innovating Subsidiaries in the Multinational Corporation' (2014) *International Business Review* 23 897–909, p. 897.

138 Yves Doz and Jose F.P. Santos, 'On the Management of Knowledge: From the Transparency of Collocation and Co-Setting to the Quandary of Dispersion and Differentiation' (1997) INSEAD, Fontainebleau, France, p. 6.

139 The key resource could be the network itself. It could be the case that two companies combine their resources in a unique way and thereby gain competitive advantages over other companies, which can be achieved through such combination. Jeffrey H. Dyer and Harbir Singh, 'The Relational View: Cooperative Strategy and Sources of Inter-Organisational Competitive Advantage' (1998) *The Academy of Management Review* 23(4) 660–679, p. 661; Ranjay Gulati *et al.*, 'Strategic Networks' (2000) *Strategic Management Journal* 21 203–215, p. 207.

140 In an extreme case, it is even possible for one subsidiary to lose all the going concern value if its network is cut off. For example, if a factory loses an important IP licence, the remaining assets may have no going concern value higher than liquidation value.

141 Commission staff working document, impact assessment, accompanying the document Revision of Regulation (EC) No. 1346/2000 on insolvency proceedings SWD(2012) 416 final, p. 15.

142 Lex Donaldson, *The Contingency Theory of Organizations* (Sage Publications 2001), p. 2.

34 Rescue of multinational groups of companies

an MCG may be the result of its exploration of the 'fit', i.e. suitable configuration. Therefore, the control that the parent company may exert is uncertain and evolving; the fit itself may be of great value as it allows the MCG to work effectively. From the perspective of business network theory, the dynamics of relationships and control between group members have been recognized by scholars embracing a business network perspective on MCGs.[143] Unlike the traditional view that considers MCGs as hierarchies,[144] the business network perspective believes that most of the organizations can be seen as bundles of different networks.[145] In reality, the relationships of multinational companies may be more similar to differentiated networks than they are to hierarchies. Regarding the task of governing multinational subsidiaries, it is beyond the capacities of any homogeneous organizational structures to capture and respond to the characteristics of MCGs with subsidiaries operating under various environments.[146]

A subsidiary both is embedded[147] in the internal and external networks containing unique features and roles to contribute to the group, and retains a certain level of autonomy in some aspects in which they have expertise and resources.[148]

---

143 Mats Forsgren, *Theories of the Multinational Firm* (2nd edn, Edward Elgar publishing Limited 2013), p. 107.

144 Following this assumption, a group is called a hierarchically centralized group when parent companies make all the decisions on behalf of the group's subsidiaries. Also, if the business of group members is interdependent, the group can be called a business integrated group. Centralization and integration can be seen as two variables of headquarter and subsidiaries relationships. Julian M. Birkinshaw and Allen J. Morrison, 'Configurations of Strategy and Structure in Subsidiaries of Multinational Corporations' (1995) *Journal of International Business Studies*, 26(4) 729–754, p. 732; Stephen R. Gates and William G. Egelhoff, 'Centralization in Headquarters-Subsidiary Relationships' (1986) *Journal of International Business Studies* 17(2) 71–92, p. 72.

145 Jeffrey H. Dyer and Harbir Singh, 'The Relational View: Cooperative Strategy and Sources of Inter-Organisational Competitive Advantage' (1998) *The Academy of Management Review* 23(4) 660–679, p. 660.

146 Nitin Nohria and Sumantra Ghoshal, *The Differentiated Network* (Jossey-Bass Inc. 1997), p. 4; K. Asakawa, 'Organizational Tension in International R&D Management: The Case of Japanese Firms' (2001) *Research Policy* 30(5) 735–757. J. Birkinshaw and N. Fry 'Subsidiary Initiatives to Develop New Markets' (1998) *Sloan Management Review* 39(3) 51–61; D.C. Galunic and K.M. Eisenhardt, 'The Evolution of Intra-Corporate Domains: Divisional Charter Losses in High Technology, Multidivisional Corporations' (1996) *Organization Science* 7(3) 255–282; R. Mudambi and P. Navarra, 'Is Knowledge Power? Knowledge Flows, Subsidiary Power and Rent-Seeking within MNCs' (2004) *Journal of International Business Studies* 35(5) 385–406.

147 Subsidiaries' embeddedness means that they form long-term business relationships through which they adapt to each other's production process; this can lead to innovation so that valuable knowledge and technology are transferred to other parties of group members, which enhances the competence of the whole MNC. See Mo Yamin and Ulf Andersson, 'Subsidiary Importance in the MNC: What Role Does Internal Embeddedness Play?' (2011) *International Business Review* 20 151–162, p. 152.

148 U. Andersson and M. Forsgren, 'In Search of Centre of Excellence: Network Embeddedness and Subsidiary Roles in Multinational Corporations' (2000) *Management International Review* 40(4) 329–350, p. 332; see also Eva A. Alfoldi *et al.*, 'Coordination at the Edge of the Empire: The Delegation of Headquarters Functions through Regional Management Mandates' (2012) *Journal of International Management* 18 276–292, p. 276.

The new roles that subsidiaries play and the complex environments in which they need to confront help them gain power from their parent companies.[149] Where the subsidiaries have expertise in certain areas, such as R&D, they may form specific advantages which can be used uniquely in their local market; the advantages can even be spread out to the whole group, making them 'non-location-bound company's specific advantages'.[150] The transfer frequency of knowledge from top to bottom and from subsidiary to subsidiary is the same, which indicates that structures of MCGs are better described as networks than hierarchical as they may directly share knowledge with other sister subsidiaries rather than via a joint head office[151] of MCGs.[152]

Networks may form relational economic rents which cannot be gained from regular market relationships. Such relationships do not contain idiosyncrasies by which the parties can gain an advantage over rivals.[153] Business relationships are the pipes of information, resources, technologies and marketing between member companies, and they can be seen as important, intangible company resources.[154] Therefore, group members who are in powerful networks may be in an advantageous position compared to their rivals. A single company's competition becomes the networks' competition.[155] This reality provides us with a business network perspective that reveals that the companies in networks do not necessarily need to have the ownership of certain important resources as long as they can have access to the resources from other parties.[156] Subsidiaries not only contribute value but also receive the benefits from other member companies, despite distance.[157]

For this purpose, group members need to form close relationship whereby they can facilitate the formation and digestion of knowledge gained by subsidiaries

---

149 Ram Mudambi *et al.*, 'How Subsidiaries Gain Power in Multinational Corporations' (2014) *Journal of World Business* 49 101–113, p. 109.

150 Alan M. Rugman and Alain Verbeke, 'Subsidiary-Specific Advantages in Multinational Enterprises' (2001) *Strategic Management Journal* 22(3) 237–250, p. 246; Sharon Watson O'Donnell, 'Managing Foreign Subsidiaries: Agents of Headquarters, or an Interdependent Network' (2000) *Strategic Management Journal*, 21 525–548.

151 'Head office' is a term generally describing an organization that is responsible for the long-term strategies of a company.

152 Cátia Fernandes Crespo, 'The Performance Effects of Vertical and Horizontal Subsidiary Knowledge Outflows in Multinational Corporations' (2014) *International Business Review* 23 993–1007, p. 1003.

153 Jeffrey H. Dyer and Harbir Singh, 'The Relational View: Cooperative Strategy and Sources of Inter-Organisational Competitive Advantage' (1998) *The Academy of Management Review* 23(4) 660–679, p. 662.

154 Mats Forsgren, *Theories of the Multinational Firm* (2nd edn, Edward Elgar 2013), p. 108.

155 Jeffrey H. Dyer and Harbir Singh, 'The Relational View: Cooperative Strategy and Sources of Inter-Organisational Competitive Advantage' (1998) *The Academy of Management Review* 23(4) 660–679, p. 675.

156 Doven Lavie, 'The Competitive Advantage of Interconnected Firms: An Extension of the Resource-Based View' (2006) *The Academy of Management Review* 31(3) 638–658, p. 641.

157 Ulf Andersson *et al.*, 'The Contribution of Local Environments to Competence Creation in Multinational Enterprises' (2014) *Long Range Planning* 47 87–99, p. 96.

36 Rescue of multinational groups of companies

from the external environment.[158] The complicated and dynamic foreign environment of subsidiaries leads to information asymmetry, which forces parent companies to rely on subsidiaries for information understanding and decision-making, no matter what corporate structure the MNC adopts.[159] The value that subsidiaries can generate combined with the information asymmetry make group members interdependent.[160] Attention should be paid that such interdependent relationships are distinguished from market relationships that do not yield going concern value.[161]

The interdependent relationships are generally formed over a long time.[162] It is difficult to replace the network reflecting the interdependence with a third party, at least in a short time, as this party faces difficulties in understanding the unique nature of the relationships of the previous party with regard to the interdependence, know-how and technologies.[163] This is especially true in the MCGs context, where the network is multidimensional and involves multiple parties.[164] Relying solely on the advantages of parent companies is inadequate for MCGs to outperform competitors unless they are the only holders of certain resources; they have to explore and integrate country-specific advantages as broadly as possible in order to enhance their competence.[165] So, every head office is responsible for transferring the useful knowledge gained from the local subsidiaries to other group members.[166] As a result, the parent company may rely on these contributions, such as technologies, from subsidiaries.[167]

---

158 Francesco Ciabuschi, Ulf Holm and Oscar Martin, 'Dual Embeddedness, Influence and Performance of Innovating Subsidiaries in the Multinational Corporation' (2014) *International Business Review* 23 897–909, p. 906.

159 Francesco Ciabuschi, Henrik Dellestrand and Ulf Holm, 'The Role of Headquarters in the Contemporary MNC' (2012) *Journal of International Management* 18 213–223, p. 218.

160 J.D. Thompson, *Organizations in Action* (McGraw-Hill 1967).

161 Interdependence may exist in many forms, such as sequential interdependence, where one company needs the input of other companies, and reciprocal interdependence, where such sequential input is multi-sided. Jeffrey H. Dyer and Harbir Singh, 'The Relational View: Cooperative Strategy and Sources of Inter-Organisational Competitive Advantage' (1998) *The Academy of Management Review* 23(4) 660–679, p. 662.

162 From a study by Hakansson 1982, the average age of a business relationship is more than 15 years. Hakansson, H. *International Marketing and Purchasing of Industrial Goods – An Interaction Approach* (John Wiley & Sons 1982).

163 Mats Forsgren, *Theories of the Multinational Firm* (2nd edn, Edward Elgar 2013), p. 108.

164 Håkan Håkansson and Ivan Snehota, *Developing Relationships in Business Networks* (Routledge 1995), p. 139.

165 Yves Doz, Jose F.P. Santos, 'On the Management of Knowledge: From the Transparency of Collocation and Co-Setting to the Quandary of Dispersion and Differentiation' (1997) INSEAD, Fontainebleau, France, p. 6.

166 Tina C. Ambos, 'Learning from Foreign Subsidiaries: An Empirical Investigation of Headquarters' Benefits from Reverse Knowledge Transfers' (2006) *International Business Review* 15 294–312, p. 306; Francesco Ciabuschi, Henrik Dellestrand and Ulf Holm, 'The Role of Headquarters in the Contemporary MNC' (2012) *Journal of International Management* 18 213–223, p. 215.

167 Christopher A. Bartlett and S. Ghoshal. *Managing Across Borders: The Transnational Solution* (Harvard Business School Press 1989), p. 129; Sharon Watson O'Donnell, 'Managing Foreign

Group going concern value and the allocation of head office functions in MCGs

The last section reveals that MCGs may internalize market relationships for the purpose of the group going concern value. The internalization is reflected by the control linking group member companies together. However, it does not indicate how the control is allocated inside an MCG among its subsidiaries in different member states. This question is important as even if one parent company can control its subsidiaries in theory, it may not do so in reality.[168] It is possible for the parent company to give up control and allocate certain head office functions to the foreign subsidiaries for the purpose of the group going concern value. Therefore, the analysis of this question will provide a better understanding of the relationship between the formation of group going concern value and the allocation of head office functions in MCGs. More importantly, the allocation of head office functions has an impact on insolvency jurisdiction rules, which allocate jurisdiction to the court where the head office functions of one company are carried out.[169] This section will focus on the relationship between the group going concern value and the allocation of head office functions within MCGs.

According to the resource dependence theory, the dependence can create power and control.[170] Even though parent companies have power over subsidiaries through their authority, they may be unable to exert it in some aspects. This is because subsidiaries and parents may be interdependent from each other, which prevents parent companies from exerting full control on the subsidiaries.[171]

In reality, it is possible to argue that every subsidiary may retain some degree of autonomy in order to cope with the complex local environment; this indicates that subsidiaries may keep some important functions and that they are able to influence other member companies. Beyond the value gained from foreign locations or countries, nowadays, subsidiaries increasingly take on innovation and research roles as opposed to the implementer roles which only enforce the

---

Subsidiaries: Agents of Headquarters, or an Interdependent Network' (2000) *Strategic Management Journal*, 21 525–548, p. 530; Mohan Subramaniam and Sharon Watson, 'How Interdependence Affects Subsidiary Performance' (2006) *Journal of Business Research* 59 916–924, p. 922; Ulf Andersson, Mats Forsgren and Ulf Holm, 'Balancing Subsidiary Influence in the Federative MNC: A Business Network View' (2007) *Journal of International Business Studies* 38(5) 802–818, p. 806.

168 Mats Forsgren *et al.*, *Managing the Embedded Multinational – A Business Network View* (Edward Elgar 2006), p. 93.

169 Whether the parent company can be viewed as the only character which executes the head office functions determines the certainty of rules for procedural consolidation. See Chapter 3.

170 Jeffrey Pfeffer and Gerald Salancik, *The External Control of Organizations: A Resource Dependence Perspective* (Harper & Row 1978); Mats Forsgren *et al.*, *Managing the Embedded Multinational – A Business Network View* (Edward Elgar 2006), p. 142.

171 Ranjay Gulati, Nitin Nohria and Akbar Zaheer, 'Strategic Networks' (2000) *Strategic Management Journal* 21 203–215, p. 212; see also Ranjay Gulati, 'Alliances and Networks' (1998) *Strategic Management Journal* 19 293–317, p. 310.

38 Rescue of multinational groups of companies

mandates from parent companies in traditional hierarchical structures.[172] This supports the idea that parent companies may defer to subsidiaries in some respects of daily operation and decision-making.

Furthermore, a good local research environment endows the subsidiaries with considerable potential to take on creative roles, especially in cases where the subsidiaries' functional mandates are broader; long-term development makes them able to transform from the home-country's implementer to a globally integrated creator.[173] All in all, imagining a corporate group as a simple hierarchy where the parent controls all foreign subsidiaries in the same way does not reflect the reality of how a group is organized.[174] Even though the parent company enjoys authority as a result of its top position, it rarely controls all the subsidiaries in the same way. Some of them in fact enjoy considerable autonomy in some aspects of decision-making.[175]

Research has shown that both European and UK MCGs are inclined to decentralize as their foreign subsidiaries' sizes grow. For example, UK corporate groups are prone to delegating power of marketing and manufacturing to local subsidiaries while retaining financial decision-making power.[176]

One can therefore argued that head office functions are increasingly allocated to different levels in MCGs according to strategic demand; some head office functions may be at the level of subsidiaries, while others may be at the level of regional headquarters. Head office functions could be divided into multi-divisions according to the functions, regions and businesses which exist in the same group.[177] Therefore, the place of the nominal head office does not indicate that all the head office functions occur there,[178] and it cannot be assumed that these functions always stay in one place, such as the home countries of the parents of MCGs.[179] Research has shown that with the growth of MCGs, parts of

---

172 Julian M. Birkinshaw and Allen J. Morrison, 'Configurations of Strategy and Structure in Subsidiaries of Multinational Corporations' (1995) *Journal of International Business Studies*, 26(4) 729–754, p. 733; The knowledge transferred by the implementers is low level knowledge. Larissa Rabbiosi, 'Subsidiary Roles and Reverse Knowledge Transfer: An Investigation of the Effects of Coordination Mechanisms' (2011) *Journal of International Management* 17 97–113, p. 105.

173 John Cantwell and Ram Mudambi, 'MNE Competence-Creating Subsidiary Mandates' (2005) *Strategic Management Journal* 26(12) 1109–1128, p. 1124.

174 Nitin Nohria and Sumantra Ghoshal, *The Differentiated Network* (Jossey-Bass Inc. 1997), p. 4.

175 Ibid., p. 14.

176 Stephen R. Gates and William G. Egelhoff, 'Centralization in Headquarters-Subsidiary Relationships' (1986) *Journal of International Business Studies* 17(2) 71–92, p. 88.

177 Francesco Ciabuschi, Henrik Dellestrand, Ulf Holm, 'The Role of Headquarters in the Contemporary MNC' (2012) *Journal of International Management* 18 213–223, p. 215.

178 Ibid., p. 216; see also Henrik Dellestrand, 'Subsidiary Embeddedness as a Determinant of Divisional Headquarters Involvement in Innovation Transfer Processes' (2011) *Journal of International Management* 17 229–242, p. 237.

179 Marc G. Baaij *et al.*, 'Why Do Multinational Corporations Relocate Core Parts of their Corporate Headquarters Abroad?' (2015) *Long Range Planning* 48 46–58, p. 54.

Rescue of multinational groups of companies 39

the head office functions, such as management teams and staff functions, may be moved overseas in order to better serve stakeholders.[180]

While parent companies may frequently arrange financing on behalf of MCGs, the contributions from other group members with reference to value creation are no less important than those of financing.[181] In fact, it has been argued that technological resources can generate the highest level of power over other aspects of resources, such as financial capital resources or distribution capacities.[182] Research has been done to show that strategic power which could influence the whole group is gained by subsidiaries which are in charge of technology-related functions.[183]

Therefore, the decentralization and centralization of control are two extreme ends of the spectrum of how MCGs exert control and allocate head office functions, while the reality is somewhere in the middle.[184] The hierarchical structure is only applicable to cases where the environment of a subsidiary is not complex, and the subsidiary does not control important resources.[185]

However, this does not mean that parent companies do not carry out any head office functions.[186] Parent companies are more likely to perform parts of head office functions while delegating the rest to subsidiaries. The need to balance the corporate group interest and local responsiveness requires the large companies to adjust their head office functions *vis-à-vis* every subsidiary.[187] To contribute to and control the local subsidiaries, the precondition is that head office should understand local business and have the capacity to provide support to local subsidiaries.[188] This will help the MCGs to adapt to an ever-changing environment and allow them to balance local responsiveness and integration.[189]

The head offices of corporate groups also need to adjust the proportion of power they delegate to different subsidiaries. Even if parent companies have the

---

180 Ibid., p. 46, 49.

181 Sharon D. James, 'Strategic Bankruptcy: A Stakeholder Management Perspective' (2016) *Journal of Business Research* 69, p. 2.

182 Ram Mudambi *et al.*, 'How Subsidiaries Gain Power in Multinational Corporations' (2014) *Journal of World Business* 49 101–113, p. 103.

183 Examples of technology-related functions are research and development; examples of business-related functions are marketing and distribution. Ibid., p. 109.

184 B. Ambos and B.B. Schlegelmilch, *The New Role of Regional Management* (Palgrave McMillan 2010), p. 1.

185 Nitin Nohria and Sumantra Ghoshal, *The Differentiated Network* (Jossey-Bass Inc. 1997), p. 111.

186 Kirsten Foss *et al.* 'MNC Organisational Form and Subsidiary Motivation Problems: Controlling Intervention Hazards in the Network of MNC' (2011), p. 6 (available at: http://ssrn.com/abstract=1969402).

187 Björn Ambos and Volker Mahnke, 'How Do MNC Headquarters Add Value?' (2010) *Management International Review* 50(4) 403–412, p. 404.

188 Ibid., p. 405.

189 Kirsten Foss *et al.*, 'MNC Organisational Form and Subsidiary Motivation Problems: Controlling Intervention Hazards in the Network of MNC' (2011), p. 6 (available at: http://ssrn.com/abstract=1969402).

40 Rescue of multinational groups of companies

corporate authority to make decisions superseding those of their subsidiaries, they may not do so as it is too costly to make mistakes.[190] Parent companies cannot fully control the subsidiaries, nor can they fully set subsidiaries free as that may conflict with the long-term strategic plan of the group.[191]

From this discussion, a conclusion could be drawn that the resources that foreign subsidiaries can obtain and the new roles they play make foreign subsidiaries valuable for MCGs. The network among member companies forms group going concern value as it enables MCGs to transfer these resources to other members of MCGs. As a result, the complex environment of subsidiaries[192] and the interdependence[193] between member companies require MCGs to adopt flexible control and structures as opposed to rigid hierarchies. In cases where the subsidiaries control important resources, the subsidiaries gain more bargaining power over other companies in the group.[194] Therefore, the head office functions of MCGs are frequently allocated to foreign subsidiaries for the purpose of obtaining group going concern value. This is the relationship between the formation of group going concern value and the allocation of head office functions in MCGs. Its implication is that one may not be able to identify where the head office functions of an MCG occur. This may have an implication on cross-border insolvency jurisdiction rules.

Implication on the treatment of MCGs in cross-border insolvency context

A company has independent legal status; limited liability and legal personality are core features of companies which generate economic efficiency by lowering the cost of doing business.[195] For instance, by enabling companies to own properties, shares can be transferred easily from sellers to buyers without costs arising from transfer of business; limited liabilities of investors also encourage businessmen to engage in their business activities.[196] The merits and legal endowment of legal personality and limited liabilities are widely respected and applied. It is possible in certain areas of law, such as accounting rules (consolidated account), to design rules for groups of companies as a unit due to their economic integration if the issue of

---

190 Kirsten Foss and Nicholai J Foss, 'Resources and Transaction Costs: How Property Rights Economics Furthers the Resource Based View' (2005) *Strategic Management Journal* 26 541–553, p. 544.

191 Nitin Nohria and Sumantra Ghoshal, 'Differentiated Fit and Shared Values: Alternatives for Managing Headquarters-Subsidiary Relations' (1994) *Strategic Management Journal* 15(6) 491–502, p. 492.

192 Ulf Andersson and Mats Forsgren, 'In Search of Centre of Excellence: Network Embeddedness and Subsidiary Roles in Multinational Corporations' (2000) *Management International Review* 40(4) 329–350, p. 344.

193 Mohan Subramaniam and Sharon Watson, 'How Interdependence Affects Subsidiary Performance' (2006) *Journal of Business Research* 59 916–924, p. 918.

194 Nitin Nohria and Sumantra Ghoshal, *The Differentiated Network* (Jossey-Bass Inc. 1997), p. 96.

195 Irit Mevorach, *Insolvency within Multinational Enterprise Groups* (Oxford University Press 2009), p. 41.

196 Ibid., p. 41.

Rescue of multinational groups of companies   41

protection of limited liabilities does not arise.[197] However, in the field of insolvency law, considering the group as one unit may be impossible as different companies in the group may have different profiles of creditors and respective assets. The limited liability of a company is the protection shield for stakeholders of different subsidiaries. Creditors in one subsidiary generally do not need to monitor the assets' and other creditors' behaviour as the creditors calculate risks only against the company to which they lend money. So, it may be radical to replace entity law with enterprise law in the context of insolvency of MCGs. Replacing entity law by enterprise law may cause serious conflicts among national laws in this regard.[198]

Another point worth mentioning is that corporate rescue law is in reality complex and elastic;[199] different member states have different insolvency laws and may pursue similar but different goals. For example, whereas German insolvency law may focus more on debt collection, French insolvency law focusses more on social goals, such as employment protection; UK and US insolvency laws are positioned somewhere in between.[200] The same creditors may be treated differently in different member states. Corporate rescue theories need not conform to or explain every detail of national corporate rescue law; rather, the discussion of relevant theories only aims to determine the desirable values that corporate rescue law in general should embrace.[201]

After acknowledging these facts, we can examine the implication of corporate rescue theories and multinational enterprise theories on the solutions of the cross-border insolvency of MCGs. In the cases where the MCGs have group going concern value, it is desirable to preserve this value for the purpose of corporate rescue law. According to the above sections, the goal – preserving going concern value – of corporate rescue law indicates that it is desirable to have a group-wide solution in a cross-border insolvency context.

On the other hand, the goal of certainty of corporate rescue law requires relevant methods to respect the independent legal personality of subsidiaries and the insolvency jurisdiction of each subsidiary; both affect creditors' rights in cross-border insolvency.

Therefore, the desirable solutions should be able to preserve the value of MCGs in an effective and predictable way.[202]

---

197 Ibid., p. 52.
198 Phillip I. Blumberg, 'The Corporate Entity in an Era of Multinational Corporations' (1990) *Delaware Journal of Corporate Law* 15(2) 283–374, p. 365.
199 Elizabeth Warren, 'Bankruptcy Policy' (1987) *University of Chicago Law Review* 54 775, p. 777, p. 811.
200 Horst Eidenmüller, 'Comparative Corporate Insolvency Law' (2016) European Corporate Governance Institute (ECGI) – Law Working Paper No. 319, p. 10.
201 Charles W. Mooney, Jr., 'A Normative Theory of Bankruptcy Law: Bankruptcy As (Is) Civil Procedure' (2004) *Washington and Lee Law Review* 61 931, p. 937.
202 With regard to methods dealing with group insolvency without conflicting limited liability, see Irit Mevorach, 'Appropriate Treatment of Corporate Groups in Insolvency: A Universal View' (2007) *European Business Organization Law Review* 8 179–194; see also Irit Mevorach, 'The "Home Country" of a Multinational Enterprise Group Facing Insolvency' (2008) *International & Comparative Law Quarterly* 57 427–448.

42 Rescue of multinational groups of companies

Generally speaking, there are four ways in which to deal with the cross-border insolvency of groups of companies. These are: substantive consolidation, procedural consolidation, market/hybrid legal solutions and cooperation/coordination. The common ground is that all of these solutions have the potential to provide solutions to preserve group going concern value.

Substantive consolidation views all the member companies in the group as if they were one company. It aims to distribute the total assets of the group to all the creditors under one set of priority rules. Substantive consolidation is a method mainly used by the US courts to pull the assets and liabilities of companies together for the purpose of insolvency. Even in US case law, the conditions for using substantive consolidation are not clear.[203] This is only applied in extreme cases. Examples include situations in which one subsidiary's veil needs to be lifted or in which the assets of one corporate group are mixed together, which makes it costly to divide them into respective companies.[204]

The UK court may show reluctance to apply substantive consolidation. In the UK case of Re Polly Peck International plc,[205] the administrator requested substantive consolidation, and the UK court denied the argument that one SPV subsidiary is just the façade of the given company, and thereby they should be substantively consolidated. The UK court insisted that to use SPV solely for the purpose of finance is just a common commercial use of a corporate group structure, even if creditors are harmed.[206] There is no necessity to transplant the concept of substantive consolidation to UK case law.[207]

In Europe, such a concept may be subject to different interpretations by various member states, and therefore it could be difficult to reach consensus regarding its use. Also, substantive consolidating companies being located in different member states within one country will dramatically change the applicable insolvency law, which local creditors may not expect.[208] The best example is the different priority rankings of creditors in different member states' insolvency law. One creditor may be in the top ranking under local insolvency law, but he may be demoted to the second or to an even lower ranking under another country's insolvency law. Transaction avoidance rule is also a good example to illustrate the risk issue. A conduct may be avoidable under one country's law that is not avoidable under another's. The size of each debtor's assets is also different, so the result of substantive consolidation will benefit some general creditors at the expense of others.

---

203 Douglas G. Baird, 'Substantive Consolidation Today' (2005–2006) *Boston College Law Review* 47 5, p. 21.
204 Ibid., p. 21.
205 Polly Peck International plc (In Administration) (No. 4), Re [1996] 1 B.C.L.C. 428.
206 Simon Bowmer, 'To pierce or not to pierce the corporate veil- why substantive consolidation is not an issue under English law' (2000) *Journal of International Banking Law* p. 6.
207 Ibid., p. 8.
208 Robert van Galen, 'Insolvent Groups of Companies in Cross Border Cases and Rescue Plan' Report to the Netherlands Association for Comparative and International Insolvency Law (2012), p. 32.

Rescue of multinational groups of companies 43

In a typical cross-border insolvency case involving groups of companies, the issue is not whether the veil of subsidiary should be lifted or whether one should pull the assets of the group together due to the liability of the parent company; rather, the issue is how to preserve the going concern value in a predictable way. Therefore, the substantive consolidation is not the means urgently needed to deal with cross-border insolvency challenges. More importantly, bringing group members together does not necessarily require the group to be treated as one company; for instance, procedural consolidation and cooperation mechanisms may be more frequently used to achieve efficient insolvency results for MCGs.[209] Therefore, the book will exclude substantive consolidation as the desirable option for the cross-border insolvency of MCGs.

Procedural consolidation aims to use cross-border insolvency jurisdiction rules to preserve group going concern value. It tries to allocate the insolvency proceedings of group members into one court or as small a number of courts as possible. In terms of procedural consolidation, Professor Mevorach pointed out that the degree of integration and interdependence of group members seems to be very relevant in this regard.[210] She believed that in groups of companies where one company's tasks closely relate to the tasks of others, connecting them through procedural consolidation may be desirable.[211] As a result, all entities in the same group coming to one court to open insolvency proceeding may be beneficial as all members can be subject to the same administration, and to a large extent this helps preserve the value of the corporate groups.[212]

However, the certainty requirement indicates that rules as such should be predictable so that the creditors can assess risks and benefits *ex ante*. Preservation of value should not trump the important goal of certainty. Even though the merit of procedural consolidation regarding preservation of value can be appreciated, one still needs to examine whether such a rule is predictable. One gap left here is whether, based on the current insolvency jurisdiction rule and the features of MCGs, the groups of companies can be procedurally consolidated in front of one court in a predictable way.[213] The danger is that pulling subsidiaries in front of one court and subjecting them to one national insolvency law may change many creditors' expectations. Therefore, one should be careful to design conditions for procedural consolidation such that these rules have as little impact on creditors' expectations as possible. Procedural consolidation will be examined in Chapter 3.

---

209 Irit Mevorach, 'The "Home Country" of a Multinational Enterprise Group Facing Insolvency' (2008) *International & Comparative Law Quarterly* 57, p. 1.

210 She argued that integration is referred to as the degree to which the member companies work together as a joint business, while interdependence means the reliance of one member on the other members. Irit Mevorach, *Insolvency within Multinational Enterprise Groups* (Oxford University Press 2009), p. 131.

211 Ibid., p. 157.

212 Ibid., p. 157.

213 The insolvency jurisdiction rule – the centre of main interest – will be examined in detail in Chapter 3.

3 Cross-border insolvency theories and procedural consolidation

The previous chapter provides evidence that MCGs may have group going concern value worth preserving for the purpose of insolvency law, and it argues that the insolvency solutions of MCGs should respect the legal personality of individual subsidiaries in order to fulfil the goal of certainty.

This chapter completes the theoretical sub-objective in Chapter 1 by connecting the corporate rescue theories and multinational enterprise theories to cross-border insolvency law theories. It achieves this objective by examining universalism and territorialism, forum shopping and doctrines of CoMI. Also, it starts the examination of the first practical solution for the cross-border rescue of MCGs – procedural consolidation. In light of the conclusion of Chapter 2, this chapter will consider the ex ante and ex post approaches of procedural consolidation, and their respective merits and demerits. Corporate rescue theory provides two values – preservation of going concern value and certainty – to examine the desirability of procedural consolidation. Also, multinational enterprise theories reveal certain characteristics of multinational corporate groups which affect the insolvency jurisdictional rules on which procedural consolidation relies. All these theories and implications will be considered in this chapter. Its main purpose is to explore whether procedural consolidation is a reliable solution for the cross-border rescue of corporate groups.

In contrast to radical and unnecessary substantive consolidation which denies the independent legal status of individual companies in the group, procedural consolidation respects the legal form of each member company. It does not aim to pool the assets and creditors' liabilities of different companies together. Rather, procedural consolidation aims to pull the group members in front of the same court to open insolvency proceedings. This can be done mainly by changing insolvency jurisdiction rules such that all the subsidiaries have the right to opening insolvency proceedings in the country of their parent company.

The current insolvency jurisdiction of one company in the EU is decided by the 'centre of main interest' (hereafter CoMI) of one company according to the 'EU regulation on insolvency proceedings' recast (hereafter EIR recast). It is the cornerstone which underlies the jurisdiction-selection rules under cross-border insolvency theories, and it is widely adopted in international insolvency law

Cross-border insolvency theories   45

instruments.[1] The concept of CoMI is based on universalism theory,[2] which prescribes that the jurisdiction of insolvency of one multinational company should be allocated to the court which possesses the CoMI of that company.

Allocation of CoMIs of a group of companies into one jurisdiction can also be done by forum shopping so that the CoMIs of all the subsidiaries are moved to one country for the purpose of cross-border insolvency.

Whether procedural consolidation is a solution desirable for cross-border insolvency of MCGs will be examined with reference to its ability to preserve group going concern value and improve certainty of insolvency rules. One thing that should be noted is that in the cross-border insolvency context, procedural consolidation may still change creditors' rights by altering the insolvency law. In other words, after being pulled to a new jurisdiction, under the current choice of law rules, with certain exceptions, the insolvency law of the new jurisdiction will apply to the creditors. As a result, whether a predictable *ex ante* jurisdictional rule could be found and whether the forum shopping of insolvency courts is desirable in the EU are important questions that need to be answered. Without certainty, the procedural consolidation may face significant challenges as solutions for the cross-border insolvency of MCGs.

The structure of this chapter is as follows. First, it discusses cross-border insolvency theories which underpin the current jurisdiction rule – CoMI.[3]

---

1 Both EC regulation on cross-border insolvency proceedings 2015 and UNCITRAL Model Law on cross-border insolvency (thereafter Model law) 1997 adopt CoMI as the determinant of cross-border insolvency jurisdiction. It refers to the place where the head office functions are exercised. See later case law in this chapter.
2 See Chapter 4 for more details.
3 Hon. Samuel L. Bufford, 'International Insolvency Case Venue in the European Union: The Parmalat and Daisytek Controversies' (2005–2006) *Columbia Journal of European Law* 12 429; Aaron M. Kaufman, 'The European Union Goes CoMI-Tose: Hazards of Harmonizing Corporate Insolvency Laws in the Global Economy' (2006–2007) *The Houston Journal of International Law* 29 625; Justin Luna, 'Thinking Globally, Filing Locally, the Effect of the New Chapter 15 on Business Entity Cross Border Insolvency Cases' (2007) *Florida Journal of International Law* 19 671; Alexander J. Belohlavek, 'Center of Main Interest (COMI) and Jurisdiction of National Courts in Insolvency Matters (Insolvency Status)' (2008) *International Journal of Law and Management* 50(2) 53–86; Matteo M. Winkler, 'From Whipped Cream to Multibillion Euro Financial Collapse: The European Regulation on Transnational Insolvency in Action' (2008) *Berkeley Journal of International Law* 26 352; Simona Di Sano, 'COMI: The Sun Around Which Cross-Border Insolvency Proceedings Revolve' (2009) *Journal of International Banking Law* 24(2) 88–101; Andrew B. Dawson, 'Offshore Bankruptcies' (2009) *Nebraska Law Review* 88(2) 317; Marek, Szydlo, 'The Notion of Comi in European Insolvency Law' (2009) *European Business Law Review* 20 747; Alexandra C.C. Ragan, 'CoMI Strikes a Discordant Note, Why US Court Are Not in Complete Harmony Despite Chapter 15 Directives' (2010–2011) *Emory Bankruptcy Developments Journal* 27 117; Thomas Biermeyer, 'Case C-396/09 Interedil Sri, Judgment of the Court of 20 October 2011, Court Guidance as to the COMI Concept in Cross-Border Insolvency Proceedings' (2011) *Maastricht Journal of European and Comparative Law* 18 581; Mark Arnold (QC), 'Truth or Illusion? COMI Migration and Forum Shopping under the EU Insolvency Regulation' (2013) *Business Law International* 14 245; Dario Latella, 'The "COMI" Concept in the Revision of the European Insolvency

46 *Cross-border insolvency theories*

The purpose is to assess whether CoMI is more desirable than the jurisdictional rule offered by territorialism theory. The key parameters are the ability to preserve insolvent companies' value and certainty of rules; the group theories on the allocation of head office functions will also be considered The book believes that though CoMI has certain drawbacks, it works better than rival insolvency jurisdictional rule. Second, the chapter analyses ways in which to achieve procedural consolidation under CoMI. One way proposed by cross-border insolvency theorists is a group CoMI approach, which ex ante allocates one court as the jurisdiction for the whole group. Another way is an ex post forum shopping approach. All these will be examined, in turn. The chapter finally argues that procedural consolidation has the potential to preserve values but only in specific cases. The uncertainty of rules makes procedural consolidation difficult to apply as a general rule for insolvency of MCGs.

Cross-border insolvency law theories on jurisdiction

Introduction

As discussed in Chapter 2, insolvency law provides one set of rules to deal with collective issues. The collectivity supersedes multiple individual actions for the purpose of going concern value preservation and certainty.

The collective nature of insolvency law makes it difficult to disconnect, or replace with the insolvency law of another country. One example is the priority of creditors' rankings. Countries may give different categories of creditors preference for various reasons. In other words, a creditor under the insolvency law of country A may enjoy certain priority that he would not enjoy under the insolvency law of country B. If creditors from a single company but different countries all argue that they should be treated according to their own countries' priority, no priority of ranking can be agreed upon and formed. As a result, the collective nature of insolvency law generally requires that only one set of rules be applied to insolvency cases. That is to say, where one court is entitled to seize jurisdiction, it could apply its own insolvency law to the given case, with some exception.

EIR recast reflects this idea by incorporating a set of harmonized insolvency choice of law rules[4] (HICOL rules). The law of the court will decide the conditions of the opening of those proceedings as well as their conduct and their closure; also, it will decide many important aspects of bankruptcy law, such as creditors' priority.[5] To protect local interests, the regulation also provides certain

---

Regulation' (2014) *European Company and Financial Law Review* 11(4) 479–494; Charlotte Møller, 'COMI and Get It: International Approaches to Cross-Border Insolvencies' (2015) *Corporate Rescue and Insolvency Journal* 6 223; Sean E. Story, 'Cross Border Insolvency: A Comparative Analysis' (2015) *Arizona Journal of International and Comparative Law* 32 431.

4 EIR recast Article 7, see comments on previous EIR HICOL in general: Bob Wessels, *International Insolvency Law* (Kluwer 2006).

5 EIR recast Article 7 (2).

Cross-border insolvency theories 47

exceptions to *lexi fori concursus*;[6] for example, the effect of the insolvency proceedings on immovable property is only decided by the law of the country where the immovable assets are situated.[7]

The EIR recast requires all courts of member states to automatically recognize the insolvency proceedings opened by the courts which first seize the cases, and other courts can only challenge the jurisdiction in that court.[8] Therefore, the regulation confers much power to the court opening insolvency proceedings due to choice of law rules and automatic recognition. It is safe to say that the jurisdictional rule of cross-border insolvency law is of great importance. In the field of cross-border insolvency law, the main theories are territorialism[9] and universalism.[10] These hold different views on the means of allocation of insolvency jurisdiction. Territorialism argues that international insolvency cases should be regulated by the courts in which the assets of the debtors are located. The result is that more than one court is entitled to open insolvency proceedings due to the various locations of assets in a typical cross-border insolvency case. Universalism argues that ideally, there should be one court and one set of bankruptcy laws to be applied to one cross-border insolvency case.

In addition to universalism and territorialism, there are some other theories: contractualism[11] and universal proceduralism.[12] Since territorialism suggests that assets' location determines the insolvency jurisdiction rule, which is differ-

---

6 EIR recast Article 8–Article 18.
7 EIR recast Article 11.
8 Gerard McCormack, 'Jurisdictional Competition and Forum Shopping in Insolvency Proceedings' (2009) *The Cambridge Law Journal* 68(01) 185–186.
9 Lynn LoPucki, 'Cooperation in International Bankruptcy: A Post Universalist Approach' (1998–1999) *Cornell Law Review* 84 696; Lynn LoPucki, 'The Case for Cooperative Territoriality in International Bankruptcy' (1999–2000) *Michigan Law Review* 98 2216; Frederick Tung, 'Is International Bankruptcy Possible?' (2001–2002) *Michigan Journal of International Law* 23 31; Lynn LoPucki, 'Universalism Unravels' (2005) *American Bankruptcy Law Journal* 79 143; Lynn LoPucki, 'Global and Out of Control' (2005) *American Bankruptcy Law Journal* 79 79–104.
10 Jay Westbrook, 'Universal Priority' (1998) *Texas International Law Journal* 33 27; Jay Westbrook, 'Theory and Pragmatism in Global Insolvencies: Choice of Law and Choice of Forum' (1991) *American Bankruptcy Law Journal* 65 457; Jay Westbrook, 'Globalisation of Insolvency Reform' (1999) *New Zealand Law Review* 401; Nigel John Howcroft, 'Universal versus Territorial Models for Cross Border Insolvency: The Theory, the Practice and the Reality that Universalism Prevails' (2007–2008) *UC Davis School of Law – Business Law Journal* 8 366; Jay Westbrook, 'Priority Conflicts as a Barrier to Cooperation in Multinational Insolvencies' (2008–2009) *Penn State International Law Review* 27 869; Jay Westbrook, 'Multinational Enterprises in General Default: Chapter 15, the ALI Principles, and the EU Insolvency Regulation' (2002) *American Bankruptcy Law Journal* 76 1; Jay Westbrook, 'Locating the Eye of the Financial Storm' (2007) *Brooklyn Journal of International Law* 32 1019; Jay Westbrook, 'Breaking Away, Local Priorities and Global Assets' (2010–2011) *Texas International Law Journal* 46 601; Jay Westbrook, 'A Global Solution to Multinational Default' (1999–2000) *Michigan Law Review* 98 2276.
11 Contracts are used to allocate jurisdiction at the beginning.
12 It aims to centralize insolvency proceeding into one jurisdiction while applying local insolvency law to protect local creditors in order to avoid multiple insolvency proceedings.

48 *Cross-border insolvency theories*

ent from the other theories that generally embrace CoMI,[13] the next section will examine whether CoMI is superior to the assets jurisdiction rule.

Dichotomy on jurisdictional rules

Territorialism

Territorialism claims that the insolvency proceedings of international companies should be opened in the courts where the assets of the companies are located.[14] Extreme territorialism does not even offer measures for home jurisdictions to cooperate with foreign courts.[15] It is described as a grab rule as, under it, one court can grab all assets within its borders and apply local insolvency law to the creditors and debtors.[16]

The courts under territorialism may be reluctant to transfer assets to the foreign courts where foreign insolvency proceedings are opened as local courts insist on providing favouritism to local creditors. For example, one court provides no cooperation with foreign courts until local creditors are fully paid.[17] As all the courts can open insolvency proceedings which are equally independent, cooperation and deference from foreign courts are difficult to obtain. This is especially true if many insolvency proceedings are opened.[18]

The territorialists have realized that territorialism needs some reform to accommodate the need of going concern value preservation and international cooperation. These demands give rise to a reformed version – cooperative territorialism. Cooperative territorialism aims to achieve a wide cooperation between courts for the purpose of successful reorganization, especially in business integrated cases.[19] Professor LoPucki briefly provided possible solutions to describe a viable cooperative territorialism: there are five suggestions of how cooperative territorialism could work:

> 1. The courts may set up a regime that could share the information of claims lists; 2. The representative may file one claim of the debtor in all other

---

13 One exception is that in contractualism, it is possible for the parties to choose insolvency jurisdiction which is different from the location of CoMI.

14 An extreme form of territorialism is that in which local courts do not allow foreign creditors to file their petitions.

15 It is true that without treaties, there is no obligation for the countries to provide cooperation to the foreign courts and recognize the foreign judgements.

16 Robert K. Rasmussen, 'A New Approach to Transnational Insolvency' (1997–1998) *Michigan Journal of International Law* 19 1, p. 16.

17 Lucian AyreBebchuk and Andrew T. Guzman, 'An Economic Analysis of Transnational Bankruptcies' (1999) *The Journal of Law and Economics* 42 775, p. 782.

18 Robert K. Rasmussen, 'A New Approach to Transnational Insolvency' (1997–1998) *Michigan Journal of International Law* 19 1, p. 6.

19 Lynn. M. Lopucki, 'The Case for Cooperative Territoriality in International Bankruptcy' (1999–2000) *Michigan Law Review* 98 2216, p. 2219.

insolvency proceedings opened against the same debtor; 3. Cooperation between courts to conduct a joint sale, 4. Voluntary investment to the estate in other jurisdictions for the purpose of reorganization 5. Insolvency practitioners return the seized assets that should be returned, due to the avoidable transfer.[20]

However, the basic principle is unchanged: each bankruptcy court has jurisdiction over the assets of one multinational company situated in its jurisdiction; no more, no less.[21] Still, this does not mean that territorialism only allows local creditors to enjoy locally seized assets. In fact, most countries' insolvency laws allow cross-filing,[22] even though they are based on territorialism.[23] Also, it is possible that both of the theories may offer cross priority[24] to the foreign creditors.

Universalism

Universalism has gradually gained support from scholars and practices by assigning the insolvency jurisdiction of one company to the court where the CoMI of the company is located. The tenet of universalism is that one single court administers one multinational insolvency case by applying its own insolvency law. One important justification for universalism is that it allows one set of insolvency laws to cover the market that the company in question operates from so that the functions of insolvency law can perform.[25] As universalism respects the economic reality and business operations of the companies, reorganization of either a company or a group of companies may be facilitated.

Pure universalism is based on an ideal universalist rationale that the court of the home country of a company should have jurisdiction over all the assets of the company, even if there are some assets of the company in other jurisdictions. For insolvency law to be effective, one has to allow bankruptcy law to be applied to the extent that the debtor's business has reached in the market.[26]

As there is only one court involved, most of the insolvency-related issues are governed by the insolvency law of the court opening the insolvency proceedings.

---

20 Lynn. M Lopucki, 'Cooperation in International Bankruptcy: A Post Universalist Approach' (1998–1999) *Cornell Law Review* 84 696, p. 750.

21 Lynn. M. Lopucki, 'The Case for Cooperative Territoriality in International Bankruptcy' (1999–2000) *Michigan Law Review* 98 2216, p. 2218.

22 Cross-filing allows foreign creditors to lodge their claims in local insolvency proceedings.

23 Ulrik Rammeskow Bang-Pederse, 'Assets Distribution in Transnational Insolvencies, Combining Predictability and Protection of Local Interests' (1999) *American Bankruptcy Law Journal* 73 385, pp. 387–388.

24 As long as foreign creditors fall into the categories to which local insolvency law gives priority, they can enjoy this priority without being discriminated against due to their nationality.

25 Jay Westbrook, 'A Global Solution to Multinational Default' (1999–2000) *Michigan Law Review* 98 2276, p. 2277.

26 John A. E. Pottow, 'Procedural Incrementalism: A Model for International Bankruptcy' (2004–2005) *Virginia Journal of International Law* 45 935, p. 942.

50 Cross-border insolvency theories

In other words, *lex concursus* (the law of the opening proceeding) should be the law to administer procedural aspects of insolvency and a number of substantive insolvency issues.[27] As a result, financially weak local creditors will not suffer from uncertain assets/claims rates.[28]

Nonetheless, universalism imposes obligation on courts by forcing them to defer to foreign courts and foreign insolvency law.[29] Here universalism may create friction that territorialism does not. Generally, pure universalism extends the jurisdiction of one country to other member states, which makes these states reluctant to cede their sovereignty.[30] Where some assets appear in other countries, the courts of those countries may be inclined to apply their own insolvency laws to the cases in question. Even though certain courts advocate pure universalism, their judgements may not be recognized by the other courts involved.

Under universalism, deferring to foreign insolvency laws means that the pre-insolvency entitlements of creditors will be modified by a new set of rules. The insolvency laws of member states may vary in the approaches they take. For instance, creditors' priority is the manifestation of how one specific country has chosen its hierarchy of values according to its policies.[31] It is therefore difficult to substitute one country's priority for another's for creditors' protection.[32] It is unlikely that the same priority (in terms of order or scale of protection) of creditors could be found in two country's insolvency law systems.[33] Ignoring the priority of these preferential creditors is unfair to them.[34] The consequence is that courts may be reluctant to defer to foreign courts.[35]

Universalism may be more favourable to more developed countries as it is more likely that the multinationals incorporate in them. As a result, some highly developed countries' insolvency law and social policies may have more chance of being applied and exported to other countries.

---

27 Such as the priority of claims and avoidance of transaction.
28 John A. E. Pottow, 'Greed and Pride in International Bankruptcy: The Problems of and Proposed Solutions to Local Interests' (2005–2006) *Michigan Law Review* 104 1899, p. 1910.
29 Frederick Tung, 'Is International Bankruptcy Possible?' (2001–2002) *Michigan Journal of International Law* 23 31, p. 45.
30 John J. Chung, 'The New Chapter 15 of the Bankruptcy Code: A Step Toward Erosion of National Sovereignty' (2007) *North-Western Journal of International Law & Business* 27 89, p. 103.
31 Jose M. Garrido, 'No Two Snowflakes the Same: The Distributional Question in International Bankruptcies' (2010–2011) *Texas International Law Journal* 46 459, p. 474.
32 Ibid., p. 475.
33 See a taxonomy of creditors priorities in Jose M. Garrido, 'No Two Snowflakes the Same: The Distributional Question in International Bankruptcies' (2010–2011) *Texas International Law Journal* 46 459.
34 Alexander M. Kipnis, 'Beyond UNCITRAL: Alternatives to Universality in Transnational Insolvency' (2007–2008) *Denver Journal of International Law and Policy* 36 155, p. 175.
35 Frederick Tung, 'Is International Bankruptcy Possible?' (2001–2002) *Michigan Journal of International Law* 23 31, pp. 47–49.

Cross-border insolvency theories 51

Considering the difficulties of adopting pure universalism, a modified universalism becomes a compromise.[36] Modified universalism maintains the premise of the pure universalism by only allowing one main proceeding, but it also utilizes territorialism elements by permitting local courts which possess establishments (such as branches) to open secondary proceedings for the purpose of local interest protection and creditors' expectations.

Modified universalism takes local creditors' interests into account by opening secondary proceedings.[37] In secondary proceedings, it is the law of the court which opens the proceedings will be applied instead of the insolvency law of the main proceedings. Where one member state confers a privilege under local law to categories of creditors, such privilege may be protected by opening secondary proceedings.[38] Such compromise may provide a viable solution to protect local creditors, such as wages, taxes and secured claims.[39]

However, secondary proceedings still need to defer to the main proceedings to some degree; otherwise, the cooperation and coordination will lose their basic grounds.[40] This means that modified universalism will be the direction of the development of cross-border insolvency law and arguably 'the smoothest and fastest transition to true universalism'.[41]

Arguably, modified universalism can still achieve the same results as pure universalism. It does not preclude the situation where only one main proceeding

36 But one should not exaggerate the issue of the protection of foreign creditors in the universalism context. The fact should be noted that non-adjusting creditors' debt may be marginal in comparison to adjusting creditors' debt. Also, unsecured trade creditors do not enjoy priority in many countries' systems. Edward S. Adams and Jason K. Fincke, 'Coordinating Cross-Border Bankruptcy: How Territorialism Saves Universalism' (2008–2009) *Columbia Journal of European Law* 15 43, p. 54.

37 National priority system may be quite idiosyncratic. Arguably, the difference could be found in the size, scope and identity of creditors, and the order of priority. For example, the compensation for fishermen under US bankruptcy law only allows fishermen who have US citizenship to file such claims. Without paying the priority claims in a foreign court, it is very difficult to receive cooperation from another court, such as on remit of assets. See Allan L. Gropper, 'The Payment of Priority Claims in Cross-Border Insolvency Cases' (2010–2011) *Texas International Law Journal* 46 559, p. 562.

38 Ian Fletcher, *Insolvency in Private International Law* (2nd edn, Oxford University Press 2005), p. 431.

39 Ibid., p. 431; Jay Lawrence Westbrook 'Breaking Away, Local Priorities and Global Assets' (2010–2011) *Texas International Law Journal* 46 601, p. 615.

40 As Virgós-Schmit Report states, 'The rationale behind the rule is that economic operators conducting their economic activities through a local establishment should be subject to the same rules as national economic operators as long as they are both operating in the same market'. Virgos-Schmit Report, para. 71.

41 Jay Westbrook, 'A Global Solution to Multinational Default' (1999–2000) *Michigan Law Review* 98 2276, p. 2277; Edward S. Adams and Jason K. Fincke 'Coordinating Cross-Border Bankruptcy: How Territorialism Saves Universalism' (2008–2009) *Columbia Journal of European Law* 15 43, p. 52; Jay Lawrence Westbrook, 'Universalism and Choice of Law' (2004–2005) *Penn State International Law Review* 23 625, p. 629.

52 *Cross-border insolvency theories*

opens without other secondary proceedings. Re Nortel Networks SA case[42] concerns the insolvency of the European subgroup of the Nortel group based in North America. The English court opened the main insolvency proceedings for all the European subsidiaries in the group according to EU regulation. The joint administrators of the English insolvency proceedings applied to the English high court for a letter of request to all the courts in other member states. The aim of this letter was to request that foreign courts inform the English administrators of any application to open secondary proceedings.[43] Therefore, the English administrators could provide reasons for which the opening secondary proceedings might not be in the interests of creditors. The English court approved the request; it was of the opinion that insolvency practitioners in the main and secondary proceedings were obligated to cooperate with each other, and that insolvency practitioners in the main proceeding should be given notice of any request to open secondary proceedings which were harmful to successful corporate rescue.[44] This case shows that if the group members' insolvency proceedings are opened in one court, cooperation between member states may be desirable such that other member states will not wage secondary proceedings to act against main proceedings.

Also, modified universalism can exert a more effective cooperation than that under cooperative territorialism. This is because the cooperation is in a hierarchical structure whereby only one main proceeding can be open, and the insolvency practitioner in the main proceeding is given more power than those in secondary proceedings.[45] Insolvency practitioners in the main proceedings enjoy more power than those in the secondary proceedings.[46] Modified universalism also requires courts and insolvency practitioners in secondary proceedings to coordinate with those in the main proceeding to achieve better results.

The HIH case[47] is an example of such cooperation and deference between main courts and secondary courts. In this case, four Australian incorporated insurance companies were in insolvency, while the CoMIs of these companies were in Australia.[48] The Australian court requested that the UK court turn over the assets in the UK after paying the relevant liquidation cost; the Australian court would distribute them under Australian insolvency law. The contradiction is that Australian insolvency law grants insurance creditors priority, while under UK insolvency law, such creditors have no priority.[49] The consequence of the assets remit would lead the English general creditors to a different result as

---

42 Re Nortel Networks SA [2009] EWHC 206 (Ch) p. 1.

43 Ibid., p. 1.

44 Ibid., p. 2.

45 The impact of the secondary proceedings will be confined to the assets seized by the local court, so it will have no impact on the assets beyond local jurisdiction.

46 Main proceeding insolvency practitioners are given priority to make group rescue plan. EIR recast Article 41.

47 In re HIH Casualty and General Insurance Ltd [2008] 1 W.L.R.852.

48 Ibid., para. 31.

49 Ibid., para. 2.

Cross-border insolvency theories 53

they would not receive the distribution *pari passu* with the Australian insurance creditors.

Lord Hoffmann allowed the assets transfer to Australia as this was the embodiment of the 'unitary and universality' of cross-border insolvency law principle.[50] The task of ancillary insolvency proceedings is to assist principal proceedings. This inevitably entails the UK courts' applying foreign insolvency law but disapplying all or part of English law after the remittal of assets in some cases. Therefore, if the precondition to approve an asset remittal to a foreign court is based on the foreign law being similar to English law, then such remittal is meaningless.[51] In the HIH case, the connection of debtors was close to Australia, so applying Australian insolvency law was in line with creditors' expectations. One cannot reject it simply because another country has a different preferential creditors list because countries rarely have the same priority rankings; remitting assets does not breach the justice and public policy of English courts.[52]

In the HIH case, the CoMI was in Australia, and creditors who signed insurance contracts with those Australian insurance companies should have expected that it was Australian law that would be applied. Though there were some assets in the UK, it would not be expected that the interests provided by the Australian insurance policies should be affected by the English insolvency law.[53] The fact that different laws yield different distributional results does not breach public policy as the foreign law does not inherently treat creditors unfairly. Without convincing evidence or reason to not cooperate, courts and creditors should accept the difference under this circumstance.

Some may argue that part of the reason the UK court offered cooperation with discretion was that Australia is on the list[54] of counties to which the UK may provide recognition and cooperation. However, Lord Hoffmann's main judgement is on the basis of the principle of modified universalism which allows English courts to provide cooperation to other courts to the extent that they are not breaching English public policies.[55] One could argue that if modified universalism is the principle that underpins cooperation, the scope of countries which are qualified to enjoy cooperation under s426 should be available to other jurisdictions as well.[56] As EU regulation formally requires not only the insolvency practitioners but also the courts to cooperate with each other, there should arguably be similar deference from secondary proceedings to the main proceeding.

---

50 'There should be a unitary bankruptcy proceeding in the court of the bankrupt's domicile which receives worldwide recognition and it should apply universally to all the bankrupt's assets' In re HIH Casualty and General Insurance Ltd [2008] 1 W.L.R.852, para. 6.
51 In re HIH Casualty and General Insurance Ltd [2008] 1 W.L.R.852, para. 21.
52 Ibid., para. 34.
53 Ibid., para. 33.
54 Insolvency Act 1986 S.426.
55 Hamish Anderson, 'Ebbs and Flows of Universalism' (2015) *Recovery*, Summer, p. 8.
56 Ibid., p. 10.

54 *Cross-border insolvency theories*

In the Cambridge gas case,[57] Lord Hoffmann said that:

> The English common law has traditionally taken the view that fairness between creditors requires that, ideally, bankruptcy proceedings should have universal application. There should be a single bankruptcy in which all creditors are entitled and required to prove. No one should have an advantage because he happens to live in a jurisdiction where more of the assets or fewer of the creditors are situated; universality of bankruptcy has long been an aspiration, if not always fully achieved, of United Kingdom law. And with increasing world trade and globalization, many other countries have come round to the same view.[58]

This further confirms the merits of modified universalism.

Determining which theories can offer better solutions to cross-border insolvency entails a comparison of CoMI and grab rule in terms of respective abilities to preserve going concern value and provide certainty. The certainty of these jurisdiction rules will be affected by forum shopping. Whether the vulnerability to forum shopping is necessarily negative is largely dependent on whether the forum shopping in a cross-border insolvency context is generally desirable. If it is not, the next question to ask is whether the CoMI supported by universalists can do better than grab rules advocated by territorialism with respect to the prevention of forum shopping. The next section examines the desirability of forum shopping in cross-border insolvency in the EU.

Forum shopping

The disparities of national insolvency law and other relevant laws, such as secured credit law and employment law, may render forum shopping difficult to avoid.[59] Debtors and creditors can seek varying degrees of efficiency of insolvency proceedings, debt restructuring mechanisms, credit recovery rates and investor protection from different member states.[60]

---

57 Cambridge Gas Transportation Corpn v Official Committee of Unsecured Creditors of Navigator Holdings plc and others [2007] 1 A.C. 508.

58 Ibid., p. 9.

59 Paul J. Omar, 'The Inevitability of 'Insolvency Tourism'' (2015) *Netherlands International Law Review* 62 14.

60 For example, according to the statistics regarding the cost of bankruptcy for banking creditors, the cost of bankruptcy proceeding in the UK is lower than it is in other member states, such as Italy, France and Germany. Also, the length of the UK's bankruptcy proceeding is shorter than those in above-mentioned countries. Another thing noteworthy is in terms of percentage of credit recovery; the UK bankruptcy procedures can yield 70% percentage credit recovery for preferential creditors, which is far ahead of the French procedure performance of 14–66% preferential creditors. UK insolvency procedure is more likely to save a business as a going concern with the recovery rate of 88.6%, while French insolvency procedure achieves a recovery rate of 48.3%. Also, UK procedure needs one year on average, while French procedure needs

Cross-border insolvency theories 55

What attitude one should have towards forum shopping in a cross-border insolvency context is an important question. This section will examine whether forum shopping can preserve value and bring in certainty. The answer to this question can help to analyse the desirability of certain procedural consolidation via forum shopping.

Theoretical views on forum shopping

Forum shopping in the insolvency context may be defined as moving assets or CoMI from one country to another in order to benefit from the substantive or procedural law of the latter.[61] As insolvency laws of member states are not harmonized, creditors or debtors may have incentives to conduct forum shopping and to seek favourable insolvency law in their own interests.[62] One example could be that senior creditors may prefer UK insolvency law to French insolvency law as English insolvency law grants creditors more power to control the insolvency proceedings.[63]

There are two concerns with the consequences of forum shopping. One is whether forum shopping can benefit the creditors of one distressed company in general by allowing them to choose the more effective insolvency law of another country. The second is that even if forum shopping can maximize the value of the debtors' assets, will the uncertainty caused by forum shopping be tolerable? These two concerns will be examined below.

Maximization of value

When creditors seek forum shopping for the purpose of changing insolvency law, one may assume that the purpose of such a change is to preserve the going concern value of one distressed company in a way that the local insolvency law cannot. However, generally speaking, forum shopping is a pejorative word. Creditors with conflicting interests may be more likely to choose the insolvency law that benefits them rather than preserving value for creditors in general. No insolvency law is perfect, so the weakness of a given insolvency law can be taken advantage of by some creditors. For example, the holding companies in corporate

---

1.9 years. Moreover, the UK procedure costs 6% of the estate, while the French costs 9% of the estate. From this comparison, the UK insolvency procedure contains relative advantages over the French one so that a French company may be more likely to transfer to the UK to conduct insolvency. Impact assessment on the directive on the cross-border transfer of registered office Brussels, 12.12.2007 annex table at p. 11, 12.

61 Gerard McCormack, 'Bankruptcy Forum Shopping, the UK and US as Venues of Choice for Foreign Companies' (2014) *International and Comparative Law Quarterly* 04 63, p. 815.

62 Such as the availability of rescue or restructuring proceedings, treatment and priority of creditors, and ability to cram down dissenting creditors. Forum shopping and COMI shifting – overview Rationale Practice note, Lexis PSL.

63 Wolf-Georg Ringe, 'Forum Shopping under the EU Insolvency Regulation' (2008) *European Business Organization Law Review* 9 579, p. 599.

56 *Cross-border insolvency theories*

groups try to move CoMIs to another country with the intention of selling the whole operating subsidiaries to potential buyers via a pre-pack sale.[64] The pre-pack sale may make it difficult for junior creditors in other countries to challenge due to a lack of transparency. Such practice may be used by senior creditors to wipe out junior creditors.

Other costs of forum shopping also arise. One could be that forum shopping may overburden some courts and so reduce their efficiency in resolving insolvency cases.[65] The court's being shopped for may not necessarily provide better than average service; arguably, the Delaware court seems to be more likely to rubber-stamp the approval of the pre-pack cases without achieving more efficient and predictable reorganization results than rival courts in other states.[66]

Also, forum shopping itself will incur cost due to the relocation of CoMI. One should note that a real relocation of CoMI means that subsidiaries may truly move the main business from one country to another. In the MCG context, such practice is likely to cause significant cost as the subsidiaries' relationships with foreign suppliers and environment may be cut off. This prevents the group from gaining an advantage from the foreign countries. Last but not least, forum shopping incurs costs to local creditors as they may have to travel to participate in the foreign insolvency proceedings.

Some may argue that if forum shopping serves as a tool to maximize the bankruptcy estate on behalf of all the creditors, it should be allowed; by contrast, if forum shopping is conducted only for the purpose of transferring value from creditors to debtors, it should be prohibited.[67] Such assertion is deduced from EIR recitals[68] which pursue the goals of preservation of value and anti-fraudulent forum shopping.[69] Some believe that the goal of maximization of assets to creditors is superior to the goal of anti-forum shopping.[70]

The reasoning of the above belief relies on the fact that the EU does not take measures to fix the concept of CoMI so as to make forum shopping impossible. The uncertainty of anti-forum shopping rules will lead to increased cost; some creditors may not reject a better recovery provided by foreign insolvency law.[71] This argument is not convincing as EIR recast clearly provides a series of mech-

---

64 HHY Luxembourg S.A.R.L & Anr v Barclays Bank plc & Ors [2010] EWHC 2406.

65 Paschalis Paschalisdis, *Freedom of Establishment and Private International Law for Corporations* (Oxford University Press 2012), p. 216.

66 Gerard McCormack, 'Jurisdictional Competition and Forum Shopping in Insolvency Proceedings' (2009) *The Cambridge Law Journal* 68(01) 169–197, p. 183.

67 Horst Eidenmüller 'Abuse of Law in the Context of European Insolvency Law' (2009) *European Company and Financial Law Review* 6 1–28, p. 10.

68 Recital 2, 8, 16, 19, 20 and Recital 4.

69 Horst Eidenmüller 'Abuse of Law in the Context of European Insolvency Law' (2009) *European Company and Financial Law Review* 6 1–28, p. 8.

70 Ibid., p. 8; Federico M. Mucciarelli, 'Private International Law Rules in the Insolvency Regulation Recast: A Reform or a Restatement of the Status Quo?' (2015), p. 13.

71 Horst Eidenmüller, 'Abuse of Law in the Context of European Insolvency Law' (2009) *European Company and Financial Law Review* 6 1–28, p. 8.

Cross-border insolvency theories 57

anisms to avoid forum shopping.[72] For example, the EU Regulation on Insolvency proceedings Recast includes a suspect period for relocation of CoMI by prescribing that if the registered office has been transferred from one jurisdiction to another within three months prior to the opening of insolvency proceedings, the new registered place cannot be used as presumption of CoMI.[73] No rule can provide absolute certainty. The shortcoming of CoMI does not imply EIR's acquiescence on forum shopping.

It is true that in some cases, forum shopping is conducted solely for the purpose of seeking a flexible restructuring scheme and benefiting creditors:[74] for instance, where desirable reorganization procedures of one jurisdiction provide a good solution to conquer hold-out issues.[75] In the Schefenacker case,[76] the unanimous approval by all the bondholders inevitably made a restructuring impossible as the threshold provided bondholders significant hold-out power to hinder a rescue which would have benefited all creditors.

After consideration, among other things, it was desirable to conduct a debt to equity swap which had the effect of deleveraging; it might save the business from the threat of liquidation insolvency proceedings.[77] However, under German insolvency law (before the reform of German restructuring law), such debt to equity conversion requires a unanimous approval from the bondholders, which is not a viable option.[78] By contrast, the UK company voluntary arrangement (CVA) is very flexible as it requires 75% of bondholders' approval. Also, it allows the guarantee of the bonds given by the operational companies to be released under the same process.[79] The debt restructuring of this case was successful.[80]

---

72 See regulatory view of forum shopping below.

73 New EU regulation article 3(1).

74 Report from the commission to the European Parliament, the council and the European economic and social committee on the application of Council Regulation (EC) No. 1346/2000 of 29 May 2000 on insolvency proceedings, p. 10.

75 R.J. de Weijs, 'Comi-Migration: Use or Abuse of European Insolvency Law?' (2014) *European Company and Financial Law Review* 11(4), p. 10.

76 Schefenacker was the key manufacturer of automotive lights and mirrors. Its base was in Germany, and it occupied 28% of the market share in the world before facing financial difficulty in 2006; it would affect the market strongly, given its weight and share on the supply end. KPMG International 12 'Seeing the light' Restore October 2007; see also Samantha Bewick, 'Schefenacker plc: A Successful Debt-for-Equity Swap' (2008) *International Corporate Rescue* 5(2).

77 KPMG International 12 'Seeing the light', Restore October 2007.

78 Samantha Bewick, 'Schefenacker plc: A Successful Debt-for-Equity Swap' (2008) *International Corporate Rescue* 5(2), p. 104.

79 Ibid., p. 104.

80 It should be noted that in the Schefenacker case, the CoMI shift subject is the holding company of the group but not be the operational companies in 12 European countries. As the holding company has no employees and trading creditors, it is easier to move CoMI from one jurisdiction to another. Even so, such movement has been approved by the majority of stakeholders, which enhances the justification of such movement. Samantha Bewick, 'Schefenacker plc: A Successful Debt-for-Equity Swap' (2008) *International Corporate Rescue* 5(2), p. 104.

58 Cross-border insolvency theories

Attention should be given to the fact that the reformed German restructuring law now permits debt to equity swaps[81]; therefore, such costly CoMI shifts may be outdated and be a less attractive option. The modernized national insolvency law is a better option than forum shopping.

The Re Zlomrex International Finance SA case is another example. Zlomrex International Finance SA is the French finance company of a Polish group. Its purpose is solely to raise finance for the whole group. When it faced difficulty repaying its debts, it proposed to move CoMI to London to benefit from a scheme of arrangement for its bond notes.[82] In fact, it is very clear that the forum shopping was an attempt to use English schemes of arrangement to avoid a potential cross default of the group members, if the French restructuring law is used.[83] In such cases, the UK's flexible scheme of arrangement would allow the bonds to be substituted by new bond notes and delay them to next year; more importantly, it helped the group to avoid insolvency.[84] It is possible to argue that as the forum shopping happened at the holding company level, the financial creditors may have acknowledged the risk of change of governing law of contract or insolvency law.[85]

It seems plausible to argue that opting for a more desirable and flexible applicable law by forum shopping does not itself constitute bad forum shopping as local law may not provide a good solution to resolve the commons (collective insolvency proceeding) and anti-commons (hold-out issue by certain creditors) problems in insolvency.[86] In other words, insolvency law and restructuring law are designed to provide solutions for insolvency and restructuring issues; where the local law does not provide a solution, it seems to be tolerable to choose another set of rules simply to overcome issues such as hold-out. However, the changed substantive rights and procedural rights may affect a large number of creditors in terms of their final gain. It is difficult to determine whether the total value of the going concern value has been enlarged or whether there is value redistribution from junior creditors to senior creditors as a consequence of the forum shopping.

Certainty

As mentioned above, the main purpose of forum shopping in a cross-border insolvency context is to benefit from the insolvency law of another country.

---

81 2012, Act for the Further Facilitation of the Restructuring of Companies (Gesetzzurweiteren-Erleichterung der Sanierung von Unternehmen, ESUG).

82 Re Zlomrex International Finance SA[2013] EWHC 3866 (Ch).

83 Ibid., p. 3.

84 Ibid., p. 3.

85 Some debt instrument may contain a majority voting clause to change the key terms of the contracts. For example, it is possible to change the governing law of the contracts. The presence of such a clause may cause financial creditors to recalibrate the interest rate of loans.

86 R.J. de Weijs, 'Comi-Migration: Use or Abuse of European Insolvency Law?' (2014) *European Company and Financial Law Review* 11(4) 1, p. 9.

Cross-border insolvency theories   59

An almost inevitable consequence is that forum shopping changes the insolvency forum and applicable law, which brings in uncertainty.[87] As insolvency law is closely connected to the advance of credits, alteration of insolvency laws will cause uncertainty, which affects solvent companies.[88] In this regard, forum shopping is generally undesirable.

Financial creditors may rely on an anti-forum shopping covenant that requires debtors not to move CoMI; also, they may seek to require unanimous consent in the governing law and jurisdiction law clause.[89] However, even such a covenant may not endow adequate protection to creditors if debtors deliberately try to break this covenant and transfer CoMI to another jurisdiction.[90] When it comes to trade creditors, who in most cases do not have bargaining power to request an anti-forum shopping covenant, their risks can be more difficult to assess.

There seems to be a case to make that if forum shopping happens in the holding companies[91] and only adjusted creditors are affected, with their own consent,[92] forum shopping may not be that susceptible. Certain holding companies in the group may not conduct day-to-day activities beyond arranging financing for the group. Therefore, they do not have numerous staff and trade creditors. As a result, moving the CoMIs of financing companies to another country is easier than moving the CoMIs of operational companies. If local insolvency law will lead to the liquidation of the whole corporate group and loss of value, the justification of forum shopping may be enhanced.[93] Forum shopping of this kind may not only preserve the going concern value but also affect the creditors' expectation the least.[94] However, such cases may be limited in reality as not all the corporate groups arrange financing in the same way.

Forum shopping and freedom of establishment

It appears that forum shopping may find support from the principle of freedom of establishment. According to the Treaty on the Functioning of the European

---

87 Paschalis Paschalisdis, *Freedom of Establishment and Private International Law for Corporations'* (Oxford University Press 2012), p. 216.

88 Vanessa Finch, *Corporate Insolvency Law Perspectives and Principles* (2nd edn, Cambridge University Press 2009), p. 69.

89 Kathy Stones, 'UK Schemes and Forum Shopping' (2014) *Corporate Rescue and Insolvency Journal* 4 161, p. 4.

90 Horst Eidenmüller, 'Abuse of Law in the Context of European Insolvency Law' (2009) *European Company and Financial Law Review* 6 1–28, p. 7.

91 Due to the fact that the holding company may not have trade creditors, it is much easier for them to shift CoMI than it is for operational companies. GeoffO'dea Julian Long and Alexandra Smyth, *Schemes of Arrangement Law and Practice*, (Oxford University Press 2012), p. 25.

92 Kathy Stones, 'UK Schemes and Forum Shopping' (2014) *Corporate Rescue and Insolvency Journal* 4 161, p. 3.

93 Jennifer Payne, 'Cross-Border Schemes of Arrangement and Forum Shopping' (2013) *European Business Organization Law Review* 14(04) 563, p. 588.

94 This type of forum shopping happens with majority senior creditors' agreement, where these creditors can anticipate the risks when they lend money.

60 *Cross-border insolvency theories*

Union Art.49 and Art.54, the freedom of establishment requires that restrictions of one member state on the free movement of establishment of a person (legal person or natural person) from another member states regarding setting up branches or subsidiaries, agencies or moving to another member state are prohibitive.[95] Companies set up in one member state should be respected and recognized in other member states.[96]

The EIR sets forth that CoMI is presumed to be the registered place of one company, unless there is evidence showing it is in another country to rebut such presumption. As a result, debtors and creditors may have incentive to transfer CoMI and registered place to another member state.[97] Relocation of either CoMI or registered places will have to deal with the mixed applicable company law system of the EU: the incorporation principle that requires company law to be governed by the law of registered place; real seat principle which requires company law to be governed by the location of head offices or main business.[98]

With the influence of this mixed system, one should not assume that forum shopping can happen only by doing some paper work. For example, assume that there are two countries, A and B, both embracing the incorporation principle; moving registered place from member state A to B is not without obstacles. Country A will require the company to wind up first as the company has changed the connecting factor, i.e. registered place, such that it is no longer subject to the company law of country A.[99] The general rule is that only the CoMI of companies can be transferred from home country to host country[100] while retaining their nationality in the home country without changing which

---

95 TFEU Art. 49.

96 TFEU Art. 54.

97 Compared to moving CoMI, moving registered place may not successfully change the applicable insolvency law as creditors may challenge it by showing that the CoMI is in a country different from the new registered place.

98 Impact assessment on the directive on the cross-border transfer of registered office Brussels, 12.12.2007, p. 9.

99 C-81/87Daily Mail 1988 ECR 5483 ECJ held that free movement of establishment does not prevent member states from deciding how the companies can retain or lose legal status under their respective laws as companies are creatures of national company law.

100 Case C-212/97 Centros Ltd v Erhvervs- og Selskabsstyrelsen [1999] ECR I-1459; Case C-208/00 Überseering BV v Nordic Construction Company Baumanagement GmbH [2002] ECR I-9919; Case C-167/01 Kamer van KoophandelenFabriekenvoor Amsterdam v Inspire Art Ltd [2003] ECR I-10155; Case C-210/06 CartesioOktatóésSzolgáltatóbt [2008] ECR I-9614; W.H. Roth, 'From Centros to Ueberseering: Free Movement of Companies, Private International Law, and Community Law' (2003) *International and Comparative Law Quarterly* 52 177; J. Rickford, 'Current Developments in European Law on the Restructuring of Companies: An Introduction' (2004) *European Business Law Review* 15 1225; J. Armour, 'Who Should Make Corporate Law? EC Legislation versus Regulatory Competition' (2005) *Current Legal Problems* 58 369; W.G. Ringe, 'No Freedom of Emigration for Companies?' (2005) *European Business Law Review* 16 621; W. Schön, 'The Mobility of Companies in Europe and the Organizational Freedom of Company Founders' (2006) *European Company and Financial Law Review* 3 122; M. Siems, 'SEVIC: Beyond Cross-Border Mergers' (2007) *European Business Organization Law Review* 8 307.

Cross-border insolvency theories 61

company law is applicable to them.[101] When it comes to transfer of registered place, one company may not simply move its registered place from one country to another without winding up and dissolution since both incorporation and real seat principles prevent such movement.[102] Nonetheless, the recent Cartesio case[103] seems to indicate that home country A is enjoined to force the emigrant company to wind up, due to the requirement of free movement of establishment, while it allows receiving country B's substantive law to sidestep the requirement : for example, by forcing the company to reincorporate under country B's law.[104] There is no need to enter into the debate regarding the exact fault line between free movement of establishment of companies. Here one important point to make is that free movement does not guarantee companies in the EU to transfer registered place without any constraints.

A more important question is whether prior to insolvency, distressed companies benefit from the free movement of establishment to shop for insolvency law. One thing that should be clear is that free movement of establishment only guarantees real mobility, but it should not be interpreted as allowing parties free choice of insolvency law.[105] Also, alteration of creditors' rights in forum shopping infringes imperative policies, such as creditors' protection – the Gebhard test.[106] Therefore, the European Court of Justice (ECJ) clarifies that freedom

---

101 Impact assessment on the directive on the cross-border transfer of registered office Brussels, 12.12.2007, p. 9.

102 As a result, moving registered place as a way of forum shopping for insolvency law will incur a significant cost as winding up entails paying debts, which may trigger the insolvency proceeding immediately. See also that the proposal for 14th company directive is again put on the agenda of EU Parliament. In its recommendation 6 (on protective measures), it clearly says:

> Any company against which proceedings for winding-up, liquidation, insolvency or suspension of payments or other similar proceedings have been brought should not be allowed to undertake a cross-border transfer of seat. For the purposes of ongoing judicial or administrative proceedings which commenced before the transfer of seat, the company should be regarded as having its registered office in the home Member State. Existing creditors should have the right to a security deposit.

Such protective provision shows that the EU is cautious of the transfer of registered place of companies in the context of insolvency. European Added Value Assessment EAVA 3/2012, Directive on the cross-border transfer of a company's registered office 14th Company Law Directive, European Parliament resolution of 2 February 2012 with recommendations to the Commission on a 14th company law directive on the cross-border transfer of company seats (2011/2046(INI)) p. 44.

103 Case C-210/06 Cartesio Oktató Szoláltató bt [2008] ECR I-9641.

104 The ECJ held that member states have the right to choose connecting factors to determine the applicable company law, and connecting factors, such as real seat, alone do not infringe on free movement of establishment. Paschalis Paschalisdis, *Freedom of Establishment and Private International Law for Corporations* (Oxford University Press 2012), p. 77; Carsten Gerner-Beuerle and Michael Schillig, 'The Mysteries of Freedom of Establishment after Cartesio' (2010) *International and Comparative Law Quarterly* 59(2) 303–323, p. 311.

105 Eva-Maria Kieninger, 'The Legal Framework of Regulatory Competition Based on Company Mobility: EU and US Compared' (2005) *German Law Journal* 6 741, p. 763.

106 Gebhard v. Consiglio di Milano Case C-55/94 [1995] E.C.R. 4165.

62   *Cross-border insolvency theories*

of establishment could be compromised by national law[107] and the Gebhard test.[108] Therefore, free movement of establishment is not an excuse for forum shopping prior to insolvency.

Regulatory view on forum shopping

The European Commission has acknowledged that not all the forum shopping activities that have happened in cross-border insolvency contexts are harmful.[109] As mentioned above, it is possible that the purpose of forum shopping is solely to achieve a better result than local insolvency law can provide.[110]

Some may also realize the changes of wording in the EIR recast regarding the attitude towards forum shopping.[111] Now it appears that the EIR recast is against the fraudulent and abusive forum shopping which is detrimental to general creditors.[112] Though EIR recast does not provide any explicit explanation regarding these concepts, it is not convincing to interpret these changes as permission for forum shopping in cross-border insolvency law.

EU regulation does not allow free choices of insolvency law, nor is the jurisdictional competition of insolvency law encouraged.[113] The problems of forum shopping discussed above present a case for the EU to discourage forum shopping in general. However, as long as the insolvency laws are different in member states, certain parties in companies have incentives to shop for better rules in their own interests.

Difficulties exist in judging whether forum shopping is done with the intention to defraud creditors. It could be argued that the evidence of blatant fraudulent forum shopping with the purpose of avoiding liabilities is not clearly seen.[114] The uncertainty of the valuation of the business and the senior creditors' power

107 Carsten Gerner-Beuerle and Michael Schillig, 'The Mysteries of Freedom of Establishment after Cartesio' (2010) *International and Comparative Law Quarterly* 59(2) 303–323, p. 310.
108 Gebhard v. Consiglio di Milano Case C-55/94 [1995] E.C.R. 4165.
109 COM(2012) 743 final para. 3.1.
110 COM(2012) 743 final para. 3.1.
111 In the previous version of EU regulation, the wording over forum shopping is as follows:

> Recital (4) It is necessary for the proper functioning of the internal market to avoid incentives for the parties to transfer assets or judicial proceedings from one Member State to another, seeking to obtain a more favourable legal position (forum shopping).

> Council Regulation on insolvency proceeding (EC) No. 1346/2000 Recital (4); by contrast, the EIR recast provides that Recital (29) 'This Regulation should contain a number of safeguards aimed at preventing fraudulent or abusive forum shopping'. New EU regulation on insolvency proceedings 2015.

112 Regulation (EU) 2015 2015/848 of the European parliament and of the Council of 20 May 2015 on insolvency proceedings New EU Regulation Recital 5 and Recital 29; see also Mark Arnold, 'The Insolvency Regulation: A Service or an Overhaul' (2013) *South Square Digest* February, p. 37.
113 Gerard McCormack, 'Jurisdictional Competition and Forum Shopping in Insolvency Proceedings' (2009) *The Cambridge Law Journal* 68(01) 169–197, p. 178.
114 Paul J. Omar, 'The Inevitability of 'Insolvency Tourism'' (2015) *Netherlands International Law Review* 62, p. 6.

to choose applicable law may at least make one doubt the intention of forum shopping, even though it may be just perception and not reality.[115]

The relevant provisions of EIR recast indicate that it has actually enhanced the mechanisms to prevent forum shopping. The new EU regulation contains five mechanisms to do so. These are suspect period, transparency mechanism, jurisdiction examination, creditors' challenge and secondary proceedings.

Suspect period

Art.3 of EIR recast prescribes that in terms of a legal person, the registered place is presumed to be the place of CoMI if there is no evidence to the contrary. However, provided that the registered place is moved to another jurisdiction within three months of the opening of insolvency proceeding, such presumption does not apply.[116]

This three-month suspect period is a new mechanism aiming to prevent fraudulent and abusive forum shopping. It also manifests the objective of the new EU regulation to prevent forum shopping by shifting registered place shortly before the opening of insolvency proceedings.

Transparency

The new EU regulation also introduces a registration and publication mechanism whereby the transparency of information with respect to the opening of insolvency proceedings and the appointment of insolvency creditors will be increased.

Art.24 (1) prescribes that the member state should establish an insolvency case register system, through which information regarding the opening of insolvency proceedings should be disclosed by the member states immediately after the opening of such proceedings.

Art.24 (2) goes on write:

(a) the date of the opening of insolvency proceedings;
......
(c) the type of insolvency proceedings referred to in Annex A opened and, where applicable, any relevant subtype of such proceedings opened in accordance with national law;
(d) whether jurisdiction for opening proceedings is based on Article 3 (1), 3 (2) or 3 (4);

Under Art.25 the European Commission will set up a system to interconnect the register system of each member state. This system will facilitate creditors and other parties' access to information on opening insolvency proceedings in other jurisdictions.

---

115 Ibid., p. 6.
116 EIR recast 2015 Article 3.

64 *Cross-border insolvency theories*

Art.28 imposes publication obligation:

> 1. The insolvency practitioner or the debtor in possession shall request that notice of the judgment opening insolvency proceedings and, where appropriate, the decision appointing the insolvency practitioner be published in any other Member State where an establishment of the debtor is located in accordance with the publication procedures provided for in that Member State. Such publication shall specify, where appropriate, the insolvency practitioner appointed and whether the jurisdiction rule applied is that pursuant to Article 3(1) or (2).

The merits of the transparency mechanism are twofold. On the one hand, it requires the courts opening insolvency proceedings to provide information regarding the reasons for opening insolvency proceedings. For example, the courts need to explain whether the insolvency proceedings are the main proceedings or the secondary proceedings. This implies that, for the purpose of opening main proceedings, the courts should be satisfied that the CoMIs are indeed in their territory. Compared to the EU regulation 2000, under the new EU regulation, the courts cannot assume jurisdiction without adequate reasons. Another aspect is that creditors who know about the opening of insolvency proceedings may challenge the jurisdiction provided that they possess sound evidence.

Jurisdiction examination

Under Art.4 of the EIR recast, the court of opening insolvency proceeding shall examine its jurisdiction and write reasons to assume jurisdiction in the judgement. Also, administrators are required to examine jurisdiction under Art4 (2).

Jurisdiction examination is left to the national courts, which open up cross-border insolvency proceedings. As a result, insolvency proceeding filed immediately after forum shopping may run the risk of not being recognized.[117] The English courts give more weight to external factors, such as registered office address, notification to the creditors and public, office place location and bank account.[118]

The main merit of jurisdiction examination is that it provides a safeguard mechanism so that the insolvency proceedings can be examined and challenged. Though judges enjoy discretion to interpret CoMI,[119] the inconsistence of their judgements can be mitigated by jurisdiction examination. The HBH case[120] is as an example.

HBH was a company incorporated in England and Wales. The English administrator opened a main proceeding in the UK.[121] However, the employees

---

117 Geoff O'dea Julian Long and Alexandra Smyth, *Schemes of Arrangement Law and Practice* (Oxford University Press 2012), p. 25.

118 Ibid., p. 25.

119 Michel Menjucq and Reinhard Damman, 'Regulation No. 1346/2000 on Insolvency Proceedings: Facing the Companies Group Phenomenon' (2008) *Boston University International Law Journal* 9 145, p. 149.

120 Hans Brochier Holdings Ltd v Exner[2006] EWHC 2594 (Ch)Warren J.

121 Ibid.

in Germany also applied to the German court to open an insolvency proceeding. The German Court did not realize that a UK insolvency proceeding had been opened; when the Court thereafter acknowledged the proceeding, the Court denied to recognise this proceeding based on the public interest provision in the EU Regulation as the case obviously showed the CoMI was in Germany.[122] After the administrator in England was informed that the CoMI was in Germany, the English administrator applied to the high court in England to invalidate the order to open insolvency proceeding in the UK.[123] This case happened prior to the draft of EIR recast. One may expect Art. 4 to prevent similar issues in the future.

Creditors' challenges

Art.5 of EIR recast provides that the debtor and creditors may also challenge the international proceedings before the court. Therefore, the CoMI location claimed by the debtor faces two levels of scrutiny: one is the examination of courts; another is the challenge coming from other parties. As abusive forum shopping may be unilaterally launched by the debtor, the impaired creditors have strong incentives to challenge the shift.

Creditors' challenge may correct the issue in which CoMI is shifted unilaterally. Just as Professor LoPucki asserts, current US bankruptcy forum shopping serves only the interests of the parties who conduct the forum shopping rather than the general interests of all the parties.[124]

The ultimate power to decide whether to accept or dismiss creditors' challenges is still conferred to the courts of member states. As long as the courts are convinced that CoMIs are in their territory after examination and challenge, they should be able to open international insolvency proceedings. However, with good faith and due care, the challenge from the creditors may provide courts with more information to reconsider and examine the CoMI location.

Secondary proceedings

The last recourse is secondary proceedings.[125] As it may interrupt the main proceeding, local creditors can gain some bargaining power against the insolvency practitioner in the main proceeding. Secondary proceedings can protect

---

122 Wolf-Georg Ringe, 'Forum Shopping under the EU Insolvency Regulation' (2008) *European Business Organization Law Review* 9 579, p. 586.

123 Ibid., p. 586.

124 Lynn Lopucki, *Courting Failure: How Competition for Big Cases Is Corrupting the Bankruptcy Courts* (University of Michigan Press 2006), p. 251.

125 John Armour, 'Who Should Make Corporate Law? EC Legislation versus Regulatory Competition' (2005) *Current Legal Problems* 58, p. 48. ECJ provided that any measures 'liable to hinder or make less attractive the exercise' of the freedom of establishment

> must be applied in a non-discriminatory manner; they must be justified by imperative requirements in the public interest; they must be suitable for securing the attainment of the objective which they pursue, and they must not go beyond what is necessary in order to attain it.

66 *Cross-border insolvency theories*

local creditors where obvious abusive and fraudulent forum shopping has been carried out.

All these mechanisms show that EIR recast is still cautious about forum shopping. It is submitted that the different national insolvency laws will lead to forum shopping cases, irrespective of these protection mechanisms,[126] while it is not safe to open the door for 'good forum shopping', especially when the distinction is unclear.

Arguably, forum shopping may partly result from manipulating the concept of CoMI.[127]

Some scholars suggest replacing CoMI with registered place, whereby greater predictability could be achieved.[128] However, this may be less helpful in dealing with letter box companies which are registered in country A while doing almost their entire business in country B. The result is that even though B country's interest is closely related to the business, its insolvency law cannot be applied to protect the creditors it aims to protect. Another shortcoming exists in the context of the corporate groups. Assume that CoMIs of all subsidiaries are in the same country; nevertheless, the possibility of procedural consolidation may disappear entirely as long as subsidiaries are registered in different countries.[129] Nonetheless, making a registered place more difficult to rebut as the indicator of insolvency jurisdiction may be a workable compromise.

After analysis, the author is of the opinion that, though in some limited cases forum shopping may provide benefits to creditors, in general, one should be cautious about its possible negative influence. Chances of forum shopping under EIR recast are reduced.

The next section will analyse CoMI and examine whether CoMI is a desirable jurisdiction rule to provide certainty and other benefit. A good understanding of forum shopping and CoMI together facilitates the later analysis of proposed cross-border insolvency law theories based on the group CoMI concept as a means of procedural consolidation.

Procedural significance of CoMI

Theoretical underpinnings of CoMI

In the field of cross-border insolvency law, there are mainly two rival theories governing the jurisdiction and choice of law of one multinational insolvency

---

126 Nicola de Luca, 'Cross Border Insolvency: New Trends' (2015) *European Insolvency Law*, p. 77.
127 Gerard McCormack, 'Reconstructing European Insolvency Law – Putting in Place a New Paradigm' (2010) *Legal Studies* 30(1) 126–146, p. 133.
128 J. Armour, 'Who Should Make Corporate Law? EC Legislation Versus Regulatory Competition' (2005) *Current Legal Problems* 58 369, ECGI law working paper, p. 369; see also W.G. Ringe, 'Forum Shopping under the EU Insolvency Regulation' (2008) *European Business Organization Law Review* 9 579.
129 Gerard McCormack, 'Reconstructing European Insolvency Law-Putting in Place a New Paradigm' (2010) *Legal Studies* 30(1) 126–146, p. 135.

Cross-border insolvency theories   67

case: universalism and territorialism.[130] Under both universalism and territorialism, the choice of forum will significantly determine the choice of insolvency law as the court will apply its own insolvency law with some exceptions.[131] This is an easy and low-cost way to bundle choice of forum and choice of law together.[132] The reason is that insolvency law is to a large extent procedural law, which is exclusively governed by the courts which enjoy jurisdiction; also, insolvency law stands for local values, which justifies applying the law where the insolvency proceedings are opened, i.e. *lex fori concursus.*[133]

Territorialism allocates jurisdiction to any court that can grab debtors' assets in its territory, while universalism only allows the court in which the CoMI is located to open insolvency proceedings. Therefore, CoMI is a concept based on universalism theory. CoMI is defined as 'the place where the debtor conducts the administration of its interests on a regular basis and which is ascertainable by third parties'.[134] It is presumed to be the registered place of one company. Nonetheless, such presumption could be rebutted by evidence proving that the real CoMI is in another jurisdiction.

To be more precise, the EU regulation is built up on a compromised form of universalism which is called 'modified universalism'. Under this theory, the jurisdiction to open the main insolvency proceeding of one insolvent company is allocated to a court in which the CoMI of the company is located.[135] The courts where the non-transitory operations of that company are located could open secondary insolvency proceedings.[136] This modification is to temper the universalism for local creditors' protection.

Evaluation of CoMI

Statutory definition of CoMI

Understanding the concept of CoMI is of significant importance as CoMI directly decides which country's insolvency law will be applied to a company and whether the possibility exists that the CoMIs of a group of companies could be interpreted as in the parent company's insolvency jurisdiction.

The first step is to discover what CoMI is for EIR recast purposes. The Virgós-Schmit Report, which provides explanatory notes on the predecessor of EIR

---

130 See Chapter 4 for more details.

131 New EU Regulation Article 7: the law applicable to insolvency proceedings and their effects shall be that of the member state within the territory in which such proceedings are opened (the 'State of the opening of proceedings').

132 Irit Mevorach, 'Cross Border Insolvency Law of Enterprise Groups: The Choice of Law Challenge' (2014) *Brooklyn Journal of Corporate, Financial & Commercial Law* 9 107, p. 2.

133 Ibid., p. 2.

134 EIR recast 2015 Article 3(1).

135 EIR recast 2015 Article 3(1).

136 EIR recast 2015 Article 3(2). (Such operation should be being carrying out or has been carried out three months prior to the opening of the main insolvency proceedings.)

68   *Cross-border insolvency theories*

2000, says, 'Where companies and legal persons are concerned, the Convention presumes, unless proved to the contrary, that the debtor's centre of main interest is the place of its registered office. This place normally corresponds to the debtor's head office'.[137] From this explanation, one may argue that great weight is given to the head office location when determining companies' CoMI.

In the previous version of EIR 2000,[138] no precise definition of CoMI was provided. EIR Recital 13 stated that the 'CoMI' should correspond to the place where the debtor conducts the administration of his interests on a regular basis and is therefore ascertainable by third parties; Art.3(1) says that 'in the case of a company or legal person, the place of the registered office shall be presumed to be the center of main interest in the absence of proof to the contrary'.[139] However, there is no instruction about in which circumstance a registered place could be rebutted.

Insolvency experts association Insol Europe defines CoMI as the operational head office of one company which is ascertainable to third parties.[140] The definition emphasizes the place where the head office functions of companies are carried out rather than the place where the head office functions are formed. Corresponding to the EIR 2000, the requirement 'ascertainable to third party' is given considerable weight. Insol Europe also provided a list of factors as relevant determinants of CoMI.[141] These factors count only if they are perceivable to third parties.

---

137   Virgós-Schmit Report at para. 75.
138   EIR 2000.
139   EIR recast 2015 Article 3(1).
140   Revision of the European Insolvency Regulation Proposals by INSOL Europe 2012, p. 29:

> centre of main interests shall mean in the case of companies and legal persons, the place of the registered office, except that, (i) where the operational head office functions of the company or legal person are carried out in another member state and that other member state is ascertainable to actual and prospective creditors as the place where such operational head office functions are carried out, it shall mean and refer to the Member State where such operational head functions are carried out and (ii) where the company or legal person is a mere holding company or mere holding legal person, within a group with head office functions in another member state, the centre of main interests as defined in the previous sentence is located in such other member state. The mere fact that the economic choices and decisions of a company are or can be controlled by a parent company in another member state than the member state of the registered office does not cause the centre of main interests to be located in this other member state.

141   The most important factors to deduce the CoMI, *inter alia*, include:

> *–the location of the strategic, financial and operational management;*
> *–the financial functions of the subsidiaries performed by the headquarters (factoring agreement);*
> *–financial information compiled in accordance with the requirements of the holding company (and not according to the requirements of each subsidiary);*
> *–the subsidiaries' inability to make purchases above a certain amount without the approval of their headquarters;*
> *–cash management and pooling functions;*
> *–the absence of budgeting autonomy;*
> *–the recruitment of all senior employees of the subsidiary after consultation with headquarters;*

Cross-border insolvency theories **69**

In 2012 the European Commission also provided a proposal to amend EU regulation. Among other things, it provided a definition of CoMI as follows:

> *The 'centre of main interests' of a company or other legal person should be presumed to be at the place of its registered office. It should be possible to rebut this presumption if the company's central administration is located in another Member State than its registered office and a comprehensive assessment of all the relevant factors establishes, in a manner that is ascertainable by third parties, that the company's actual centre of management and supervision and of the management of its interests is located in that other Member State. By contrast, it should not be possible to rebut the presumption where the bodies responsible for the management and supervision of a company are in the same place as its registered office and the management decisions are taken there in a manner ascertainable by third parties.'[142]*

Based on this definition, the Commission agreed that the location where head office functions are carried out, i.e. the location of the actual centre of management and supervision, is the location of CoMI.

The new EIR 2015 takes account of the development of the understanding of CoMI in recent years; in Art.3 of EIR recast, there is a definition provided as

> The centre of main interests shall be the place where the debtor conducts the administration of its interests on a regular basis and which is ascertainable by third parties; and 'the place of the registered office shall be presumed to be the centre of its main interests in the absence of proof to the contrary. That presumption shall only apply if the registered office has not been moved to another Member State within the 3-month period prior to the request for the opening of insolvency proceedings.[143]

Two recitals also help to further explain the mechanics of CoMI. Recital 28[144] immutably emphasizes the importance of the 'ascertainable to third parties'

> *–the appointment and removal of senior employees as performed by headquarters;*
> *–all information technology and support as performed by headquarters;*
> *–over 70% of the purchases negotiated and dealt with by headquarters;*
> *–the absence of independent trading by the subsidiaries; and*
> *–branding, strategy and production design considerations.*
>
> Revision of the European Insolvency Regulation Proposals by INSOL Europe 2012, p. 32.

142 Proposal for a regulation of the European parliament and of the council amending council regulation (EC) No. 1346/2000 on insolvency proceedings 2012/0360 (COD) Recital 13(a) p. 16.

143 EIR recast Article 3.

144 EIR recast Recital 28

> special consideration should be given to the creditors and to their perception as to where a debtor conducts the administration of its interests. This may require, in the event of a shift of centre of main interests, informing creditors of the new location from which the debtor is carrying out its activities in due course, for example by drawing attention to the change of address in commercial correspondence, or by making the new location public through other appropriate means.

70 Cross-border insolvency theories

requirement of CoMI; it provides an example whereby if there is a shift of CoMI, proper notice should be given to creditors. Also, Recital 30[145] imposes obligations on member states to carefully examine whether the CoMI is indeed in their territory before opening proceedings.

From the statutory definition of CoMI, one could argue that it is presumed to be the registered place of one company. This presumption provides the most predictable result for the third party to check and confirm the location of CoMI for one specific company. The presumption can be rebutted only when evidence appears that the real head office functions are carried out from another member state, and this is ascertainable to the third parties. When the head office functions location and registered place are in the same place, and this could be ascertainable to third parties, the CoMI place cannot be challenged. Where the central administration and the registered place are in two different places, a comprehensive assessment of all factors needs to be conducted so as to determine the real CoMI. In either case, relevant factors used for analysis and the purported central administration need to be ascertainable to the public.

The CoMI of one company is, in many cases, likely to be in the same location as its registered place. It is sensible to attach great importance to registered place by making it difficult to rebut due to the need for predictability.[146] Except where the company does almost no business in its registered place, the presumption can be rebutted. The EIR should respect creditors' perception for the purpose of certainty, but this approach relies on creditors' subjective reliance. A better way to fix such drawbacks is to increase the difficulty of rebutting the presumption.[147] The next section moves to the case law and examines how it shapes the definition of CoMI.

CoMI in case law

The development of the concept of CoMI is largely fuelled by important cases at both national and EU levels. This section aims to provide an overview of relevant cases. Case law provides certain clarity and flexibility on CoMI, and some of the cases are tailored to accommodate corporate group insolvency.[148]

---

145 Recital 30

> Member State should carefully assess whether the centre of the debtor's main interests is genuinely located in that Member State. In the case of a company, it should be possible to rebut this presumption where the company's central administration is located in a Member State other than that of its registered office, and where a comprehensive assessment of all the relevant factors establishes, in a manner that is ascertainable by third parties, that the company's actual centre of management and supervision and of the management of its interests is located in that other Member State.

146 Gerard McCormack, 'COMI and Comity in UK and US Insolvency Law' (2012) *Law Quarterly Review*, p. 7.

147 Dario Latella, 'The "COMI" Concept in the Revision of the European Insolvency Regulation' (2014) *European Company and Financial Law Review* 11(4) 479–494.

148 Luci Mitchell-Fry and Sarah Lawson, 'Defining CoMI, Where Are We Now?' (2012) *Corporate Rescue and Insolvency*, p. 17.

DAISYTEK ISA

As cross-border insolvency law respects the legal person status of every company, it may be difficult for the groups of companies registered in different countries to come to one court to open insolvency proceedings. That is to say, the procedural consolidation of insolvency proceedings is not provided by the EIR 2000 or EIR 2015. The Daisytek case[149] opened an innovative way to deal with the cross-border insolvency of corporate groups. Daisytek ISA is itself a subsidiary of a US-based parent company, Daisytek, while it is also the holding company of 16 European subsidiaries in the group in Europe. Daisytek ISA is registered in the UK, with its CoMI in the UK as well. When the European subgroup became insolvent, many petitions for administration were made in the English court. The core issue of this case is whether the English court has jurisdiction to make administration orders for those foreign subsidiaries.

The UK court noted that the key to open insolvency proceeding for foreign registered subsidiaries was to rebut Art.3(1) of the EIR 2000, i.e. the UK court needed to be convinced that the CoMIs of these subsidiaries were in the UK, not in their respective registered countries. After considering the scale and importance of the interests of creditors of subsidiaries, the court confirmed that the UK was the place of CoMI of the European group.[150]

After an analysis of CoMI for all the subsidiaries, the UK court decided that the actual CoMIs of all the subsidiaries were in the UK, so the court was entitled to open insolvency proceedings on behalf of the whole group.[151] Though the UK court did not create the concept of 'group CoMI', it indeed provided an innovative interpretation of CoMI whereby the subsidiaries in other member states could be drawn to the UK to open insolvency proceedings, based on Art.3(1) of the EU regulation.

Such innovation did not come without resistance from foreign courts,[152] while the general attitude to this new way was supported later on the basis that UK courts had conducted detailed analyses of the location of CoMI for every

---

149 Re Daisytek-ISA Ltd [2004] B.P.I.R. 30.
150 Hon. Samuel L. Bufford, 'International Insolvency Case Venue in the European Union: The Parmalat and Daisytek controversies' (2005–2006) *Columbia Journal of European Law* 12 429, p. 457.
151 The factors to support such a reasoning were:

> financing of the business is from UK; 70% goods supply contracts made in UK; German subsidiary needs approval from UK if spending exceeding 5000 Euros or recruitment of senior employees; also, technology and support are from UK, pan-European customers contracted and negotiated with UK holding company, which comprise 15% sale amount of German subsidiary.
>
> Re Daisytek-ISA Ltd [2004] B.P.I.R. 30.

152 The French commercial court argued that the UK court ignored the fact that CoMI did not apply to corporate group context; the commercial court believed the CoMI was in France, while the UK only possessed one establishment of this company. It was wrong for the UK court to open main insolvency proceedings against French registered subsidiaries.

72   Cross-border insolvency theories

subsidiary rather than rubber-stamping the insolvency petitions.[153] These challenges of foreign courts could be partly understood as issues of communication between courts as the French and German courts may not have been fully aware of the reasoning of the UK court.[154] Nonetheless, one could also argue that the foreign courts may have been reluctant to give up cases to the UK court.[155] Innovative procedural consolidation may be used in limited circumstances as its uncertainty may upset the foreign creditors and foreign courts.

The innovation of the UK court is nevertheless applaudable in that it provided a way to deal with corporate group insolvency under the old framework where no helpful regimes assist the court in doing so. But we should not ignore the danger lying in this approach. One should not assume that all the courts will seize jurisdiction[156] with good faith and a robust analysis of CoMI under the EIR.

EUROFOOD

The approach taken by the UK court in the Daisytek case took issue with the Eurofood case[157] decision made later by the ECJ. The Eurofood case was an important ECJ case, emphasizing that CoMI should be decided on an entity basis while not on a group of companies basis.

Eurofood was a wholly owned subsidiary of an Italian parent company in the Parmalat Group. The registered place of Eurofood was in Ireland throughout its existence. One feature of Eurofood worth mentioning was that it was a finance company which did not hire any employees; it only made three transactions during its existence for the corporate group: two for operations in South American, and one for operation in Ireland.[158] Also, it held the certificate of the Ministry of Finance of Ireland so as to stay in an international finance service centre and take

---

153   The French court decision later was repealed by the court of appeal of Versailles as the latter believed that the UK court had conducted the CoMI analysis. German courts also supported the UK court. Hon. Samuel L. Bufford, 'International Insolvency Case Venue in the European Union: The Parmalat and Daisytek controversies' (2005–2006) *Columbia Journal of European Law* 12 429, p. 460.

154   Some foreign courts may not have been aware that the UK court had opened insolvency proceedings first, nor were they aware of how the UK court decided the CoMI. As a result, concerns regarding whether the UK court had done it in a proper way arose.

155   Matteo M. Winkler, 'From Whipped Cream to Multibillion Euro Financial Collapse: The European Regulation on Transnational Insolvency in Action' (2008) *Berkeley Journal of International Law* 26 352, p. 369.

156   Ibid., p. 369.

157   In re Eurofood IFSC Ltd [2006] Ch. 508.

158   Craig Martin, 'Eurofood Fight: Forum Shopping Under the E.U. Regs' (2005) *ABIJ* 24, p. 36; see also Hon. Samuel L. Bufford, 'International Insolvency Case Venue in the European Union: The Parmalat and Daisytek controversies' (2005–2006) *Columbia Journal of European Law* 12 429, p. 440.

Cross-border insolvency theories   73

advantage of tax benefits.[159] Any change with regard to the management or location of Eurofood required a decision by the Ministry of Finance.[160] Eurofood's business was empowered to the Bank of America at that time. All the evidence showed that the CoMI of Eurofood was in Ireland, and this was ascertainable to its creditor, the Bank of America. On the entity law basis, one could argue that the centre of gravity of Eurofood was in Ireland.

However, the Italian court believed that the CoMI of Eurofood should be in Italy, where its parent company was located. As in the Daisytek case, the Italian court argued that Eurofood was incorporated in Ireland for tax benefits and was only the financial division of the whole Parmalat Group; that all Eurofood did was to implement the decisions made by the parent company.[161] Furthermore, the creditors of Eurofood would have no difficulties knowing that Eurofood was an 'empty box', and its parent company was in Italy.[162]

The Irish court retorted that the Italian court was not aware of the fact that the creditors of Eurofood actually believed that the CoMI of Eurofood was in Ireland as their investment in Eurofood was subject to Irish fiscal regulation.[163]

Later, the Italian court referred to the ECJ for instruction, the ECJ held that the ECJ notified that the EIR did not apply to groups of companies and to the relationships amongst them thereof; the *ex ante* predictability, especially of the cross-border debt transactions was very important to the interests of creditors. When deciding the CoMI of one specific company, the ECJ considered factors relating to registered place, place of head office functions and ability by third parties to ascertain location; the ECJ also considered factors such as the location of the parent company and the control it could exert on the decision-making of subsidiaries.[164] And then it reasoned:

> ... only if factors which are both objective and ascertainable by third parties enable it to be established that an actual situation existed which was different from that which locating it at that registered office was deemed to reflect. Where a company carried on its business in the member state where its registered office was situated, the mere fact that its economic choices were or

---

159 Hon. Samuel L. Bufford, 'International Insolvency Case Venue in the European Union: The Parmalat and Daisytek controversies' (2005–2006) *Columbia Journal of European Law* 12 429, p. 440.

160 Samuel L. Bufford, 'Center of Main Interests, International Insolvency Case Venue, and Equality of Arms: The Eurofood Decision of the European Court of justice' (2006–2007) *Northwestern Journal of International Law & Business* 27 351, p. 364.

161 Ibid., p. 368.

162 Hon. Samuel L. Bufford, 'International Insolvency Case Venue in the European Union: The Parmalat and Daisytek controversies' (2005–2006) *Columbia Journal of European Law* 12 429, p. 443.

163 Samuel L. Bufford, 'Center of Main Interests, International Insolvency Case Venue, and Equality of Arms: The Eurofood Decision of the European Court of Justice' (2006–2007) *Northwestern Journal of International Law & Business* 27 351, p. 371.

164 Ibid., p. 381.

74 *Cross-border insolvency theories*

could be controlled by a parent company in another member state was not enough to rebut the presumption[165];

   The fact (assumed by the referring court) that the subsidiary conducts the administration of its interests on a regular basis in a manner ascertainable by third parties and in complete and regular respect for its own corporate identity in the member state where its registered office is situated will normally be decisive in determining the "centre of [its] main interests".[166]

The ECJ finally decided that as the registered place and CoMI were in Ireland and ascertainable to creditors, the Irish court should have jurisdiction.

The Eurofood case effectively challenged the validity of the practice from Daisytek. It argued that simply being able to exert control on subsidiaries from a parent company is not adequate to determine that the subsidiaries' CoMI is in the place where the parent's CoMI is located.[167]

As a result, every company's CoMI has to be determined in an entity-by-entity manner. This indicates that the relationship between parent and subsidiaries should not directly affect the location of the CoMIs of subsidiaries. The court also concluded that in cases where parent companies and subsidiaries are registered in different member states, the subsidiary's operating its business in its own identity in the registered place on a regular basis, and being ascertainable to third parties, is enough of a condition to determine its CoMI.[168] Conversely, if the control executed by the parent company is not ascertainable to the third parties, the presumption that the subsidiary's CoMI is in its own registered place cannot be rebutted simply on the basis that the parent company could wield its power to appoint a board of directors and affect the decision of the subsidiaries.[169]

The Eurofood case is considered a new stage of development of CoMI in that the registered place becomes harder to rebut simply due to a parent-subsidiary relationship.[170] Nevertheless, it does not completely eradicate the possibility that the CoMI of the parent company is also the CoMI of all group members. If the subsidiaries' CoMIs are indeed in their parent's location and are ascertainable to third parties,[171] the relevant insolvency proceedings of subsidiaries could still be opened in the place of the parent company. Therefore, it could be argued that there may not be serious contradictions between the Eurofood case and the Daisytek case. This is because, in the Daisytek case, the court did not locate the

---

165 Eurofood [2006] Ch.508 Held(1) p. 3.
166 Ibid., p. 20.
167 In re Eurofood IFSC Ltd [2006] Ch. 508 para. 112.
168 Ibid., para. 116.
169 Ibid., para. 126.
170 Sarah Paterson, 'COMI: The Elephant in the Room' (2012) *Corporate Rescue and Insolvency Journal* 4 135, p. 2.
171 Heribert Hirte, 'Towards a Framework for the Regulation of Corporate Groups' Insolvencies' (2008) *European Council on Foreign Relations* 5 213, p. 220; see also Christoph Paulus, 'Group Insolvencies – Some Thoughts about New Approaches' (2007) *Texas International Law Journal* 42 819–820.

Cross-border insolvency theories 75

CoMI of each subsidiary to England on the sole basis of their parent-subsidiary relationship. The court, in analysing the relevant factors of central administration of each member, decided the CoMI of the subsidiaries.

MPOTEK

After the Eurofood case, the MPOTEK case[172] showed that the pragmatic approach to allocating the jurisdiction of subsidiaries to one country is still possible in cases where businesses of group members are interwoven, and subsidiaries are centrally controlled.

MPOTEK, as a subsidiary of the French Emtek Group, had its registered place in Germany. While the presumption of registered place indicated that Germany should be the insolvency jurisdiction, the application for administration was delivered to the French Commercial Court of Nanterre.[173] The whole group is business-integrated. For example, one subsidiary controls human resources, management and development of strategy, while another is in charge of commercial policy, supermarket distribution and management of purchases of merchandize.[174] The French court reasoned that the head office functions of MPOTEK are in France and are ascertainable to third parties, so the court has jurisdiction to open insolvency proceeding for MPOTEK.[175] As a result, the insolvency proceedings are held in France, so a cross-country reorganization rescue is possible. The value of the group in the trademark and distribution network could be retained.[176]

One important point to bear in mind is that the French court did not seize jurisdiction purely on the basis of the integrated business characteristics of the group. Rather, it analysed the CoMI of MPOTEK subsidiary according to 'head office functions' and 'ascertainable to third party' tests. The special feature of the Emtek group is that other subsidiaries, except MPOTEK, consisting of the integrated business network, are based in France. If they are located in different countries, the result of the case may change. Since each subsidiary controls certain head office functions ascertainable to third parties, it is difficult to allocate all the jurisdictions to French court.

STANDFORD

In the leading UK case Re Standford International Bank Ltd,[177] Lewison J stressed the importance of certainty of CoMI. This is a fact-oriented concept in the sense that it is built on the basis of objective factors. It is the head office func-

---

172 MPOTEC GmbH [2006] B.C.C. 681.
173 Ibid., p. 1.
174 Ibid., p. 4.
175 Ibid., p. 2.
176 Ibid., p. 2.
177 Re Stanford [2010] EWCA Civ 137.

76   Cross-border insolvency theories

tion of one company determined on the basis of objectivity and ascertainability.[178] In the Standford case, the court of appeal agreed with Lewison J and confirmed that it is important to consider whether the factors determining head office functions are ascertainable to third parties. The EIR aims not only to allocate the jurisdiction to the court which possesses the actual CoMI but also to ensure that it could be perceived by third parties. Perception is closely related to predictability, which is an important requirement for creditors to calculate risks.[179] The being ascertainable to third party test ensures that all the necessary information to decide the location of CoMI is in the public domain.

INTEREDIL CASE

The Interedil case is another influential ECJ case on the definition of CoMI. The company Interedil is an Italian company registered in Italy. In July 2001, it was registered in London as a foreign company, and on the same day it removed its registered office from the Italian Register Office.[180]

The dispute over the jurisdiction of Interedil started on 28 October 2003. On that day, an Italian creditor, Intesa, filed an insolvency proceeding against Interedil in Italy. However, the Interedil company argued that since the register office had been transferred to the UK, the Italian court should not have jurisdiction as the registered place was assumed to be the CoMI.[181] The Italian court disagreed and believed the CoMI was in Italy as Interedil still owned real estate, bank accounts and a leased hotel in Italy.[182] Italian court also argued that Interedil, after transfer of registered place, did not carry out any transactions, so the central administration was not transferred.[183]

The ECJ refereed the judgement of the Eurofood case and rendered the opinion that central administration of one company is the decisive factor for the purpose of determination of CoMI. The factors assessed should be objective and ascertainable to the creditors.[184] The ECJ went on to state that when the registered place and 'management and supervision place' are in the same place and ascertainable to third parties, the CoMI cannot be rebutted; when they are in different places, the mere fact that one country possesses assets and contracts is not sufficient to determine CoMI; a comprehensive assessment of all the relevant

---

178 Luci Mitchell-Fry and Sarah Lawson, 'Defining CoMI, Where Are We Now?' (2012) *Corporate Rescue and Insolvency*, p. 16.

179 In re Stanford International Bank Ltd and another [2010] Bus. L.R. 1270 p. 21.

180 For a detailed depiction of the fact of Interedil case, see Federico M. Mucciarelli, 'The Hidden Voyage of a Dying Italian Company, from the Mediterranean Sea to Albion' (2012) *European Company and Financial Law Review* 9(4), p. 2.

181 Interedil case [2012] B.C.C. 851 p. s2.

182 Federico M. Mucciarelli, 'The Hidden Voyage of a Dying Italian Company, from the Mediterranean Sea to Albion' (2012) *European Company and Financial Law Review* 9(4), p. 3.

183 Opinion of advocate general kokott delivered on 10 March 2011, para. 55.

184 Interedil Srl (in liquidation) v Fallimen to InteredilSrl and another [2012] Bus. L.R. 1582 p. 2.

Cross-border insolvency theories 77

factors is needed in order to prove that central administration is ascertainable to third parties in the state.[185]

Two parts of the court judgement are worth particular attention. One is that the ECJ used the words 'management and supervision place' of a company as a representation of CoMI.[186] This leads some scholars to argue that the Interedil case narrowed the factors needed to determine the CoMI.[187] If this is true, the approach may facilitate the corporate group insolvency as it enables the court to seize the jurisdiction if it can show that the management and supervision place of the entire EU-wide group or European subgroup of a US corporate group is in its territory.[188] This interpretation may nonetheless ignore the fact that the Interedil reasoning does not necessarily deviate from Eurofood.[189] Putting it in the context of the case, the court required a comprehensive assessment of all the objective factors ascertainable to the third parties to determine CoMI, so only considering the place of the nominal head office is not sufficient. Moreover, the location of management and supervision should only be ascertainable after considering all the objective factors which are ascertainable to the third parties, that is to say, management and supervision is the result of the analysis, rather than an independent factor to determine CoMI.

Another part is that the court gave more weight to the 'ascertainable to third party' test of CoMI.[190] This is understandable because one important goal of insolvency is certainty, as mentioned in Chapter 2. Therefore, the creditors should enjoy the right to know beforehand which jurisdiction's law they are going to deal with and how rights are going to be affected under a specific law.[191] So, the location of CoMI should be decided in line with what creditors understand.[192] Some scholars, from the viewpoint of the ECJ in the Interedil case, argue that creditors may have the inclination to believe that the place of operational factories rather than the place of management and supervision is the location of CoMI.[193] That is to say, creditors' perception may be subjective and therefore different

---

185 Interedil case [2012] B.C.C. 851, p. 3.
186 Gabriel Moss (QC), 'Group Insolvency-Forum-EC Regulation and Model Law Under the Influence of English Pragmatism Revisited' (2014–2015) *Brooklyn Journal of Corporate, Financial & Commercial* 9 179, p. 4.
187 Thomas Biermeyer, 'Case C-396/09 Interedil Sri, Judgment of the Court of 20 October 2011, Court Guidance as to the COMI Concept in Cross-Border Insolvency Proceedings' (2011) *Maastricht Journal of European and Comparative Law* 18 581, p. 587.
188 Gabriel Moss (QC), 'Group Insolvency-Forum-EC Regulation and Model Law Under the Influence of English Pragmatism Revisited' (2014–2015) *Brooklyn Journal of Corporate, Financial & Commercial* 9 179, p. 5.
189 Adrian Cohen, 'Eurofood for Thought: Additional Guidance on COMI' (2012) *Journal of International Banking and Financial Law* 1 52, p. 3.
190 Sarah Paterson, 'COMI: The Elephant in the Room' (2012) *Corporate Rescue and Insolvency Journal* 4 135, p. 1.
191 Ibid., p. 2.
192 Ibid., p. 3.
193 Luci Mitchell-Fry and Sarah Lawson, 'Defining CoMI, Where Are We Now?' (2012) *Corporate Rescue and Insolvency*, p. 17.

78 Cross-border insolvency theories

from reality. However, after careful analysis of the Eurofood and Interedil cases, one may argue that creditors' perception should not be based on their respective subjective views. Rather, they should predict the location of CoMI on the basis of objective factors available in the public domain. Therefore, such a test is still an independent and objective test.[194] After processing all the relevant objective factors, most creditors will reach the same conclusion regarding the location of CoMI of a given debtor. Any hidden information known only by sophisticated creditors or debtors will be excluded from consideration.

Certainty of CoMI

Insolvency law relates to lending interest rate, which is expected to be ex ante predictable. In cross-border insolvency context, which set of insolvency laws will be applied to a given case is determined by insolvency jurisdiction rules. CoMI, as a jurisdiction rule, assigns insolvency proceedings to the court of CoMI, irrespective of where the debtors do businesses. This choice of forum rule generates predictability and uniformity.[195] Nevertheless, the concept of CoMI could be criticized as not being clear enough; this is especially true in cases where the main assets and operations of the companies are not in the same place.[196]

As CoMI also needs to be ascertainable to the third parties,[197] the importance of the place of decision-making seems to be subordinate to the importance of the place where the decision-making is carried out, i.e. the place of operation.[198] That is because the creditors are arguably more likely to identify the objective operation places than the subjective and abstract decision-making places. However, it is possible that certain senior creditors, such as banks that play monitoring roles, may more readily ascertain the real decision-making location of a given company. This begs the question of whose expectation needs to be served in terms of the requirement of 'ascertainable to third party'. The solution seems to require the debtors to disclose as much information as possible to the public so that creditors can roughly make the same conclusion regarding the place of CoMI.

---

194 Federico M. Mucciarelli, 'Private International Law Rules in the Insolvency Regulation Recast: A Reform or a Restatement of the Status Quo?' (2015), p. 11 (available at: http://ssrn.com/abstract=2650414).

195 The choice of law theory of CoMI is based on multilateralism theory, which analyses the connection between legal relationship and one court; thereafter, the theory assigns the legal relationship to one court, which arguably generates predictability and uniformity; see Hannah L. Buxbaum, 'Rethinking International Insolvency: The Neglected Role of Choice of Law Rules and Theory' (2000) *Stanford Journal of International Law* 36 23, p. 39, p. 60.

196 Gerard McCormack, 'Jurisdictional Competition and Forum Shopping in Insolvency Proceedings' (2009) *The Cambridge Law Journal* 68(01), pp. 185–186.

197 Samuel L. Bufford, 'Center of Main Interests, International Insolvency Case Venue, and Equality of Arms: The Eurofood Decision of the European Court of justice' (2006–2007) *Northwestern Journal of International Law & Business* 27 351, p. 419.

198 André J. Berends, 'The Eurofood Case: One Company, Two Main Insolvency Proceedings: Which One Is the Real One' (2006) *Netherlands International Law Review* 53(2) 331–361, p. 345.

One may also notice the difficulties of fixing the above problem if the elements making up the CoMI cannot be defined as different industries may comprise different important elements which affect the determination of the location of the CoMI.[199] The development of case law tries to enhance the objectivity of CoMI by providing that it should be decided by objective factors which are ascertainable to third parties. Though this requirement may help to depict the frame of the CoMI, in practice creditors may still have different views as they perceive different facts. Therefore, case law so far does not provide a highly predictable CoMI concept.

Replacing CoMI with registered place may be beneficial in that it increases predictability, but a caveat is its ineffectiveness when dealing with letterbox companies.[200] As insolvency law reflects one country's social policies and priority of values, it is not justifiable to replace the insolvency policies of the country which has most stake in the risk with those of the countries of the letterbox companies. Also, such change of EIR may create inconsistency of the CoMI test as the UNCITRAL Model Law also uses the CoMI concept.[201] Therefore, increasing the threshold to rebut the registered place presumption may be better. More effort should be put in by further legislation and case law in order to enhance the predictability of CoMI. For example, Recital 32 of the EU regulation provides that where debtor's opinion with regard to the location of CoMI causes doubt, debtors may need to provide further evidence, and creditors are also given opportunities to express their opinions.[202]

Another merit of the rule keeping the CoMI as the jurisdiction is its relatively unbiased function regarding jurisdiction allocation. If CoMI is interpreted as simply the head office, it generally works in the interest of more developed countries, such as the UK, rather than in that of less developed countries, even though operations take place in the territory of the latter. Since it is more likely that the head office of a company is located in the more developed location, such as London, the UK may seize jurisdiction more frequently than other foreign courts.[203] Adopting 'group CoMI' for cross-border insolvency of MCGs will further exaggerate the uneven allocation of insolvency proceedings.[204]

Evaluation of territorialism and universalism

With the understanding of the concept of CoMI, it is possible to evaluate territorialism and universalism in terms of their abilities regarding the preservation of going concern value and certainty.

---

199 Ibid., p. 338.
200 Gerard McCormack, 'Something Old, Something New: Recasting the European Insolvency Regulation' (2016) *The Modern Law Review* 79(1) 102–146, p. 130.
201 Ibid., p. 130.
202 Ibid., p. 131.
203 Robert W. Miller, 'Economic Integration: An American Solution to the Multinational Enterprise Group Conundrum' (2011–2012) *Richmond Journal of Global Law and Business* 11 185, p. 199.
204 Ibid., p. 199.

80 *Cross-border insolvency theories*

Ability to preserve value

Territorialism may not be able to preserve going concern value for a single company, let alone MCGs. It ignores the economic reality of international business as it allows borders of countries to sever the business which would have been one integrated part. Such weakness of territorialism also exists in cooperative territorialism[205]. Though it is possible that an agreement will be achieved by creditors scattered in different member states, it is also possible that no consensus will be achieved if it is harmful to local creditors. Also, the cooperation under cooperative territorialism may be disorganized due to the fact that there is no leading court to coordinate the whole process. It is desirable to have one leading court (or coordinator), taking into account other courts' (or insolvency practitioners') opinions, to propose a reorganization plan such that a well-functioning and effective group reorganization plan can be achieved.[206]

One may argue that territorialism may reduce costs as it is convenient for the local creditors to lodge debtors locally. However, such an advantage is not obvious any more as the new EU Regulation Recast Art.45 states that insolvency practitioners may help creditors to lodge claims in every opened insolvency proceeding.[207] With the support of representatives, the cost to local creditors of lodging claims in foreign courts will be reduced.

In the typical universalism paradigm, one representative or trustee of an insolvency case can be entrusted to communicate with all the creditors; one single set of insolvency law, which is the law of the opening state, will be applied to the whole case wherever creditors are located. Therefore, territorialism is very likely to be more inefficient than universalism in the sense that it increases the information cost of adjusting creditors.[208] The same is true for non-adjusting creditors as under universalism they may be able to collect information regarding foreign bankruptcy regimes at a low cost compared with collecting information of every creditor under territorialism; only dealing with one country may allow non-adjusting creditors to decide interest rates.[209]

---

205 Lynn. M. Lopucki, 'The Case for Cooperative Territoriality in International Bankruptcy' (1999–2000) *Michigan Law Review* 98 2216, p. 2220.

206 External evaluation of regulation no. 1346/2000/EC on insolvency proceedings p. 234; later, see 'Group coordination proceeding' in the new EIR Recast 2015 Art.61. Also, Art.70 of EIR Recast provides that the coordinators of group coordination proceedings may suggest a group coordination plan, though the insolvency practitioners representing other companies in the same group have no obligation to follow it.

207 EU regulation on insolvency proceedings recast, Art.45.

208 Adjusting creditors, defined by Andrew Guzman as creditors who can and will adjust their interest rate in terms of risks of lending; by contrast, none-adjusting creditors are ones who will not or cannot adjust interest rates either due to the high cost involved (such as credit card companies, which generally charge the same rate to everyone) or inability to adjust interest rates (tort creditors or tax authorities).

209 Andrew T. Guzman, 'International Bankruptcy: In Defence of Universalism' (1999–2000) *Michigan Law Review* 98 2177, p. 2198.

Cross-border insolvency theories 81

Universalism also avoids multiple insolvency proceedings being opened against the same debtor, so administration fees and cooperation costs can be reduced.[210] One court with one set of insolvency rules ensures that a cross-border sale or rescue is achieved quickly. As a result, pure universalism, by reducing the international transaction cost[211] (especially the debt collection cost), achieves the goal of maximization of value. Modified universalism potentially allows more than one insolvency proceeding against the same company to open.[212] Nevertheless, this does not necessarily mean that secondary proceedings have to be opened. Re MG Rover Espana SA case[213] exemplifies such situation.

In this case, the English court appointed joint administrators on behalf of eight foreign national sales companies in Europe. An issue was that the local employees might have been treated less favourably by the English insolvency law, which would have given rise to secondary proceedings.[214] The English court and joint administrators were of the opinion that the purpose of the administration of MG Rover group was to rescue it as a going concern and preserve its distribution networks; the English court believed that the administrators could make certain payments to local employee creditors under their own local law.[215]

Even though secondary proceedings are opened, modified universalism may not lead to a large number of insolvency proceedings in the way that cooperative territorialism does. As opposed to the low threshold to open jurisdiction in territorialism, there is a relatively high threshold to open secondary proceedings: namely establishment test.[216] In the case of Olympic Airline, the courts reasoned that '*the existence of an establishment must be determined, in the same way as the location of the centre of main interests, on the basis of objective factors which are ascertainable by third parties*'.[217] Also, a winding-up proceeding alone does not

---

210 Alexander M. Kipnis, 'Beyond UNCITRAL: Alternatives to Universality in Transnational Insolvency' (2007–2008) *Denver Journal of International Law and Policy* 36 155, p. 173.
211 Edward S. Adams and Jason K. Fincke 'Coordinating Cross-Border Bankruptcy: How Territorialism Saves Universalism' (2008–2009) *Columbia Journal of European Law* 15 43, p. 49.
212 Ibid., p. 55.
213 Re MG Rover Espana SA [2006] B.C.C. 599.
214 Ibid., p. 3.
215 Without taking into account the local creditors' interests, the secondary proceedings may be opened, and this would make it impossible to rescue the group. The English courts believed that it was correct to interpret para. 66 of Sch.B1 of insolvency law act 1986 as giving the administrators the power to make payment for the purpose of achieving the goals of administration, even though such payment is not consistent with the rank of insolvency law. The administrators themselves need to think about whether payment to avoid secondary proceeding can lead to a better result. Re MG Rover Espana SA [2006] B.C.C. 599, p. 6.
216 Under territorialism, one court could open insolvency proceedings as long as it possesses assets of the debtor; EU regulation only allows local courts to open secondary proceeding if they possess establishment of the debtor. According to EU regulation art. 2 (10), 'establishment' means any place of operations where a debtor carries out or has carried out in the three-month period prior to the request to open main insolvency proceedings a non-transitory economic activity with human means and assets.
217 Trustees of the Olympic Airlines SA Pension & Life Assurance Scheme v Olympic Airlines SA [2015] UKSC 27, p. 6.

82 Cross-border insolvency theories

meet the establishment threshold.[218] Furthermore, the mere existence of an office or branch is not enough to convince a court that the debtor has an establishment; it should be a real operation involving human resources and assets.[219] To meet the establishment test, the business should be conducted in a fixed place, and it should deal with the third parties in the market.[220]

Secondary proceedings can be utilized as a cost-effective tool to resolve local complex issues through advantageous local law.[221] Also, certain EU regulation provisions can be used to reduce the number of them.[222] To sum up, universalism can preserve going concern value better than territorialism.

Certainty-forum shopping

Certain advocates of territorialism argue that territorialism yields a higher level of predictability than universalism.[223] Though assets may be transferred from one jurisdiction to another, even in the vicinity of the insolvency proceedings, defenders of territorialism assert that the effect of such transfer is only limited to the assets being transferred; also, the local creditors can file their claims in the country to which the assets are transferred to require distribution in that insolvency proceeding.[224]

As with forum shopping in territorialism, CoMI can also be manipulated under universalism for the purpose of forum shopping.[225] Universalism as-

---

218 Ronan McNabb, 'Olympic Airlines: A First Step to Tighter Controls in Secondary Proceedings?' (2013) *Corporate Rescue and Insolvency* 5 129, p. 130.

219 Trustees of Olympic Airlines SA Pension & Life Assurance Scheme v Olympic Airlines SA [2013] EWCA Civ 643.

220 Trustees of the Olympic Airlines SA Pension & Life Assurance Scheme v Olympic Airlines SA [2015] UKSC 27, p. 6.

221 Ian Fletcher, *Insolvency in Private International Law* (2nd edn, OUP Oxford 2005), p. 432.

222 Recital 42 EU regulation

> ...this Regulation confers on the insolvency practitioner in main insolvency proceedings the possibility of giving an undertaking to local creditors that they will be treated as if secondary insolvency proceedings had been opened. That undertaking has to meet a number of conditions set out in this Regulation, in particular that it be approved by a qualified majority of local creditors. Where such an undertaking has been given, the court seized of a request to open secondary insolvency proceedings should be able to refuse that request if it is satisfied that the undertaking adequately protects the general interests of local creditors. When assessing those interests, the court should take into account the fact that the undertaking has been approved by a qualified majority of local creditors.

223 Edward S. Adams and Jason K. Fincke, 'Coordinating Cross-Border Bankruptcy: How Territorialism Saves Universalism' (2008–2009) *Columbia Journal of European Law* 15 43, p. 67; and see generally Lynn LoPucki, 'Universalism Unravels' (2005) *American Bankruptcy Law Journal* 79 143; Lynn LoPucki, 'Global and Out of Control' (2005) *American Bankruptcy Law Journal* 79 79–104.

224 Edward S. Adams and Jason K. Fincke, 'Coordinating Cross-Border Bankruptcy: How Territorialism Saves Universalism' (2008–2009) *Columbia Journal of European Law* 15 43, p. 58.

225 Sefa M. Franken, 'Three Principles of Transnational Corporate Bankruptcy Law: A Review' (2005) *European Law Journal* 11(2) 233–258, p. 236.

signs jurisdiction to CoMI, which is unchanged no matter how assets are relocated.[226] Transferring assets is easier than transferring CoMI, so moving assets is more easily manipulated in this regard. Also, if the local creditors' priority is not recognized in the foreign courts, local creditors are unlikely to recover their losses by filing their claims in those courts. This is probably the main reason that certain creditors or debtors initiate such a transfer of assets in the first place.

When debtors transfer assets from one member state to another on the eve of the insolvency, creditors in different member states do not need to worry about the location of the assets as the court possessing CoMI will govern the case. Territorialism makes non-adjusting creditors even worse off due to the manipulation. The information cost for adjusting creditors is very high as they have to ascertain a number of factors on the location of assets and the priority of creditors in different jurisdiction. Also, as it is difficult to predict the chances of transfer of assets, the adjusting creditors can hardly fully adjust their interest rates. This leads to inefficient results as the interest rates will increase.[227]

Also, universalism prevents unfair situations in which some creditors receive nothing just because they are in a member state that possesses no assets. As moving assets is easier than moving CoMI, universalism is generally more predictable[228] than territorialism because it provides a uniform way to select jurisdiction.

Another reason territorialism provides higher predictability than rival regimes is that local creditors may expect local law to be applied to them.[229] Therefore, territorialism may be adopted with modest friction from member states.[230] This assumption may ignore the fact that the categories of creditors are highly diverse; among them, there are sophisticated creditors who do not base their expectations on the application of local insolvency law and local assets as the only resources available to them. For example, certain banks enjoy cross-guarantee from all the subsidiaries in corporate groups.[231] Also, not all local creditors are offered priority by the local law, so they may not have to be protected under local law. More importantly, protecting local creditors through local assets may either

---

226 Jay Lawrence Westbrook, 'Universalism and Choice of Law' (2004–2005) *Penn State International Law Review* 23 625, p. 630.

227 Andrew T. Guzman, 'International Bankruptcy: In Defence of Universalism' (1999–2000) *Michigan Law Review* 98 2177, pp. 2199–2022.

228 See Ulrik Rammeskow Bang-Pederse, 'Assets Distribution in Transnational Insolvencies, Combining Predictability and Protection of Local Interests' (1999) *American Bankruptcy Law Journal* 73 385 which argues that universalism with cross priority is a better principle with regard to predictability and local creditors' protection than different forms of territorialism.

229 Alexander M. Kipnis, 'Beyond UNCITRAL: Alternatives to Universality in Transnational Insolvency' (2007–2008) *Denver Journal of International Law and Policy* 36 155, p. 168; Lynn. M Lopucki, 'Cooperation in International Bankruptcy: A Post Universalist Approach' (1998–1999) *Cornell Law Review* 84 696, p. 751.

230 Hannah L. Buxbaum, 'Rethinking International Insolvency: The Neglected Role of Choice of Law Rules and Theory' (2000) *Stanford Journal of International Law* 36 23, p. 26.

231 Jay Lawrence Westbrook, 'Multinational Financial Distress: The Last Hurrah of Territorialism' (2006) *Texas International Law Journal* 41 321, p. 333.

84 Cross-border insolvency theories

make them receive a windfall where the assets/claims rate is high or make them suffer where the rate is low. By contrast, under universalism, the creditors generally enjoy rights to file their claims in other countries, and they may be given priority under foreign insolvency law. As a result, local creditors can be better protected in many cases.

The incentive for forum shopping under modified universalism is not as strong as that in universalism due to the possibility to open secondary proceedings.[232] One may criticize that the conditions to open secondary proceedings are not entirely clear.[233] Courts may decide to open secondary proceedings or dismiss the application at their discretion. However, this argument should not be overstated. One reason is that secondary proceedings may not have even commenced in many cases. This is especially true in cases where local creditors and courts are happy to defer to the main proceeding either because local creditors' rights are respected or because certain compensation is made to local creditors under local law. Also, as the case of Public Prosecutor v Segard shows,[234] under EU regulation and the development of case law, common principles are built up. The French court requested that the French court of appeal ignore UK judgement by invoking public interest, arguing that the UK court did not protect French employees by allowing them to be represented in court.[235]

However, the French Court of Appeal was of the opinion that though Art.26 of EU regulation confers member states the right to refuse foreign main proceedings on the basis of public policy provision, the conditions to use public policy as a defence should be limited to the minimum.[236] The English court's arrangement neither deprived French employee's rights nor prevented them from claiming their preference; also, the consultation of the workers' council and staff representatives was conducted by the English administrator under French employment law; the opening of secondary proceedings should be purposeful and bring benefits to creditors, but in this case there was no reason to open it.[237]

One aim of secondary proceedings is to cooperate with main proceedings to achieve a good reorganization result for creditors rather than to act against main proceedings. Therefore, member states may not allow secondary proceedings to be opened without any meaningful reasons, even though local applicants would like to open them. Therefore, in cases where the courts find that the opening of secondary proceeding is of no utility, they may reject the application.

---

232 Edward J. Janger, 'Virtual Territoriality' (2009–2010) *Columbia Journal of Transnational Law* 48 401.

233 Hannah L. Buxbaum, 'Rethinking International Insolvency: The Neglected Role of Choice of Law Rules and Theory' (2000) *Stanford Journal of International Law* 36 23, p. 30.

234 Public Prosecutor v Segard [2006] (As Administrator for Rover France SAS) I.L.Pr. 32, p. 8.

235 Ibid., p. 8.

236 Ibid., p. 8.

237 Public Prosecutor v Segard [2006] (As Administrator for Rover France SAS) I.L.Pr. 32, p. 2.

Summary

Territorialism has two drawbacks: high cost and low predictability. Multiple insolvency proceedings make territorialism costly; the unpredictability gives rise to inefficient strategic behaviours, such as forum shopping by moving assets.[238] Cooperative territorialism does not make such cooperation mandatory like EIR. Another problem is that it makes value preservation difficult to achieve: for example by selling businesses as a whole.[239] Cooperative territorialism may not do better than modified universalism in cases of MCGs reorganization.[240]

A desirable cross-border insolvency theory should respect the economic reality of international businesses and provide mechanisms to encourage cooperation or even deference between courts and insolvency practitioners in order to preserve going concern value and yield predictability. Universalism based on CoMI as the insolvency jurisdiction rule has considerable advantages. The next section will further examine whether CoMI can be applied to MCGs, i.e. group CoMI.

Puzzles of group CoMI

Definition of group CoMI

One may consider whether a given MNC can have a joint group CoMI so that one court can deal with the cross-border insolvency of the entire group. More complexity may be introduced by MCGs in terms of assessing the CoMI for a whole group of companies. EIR recast does not provide the concept of group CoMI. Also, following the Eurofood case tenet, it is the attitude of the ECJ that corporate groups should be treated in an entity-by-entity fashion.

However, there are good reasons to consider the concept of group CoMI: procedural consolidation. The benefits of centralizing insolvency proceedings of group members into one jurisdiction (in most cases, the parent's jurisdiction) have long been recognized. Some scholars have tried to provide a group CoMI concept for the insolvency of corporate groups.[241] The main reason to employ this concept is to centrally control the insolvency proceedings and maximize the recovery of corporate group insolvency for creditors due to the higher likelihood of successful insolvency reorganization.[242]

It is correct to note that modern global business may be conducted in a cross-division way in the corporate group rather than in an entity-by-entity way.

---

238 Alexander M. Kipnis, 'Beyond UNCITRAL: Alternatives to Universality in Transnational Insolvency' (2007–2008) *Denver Journal of International Law and Policy* 36 155, p. 170.

239 Jay Lawrence Westbrook, 'Multinational Financial Distress: The Last Hurrah of Territorialism' (2006) *Texas International Law Journal* 41 321, p. 333.

240 Ibid., p. 334.

241 For example, Professor Irit Mevorach and Samuel Bufford.

242 Samuel L. Bufford, 'Coordination of Insolvency Cases for International Enterprise Groups: A Proposal' (2012) *American Bankruptcy Law Journal* 86 685, p. 712.

86 *Cross-border insolvency theories*

That is to say that the business integration of group members may not be served well by traditional insolvency law, especially in corporate rescue situations.[243]

One may therefore argue that it is desirable to have provisions in the EIR to allow one court to open insolvency proceedings for all group members if it is clear that the whole group is run as one entity. In this situation, one court could administer the group insolvency without the need to design new provisions specific to group insolvency.[244]

The group CoMI concept helps to centralize insolvency proceedings in one place, especially in terms of the types of corporate groups which are business-integrated and centrally controlled by one parent company.[245] Such conduct will reduce the cost of multiple insolvency proceedings and avoid the difficulty of court-to-court cooperation. CoMI is the place where the head office functions are carried out, and the same may apply to corporate groups, i.e. the place where the head office function is centrally carried out and controlled.[246]

Some scholars also endorsed the necessity to introduce a group CoMI concept so that the court possessing group CoMI could have jurisdiction to open insolvency proceedings for all the group members.[247] One may suggest that the group CoMI concept could free-ride the development of CoMI, and group CoMI can be defined as the location where the group collectively organizes and manages its interests and is perceptible to third parties.[248] Such a place corresponds to the place where the group's actual head office functions are carried out.[249]

Another scholar's proposal – virtual territoriality – also suggests a group CoMI to regulate corporate group insolvency.[250] Professor Janger believes that corporate groups' insolvency proceedings can be centralized in the group CoMI jurisdiction. While the court possessing group CoMI can decide whether to open secondary proceedings, it should apply the law of subsidiaries' CoMI to each group member. In other words, the court of group CoMI should only control the multiple insolvency proceedings with regard to administrative or procedural matters, leaving the substantive insolvency issues to the law of subsidiaries' home countries.[251] The effect is that though only one court governs the group's insolvency cases, the creditors of subsidiaries are treated as if subsidiaries' insolvency

---

243 Gabriel Moss and Christoph G. Paulus, 'The European Insolvency Regulation – The Case for Urgent Reform' (2006) *Insolvency Intelligence* 19(1) 1–5, p. 5.

244 Ibid., p. 5.

245 Irit Mevorach, 'The "Home Country" of a Multinational Enterprise Group Facing Insolvency' (2008) *International & Comparative Law Quarterly* 57 427–448, p. 8.

246 Ibid., p. 8.

247 Samuel L. Bufford, 'Coordination of Insolvency Cases for International Enterprise Groups: A Proposal' (2012) *American Bankruptcy Law Journal* 86 685, p. 711.

248 Ibid., p. 716.

249 Ibid., p. 716.

250 Edward J. Janger, 'Virtual Territoriality' (2009–2010) *Columbia Journal of Transnational Law* 48 401, p. 434.

251 Ibid., p. 435.

proceedings are opened in their own countries.[252] Such a decentralized choice of law practice may be better implemented in a business-integrated, centrally controlled corporate group context; otherwise, it may create an unjustified disturbance to the sovereignty of subsidiaries' countries.[253]

There is no census in terms of the definition of group CoMI.[254] Though it is desirable for business integrated and control centralized corporate groups to open insolvency proceedings in one court, such types of corporate group may be difficult to define, and they may not be the majority of the types of corporate groups. It is possible for a corporate group to possess more than one entity which performs the head office functions. In such circumstance, the efficacy of group CoMI will be noticeably reduced as there will still be multiple courts to apply multiple sets of insolvency laws in multiple insolvency proceedings. The next section will consider whether group CoMI can be easily identified under its current definition – place where the head office functions are conducted.

Implications of MCG theories on procedural consolidation

Large corporate groups in Europe typically operate through the network of subsidiaries.[255] When upstream or downstream subsidiaries face financial difficulties, other subsidiaries in other member states will also suffer.[256] A lack of provisions for groups of companies is one problem identified by the European Commission, even though the number of group cases is large.[257] To achieve the goals of insolvency law, it is desirable if certain rules allow group going concern values to be preserved on the one hand, and such rules also provide certainty on the other hand. Based on the insolvency jurisdictional rule-CoMI, it seems to be desirable that the CoMIs of all the subsidiaries be found in one place in terms of head office functions.[258] This requires an analysis regarding whether the head office function-related control on subsidiaries is executed in one place.

252　Robert W. Miller, 'Economic Integration: An American Solution to the Multinational Enterprise Group Conundrum' (2011–2012) *Richmond Journal of Global Law and Business* 11 185, p. 213.

253　Ibid., pp. 213–214.

254　Lynn M. LoPucki, 'Universalism Unravels' (2005) *American Bankruptcy Law Journal* 79 143, p. 153.

255　Commission staff working document executive summary of the impact assessment – accompanying the document-commission recommendation on a new approach to business failure and insolvency SWD(2014) 61 final, p. 20.

256　Commission staff working document executive summary of the impact assessment – accompanying the document-commission recommendation on a new approach to business failure and insolvency SWD(2014) 62 final, p. 2.

257　Commission staff working document, impact assessment, accompanying the document Revision of Regulation (EC) No. 1346/2000 on insolvency proceedings SWD(2012) 416 final, p. 10 (available at ec.europa.eu/justice/civil/files/insolvency-ia_en.pdf).

258　For a discussion of the relationship between the allocation of head office functions and group going concern value, see Daoning Zhang, 'Reconsidering Procedural Consolidation for Multinational Corporate Groups in the Context of the Recast European Insolvency Regulation' (2017) *International Insolvency Review* 26(3) 241–357. This part is partly built on it.

88   Cross-border insolvency theories

The business network perspective[259] provides useful insights into the head office and subsidiaries' relationships, which have a bearing on insolvency jurisdiction. The theory reveals that the relationships between head office and subsidiaries should not be simplified to one parent company controlling all the subsidiaries in a hierarchical structure. The danger of such simplicity is that it fails to reflect the reality of how control is exerted in the group.

The deeper the subsidiaries are embedded in the internal network, the stronger the parent company's power to exert control on subsidiaries.[260] Nevertheless, even though parent companies may acquire control through their ownership,[261] they may not exert this control. The precondition to exert control is that the parent company makes sure that its allocation of resources to one company does not harm the opportunities of other subsidiaries.[262] A parent company therefore needs to balance its control on subsidiaries and subsidiaries' control on other subsidiaries and the parent itself. This does not deny the existence and importance of the hierarchical structure of MCGs; it argues that the real structures of MCGs and control from the parent are better represented from a business network perspective than by a strict hierarchy.

The phenomenon can be explained as the change of the subsidiaries' roles. The roles of the subsidiaries expand from a local implementer of the parent company to those in charge of certain technological and business-related resources, such as research and development (R&D) and marketing, as mentioned above.[263] From resource dependence theory, the parent has to rely on their resources as it cannot understand how to properly use these resources without the facilitation

---

259 Mats Forsgren *et al.*, *Managing the Embedded Multinational – A Business Network View* (Edward Elgar 2006); Jeffrey H. Dyer and Harbir Singh, 'The Relational View: Cooperative Strategy and Sources of Inter-Organisational Competitive Advantage' (1998) *The Academy of Management Review* 23(4) 660–679; Bernard Surlemont, 'A Typology of Centres within Multinational Corporations: An Empirical Investigation', in J. Birkinshaw and N. Hood (eds.), *Multinational Corporate Evolution and Subsidiary Development* (Macmillan Press 1998); Mats Forsgren, *Theories of the Multinational Firm* (2nd edn, Edward Elgar 2013); Ulf Andersson, Mats Forsgren and Ulf Holm, 'Balancing Subsidiary Influence in the Federative MNC: A Business Network View' (2007) *Journal of International Business Studies* 38(5) 802–818; Håkan Håkansson and Ivan Snehota, *Developing Relationships in Business Networks* (Routledge 1995); Kirsten Foss *et al.*, 'MNC Organisational Form and Subsidiary Motivation Problems: Controlling Intervention Hazards in the Network of MNC' (2011) (available at: http://ssrn.com/abstract=1969402).

260 Ulf Andersson and Mats Forsgren, 'Subsidiary Embeddedness and Control in the Multinational Corporation' (1996) *International Business Review* 5(5) 487–508, p. 504.

261 For instance, one holding company stays at the apex of the whole group; in chain style shareholding, the head of the chain owns the majority of shares of its subsidiary, and, in turn, the subsidiary owns the majority of shares of its sub-unit. Bob Tricker, *Corporate Governance Principles, Policies, and Practices* (Oxford University Press 2009), p. 76.

262 Mo Yamin and Ulf Andersson 'Subsidiary Importance in the MNC: What Role Does Internal Embeddedness Play?' (2011) *International Business Review* 20 151–162, p. 153.

263 Ram Mudambi *et al.* 'How Subsidiaries Gain Power in Multinational Corporations' (2014) *Journal of World Business* 49 101–113, p. 109.

of subsidiaries.[264] As a result, the subsidiaries can use these resources to obtain power and autonomy in certain areas of decision-making, irrespective of the desire of the parent. In other words, certain subsidiaries' strategies derived from their networks will counterbalance control from the parent company.[265] This is especially true for the subsidiaries which possess technological-related power and may shape the decision-making of the parent company in the area of R&D. Similarly, subsidiaries which possess business-related resources may make decisions for the group regarding marketing strategies.[266]

The parent may also delegate certain head office functions to other places, either through a regional head office or directly to some eligible subsidiaries. Therefore, there is more than one head office in a given MNC, with different head office functions spread across different levels. Research has shown that relatively decentralized subsidiaries are more likely to learn and create value.[267] The relative decentralized decision-making mandate allows subsidiaries to adapt to the local environment and respond to the exigencies quickly. By contrast, a hierarchical and centralized corporate group may not be able to cope with more and more complex environments and win in fierce competition.[268]

All this encourages international companies not to adopt a purely centralized and integrated business form of group as it prevents the subsidiaries from learning from their environments and contributing to the group. As a result, parent companies need to allow certain subsidiaries to retain decision-making power in the areas where they have valuable expertise. The parent may also delegate certain head office functions to subsidiaries by forming regional head offices. Therefore, there is more than one head office in a given MNC with different head office functions spread across different levels.

For example, the parent company can control the financial arrangements of all the subsidiaries, while certain subsidiaries may control R&D functions, which are at least equally important. As technology-related functions can arguably yield the strongest control,[269] it is difficult to assert that the CoMIs of these subsidiaries are in the location of the parent company.

As a result, it is difficult to argue that subsidiaries' CoMIs are in the same location as the parents'. This makes a group CoMI approach difficult. It is widely accepted that certain types of groups may be better treated in a centralized way.

---

264 Reason could be, for example, causal ambiguity, which means difficulty for others in understanding the better performance of one player.
265 Mats Forsgren *et al.*, *Managing the Embedded Multinational – A Business Network View* (Edward Elgar 2006), p. 133.
266 Ram Mudambi *et al.* 'How Subsidiaries Gain Power in Multinational Corporations' (2014) *Journal of World Business* 49 101–113, p. 103.
267 Kirsten Foss *et al.*, 'MNC Organisational Form and Subsidiary Motivation Problems: Controlling Intervention Hazards in the Network of MNC' (2011) (available at: http://ssrn.com/abstract=1969402), p. 6.
268 Ibid., p. 6.
269 Ram Mudambi *et al.*, 'How Subsidiaries Gain Power in Multinational Corporations' (2014) *Journal of World Business* 49 101–113, p. 109.

90 Cross-border insolvency theories

The networks that the embedded members have internally and externally are strategic resources.[270] It could be the case that two companies combine their resources in a unique way, thereby gaining group going concern value.[271] It is also possible that two companies in a group exchange technologies and adapt to each other by mutual investment.

Networks may also form relational economic rents which cannot be gained by regular market relationships.[272] Business relationships are the pipes of information, resources, technologies and marketing between member companies, and they can be seen as important intangible resources.[273] Therefore, it is desirable to have group cross-border insolvency solutions to preserve the group going concern value.

This chapter examines the pivotal concept of CoMI in the EIR context. It argues that CoMI is not a very clear concept, while its predictability has been improved by the EIR recast and case law. The chapter further moves to consider the concept of group CoMI. Drawing from insights from a business network perspective, it concludes that group CoMI is not a predictable concept that can be widely applied to many groups of companies. The next chapter will examine cross-border insolvency theories for corporate groups with reference to this conclusion, especially the theories which are based on the group CoMI approach.

Theoretical proposals and procedural consolidation

There is no group procedural consolidation solution for the cross-border insolvency of MCGs under EIR.[274] Based on the previous discussion of various cross-border insolvency theories, it is possible to speculate whether some of these theories may be applied to MCGs. This section will examine the proposed theories for procedural consolidation in an ex ante way and practice for procedural consolidation in an ex post way. The aim is to consider whether procedural consolidation is possible and desirable as a solution for cross-border insolvency of MCGs.

Ex ante approach – group cross-border insolvency theories

This section examines proposals for group procedural consolidation using an ex ante approach. Arguably, modified universalism, contractualism and universal

---

270 Jeffrey H. Dyer and Harbir Singh, 'The Relational View: Cooperative Strategy and Sources of Inter-Organisational Competitive Advantage' (1998) *The Academy of Management Review* 23(4) 660–679, p. 661.

271 Ibid., p. 661.

272 Ibid., p. 662.

273 Mats Forsgren, *Theories of the Multinational Firm* (2nd edn, Edward Elgar 2013), p. 108.

274 From one study, it seems that EIR 2000 does not obtain a desirable satisfaction level from the respondents with regard to group insolvency. 'Almost half of respondents (49%) felt the EIR does not work efficiently for multinational group insolvencies with 30% feeling it does'. Commission staff working document impact assessment. Revision of Regulation (EC) No. 1346/2000 on insolvency proceedings Strasbourg, 12.12.2012, p. 52.

proceduralism can all be used as ex ante solutions for cross-border insolvency of MCGs.

Though cooperative territorialism could solve group insolvency issues, it does not support procedural consolidation. This is because insolvency proceedings may be opened wherever the local courts can find assets belonging to the corporate group, which is especially true in an MNC cross-border insolvency case. Therefore, cooperative territorialism does not offer solutions to pull insolvency proceedings into one court. The following will examine the other three possible solutions.

Contractualists

Contractualists propose to replace regulations with contracts.[275] In the cross-border insolvency context, the main tenet of contractualism is that companies should be allowed to have bankruptcy-selection clauses in their charters.[276] The chosen bankruptcy law by a company will be the one most suitable to administering the bankruptcy affairs of that company.[277] Members of companies make the choice of their bankruptcy laws at the time of incorporation, and it can be changed later with creditors' consent.[278] In the case of MCGs, it is possible that many subsidiaries choose the same jurisdiction as the insolvency jurisdiction in order to achieve procedural consolidation. However, without insolvency, it may be difficult to find one country whose insolvency law is the best option for all foreign subsidiaries as they may all have different demands. Contractualism leads to complexity and inflexibility. Companies may need to change their places of business during development, or at a certain stage, another insolvency law may be more suitable to their needs.[279] An insolvency law chosen early on may not be a favourable option for the company years later.

One merit of contractualism is that it is purported to be highly predictable. As the chosen jurisdiction and insolvency law will be written in the charters of the companies, creditors can calculate interest rates accordingly. Also, as the

---

275 Lynn Lopucki 'The Case for Cooperative Territoriality in International Bankruptcy' (1999–2000) *Michigan Law Review* 98 2216, p. 2242.

276 Robert K. Rasmussen, 'A New Approach to Transnational Insolvency' (1997–1998) *Michigan Journal of International Law* 19 1; Robert K. Rasmussen, 'Resolving Transnational Insolvency through Private Ordering' (1999–2000) *Michigan Law Review* 98 2252; Robert K. Rasmussen, 'Where Are All the Transnational Bankruptcies, the Puzzling Case for Universalism' (2006–2007) *Brooklyn Journal of International Law* 32 983; Mihailis E. Diamantis, 'Arbitral Contractualism in Transnational Bankruptcies' (2005–2007) *Southwestern University Law Review* 35 327.

277 Robert K Rasmussen. 'A New Approach to Transnational Insolvency' (1997–1998) *Michigan Journal of International Law* 19 1, p. 5.

278 Ibid., p. 5.

279 Gerard McCormack, 'Jurisdictional Competition and Forum Shopping in Insolvency Proceedings' (2009) *The Cambridge Law Journal* 68(01) 169–197, p. 178.

92   Cross-border insolvency theories

jurisdiction has been decided ex ante by contracts, forum shopping may also be reduced. Contractualists believe that companies are in a better position than governments to choose the insolvency law that is best suited to their business.[280] Also, governments and courts have little information about the condition of the company, so the company and its creditors are in the best position to decide where to conduct insolvency and which jurisdiction's insolvency laws are best suited to them.

It is, however, possible for influential creditors to choose insolvency law that only benefits them while bypassing the protection offered to the non-adjusting creditors or stakeholders. Non-adjusting creditors, such as tort creditors, who cannot bargain for their payment, will become victims since senior creditors can externalize loss to them under contractualism. Debtors and senior adjusting creditors may choose haven countries to preclude non-adjusting creditors from claiming money. For example, high petition fees discourage creditors with small claims from joining the insolvency proceedings.[281]

If most of creditors are adjusting creditors in insolvency cases, one may find a plausible reason to support contractualism. However, the number and size of non-adjusting creditors' claims may not be as small as contractualists suggest.[282] According to Westbrook's research, small claims pervasively exist in most of the cases and account for a considerable portion of unsecured claims.[283] This finding reveals a problem of contractualism in that it may neglect that there are many unsecured creditors and other involuntary creditors who probably have no power to change the content of contracts; thus, the contracts will be used as a tool biased towards the interests of debtors and big creditors.[284] The contracts will choose a jurisdiction which can maximize senior creditors' value rather than maximizing value for the stakeholders as a whole.

Contractualism lacks measures for assets control and transparency.[285] Without mechanisms to control the assets of debtors, the agreement is unenforceable in that the debtor could transfer assets to other subsidiaries or somewhere else.[286]

Also, the tailored insolvency law template designed by contractualism may not be broadly replicated by other companies as unfamiliarity with the chosen

---

280 Robert K. Rasmussen. 'A New Approach to Transnational Insolvency' (1997–1998) *Michigan Journal of International Law* 19 1, p. 20.

281 Lynn Lopucki, 'The Case for Cooperative Territoriality in International Bankruptcy' (1999–2000) *Michigan Law Review* 98 2216, p. 2247.

282 Robert K. Rasmussen, 'Resolving Transnational Insolvency through Private Ordering' (1999–2000) *Michigan Law Review* 98 2252, p. 2273.

283 Elizabeth Warren and Jay Westbrook, 'Contracting Out of Bankruptcy: An Empirical Intervention' (2004–2005) *Harvard Law Review* 118 1197, p. 1245.

284 Lynn Lopucki, 'Cooperation in International Bankruptcy: A Post Universalist Approach' (1998–1999) *Cornell Law Review* 84 696, p. 739.

285 Jay Lawrence Westbrook, 'A Global Solution to Multinational Default' (1999–2000) *Michigan Law Review* 98 2276, p. 2304.

286 Ibid., p. 2305.

Cross-border insolvency theories **93**

insolvency law and risks may make the cost of replication high.[287] As a result, contractualism may be costly as every company needs to design its own template of insolvency law.

Free choice of insolvency law also ignores the interaction of insolvency law and other laws within a country. Insolvency law closely connects to employment law, corporate governance and secured credit law.[288] Allowing parties to choose foreign insolvency law will break such interaction; also, parties may not be familiar with the chosen foreign law.[289]

Contractualists try to cure this issue by arguing that forums can refuse to assume or recognize the choice if they think it is unjust and unreasonable; involuntary creditors could not be in a worse position under the chosen law than they would be in their own jurisdiction.[290] However, the rejection of recognition itself causes uncertainty.

The *ex ante* determination of jurisdiction and insolvency law under contractualism may provide predictability to stakeholders. But one may argue that a consensus regarding which insolvency law will be chosen may be difficult to achieve; the multiple bankruptcy law options give rise to transaction costs to negotiate an agreement.[291] Also, there are significant numbers of creditors in an insolvency case, so the cost of negotiation will balance out the efficiency of contractualism.[292] As Professor LoPucki identified, the cost to conclude such contracts may be very high as every creditor needs to analyse and understand the chosen law and efficiency of the chosen court to calculate the risks therein, even when the firm is healthy.[293] Free choice of insolvency law is likely to introduce heavy transaction costs as it does not offer an efficient disclosure system to inform creditors to which insolvency law they will be subject.[294]

All these transaction costs will increase in the context of cross-border insolvency of MCGs as more creditors are expected to join in the process of contracts negotiation. Also, it is difficult to obtain all their approval to change insolvency law.

---

287 Robert K Rasmussen. 'A New Approach to Transnational Insolvency' (1997–1998) *Michigan Journal of International Law* 19 1, p. 27.

288 For the interaction between insolvency law and corporate governance, see John Armour, Brian R. Cheffins and David A. Skeel, Jr., 'Corporate Ownership Structure and the Evolution of Bankruptcy Law: Lessons from the United Kingdom' (2002) *Vanderbilt Law Review* 55 1699, p. 1701.

289 Gerard McCormack, *Secured Credit and the Harmonisation of Law, the UNCITRAL Experience* (Edward Elgar Publishing Limited 2011), p. 49.

290 Robert K Rasmussen. 'A New Approach to Transnational Insolvency' (1997–1998) *Michigan Journal of International Law* 19 1, p. 35.

291 Elizabeth Warren and Jay Westbrook, 'Contracting Out of Bankruptcy: An Empirical Intervention' (2004–2005) *Harvard Law Review* 118 1197, p. 1249.

292 Ibid., p. 1219.

293 Lynn Lopucki, 'Cooperation in International Bankruptcy: A Post Universalist Approach' (1998–1999) *Cornell Law Review* 84 696, p. 739.

294 Jay Lawrence Westbrook, 'A Global Solution to Multinational Default' (1999–2000) *Michigan Law Review* 98 2276, p. 2306.

94 *Cross-border insolvency theories*

To make contractualism practicable, all participating countries should accept free choice of insolvency law regimes. Currently, contractualism does not have a wide support base. No countries allow participants to decide jurisdiction and choice of law beforehand. As a result, contractualism does not necessarily prove it has the ability to preserve going concern value and provide high certainty. It may not be the desirable option for cross-border insolvency of MCGs.

The modified universalism solution to MCGs

Modified universalism is only applied to an individual company. However, by analogy, one could argue that the insolvency proceedings of subsidiaries in a corporate group may be treated like secondary proceedings available under EIR.

Insol Europe suggested a similar solution by designing a concept called 'group main proceeding'. Group main proceeding is the insolvency proceeding of the ultimate parent. The power enjoyed by insolvency practitioners in a group main proceeding vis-à-vis the main proceedings of subsidiaries is similar to the power of the insolvency practitioners in a main proceeding of a company vis-à-vis a secondary proceeding of the same company.[295] Insol Europe believed that it is a modest proposal to apply the current regime to the corporate group, especially where the parent and the subsidiaries are all in insolvency.[296]

Samuel L. Bufford[297] and Ralph R. Mabey[298] also designed a universalist concept named Enterprise – CoMI, arguing that the home country of the group is where the CoMI of the group is located. Insol Europe's proposed group main proceeding is the insolvency proceeding opened in the ultimate parent company's CoMI place.[299] Though there are some nuances between the group main proceeding approach and the Enterprise CoMI approach, the rationales behind them are nearly the same: all these proposals try to achieve procedural consolidation by designing a group CoMI concept and locating group CoMI in the place of the ultimate parent company. Such suggestions have the benefit of free-riding existing concepts and mechanisms underpinned by modified universalism.

However, it may not be justified to equate the CoMI of the ultimate parent company with the CoMI of the group. A business network perspective provides useful insights in this regard. CoMI means the place where the head office functions are carried out, and these functions should be ascertainable to third parties. In reality, in order to gain group going concern value, many head office functions are mandated to subsidiaries and ascertainable to third parties. Also, the ultimate parent company may not be an active group member and might not

---

295 Revision of the European Insolvency Regulation Proposals by INSOL Europe 2012, p. 96.
296 Proposal by INSOL Europe revision of EIR, p. 93.
297 See Samuel L. Bufford, 'Coordination of Insolvency Cases for International Enterprise Groups: A Proposal' (2012) *American Bankruptcy Law Journal* 86 685.
298 Ralph R. Mabey and Susan Power Johnston, 'Coordination among Insolvency Courts in the Rescue of Multi-National Enterprises' (2008) *34th Lawrence P. King & Charles Seligson Workshop on Bankruptcy and Business Reorganization*, New York. University School of Law.
299 Revision of European insolvency regulation proposed by Insol Europe, p. 95.

Cross-border insolvency theories 95

be involved in subsidiaries' operations at all. Therefore, the concept of group CoMI may not qualify as the CoMI of the group. The challenge of applying universalism to deal with the insolvency of MCGs is that it cannot provide a clear enough group CoMI concept.[300]

Another drawback of the group CoMI approach is that there is no effective way, so far, to eliminate secondary proceedings, never mind the main proceeding of subsidiaries. The purpose of secondary proceedings is, among other things, to protect local creditors' interests according to local insolvency law.[301] The most obvious reason for the opening of secondary proceedings is explained by the difference of priority of creditors.[302] Secondary proceedings may be avoided in some cases, such as employment preservation, where the claims of the creditors can be acceptably reduced to the pecuniary repayment.[303] Nonetheless, in some cases, national insolvency law provides creditors with not just a monetary priority and repayment, but also a policy-based judicial intervention which cannot be simply reduced to a monetary payment.[304]

Therefore, modified universalism may not provide a desirable solution for consolidating insolvency proceedings in the group CoMI place; among other reasons, according to insights from the business network perspective, such a place may not exist at all.

The universal proceduralism solution to MCGs

Compared with territorialism and universalism, universal proceduralism (sometimes called 'virtual territoriality') is a relatively new theory proposed by Professor Janger.[305] The main tenet of universal proceduralism is that one court should control one cross-border insolvency case, and it should apply decentralized choice of law rules to decide substantive rights of foreign creditors. The effect of universal proceduralism is that the court which opens the insolvency proceeding should treat the foreign assets and foreign claims as close as possible to the treatment available under local law had the local insolvency proceedings been opened.[306] The court only controls the case at issue, while the substantive insolvency rules that have distributional effects, such as priority, avoidance law

---

300 Lynn Lopucki, *Courting Failure: How Competition for Big Cases Is Corrupting the Bankruptcy Courts* (University of Michigan Press 2006), p. 209.
301 John A. E. Pottow, 'A New Role for Secondary Proceedings in International Bankruptcies' (2010–2011) *Texas International Law Journal* 46 579, p. 580.
302 Ibid., p. 580.
303 Ibid., p. 587.
304 Ibid., p. 588.
305 Edward J. Janger, 'Universal Proceduralism' (2006–2007) *Brooklyn Journal of International Law* 32 819; Edward J. Janger, 'Virtual Territoriality' (2009–2010) *Columbia Journal of Transnational Law* 48 401; Edward J. Janger, 'Reciprocal Comity' (2010–2011) *Texas International Law Journal* 46 441; Edward J. Janger, 'Silos, Establishing the Distributional Baseline in Cross Border Bankruptcies' (2014–2015) *Brooklyn Journal of Corporate, Financial & Commercial Law* 9 85.
306 Edward J. Janger, 'Virtual Territoriality' (2009–2010) *Columbia Journal of Transnational Law* 48 401, p. 408.

96 Cross-border insolvency theories

and reorganization plan, should be replaced by foreign local insolvency law.[307] As the power of court in which the insolvency proceedings are centralized is reduced, the incentive of forum shopping is lower than that in universalism. Any change of the forum will not necessarily change the applicable law to certain claims and assets.

Professor Janger believes that universal proceduralism has an advantage over modified universalism. He argues that in the corporate groups context, it is desirable to allow the court of group CoMI to administer proceedings on behalf of group members while requiring the court to apply the local law of subsidiaries' jurisdictions, determined by their respective CoMIs.[308]

Applying local substantive insolvency law could be seen as reciprocal comity in the sense that not only do local courts defer to the court of the main proceeding, but also the main proceeding respects local interests.[309] Universal proceduralism provides balance between the desirable result of centralized insolvency proceedings and the protection of local creditors. Local creditors' reliance[310] on local law vindicates the need to protect local interests by applying local law.[311] For example, if local employment law provides local workers with certain benefits which are not available under foreign insolvency law, local workers expect that local law will be applied to protect them. Designing rules solely based on local creditors' various or even conflicting expectations may be too subjective.[312] A better solution is to replace subjective creditors' reliance with harmonized choice of law rules. This approach may require the law to determine what local interests are, who local creditors are and what local assets are. For example, it may be the case that local interests are protected by the court of main proceeding only to the extent of local establishment-related local assets. Such rules provide objective rules to direct local creditors' expectations.[313] In the case where the local court does not possess CoMI or establishment, neither do creditors have *right in rem* locally, such creditors cannot subjectively argue that they base their expectations on local insolvency law rather than the insolvency law of the main proceeding.[314]

---

307 Ibid., p. 435.
308 Ibid., p. 434.
309 Edward J. Janger, 'Reciprocal Comity' (2010–2011) *Texas International Law Journal* 46 441, p. 456.
310 EU regulation on insolvency proceedings recast 2015 Article 2 definitions: 'local creditor' means a creditor whose claims against a debtor arose from or in connection with the operation of an establishment situated in a member state other than the member state in which the centre of the debtor's main interests is located.
311 John A. E. Pottow, 'Beyond Carve-Outs and Toward Reliance: A Normative Framework for Cross-Border Insolvency Choice of Law' (2014) *Brooklyn Journal of Corporate, Financial & Commercial Law* 9 202, pp. 212–214.
312 Charles W. Mooney, Jr., 'Harmonisation Choice of Law Rules for International Insolvency Cases: Virtual Territoriality and Virtual Universalism and the Problem of Local Interests' (2014) *Brooklyn Journal of Corporate, Financial and Commercial Law* 9 120, p. 144.
313 Ibid., p. 146.
314 Ibid., p. 141.

Cross-border insolvency theories 97

There are many drawbacks to procedural universalism. One is that similar to rival theories such as virtual territoriality, and universalism, procedural universalism relies on the 'group CoMI' concept in order to centralize insolvency proceedings in corporate group cases.[315] It is impossible to broadly apply this one size fits all approach to many cross-border insolvency context of MCGs as procedural universalism does not provide clues regarding the group CoMI location and neither it is always desirable to allocate the CoMIs of subsidiaries to one place.

Universal proceduralism may also be criticized because it connects local assets to local interests.[316] The assets situated in one jurisdiction do not by themselves mean that such assets are local assets. Conferring jurisdiction by assets is not reasonable; it gives too much power to the local law and benefits local creditors without justification.[317] The location of assets by itself is not the relevant test which support the court of main proceeding to apply local insolvency law; it is the actual local interests that deserve local law protection.[318] Also, not all creditors should be protected by local insolvency law if they are not offered priority.

Another thing worth mentioning is that the scope of local assets under procedural universalism may be too broad if they are roughly defined as all the assets that are located locally. Some assets may not be connected to the local establishment and local operation, so local interests should not benefit from this windfall simply because they are lucky enough to be the local creditors of the country.[319] The Nortel case[320] provided an example of this. The proceeds from the sale of the IP assets of the corporate group were pro rata allocated to member companies, rather than only to the creditors of the company that holds the property.

Under modified universalism, there are certain rules, such as the establishment test to restrict opportunist debtors or creditors from opening secondary proceedings and using local laws in their own interests.[321] By contrast, under

---

315 Edward J. Janger, 'Virtual Territoriality' (2009–2010) *Columbia Journal of Transnational Law* 48 401, p. 434.

316 Jay Lawrence Westbrook, 'Comments on Universal Proceduralism' (2009–2010) *Columbia Journal of Transnational Law* 48 503, p. 509.

317 Charles W. Mooney, Jr., 'Harmonisation Choice of Law Rules for International Insolvency Cases: Virtual Territoriality and Virtual Universalism and the Problem of Local Interests' (2014) *Brooklyn Journal of Corporate, Financial and Commercial Law* 9 120, p. 10.

318 Jay Lawrence Westbrook, 'Comments on Universal Proceduralism' (2009–2010) *Columbia Journal of Transnational Law* 48 503, p. 514.

319 One may further suggest that even though the secondary proceedings are initiated by local courts, the non-establishment assets (the assets that are not relevant to local operation) should be subject to the insolvency law of the main insolvency proceeding. This makes the regime more like universalism. Charles W. Mooney, Jr., 'Harmonisation Choice of Law Rules for International Insolvency Cases: Virtual Territoriality and Virtual Universalism and the Problem of Local Interests' (2014) *Brooklyn Journal of Corporate, Financial and Commercial Law* 9 120, p. 141, p. 146.

320 In re Nortel Networks, Inc., 532 BR 494 Bankr D Del 2015.

321 Ian F. Fletcher *Insolvency in Private International Law* (2nd edn, Oxford University Press 2005), p. 376.

98　Cross-border insolvency theories

universal proceduralism, debtors and creditors without similar constraints may abuse local insolvency law and gain at a cost to other creditors. The court may also be overburdened by dealing with multiple sets of local insolvency laws, and the court may have difficulties in understanding local law.

Another practical difficulty that of classifying procedural and substantive insolvency laws. In order to make virtual territoriality practical, one has to clearly divide national insolvency laws into procedural rules which do not have distributional effects and other procedural and substantive insolvency rules that do. What makes it even more complex is that certain procedural rules, such as the stay provisions in insolvency laws, could cause substantive consequences as these procedural rules affect secured creditors' rights.[322]

Janger is of the view that the Collins and Aikman case[323] is a manifestation of virtual territoriality.[324] The Collins and Aikman group (CA group) is a corporate group that manufactures car parts. The European subsidiaries entered into administration insolvency proceedings in the English high court. Even though the subsidiaries were incorporated in different member states, the joint administrators were appointed by the English court for the purpose of a better recovery.[325] To prevent the local creditors from opening secondary proceedings, the joint administrators promised that their priority would be treated as if the secondary proceedings had been opened in their respective member states. The result would be a higher sale price and a higher return to all the creditors.[326]

The English court and administrators clearly understand that to achieve a better result, procedural consolidation alone is not enough; they also need to avoid secondary proceedings, as otherwise multiple proceedings and laws will interrupt the rescue in the main proceeding.[327] This pragmatic path of the CA group case is called 'synthetic secondary proceedings'. The rationale behind synthetic insolvency proceedings is that they serve the goal of maximization of the insolvency estate by procedural consolidation. In some cases, the opening of secondary proceedings will dismember the whole business of a distressed group, thus impeding the possibility of group reorganization. Also, the cost may be high due to the opening of numerous insolvency proceedings. The entity law approach prevents the reorganization procedure from achieving value maximization goals.[328]

---

322 Jay Lawrence Westbrook, 'Comments on Universal Proceduralism' (2009–2010) *Columbia Journal of Transnational Law* 48 503, p. 515.

323 In the Matters of Collins & Aikman Europe SA and Others [2006] EWHC 1343 (Ch).

324 Edward J. Janger, 'Virtual Territoriality' (2009–2010) *Columbia Journal of Transnational Law* 48 401, p. 434.

325 In the Matters of Collins & Aikman Europe SA and Others [2006] EWHC 1343 (Ch), p. 1.

326 Christoph G. Paulus, 'Group Insolvencies – Some Thoughts about New Approaches' (2007) *Texas International Law Journal* 42 819, p. 826.

327 Gabriel Moss (QC), 'Group Insolvency – Choice of Forum and Law: The European Experience under the Influence of English Pragmatism' (2006–2007) *Brooklyn Journal of International Law* 32 1005, p. 1017.

328 Christoph G. Paulus, 'Group Insolvencies – Some Thoughts about New Approaches' (2007) *Texas International Law Journal* 42 819, p. 826.

Cross-border insolvency theories 99

The precondition of the viability of synthetic secondary proceedings is that all the CoMIs of subsidiaries can be argued in the location of one member state; the court that opens main insolvency proceeding should have the authority to guarantee monetary compensation to the aggrieved creditors in other member states; the other member states may also agree to compromise such synthetic treatment of creditors without applying their own insolvency law.

However, neither of these conditions can be met in reality. From a business network perspective, certain subsidiaries can take on innovative roles and implement head office functions. It is difficult to justify procedural consolidation. One should note that it is difficult for other courts of civil law countries to approve undertakings in the same fashion as civil law courts may not enjoy the same flexible discretion as case law jurisdictions.[329] Without the flexibility of the English court and the acceptance of local creditors, the CA case is difficult to replicate.[330]

More importantly, it is not clear whether such practice is cost-efficient due to the uncertainty in the content of promises, valuation of assets and reaction of creditors.[331] Without evidence to show that local creditors benefit from such practice but do not fall victim to it, it is also hard to say whether synthetic secondary proceeding is a reliable solution.

Universal proceduralism and modified universalism may not be too different in practice. While modified universalism applies the rule of main proceeding to decide control, priority, avoidance rules and reorganization plan,[332] universal proceduralism insists that local insolvency law should be applied to decide local creditors' priority.[333] In cross-border insolvency of MCGs cases, both universal proceduralism and modified universalism rely on a group CoMI concept to achieve procedural consolidation.

It is worth noting that the CA case is not based on virtual territoriality but still on modified universalism. The prerequisite of opening main proceedings for the European subsidiaries is that their CoMIs are in the jurisdiction of the English court. Without this precondition, the CA case would have caused considerable uncertainty in that all the subsidiaries' insolvency proceedings could have been reallocated to the parent company's jurisdiction, even if their CoMIs were not in that country. Therefore, it appears that virtual territoriality does not provide a new jurisdiction-selection rule for corporate group cases. It ends up with unclear rules on insolvency proceedings, making it unpredictable.

---

329 It appears that the EIR recast has codified synthetic secondary proceedings in Recital 42, while how it will be practiced remains to be seen.
330 Eyal Z. Geva, 'National Policy Objectives from an EU Perspective: UK Corporate Rescue and the European Insolvency Regulation' (2007) *European Business Organization Law Review* 8(4) 605–619, p. 619.
331 Ibid., p. 618.
332 Jay Lawrence Westbrook, 'Locating the Eye of the Financial Storm' (2007) *Brooklyn Journal of International Law* 32 1019, p. 1021.
333 Edward. J. Janger, 'Reciprocal Comity' (2010–2011) *Texas International Law Journal* 46 441, p. 445.

100 *Cross-border insolvency theories*

The unclear group CoMI rule will invite forum shopping, especially in the EIR, which confers the obligation of automatic recognition of the main proceeding's jurisdiction. This automatic recognition entails the cooperation of all relevant member states in that they need to accept to apply a different country's insolvency law. Considering the unclear group CoMI and the notable discretion of courts, the possibilities of forum shopping cannot be ignored.[334] Forum shopping may be more fierce and harmful at an international level as the changed applicable laws provide creditors with strong incentives.[335]

By exploring all three proposals for cross-border insolvency of MCGs, one may draw the conclusion that current cross-border theories may not provide a predictable and desirable solution for dealing with MCGs in an ex ante way. This is at least partly because no proposal can provide a clear jurisdiction rule. The next part will examine ex post procedural consolidation solutions and check their desirability.

Ex post approach of procedural consolidation

Procedural consolidation may be arranged ex post by means of insolvency jurisdictional rules. Senior creditors may persuade a court to seize jurisdiction of many group member companies, even if the CoMIs of group member companies may not be in the territory of that court. Alternatively, creditors or debtors may move CoMI to other countries to make their companies eligible to use foreign insolvency laws, such as pre-pack administration.

The ex post approach may overcome the obstacles of varying member states' insolvency laws and avoid the cost of opening many parallel insolvency proceedings. However, foreign insolvency law may not be used to serve the interests of creditors in general. Rather, it may be the tool exploited by the senior creditors to redistribute the value from junior creditors to senior ones. Another aspect is that alteration of jurisdiction means alteration of creditors' rights under cross-border insolvency law. The cost of uncertainty may be significant.

Ex post approach by CoMI interpretation

The English courts provide examples of how to deal with the insolvency of MCGs under EIR. One of the cases is the Daisytek case.[336] The English court, after analysing the factors determining CoMI, held that all the CoMIs of the subsidiaries in Europe are in the UK. Based on this evidence, the English court opened the main insolvency proceedings regarding all these subsidiaries. The effect of procedural consolidation was achieved. It may be argued that this case

---

334 Michel Menjucq, 'EC-Regulation No. 1346/2000 on Insolvency Proceedings and Groups of Companies' (2008) ECFR, p. 140.

335 Lynn Lopucki *Courting Failure: How Competition for Big Cases Is Corrupting the Bankruptcy Courts* (University of Michigan Press 2006), p. 207.

336 Re Daisytek-ISA Ltd [2004] B.P.I.R. 30.

Cross-border insolvency theories   101

confirmed the 'head office test' developed by the English court and that it is useful to resolve corporate group insolvency cases.[337] The English court was also convinced that elements used to determine head office functions are on the basis of objective factors which are ascertainable to the third parties.[338]

However, one should not be so optimistic as to believe that this is the perfect and easy solution to corporate groups. As mentioned, in many other cases, the CoMIs of subsidiaries may not be coincidently in one jurisdiction. If the court still wants to achieve procedural consolidation by interpretation, it will damage creditors' expectations. Only in the corporate groups whose businesses are neatly, centrally controlled and integrated it is possible to achieve a result similar to that of the Daisytek case, where one forum and one set of insolvency law were applied.[339] However, as discussed, in reality, head office functions are not neatly located in one company in a given group, which may render this approach implausible to apply in many cases.

To allow courts to seize insolvency jurisdiction by interpretation of CoMI is not without controversy. It is argued, especially in the US context, that the insolvency courts are not reliable enough to determine CoMI as they may compete for the insolvency jurisdiction; the courts are more likely to act in favour of managers and other allies than in favour of the unsecured creditors.[340] As big cases are usually lucrative, the courts and insolvency practitioners cannot be expected to give them up to other jurisdictions.[341]

Though the effect of CoMI interpretation can be tempered by secondary proceedings under EIR,[342] the uncertainty that such practice can cause should not be underestimated. From a business network perspective, foreign subsidiaries may have been allocated head office functions for the purpose of generating group going concern value. Local creditors may well believe that the local subsidiaries are not fully controlled by the parent companies, so it is the local insolvency law that should be applied to these creditors. CoMI interpretation changes the law applicable to those creditors. Whether a centralized group rescue plan can bring a good result to the creditors or not, the uncertainty may likely give rise to an increase in interest rate. As predictability is an important goal that cross-border insolvency law aims to pursue,[343] CoMI interpretation runs the risk of creating uncertainty.

---

337   Gabriel Moss (QC), 'Group Insolvency-Forum-EC Regulation and Model Law Under the Influence of English Pragmatism Revisited' (2014–2015) *Brooklyn Journal of Corporate, Financial & Commercial* 9 179, p. 186.

338   Ibid., p. 181.

339   Irit Mevorach, 'Cross Border Insolvency Law of Enterprise Groups: The Choice of Law Challenge' (2014) *Brooklyn Journal of Corporate, Financial & Commercial Law* 9 107, p. 6.

340   Lynn M. LoPucki, *Courting Failure: How Competition for Big Cases Is Corrupting the Bankruptcy Courts* (University of Michigan Press 2006), p. 243.

341   Ibid., p. 221.

342   David A. Skeel, 'European Implications of Bankruptcy Venue Shopping in the US' (2006–2007) *Buffalo Law Review* 54 439, p. 459.

343   Jay L. Westbrook, 'Locating the Eye of the Financial Storm' (2007) *Brooklyn Journal of International Law* 32 1019, p. 1032.

102 *Cross-border insolvency theories*

Ex post approach by forum shopping

Using forum shopping as a method of achieving procedural consolidation is dangerous for several reasons. Foremost is that forum shopping may destroy group going concern value. From a business network perspective, the relationships between member companies are the main component of the group going concern value of MCGs. Part of the group going concern value is gained through the foreign subsidiaries in that they can absorb foreign countries' specific advantages. Forum shopping, under EIR recast, generally requires debtors to move CoMI to another country for the purpose of procedural consolidation. This may change the environment where foreign subsidiaries are embedded and cut off the conduits on which they rely to gain foreign resources and capacities.

As a result, a real transfer of CoMI means that foreign subsidiaries cannot transform the advantages of foreign countries into the group going concern value as their business locations have been changed. These transferred subsidiaries cannot transform the country-specific resources into company-specific resources and transfer these values to the MNCs. The decrease in value as a result of a forum shopping may outweigh the cost saved by procedural consolidation.

Also, procedural consolidation by forum shopping will give rise to uncertainty as junior creditors are less likely to have decision-making power to decide where the CoMI should be transferred. Furthermore, certain foreign insolvency law procedures, such as pre-pack administrations, may benefit senior creditors at the expense of junior ones.[344] The main reason that debtors and certain senior secured creditors prefer pre-pack sales is because this serves their own interests.

The Wind Hellas case is a notorious example of forum shopping for the purpose of making use of UK pre-pack administration and schemes of arrangement. This is also the case that involves procedural consolidation as six companies in the group transferred CoMIs to the UK. The result attracted heavy criticism as it left the unsecured creditors with 1.5 billion Euros unpaid.[345]

The Hellas Group has business in the telecom industry in Greece; in this group, Wind Hellas is the main operating subsidiary.[346] Hellas II is the parent of Wind Hellas. Hellas II was likely to default on its debt, so it decided to move its CoMI to the UK to utilize the UK pre-pack administration and sell its shares in Wind Hellas to the buyer. Hellas II transferred its CoMI three months before the opening of insolvency proceedings.[347] As Hellas II is a financing company,

---

344 Pre-pack blurs the line between formal and informal rescue procedures; further, it gains popularity gradually as it accounts for almost a third of all going concern sales. S. Davies (QC), 'Pre-Pack-He Who Pays the Piper Calls the Tune' (2006, summer) *Recovery* 16, p. 17 (cited by Vanessa finch *Corporate Insolvency Law Perspectives and Principles* (2nd edn, Cambridge University Press 2009), p. 456).

345 M. Rustein and L. Bloomberg, 'A Wind Blow through an English Brothel' (2010) *Corporate Rescue and Insolvency Journal*, p. 156.

346 Financing briefing, Slaughter and May, December 2009.

347 Re Hellas Telecommunications [2009] EWHC 3199 (Ch) p. 4.

even though the judge recognized that it did not possess much property in the UK, the court was convinced that its CoMI had been shifted.[348]

However, such enforcement sale had to be conducted according to certain terms of the inter-creditor agreement, and, among other things, the agreement did not allow security agents to release principal and interests of inter-company debts between Wind Hellas and other holding companies.[349]

Hellas III, Hellas IV, Hellas V and Hellas VI are all holding companies in the group which bear debt and obligation of guarantees stipulated in the same inter-creditor agreement. As a result, the holding companies and the parent of Wind Hellas all decided to move CoMI to the UK to use schemes of arrangement and pre-pack administration to facilitate such a sale. As a result, Wind Hellas shares could be sold free of any subsidiaries, principal and interest obligations.[350]

The UK court found that there were two bids to purchase the Wind Hellas shares available: one provided by senior creditors and another provided by the subordinated notes creditors.[351] As the inter-creditor agreement required the proposal supported by subordinated notes creditors to be approved by senior creditors, when the senior creditors did not approve it, the only bid remaining was the senior creditors'.[352] Therefore, the subordinated creditors were not contractually entitled to receive compensation.

One may find a good reason to support forum shopping in this case as, if the restructuring were not to happen, the whole group value would dissipate quickly; in a hypothetical liquidation proceeding under the insolvency law of Luxembourg, the creditors holding subordinated notes may not receive anything, while senior creditors were left worse off. However, one may also note that subordinated notes creditors complained about the bid method of Wind Hellas in pre-pack. The whole process was suspiciously rigged by the debtor since some information was available only to the successful bidder and not to others.[353] It was because there was only one bidder in this case that the court had no alternative option but to approve the only pre-pack sale bid.[354]

In the Wind Hellas case, the terms in the inter-creditor agreement prevent senior creditors from releasing junior creditors' rights; the terms can be seen as a protection of junior creditors. However, the group, controlled by the senior creditors, successfully went around the protection by forum shopping six financing companies. This was intended to overcome the obstacles by using a more favourable and flexible restructuring law. However, the change dramatically

---

348 Ibid., p. 4.
349 Christian Pilkington *et al.*, *Wind Hellas a Complex Restructuring in Global Recession* (Practical Law Publishing Limited 2011).
350 Ibid.
351 Katrina Buckley, 'Wind Hellas: Pre-packs and COMI Shift; Abuse or Innovation?' (2010) *Journal of International Banking & Financial Law* 6 342, p. 4.
352 Ibid., p. 4.
353 Re Hellas Telecommunications [2009] EWHC 3199 (Ch) p. 5.
354 Ibid., p. 5.

104 *Cross-border insolvency theories*

modified junior creditors' expectations, and the drawbacks of many national restructuring rules, such as pre-packs, could be revealed if it was not used properly. Therefore, one should be doubtful about ex post procedural consolidation by forum shopping. Also, as mentioned, if forum shopping happens at the level of operating companies, the result may be far more harmful.

Conclusion

As the above analysis indicates, cross-border insolvency law theories face difficulties in being transformed to their group version. Though cost may be reduced by centralizing the insolvency proceedings of subsidiaries to those of their ultimate parents, the cost from the uncertainty may outweigh the benefits from centralization.

The main difficulty arises from the group CoMI concept. As in many corporate group cases, the CoMIs of the subsidiaries are not in the place of the parent company, so the practice of procedural centralization may cause uncertainty.

Procedural consolidation may contain inherent drawbacks in solving cross-border insolvency issues for MCGs. The next two chapters will examine how the market develops solutions for MCGs and whether the group coordination proceedings can be used as better solutions.

4 Market/hybrid approaches to cross-border insolvency of MCGs in the EU

Chapters 2 and 3 provide theoretical and factual grounds to analyse existing solutions to cross-border insolvency of groups of companies and show that procedural consolidation has serious limitations and drawbacks. The uncertainty of group CoMI location poses a difficult question for cross-border insolvency law theorists. At least from a theoretical standpoint, insolvency jurisdictional rules may not be used to achieve procedural consolidation.[1] As insolvency law is closely connected with the advance of credits, uncertainty created by procedural consolidation may negatively affect credit arrangements with regard to solvent companies.[2]

Parallel to theoretical solutions for cross-border insolvency of MCGs, market solutions alone or in combination with insolvency proceedings are also used as solutions in practice.

The task of this chapter is to examine advantages and limitations of the second practical solution: market solutions/hybrid solutions dealing with the cross-border rescue of MCGs. It begins with an overview of categories of rescue. It includes private restructuring solutions, hybrid restructuring solutions and insolvency protocols. Then the chapter moves to examine the limitations of private solutions from both practical and theoretical points of view. Next, two group market/hybrid solutions will be examined. These could prevent corporate groups from entering into insolvency through renegotiation of debt agreements at the holding companies level.

Sometimes, the complicated categories of debts and creditors render private solutions unable to deal with the debt renegotiation; debtors and creditors in these situations are forced to seek the recourse of hybrid solutions, such as a pre-pack sale of shares in operating subsidiaries to the company owned by senior creditors. Also, it is possible for creditors to reach cooperation protocols to deal with cross-border insolvency issues. This chapter analyses whether these

---

1 By allocating insolvency jurisdiction of subsidiaries to the court possessing group CoMI, the insolvency of the whole group can be handled in only one court.
2 Vanessa Finch, *Corporate Insolvency Law Perspectives and Principles* (2nd edn, Cambridge University Press 2009), p. 69.

106 *Cross-border insolvency of MCGs in the EU*

solutions provide desirable results for cross-border insolvency of MCGs and whether they have limitations.

Types of rescue

There is no universally acknowledged definition or method of rescue. Formal rescue regimes, such as administration; hybrid regimes, such as a 'pre-pack' sale of business; and informal rescue, such as private negotiations between debtors and creditors, can all be seen as rescue methods.[3] The measures of rescue could be in either informal (i.e. workout by private negotiation) fashion; formal (court supervised insolvency proceedings) fashion; or a hybrid way, such as pre-pack.

In many rescue cases involved with informal rescue methods, the categories of creditors are various, and the number of them is notably large, and the hold-out issues may not be easily solved by private contracts, which require unanimity.[4] Creditors may only be able to reach a private agreement regarding how to distribute the assets of the insolvent debtors when the number of creditors is small.[5] In other words, when the numbers of creditors are very large, and categories are complex, the chances of drafting a private plan among all creditors may fade away.

Formal rescue procedures are court supervised, so their benefits is that many useful insolvency mechanisms can be used, such as stay and refinancing. Also, a broader range of interests can be protected by the bankruptcy policies. Therefore, informal and formal rescue measures can be considered a supplement to each other. The aim of both formal and informal rescue measures is to keep the business running as a going concern.[6]

Hybrid rescue procedures are also called pre-insolvency procedures, and they purport to mix the benefits of both formal and informal insolvency measures. Taking pre-pack as an example, it is said that pre-pack could reduce the cost of rescue and save time.[7] Its main feature is that a reorganization plan is drafted and confidently approved with the consent of only secured creditors, by out-of-court appointed administrators, before the opening of administration proceedings.[8]

---

3 Vanessa Finch, 'Corporate Rescue: A Game of Three Halves' (2012) *Legal Studies* 32(2) 302.
4 Bolanle Adebola, 'A Few Shades of Rescue: Towards an Understanding of the Corporate Rescue Concept in England and Wales' (2014), p. 4 (available at: http://ssrn.com/abstract=2524488).
5 Thomas H. Jackson, *The Logic and Limits of Bankruptcy Law* (Harvard University Press 1986), p. 19.
6 Alice Belcher, *Corporate Rescue* (Sweet & Maxwell 1997), p. 72.
7 IMF Orderly & Effective Insolvency Procedures 2000 at www.imf.org/external/pubs/ft/orderly/index.htm.
8 John Armour, 'The Rise of the Pre-Pack, Corporate Restructuring in the UK and Proposal for Reform' (2012), p. 16 (available at: http://ssrn.com/abstract=2093134).

The limitation of alternative approaches to insolvency law and out-of-court solutions

Theoretical limitations of contract approaches

Some scholars claim that contracts may be used to replace corporate rescue regimes.[9] The common ground of such approaches is that creditors and companies can negotiate contracts *ex ante* regarding how to deal with the insolvency of debtors.

The main thread of these alternative methods argues that contracts and markets could provide a lower-cost solution than traditional rescue regimes. For example, auction may be used to implement a sale of the business to third parties at a fair price; auction could also help to preserve the going concern value by selling the business as a whole.[10] The benefit yielded from substituting auction for rescue is that auction can avoid delay and redistribution in traditional rescue proceedings. The selling price can indicate which parties are still have money and which parties do not. The court only needs to distribute the proceeds from the auction along with the priority of relevant stakeholders.

Other approaches focus on contracts whereby the shares of insolvent companies are reallocated into the hands of creditors; the creditors in the lower ranking have the right to buy shares from the senior creditors if they believe the going concern value is large. These similar approaches assume that the court should sell the distressed business and then distribute the proceeds to the senior creditors; the lower creditors are allocated options to buy the shares from the senior creditors.[11] Also, parties could negotiate contracts regarding how to distribute assets when the debtors are bankrupt. For example, Professor Adler provided the idea of chameleon equity to resolve insolvency issues. When a company is insolvent, the equity of shareholders will be cancelled; the highest residual claimants will become the new shareholders. If the lower residual claimants believe that the going concern value is higher, they may bid for the shares from the senior creditors. This activity provides senior creditors with a way to exit.[12]

---

9 Douglas G. Baird, 'The Uneasy Case for Corporate Reorganizations' (1986) *The Journal of Legal Studies* 15 127; Lucian A. Bebchuk, 'A New Approach to Corporate Reorganizations' (1988) *Harvard Law Review* 101 775–804, pp. 775, 785; Barry E. Adler, 'Bankruptcy and Risk Allocation' (1992) *Cornell Law Review* 77 439–489, pp. 439, 489; Michael Bradley and Michael Rosenzweig, 'The Untenable Case for Chapter 11' (1992) *The Yale Law Journal*, 101 1043; Lucian Ayre Bebchuk, 'Using Options to Divide Value in Corporate Bankruptcy' (2000) *European Economic Review* 44 829; Douglas G. Baird and Robert K. Rasmussen, 'The End of Bankruptcy' (2002) *Stanford Law Review* 55 751, pp. 751–752.

10 Douglas G. Baird, 'The Uneasy Case for Corporate Reorganizations' (1986) *The Journal of Legal Studies* 15 127.

11 Lucian Arye Bebchuk, 'A New Approach to Corporate Reorganizations' (1988) *Harvard Law Review* 101 775–804.

12 Barry E. Adler, 'Bankruptcy and Risk Allocation' (1992) *Cornell Law Review* 77 439–489, pp. 439, 489.

108   Cross-border insolvency of MCGs in the EU

Contract and market approaches bear three main drawbacks which make them almost impossible to adopt. The first is the significant transaction costs arising from these approaches. The efficient solutions of contract and market approaches assume a perfect market with zero transaction cost. However, in the complex world of insolvency or international insolvency, this assumption is far from the reality. Insolvency law is incredibly complex, more so when many insolvency jurisdictions are involved. The capital structures of most international companies are very complex, the categories of creditors are various, the conflicts of interests between different parties are serious and the access to information is asymmetrical among different parties. The complicated relationships between debtors and the myriad of creditors and national insolvency laws make such contracts difficult and costly to draft, if not impossible to do *ex ante*.

One could imagine the difficulties for parties who would like to buy the shares from senior creditors to raise capital. The reorganization procedure may keep the distressed companies in the hands of existing creditors and shareholders without the need to raise money if a compromise among them could be reached. In the contract and market approach, either auction or buying shares from senior creditors will incur costs arising from the need to raise capital; the costs may outweigh the cost of a traditional reorganization procedure.[13] What one also needs to bear in mind is that sometimes the bankruptcy market is too thin to support auctions, so a more likely result will be an undervalued sale of the business[14]; a distressed company may have to rely on existing managers, shareholders or creditors for liquidity. Such illiquidity issues can be better eased by reorganization procedures, giving some breathing space to the debtors. Other costs, such as negotiation and communication fees, are very likely to be huge, considering the number of creditors and categories of debts.[15]

The second problem is that contracts cannot easily resolve the conflicts of interests of complex insolvency cases.[16] As different classes of creditors do not share the same interests, the decision-making of any class of creditors may not be in the interest of the general creditors.[17] It is almost intractable for the contract to identify the residual claimants in advance. Without knowing the entitlements of each creditor, there is no way to either allow the court to distribute proceeds

---

13 Charles W. Adams, 'An Economic Justification for Corporate Reorganisation' (1991–1992) *Hofstra Law Review* 20 117, p. 143.

14 Lynn M. LoPucki, 'The Trouble with Chapter 11' (1993) *Wisconsin Law Review* 729, p. 759.

15 Lynn M. LoPucki, 'Strange Visions in a Strange World: A Reply to Professors Bradley and Rosenzweig' (1992–1993) *Michigan Law Review* 91 79, pp. 100–102.

16 Lynn M. LoPucki, 'The Nature of the Bankrupt Firm: A Response to Baird and Rasmussen's "The End of Bankruptcy"' (2003) *Stanford Law Review* 56(3) 645–671, p. 661; The collective nature of insolvency law necessitates it having to deal with competing interests as the common pool arises only when the companies become insolvent. Richard. V. Butler and Scott. M. Gilpatric, 'A Re-Examination of the Purposes and Goals of Bankruptcy' (1994) *The American Bankruptcy Institute Law Review* 2 269, p. 277.

17 George G. Triantis, 'A Theory of the Regulation of Debtor-in-Possession Financing' (1993) *Vanderbilt Law Review* 46 901, p. 916.

Cross-border insolvency of MCGs in the EU 109

or allow creditors to bid for the shares of insolvent companies.[18] As a result, a contract that requires shareholders to automatically pass control and interests to the higher-ranking parties is difficult to draft.[19] Drafting such contracts for every company, many of which will not be insolvent in the future, will introduce significant cost. Even if parties could draft such unusual contracts, the changing nature of the world and business would force terms of contracts and solutions to be regularly reconsidered. That is why there is a role for rescue procedures to play in the insolvency context.[20]

The third drawback of the contract and market approach is that no neutral platform as courts exists in reorganization procedures to provide information and resolve disputes for all the relevant parties.[21] The rescue procedure imposes obligations on relevant parties to disclose information and punish those who provide false information. Also the traditional rescue procedure can provide a clean title after the sale of debtors' assets; without such an insolvency procedure, it is almost impossible to achieve the same result.[22] The traditional rescue regime also encourages parties to cooperate: for example, by paying certain important trade creditors first in exchange for their support. Without such mechanisms, if the auction takes a period of time, and suppliers stop cooperating, the sale will be frustrated as the value of the business drops significantly.[23]

The proposal to use contracts and markets to replace traditional rescue procedures may not be workable. The traditional rescue procedures, though far from perfect, still have very important roles to play.

Practical limitations of out-of-court approaches

In theory, insolvency law cannot be replaced completely by contracts. This section goes on to examine whether, without the support of insolvency tools, insolvency issues are increasingly difficult to resolve with out-of-court solutions.

Hold-out

When considering the weakness of market solutions for insolvency of companies, the starting point is the collective nature of the insolvency law. Insolvency law deals with a group of creditors and stakeholders rather than a handful of people. As a result, each creditor may either take individual action against debtors or veto

---

18 David A. Skeel, Jr., 'Markets, Courts, and the Brave New World of Bankruptcy Theory' (1993) *Wisconsin Law Review* 2 465, p. 481.
19 Lynn M. LoPucki 'Strange Visions in a Strange World: A Reply to Professors Bradley and Rosenzweig' (1992–1993) *Michigan Law Review* 91 79, p. 99.
20 Douglas G. Baird, 'The Hidden Virtues of Chapter 11: An Overview of the Law and Economics of Financially Distressed Firms' (1997), Working Paper No. 43, p. 33.
21 Ibid., p. 34.
22 Ibid., p. 34.
23 Stephen J. Lubben, 'Some Realism about Reorganization: Explaining the Failure of Chapter 11Theory'(2001–2002) *Dickinson Law Review* 106 267, p. 296.

110   *Cross-border insolvency of MCGs in the EU*

the rescue agreement which is negotiated on the basis of the contracts. Without all the creditors' approval, the drafted plan cannot be executed as contracts cannot be negotiated without other parties' consent. This creates a hold-out issue.

The hold-out problem is probably the most conspicuous weakness of informal rescue as unanimity is a requirement of private rescue by contracts. Compared to the formal insolvency proceedings, the most notorious disadvantage of informal rescue is that it is contract-based. Therefore, in most cases, unanimous agreements have to be achieved.[24] Where the dissenting creditors are not happy with the terms of contract, including wavier of debt or postponing payment, they may choose not to accept the informal rescue plan and file for insolvency proceedings in the courts.[25]

Since 2000, companies have started to borrow from a wide range of lenders, including banks, bondholders, hedge funds and private equities. This leads to a complex and fragmented corporate debt structure such that negotiating the informal restructuring of debts is a challenging task, while formal insolvency proceedings may have more chances to be initiated.[26] To put it in a cross-border insolvency context, it is less likely for the banks to achieve consensus among all affected creditors.[27] In a modern restructuring case, banks may be substituted by various distressed debt investors who do not have existing lending relationships with debtors.[28]

Furthermore, the prevalence of the use of credit derivatives, such as credit default swaps (CDS), may cause trouble for distressed companies waiting to be rescued.[29] Since some creditors are also buyers of CDS, they may benefit more from an expected default of their debts than from waiting for debtors' limited payment in the upcoming corporate rescue attempt. As a consequence, these creditors even have incentives to not rescue the company. Therefore, the informal corporate rescue cooperation may be stymied by different creditors' conflicting incentives.[30]

The distressed debt market may increase the difficulty that the creditors face in reaching a restructuring plan at a low price due to the continuous change of creditors.[31] When hedge funds and private equity join in the debt finance group, coordination between those who hold different strategies and objectives is more

---

24 Vanessa Finch, *Corporate Insolvency Law Perspectives and Principles* (2nd edn, Cambridge University Press 2009), p. 253.

25 Ibid., p. 253.

26 John Armour, 'The Rise of the Pre-Pack, Corporate Restructuring in the UK and Proposal for Reform'; 'Restructuring Companies in Troubled Times: Director and Creditor Perspectives' (2012) Ross Parsons Centre Sydney Law School, p. 1.

27 Finch Vanessa, 'Corporate Rescue in a World of Debt' (2008) *Journal of Business Law* 8 756–777, p. 9.

28 Paul M. Goldschmid, 'More Phoenix than Vulture: The Case for Distressed Investor Presence in the Bankruptcy Reorganization Process' (2005) *Columbia Business Law Review* 191, p. 202.

29 Vanessa Finch, *Corporate Insolvency Law Perspectives and Principles* (2nd edn, Cambridge University Press 2009), p. 139.

30 Ibid., p. 139.

31 John Armour and Simon Deakin, 'Norms in Private Insolvency: The "London Approach" to the Resolution of Financial Distress' (2001) *Journal of Corporate Law Studies* 1(1) 21–51, p. 49.

Cross-border insolvency of MCGs in the EU 111

difficult to achieve.[32] Hedge fund managers often favour short-term investment. Unlike banks which get involved in private restructuring at an earlier date to try to rescue companies, hedge funds may have short-term conflicts of interests over other parties.[33] For example, hedge funds may either have strong incentives to conduct a pre-pack fire sale to reap the value or hold-out for a favourable deal where they are junior creditors but can control a voting class.[34]

Also, when the creditors buy CDS, their exposure to the distressed company is insured at the time of the negotiation of the private restructuring plan as the CDS will be triggered should credit events such as 'bankruptcy', 'restructuring'[35] or 'failure to pay' happen before the maturity date.[36] These creditors may decide not to leave the bargaining tables, and they do not want to support promising rescue plans, as they may get more if the company defaults, even at the expense of other creditors.[37] All these examples show that creditors are of different categories, and their motives vary, so private restructuring may not work in all cases. During the negotiation stage of an informal rescue plan, the buyers may have a strong incentive to file for bankruptcy petitions in order to trigger the credit event.[38] In the case of restructuring, even though the prospect of restructuring may benefit the CDS rights-holder, it may not be as favourable as what the rights-holders would get from a default, so the CDS rights-holder may still choose not to cooperate.

Arguably, distressed investors may be incentivized to capture long-term interest from the insolvent companies and control them, unlike short-term creditors, who do not purchase enough shares or debts of insolvent companies to be able to do so.[39] Senior creditors have obtained favorable terms in their debt covenants from which the control of the distressed companies is switched to them both before and after the insolvency proceedings.[40] Investors may still hold the stakes of the debtors for a long time to reap maximum interests after

---

32 Vanessa Finch, *Corporate Insolvency Law Perspectives and Principles* (2nd edn, Cambridge University Press 2009), p. 297.

33 Robert J. Rosenberg and Michael J. Riela, 'Hedge Funds, the New Masters of the Bankruptcy Universe' (2008) International Insolvency Institute Eighth Annual International Insolvency Conference, p. 3.

34 Bo J. Howell, 'Hedge Funds: A New Dimension in Chapter 11 Bankruptcy Proceedings' (2008–2009) *The DePaul Business and Commercial Law Journal* 7 35, p. 42.

35 Restructuring here only refers to the ones that give creditors less favourable terms of rights or priority, not including the ones that could improve the financial status of creditors. See ISDA Credit Event definitions http://credit-deriv.com/isdadefinitions.htm.

36 Stephen. J. Lubben, 'Credit Derivatives and the Future of Chapter 11' (2007) *The American Bankruptcy Law Journal* 81(4) 409–412, p. 411.

37 Frank Partnoy and David A. Skeel, Jr., 'The Promises and Perils of Credits Derivatives' (2006–2007) *The University of Cincinnati Law Review* 75 1019, p. 1035.

38 Stephen. J. Lubben, 'Credit Derivatives and the Future of Chapter 11' (2007) *The American Bankruptcy Law Journal* 81(4) 409–412, p. 427.

39 Paul M. Goldschmid, 'More Phoenix than Vulture: The Case for Distressed Investor Presence in the Bankruptcy Reorganization Process' (2005) *Columbia Business Law Review* 191, p. 271.

40 Douglas G. Baird and Robert K. Rasmussen, 'Chapter 11 at Twilight' (2003) *Stanford Law Review* 56, p. 674.

112 *Cross-border insolvency of MCGs in the EU*

they emerge from the bankruptcy.[41] Where the distressed investors inject new capital as debtor-in-possession financing (DIP financing),[42] their interests are deeply tied with distressed companies; investors as such have incentive to maximize the whole value of the companies.[43] Nevertheless, uncooperative strategies cannot be ruled out.

Also, some believe that such cases will help restructuring as the creditors who do not want to stay in the restructuring plan can find ways to leave without risk of further enforcements.[44] This argument may be undermined by the fact that whether creditors decide to leave or not depends on their positions in the negotiation. If they can exert some control of the plan, they may decide not to leave at a discounted price in the distressed debt market.

To sum up, private restructuring faces significant challenges as the creditors and categories of debts are so fragmented.[45] It could be argued that private restructuring is not always an option or that it is not necessarily cheaper than insolvency procedures as the transaction cost may rise sharply due to difficulties in negotiations. The more creditors are involved, the more possible it is that the private restructuring is not available.[46]

The implication of these changes poses significant challenges to MCGs. As MCGs may have fragmented categories of debts and creditors, private market solutions may not always be available. The limitations of market solutions will be further examined in 'A typical market solution – London approach'.

Narrow protection

Arguably, another weak point of the informal restructuring is that certain junior creditors on the lower rungs of the creditors' ladder may be unfairly treated by the proposed plan of senior creditors due to a lack of bargaining and monitoring power.[47] Unlike insolvency law, which provides a forum to monitor the behaviour of relevant parties, unbalanced bargaining power and asymmetric availability of information make junior creditors unable to protect themselves using contracts.

---

41 Paul M. Goldschmid, 'More Phoenix than Vulture: The Case for Distressed Investor Presence in the Bankruptcy Reorganization Process' (2005) *Columbia Business Law Review* 191, p. 272.
42 'DIP financing is financing arranged by a company while under the Chapter 11 bankruptcy process. DIP financing is unique from other financing methods in that it usually has priority over existing debt, equity and other claims'. www.investopedia.com/terms/d/debtorinpossessionfinancing.asp.
43 Paul M. Goldschmid, 'More Phoenix than Vulture: The Case for Distressed Investor Presence in the Bankruptcy Reorganization Process' (2005) *Columbia Business Law Review* 191, p. 255.
44 Sarah Paterson, 'Rethinking the Role of the Law of Corporate Distress in the Twenty-First Century' (2014) *LSE Law, Society and Economy Working Papers* 27, p. 6.
45 Douglas G. Baird and Robert K. Rasmussen, 'Anti-Bankruptcy' (2010) *The Yale Law Journal* 119(4) 648, p. 652.
46 J. Bradley Johnston, 'The Bankruptcy Bargain' (1991) *American Bankruptcy Law Journal* 65 213, p. 231.
47 Vanessa Finch, *Corporate Insolvency Law Perspectives and Principles* (2nd edn, Cambridge University Press 2009), p. 253.

Cross-border insolvency of MCGs in the EU   113

As a result, informal rescue may not fairly consider the interests of some junior creditors as they are too short of investigation and bargaining power to discuss a possible rescue plan.[48] Where the transparency of procedure and adequate information cannot be provided, junior creditors' interests may be seriously damaged. It provides only narrow consideration to the companies and senior bank creditors, while it may undervalue the protection of other stakeholders who deserve protecting. By contrast, formal insolvency proceedings provide a platform to all stakeholders to decide the future of the companies.[49]

To sum up, even though an out-of-court approach has some benefits, such as lower costs, insolvency rescue law cannot be replaced by contacts and out-of-court private solutions. Out-of-court corporate rescue solutions based on contracts have limitations when it comes to resolving insolvency issues, such as hold-out. Hence, corporate rescue needs insolvency law tools for support if desirable results are to be achieved.

A typical market solution – London approach

It is true that informal restructuring solutions can be exploited for cross-border group insolvency. If creditors of one viable but financially distressed group[50] can contractually reach a new agreement so that the group can recover from unsustainable indebtedness, a group-wide insolvency will be avoided. In cases where evidence could be obtained that private restructuring could be cheaper than formal full-scale insolvency proceedings, rational parties may choose private restructuring.[51] Many corporate rescues are carried out in informal fashions. It holds that informal rescue may reduce the insolvency stigma as it does not require publicity.[52] Also, the cost of informal rescue may be cheaper as courts are not involved (or are involved at a minimal level).[53] Besides these benefits, managers and directors need not worry about displacement by insolvency practitioners in a formal rescue.[54] Furthermore, unlike formal insolvency procedures, which

---

48 Ibid., p. 253.

49 Gerard McCormack, *Corporate Rescue Law – An Anglo-American Perspective* (Edward Elgar Publishing Limited 2008), p. 18.

50 When one company suffers economic insolvency, as Chapter 2 discussed (for example, distress arises from that fact that it loses the core competitive advantage), the only possible recourse is selling its assets in liquidation proceedings, not restructuring. Roy Goode, *Principle of Corporate Insolvency Law* (4th edn, Sweet Maxwell London 2011), p. 476.

51 John Armour and Simon Deakin, 'Norms in Private Insolvency: The "London Approach" to the Resolution of Financial Distress' (2001) *Journal of Corporate Law Studies* 1(1) 21–51, p. 25.

52 Vanessa Finch, *Corporate Insolvency Law Perspectives and Principles* (2nd edn, Cambridge University Press 2009), p. 251.

53 Insolvent companies will suffer indirect bankruptcy cost, such as higher interest rates and decreased power to bargain for favourable terms of contracts. The indirect cost also includes the negative impact on the parties in the same network, which is difficult to estimate. Wilbur N. Moulton and Howard Thomas, 'Bankruptcy as a Deliberate Strategy: Theoretical Considerations and Empirical Evidence' (1993) *Strategic Management Journal* 14(2) 125–135, pp. 127.

54 Vanessa Finch, *Corporate Insolvency Law Perspectives and Principles* (2nd edn, Cambridge University Press 2009), p. 252.

114 *Cross-border insolvency of MCGs in the EU*

impose disclosure obligations on debtors to make sensitive information available to the public, informal and private negotiation may prevent a sudden plummet of the value of a distressed business and prevent uncooperative behaviour by potential suppliers and customers.[55]

The London approach is the typical example of an out-of-court solution for insolvent companies which are financed by multi-banks syndicated loans. The main idea of this private solution is similar to a court-supervised insolvency proceeding. A typical London approach agreement comprises components such as a standstill period, coordination between parties, information exchange and a refinancing plan.[56] The Bank of England monitors and deters the non-cooperative opportunist behaviours of the other banks in a syndicate loan.[57]

The London approach first contains a standstill period for the banks not to take individual actions against the debtors, and second it contains a negotiation stage organized by debtors' leading the bank to develop a restructuring plan.[58] The viability of the London approach heavily relies on the support of lending banks, information sharing, financing approval from coordinated creditors and apportioning cost and benefits among all parties.[59] The success of the London approach depends on a leading bank organizing the whole restructuring procedure and a small number of creditors.

However, this requirement for success contrasts with reality. Many financial creditors actively provide credit with different motives.[60] Also, an increasing use of other sources of finance, such as bonds, along with the syndicated bank loan, makes it difficult to find out leading banks in the cases of private restructuring of large companies. Therefore, the London approach is facing significant challenges due to the fragmented categories of debts and creditors. The transaction costs increase due to the rise of these categories. Also, serious conflicts of interest among creditors create hold-out issues that make consensual agreement more and more difficult to achieve.

To sum up, cross-border insolvency of MCGs may be resolved by means of private restructuring. However, when there are so many creditors with different motivations, it is a challenging task to organize such restructuring.

---

55 Michelle M. Harner and Jamie Marincic, 'Behind Closed Doors: The Influence of Creditors in Business Reorganizations' (2010–2011) *The Seattle University Law Review* 34 1155, p. 1156. Advantages of a workout: lower administrative costs; lower professional fees; increased control and flexibility; less management distraction; generally, no loss of management control; better preservation of going concern value than reorganizations' disadvantages of a workout: no ability to bind dissenting creditors or classes of creditors; no automatic stay protection; no ability to recover preferences; no ability to recover fraudulent conveyances. Rodrigo Olivares-Caminal *et al.*, *Debt Restructuring* (Oxford University Press 2011), pp. 83–84.

56 Roy Goode, *Principle of Corporate Insolvency Law* (4th edn, Sweet Maxwell London 2011), p. 477.

57 John Armour and Simon Deakin, 'Norms in Private Insolvency: The "London Approach" to the Resolution of Financial Distress' (2001) *Journal of Corporate Law Studies* 1(1) 21–51, p. 40.

58 Ibid., p. 35.

59 Finch Vanessa, 'Corporate Rescue in a World of Debt' (2008) *Journal of Business Law* 8 756–777, p. 8.

60 Ibid., p. 3.

Cross-border insolvency of MCGs in the EU   115

Court-supervised insolvency proceedings, though arguably expensive, provide useful legal tools to overcome the opportunism of each party involved and to provide more transparent information to all the creditors and a lower threshold of approval standards.[61] For the purpose of a successful rescue, sometimes creditors have to implement a private negotiation by mixing legal tools. The next section will examine hybrid solutions.

The implication of the proposed Directive on preventive restructuring frameworks

As mentioned above, market solutions face serious limitations, such as hold-out problems. Acknowledging the difficulties of solely relying on private solutions for group rescue, debtors and creditors have developed hybrid solutions to resolve cross-border group restructuring issues. Hybrid solutions are the middle ground between formal insolvency proceedings and informal contractual solutions. Unlike formal rescue, such as administration and corporate voluntary arrangements, hybrid rescue measures have the characteristics of no court involvement or a minimum court involvement. The informal solutions are done mainly by private contracts, while hybrid ones may be facilitated by insolvency law-related tools/procedures, such as UK schemes of arrangement and pre-packs.[62] The main purpose of hybrid group insolvency solutions is to preserve the group going concern value by incentivizing creditors either to renegotiate their loan agreement in order to avoid a group-wide insolvency[63] or to sell the whole group to the newly formed companies owned by senior creditors at the holding companies level. At the EU level, a Directive on preventive restructuring frameworks can be seen as a codified statute which aims to equip member states with effective rescue-oriented rules.[64] The next section will examine this new piece of legislation together with its previous versions.[65]

---

61 Wilbur N. Moulton and Howard Thomas, 'Bankruptcy as a Deliberate Strategy: Theoretical Considerations and Empirical Evidence' (1993) *Strategic Management Journal* 14(2) 125–135, p. 132.

62 Though schemes of arrangement are categorized as company law tools, creditors' schemes are frequently used in an insolvency context. In this thesis, hybrid legal solutions mean the solutions that contain a mix of contractual solutions and legal solutions.

63 The debtor may choose to renegotiate with existing creditors for debt waivers, be provided means to sell the assets free of liens to creditors or be provided means to offer new creditors super-priority to refinance debts. Kenneth Ayotte and David A. Skeel, Jr., 'Bankruptcy Law as a Liquidity Provider' (2013) *University of Chicago Law Review* 80 1557, pp. 1573–1579.

64 European Parliament legislative resolution of 28 March 2019 on the proposal for a directive of the European Parliament and of the Council on preventive restructuring frameworks, second chance and measures to increase the efficiency of restructuring, insolvency and discharge procedures and amending Directive 2012/30/EU (COM(2016)0723 – C8-0475/2016 – 2016/0359(COD)).

65 For a detailed discussion as to how English schemes of arrangement meet the requirements of the Directive on preventive restructuring frameworks, see Daoning Zhang, 'Preventive Restructuring Frameworks: A Possible Solution for Financially Distressed Multinational Corporate Groups in the EU' (2019) *European Business Organization Law Review*. https://doi.org/10.1007/s40804-018-0125-3; T.M.C. Asser Press.

116   *Cross-border insolvency of MCGs in the EU*

An introduction to the Directive on preventive restructuring frameworks

At the end of 2018, the European Parliament and the Council reached an agreement with regard to the main text of the draft of the Directive on preventive restructuring frameworks.[66] The final text largely respects previous proposals regarding principles and text published by the European Commission,[67] with only a few modifications or additions in certain areas. At the end of March 2019, the EU Parliament approved the final version of its text.[68] Later, the Council formally approved the Directive on June 2019.[69] This section examines four aspects where the original proposal was modified notably: early warning tool and information,[70] viability test of companies,[71] the grant of stay,[72] and cross-class cram-down.[73]

Recital 16 prescribes that early warning tools and procedures should be available in each member state, and information relating to these tools and procedures should be made public. Clearly, there are no one-size-fits-all tools or procedures, so the Directive provides that tools may be different for companies of different sizes, including corporate groups.[74] The signal of early warning tools indicates that one given company is likely to enter into insolvency in the near future.[75] Should there be national early warning signs for corporate groups, it will be possible for them to be used similar to recovery plans and resolution plans. Corporate groups need to consider whether the whole group or part of the group may enter into financial difficulties and take actions in a timely way.

In this final draft, three possible early warning tools are envisioned by the Parliament and the Council: not paying certain types of payment, advisory services by public or private organizations and information from certain third parties.[76]

---

66 Proposal for a Directive of the European Parliament and of the Council on preventive restructuring frameworks, second chance and measures to increase the efficiency of restructuring, insolvency and discharge procedures and amending Directive 2012/30 – Confirmation of the final compromise text with a view to agreement 15556/18, available at https://data.consilium. europa.eu/doc/document/ST-15556-2018-INIT/en/pdf (thereafter Directive on preventive restructuring frameworks final version 2018).

67 Proposal for a Directive of the European Parliament and of the Council on preventive restructuring frameworks, second chance and measures to increase the efficiency of restructuring, insolvency and discharge procedures and amending Directive 2012/30/E 2016/0359 (COD).

68 European Parliament legislative resolution of 28 March 2019 on the proposal for a directive of the European Parliament and of the Council on preventive restructuring frameworks, second chance and measures to increase the efficiency of restructuring, insolvency and discharge procedures and amending Directive 2012/30/EU (COM(2016)0723 – C8-0475/ 2016 – 2016/0359(COD)).

69 Directive (2019) of the European Parliament and of the Council on preventive restructuring frameworks, on discharge of debt and disqualifications, and on measures to increase the efficiency of procedures concerning restructuring, insolvency and discharge of debt, and amending Directive (EU) 2017/1132 (Directive on restructuring and insolvency).

70 Art.3 Directive on preventive restructuring frameworks final version 2018.

71 Art.4(1)a Directive on preventive restructuring frameworks final version 2018.

72 Art.6 Directive on preventive restructuring frameworks final version 2018.

73 Art.11 Directive on preventive restructuring frameworks final version 2018.

74 Recital 16 Directive on preventive restructuring frameworks final version 2018.

75 Art.3(1) Directive on preventive restructuring frameworks final version 2018.

76 Art.3(1)a Directive on preventive restructuring frameworks final version 2018.

Cross-border insolvency of MCGs in the EU   117

Even though it is not entirely clear which approach member states may take, the first early warning tools and examples of early warning tools will make the preventive restructuring framework more practical. In other words, without early warning tools, debtors and creditors may not be sure when a preventive procedure will be opened. Since the procedure may change creditors' rights and interests, the availability of precise early warning tools will be a welcome change.

The Directive also requires member states to design a viability test of companies wanting to make use of the preventive restructuring frameworks.[77] This requirement, again, aims to substantiate the classification of financially distressed companies and economically distressed companies. As insolvent companies which do not have viable business plans or technologies should be moved out from the market, this viability test is important to make sure that such companies will not reborn under the Directive.

The new Directive grants a pre-emptive and supportive stay for pre-insolvency proceedings which support the negotiation of restructuring plans before the opening of insolvency proceedings.[78] This stay, to some degree, is different from the stay in traditional insolvency proceedings as it may prevent creditors from opening insolvency proceedings or suspend debtors' obligation to file for insolvency proceedings.[79] Indeed, in many European countries, directors have duties to file a petition for an insolvency proceeding if they think the companies are about to become insolvent. Similarly, in the UK, directors of insolvent companies are subject to wrongful trading claims if they keep trading during insolvency unless the purpose of doing so is to minimize the losses for creditors.[80] Another important aspect of this stay power is that it does not intend to cover all creditors' actions, or exclude certain creditors from the scope of stay, if the goal of restructuring is not affected by their individual actions or if certain creditors are unfairly prejudiced.[81]

The Directive helps member states to remove burdens imposed on directors which prevent them from seeking cooperative remedies from other group members. For example, if the directors have an obligation to enter into insolvency as soon as they identify a decrease in the financial performance of their companies, they have no desire to consider a group rescue plan as doing so would make them liable under national law. Since one of the purposes of preventive restructuring proceedings is to facilitate the restructuring of corporate groups in the EU, the removal of certain directors' duties may encourage them to cooperate with each other at the stage of group-wide restructuring planning.

More importantly, the Directive prevents creditors from terminating or accelerating executory contracts at the expense of debtors only on the basis of a request for a preventive restructuring procedure or a stay, or the opening of

---

77 Art.4(1)b Directive on preventive restructuring frameworks final version 2018.
78 Recital 19 Directive on preventive restructuring frameworks final version 2018.
79 Recital 21 Directive on preventive restructuring frameworks final version 2018.
80 Art.214 Insolvency Act 1986.
81 Article 6(1) and Article 6(2)b Directive on preventive restructuring frameworks final version 2018.

118 *Cross-border insolvency of MCGs in the EU*

a preventive proceeding.[82] This requirement affects the effect of termination clauses and acceleration clauses in the contracts between debtors and creditors to the extent that these clauses may not be effective in preventive restructuring setting. This shows that the Directive aims to foster a cooperative environment for creditors and debtors to pursue a goal which may be in the interest of all parties.

To avoid individual creditors or groups of creditors vetoing a restructuring plan, even if it is not detrimental to them, it is necessary for restructuring mechanisms to include resolutions for anti-commons issues. One preliminary way to achieve it is to limit the categories of creditors or shareholders to those who are affected by the restructuring plans and exclude equity holders and certain low-ranking creditors who are out of money from participating in a plan.[83] The Draft Directive goes on to introduce a detailed cross-class cram-down mechanism.[84] The main purpose of this cross-class cram-down mechanism is to overcome the issue of creditor hold-out. Therefore, the need to obtain approval from all classes of affected creditors is not necessary if certain conditions are met. So far as certain impaired classes of creditors are adequately protected according to the tests prescribed by the Directive, subject to further development by EU case law, the dissident classes of creditors' approval of a restructuring plan are not required for the purpose of approving the plan by judicial authorities.[85]

Drawing from the US experience, the Directive posits that restructuring plans can be confirmed, if

> (a) at least one voting class of affected parties, or, where so provided under national law, impaired parties, other than an equity-holders class or any other class which, upon a valuation of the debtor as a going concern, would not receive any payment or keep any interest, or, where so provided under national law, can be reasonably presumed not to receive any payment or keep any interest, if the normal ranking of liquidation priorities were applied under national law; or (b) a majority of voting classes of affected parties, provided that at least one of those classes is a secured creditor class or is senior to the ordinary unsecured creditors class.[86]

Also, member states should introduce one previously named 'fairness test' which requires that (a) a dissenting voting class of affected creditors is satisfied in full by the same or equivalent means if a more junior class is to receive any payment or keep any interest under the restructuring plan, or (b) dissenting voting classes of

---

82 Article 7(5) Directive on preventive restructuring frameworks final version 2018.

83 Art.9 Directive on preventive restructuring frameworks final version 2018.

84 Art.11 Directive on preventive restructuring frameworks final version 2018.

85 Isaac M. Pachulski, 'The Cram Down and Valuation under Chapter 11 of the Bankruptcy Code' (1980) *The North Carolina Law Review* 58 925; Kenneth N. Klee, 'Cram Down II' (1990) *American Bankruptcy Law Journal* 64 229.

86 Art.11(1) Directive on preventive restructuring frameworks final version 2018.

Cross-border insolvency of MCGs in the EU 119

affected creditors are treated at least as favourably as any other class of the same rank and more favourably than any junior class.[87]

One twist of the newest version (December 2018) of this proposed Directive, as some scholars have identified, is that under the Directive dissenting creditors in a higher ranked group may be voted down as long as they are treated more favourably than the junior class of creditors or shareholders.[88] Arguably, this provision is not the traditional absolute priority rule, which does not allow the court to sanction a cross-class cram-down against an entire class of creditors who vote against the plan unless the lower class of creditors do not receive anything.[89] The current Directive may allow shareholders to gain going concern value while leaving unsecure creditors with the liquidation value of the insolvent company, given the test of the no-creditor-worse-off principle is based on the valuation of liquidation value of the company. One may therefore expect that the proposed cross-class cram-down rule will be changed later, or the member states will still apply absolute priority rules, even though the relative priority rules are kept in the final version of the Directive.

As one of the most popular debt restructuring jurisdictions, English schemes of arrangement, together with Insolvency Act 1986, provides debtors in the other corners of the world a flexible choice for debt restructuring demands, including MCG cases. Arguably, schemes of arrangement, together with administration procedures, meet all the requirements prescribed in the Directive. Therefore, the next task is to provide some examples of how the Directive, if adopted by other member states, may improve the success of MCG debt restructurings.

Examples

Renegotiation of debt agreements at holding companies level

For the purpose of preserving group going concern value, it is useful to renegotiate the debt contracts.[90] When the debts of the groups of companies are mainly incurred at the holding companies level, it is possible to avoid a potential group insolvency by forming a new agreement between debtor holding companies and their creditors.[91] If a debt agreement includes a majority voting clause which

---

87 Art.11(1) c, ca and 2a of Directive on preventive restructuring frameworks final version 2018.
88 Art.11 Directive on preventive restructuring frameworks final version 2018.
89 Article 1129 US Bankruptcy Code 1978; see also R.J. de Weijs and others 'The Imminent Distortion of European Insolvency Law: How the European Union Erodes the Basic Fabric of Private Law by Allowing 'Relative Priority' (RPR) (2019) Centre for the Study of European Contract Law available at: https://ssrn.com/abstract=3350375, p. 9.
90 'Examples' is based on my publication in European business and organization law review. See Daoning Zhang, 'Preventive Restructuring Frameworks: A Possible Solution for Financially Distressed Multinational Corporate Groups in the EU' (2019) *European Business Organization Law Review*. https://doi.org/10.1007/s40804-018-0125-3; T.M.C. Asser Press.
91 'Examples' is built on my article Daoning Zhang, 'Preventive Restructuring Frameworks: A Possible Solution for Financially Distressed Multinational Corporate Groups in the EU' (2019) *European Business Organization Law Review*. https://doi.org/10.1007/s40804-018-0125-3; T.M.C. Asser Press.

120   *Cross-border insolvency of MCGs in the EU*

allows certain debts to be modified without the approval of all relevant creditors, the hold-out issue is not serious. However, in practice, only in complex leveraged loan agreement can one find such a clause.[92] To facilitate reaching such a new agreement, certain legal tools with cram-down functions are necessary.

UK schemes of arrangement can be viewed as useful tools to encourage dissident senior creditors to accept a new deal with debtors using a cram-down mechanism.[93] In essence, schemes of arrangement can be considered a compromise made between the company as one party and the creditors or members as another party. 'Sufficient connection' is a jurisdictional standard of companies to use schemes. Generally speaking, as long as the loan contracts between the debtors and the creditors are subject to English law, the sufficient connection test is met.[94]

There are three main stages in which a scheme comes into effect.[95] First the company needs to apply to court to notice that a meeting will be convened; then creditors need to vote on the plan, and each class needs to approve it. The ensuing stage is for the court to sanction the plan. [96] One feature of schemes is their cram-down power: as long as a majority in number of creditors (with 75% in value) in each class supports a plan, the dissident creditors are bound by the terms.[97]

Schemes have the potential to deal with some debt restructurings involving cross-border groups of companies. When one group of companies encounters financial distress, the main task of the schemes is to facilitate parties to reach a new deal: for example, by extension of the maturity date of the debts.[98] If the main borrower of the group is a holding company, it may be best to renegotiate a deal between the holding company and the senior creditors. The benefit would be that there is no need to worry that multiple local insolvency proceedings have been opened. The value of the group can be protected as the operating subsidiaries have not been disturbed. For example, the new arrangement could include: issuing new shares to provide necessary funds for the group, conducting a debt-for-shares swap to settle part of the due claims or converting the lower ranked debt to higher ranked debt in exchange for extension of debt maturity or waivers.[99] Also, these schemes respect the expectation of those financial credi-

---

92 Chris Howard and Bob Hedge, *Restructuring Law and Practice* (2nd edn, LNUK 2014), p. 337.

93 Scheme of arrangement is 'a compromise or arrangement between a company and its creditors, or any class of them, or its members, or any class of them'. Section 895 Company Act 2006.

94 Re Rodenstock GmbH [2011] EWHC 1104 (Ch).

95 David Milman, 'Schemes of Arrangement and Other Restructuring Regimes under UK Company Law in Context' (2011) *Company Law Newsletter* 301, pp. 1–4.

96 Ibid., pp. 1–4.

97 Gerard McCormack, 'Bankruptcy Forum Shopping, the UK and US as Venues of Choice for Foreign Companies' (2014) *International and Comparative Law Quarterly* 04 63, p. 826.

98 Apcoa Parking (UK) Ltd, Re [2014] EWHC 997 (Ch).

99 Christian Pilkington, *Schemes of Arrangement in Corporate Restructuring* (Sweet & Maxwell 2013), p. 151.

Cross-border insolvency of MCGs in the EU   121

tors as they may draft contracts before lending which explain how to control the business and how to distribute the value.

The Primacom Holding GmbH case[100] exemplifies a vivid cram-down scheme case[101] in which a potential corporate group insolvency can be avoided using the UK scheme. In this case, the ultimate parent companies are two companies incorporated in Luxembourg. An intermediate company is Primacom, which, along with its subsidiaries, operates mainly in Germany. In this case, most of the loan facilities were owed by Primacom, and the company could not serve its debt when they fell due. As a result, the company was of the opinion that debt restructuring could yield a better result than the German insolvency proceeding, so the company sought recourse to UK schemes on the basis that its financial documents were governed by UK law.[102] The scheme helped the company and its creditors to renegotiate debts.

The scheme provided new liquidity and deleveraged the group. Notably, the debts of the operating companies were novated to the holding company so that the German directors' duty under German insolvency law, requiring directors to file an insolvency petition when the company cannot pay the debt, could be avoided.[103] One important part of the deal was that Primacom's parent company agreed to take on certain debt so that it would not be forced into a German insolvency proceeding. The flexibility of the private restructuring solutions provided useful tools to support such planning and debt renegotiation. As a result, a potential cross-border insolvency of a group of companies could be resolved in only one jurisdiction.

The La Seda case[104] is another example. The company La Seda is the Spanish parent company of a group whose main business is packaging substance manufacturing across the EU. The scheme was used to amend senior debts governed by English law with a UK jurisdiction clause.[105] La Seda was the borrower of senior facilities which were guaranteed and secured by most of the group members with their shares.[106] The purpose of the restructuring was to inject new money into the group[107] such that it would not fall into fragmented insolvency proceedings in member states. As a result, the restructuring gave senior creditors more than 69% recovery, as opposed to insolvency, which would have given

---

100 Primacom Holding GmbH v A Group of the Senior Lenders & Credit Agricole [2011] EWHC 3746 (Ch) [2013] B.C.C. 201.
101 The cram-down schemes mean the schemes are used to cram down junior financial creditors so that hold-out issues can be mitigated.
102 Primacom Holding GmbH v A Group of the Senior Lenders & Credit Agricole [2011] EWHC 3746 (Ch) [2013] B.C.C. 201, p. 2.
103 German directors have to file for insolvency petition within 21 days of the insolvency situation appearing. Ibid., p. 9.
104 Re La Seda De Barcelona Sa [2010] EWHC 1364 (Ch).
105 Ibid., p. 1.
106 K. Asimacopoulos and J. Bickle, *European Debt Restructuring Handbook: Leading Case Studies from the Post-Lehman Cycle* (Globe Law and Business 2013), p. 105.
107 Ibid., p. 108.

122   *Cross-border insolvency of MCGs in the EU*

them less than 40% recovery. The group used the UK scheme to cram down the dissident minority of senior creditors. The restructuring plan included, among other things, agreements which amended the terms of the senior loan facilities with senior creditors and added more group members to act as guarantors to the senior loan facilities.[108]

All these cases show that when the debt contracts which cause the MCGs to be distressed can be renegotiated, the group can be kept intact. As a result, it is likely that the group going concern value is also preserved as the operating subsidiaries can be isolated to the restructuring process. Financial creditors may renegotiate contracts in accordance with the terms of inter-creditor agreements. This provides certainty to them as well as they accept the terms when they decide to lend money. However, this option is more likely to be available in concentrated syndicated loan cases. Therefore, one may not assume that all cross-border insolvency cases involving MCGs can be resolved in this way.

Group pre-pack sale

Another way to preserve the going concern value of a group is to conduct a pre-pack sale of the whole group to new companies formed by senior creditors. Along with the sale, operating companies are still largely intact, and the junior creditors will bear the most loss due to their ranking. Inter-creditor agreements prescribe the priority and enforcement methods among financial creditors in an out-of-court fashion.[109] Such a sale may happen at the intermediate holding companies' level so that the group will 'break the neck' and transfer the main assets-operating subsidiaries to the senior creditors.

In many cases, with the help of the contracts and restructuring laws, holding companies could sell the shares of all operating subsidiaries to the senior creditors without the claims from junior creditors, provided that junior creditors have security and guarantee from the operating subsidiaries. Taking UK law as an example, the above aim could be achieved through a transfer scheme and inter-creditor agreement. Transfer schemes allow shares or assets of the operating group to be sold to companies formed by senior creditors while leaving out-of-money creditors behind against the assets-stripped holding companies. Junior creditors' claims are released by the inter-creditor agreement so that they will not benefit from the assets of the newly formed companies.[110] The aim of the transfer schemes is twofold: one aim is to cram down unsupportive senior creditors' hold-out issues; another is to allow the new company to be clear of debt from out-of-money creditors so as to avoid insolvency.[111]

---

108 La Seda de Barcelona SA, re [2010] EWHC 1364 (CH).

109 Lauren Hanrahan and Suhrud Mehta, 'A Comparative Overview of Transatlantic Inter-creditor Agreement' in *The International Comparative Legal Guide To: Lending & Secured Finance* (2nd edn, GLG 2014), p. 46.

110 Christian Pilkington, *Schemes of Arrangement in Corporate Restructuring* (Sweet & Maxwell 2013), p. 19.

111 Ibid., p. 19.

Cross-border insolvency of MCGs in the EU 123

The junior claims can be legally released because of inter-creditor agreements. In a typical inter-creditor agreement, the priority and enforcement method of financial creditors are regulated by relevant provisions in it; one example of the term is as follows:

a the Junior Note-holders may not take any action to enforce their rights while the Senior Liabilities remain outstanding;
b the Secured Parties have no independent power to enforce or have recourse to any of the Transaction Security, or to exercise any rights or powers with respect thereto, except through the Security Agent.[112]

The fundamental result that an inter-creditor agreement would like to achieve is one in which the claims, guarantee and security of junior creditors, who, by the evidence of valuation, have no economic interests in the corporate group, are released along with the security enforcement instructed by the senior creditors. As a result, the senior creditors could maximize the value of the corporate group as it is free of claims and encumbered assets from the junior creditors; it is not unusual that the terms of inter-creditor agreement put the right of control of enforcement in the hand of senior creditors by constraining the junior creditors' rights of enforcement.[113] For example, in a European mezzanine inter-creditor agreement, the release provisions provide that junior creditors' security and guarantee will automatically be released if the senior creditors have instructed the agent to release their security on the debtor's assets in accordance with the senior and second-lien facilities.[114]

This is to say that the debtor in the restructuring could sell the whole group, encumbered by the security and guarantee of all financial creditors, to the Newco formed by the senior creditors, free of encumberment.[115] It has been expounded in the Barclays Bank Plc v HHY Luxembourg Sàrl case[116] that the operational subsidiaries could be sold to the senior creditors as a whole through a sale of shares in the holding companies, with all the guarantee and security on the assets of subsidiaries released on the basis of release provisions in the inter-creditor agreement between senior financial creditors and junior financial creditors.

The IMO car wash case[117] is a good example of a pre-pack sale of an insolvent MNC. IMO is the world's largest car wash company group based in the EU, stretching across 14 countries. The group was funded by one senior facility agreement and one mezzanine facility agreement. When the group was having

---

112 In the Matter of Christophorus 3 Limited [2014] EWHC 1162 (Ch), p. 3.
113 Lauren Hanrahan and Suhrud Mehta, 'A Comparative Overview of Transatlantic Inter-creditor Agreement' in *The International Comparative Legal Guide To: Lending & Secured Finance* (2nd edn, GLG 2014), p. 47.
114 Ibid., p. 48.
115 Richard Hooley, 'Release Provisions in Intercreditor Agreements' (2012) *Journal of Business Law* 3 213–233, p. 2.
116 Barclays Bank Plc v HHY Luxembourg Sàrl [2011] 1 B.C.L.C. 336.
117 Re Bluebrook Ltd [2010] B.C.C. 209.

124   *Cross-border insolvency of MCGs in the EU*

financial difficulties, it decided to transfer the business to Newcos, owned by senior creditors with shares apportioned by them. Three of the main holding companies were put in administration to sell the business to the Newcos. The claims of the mezzanine creditors against the subsidiaries of the group were released by the security agent in accordance with the inter-creditor agreement.[118] As a consequence, the group was transferred to the senior creditors, and the going concern value was preserved.

The European Directories case[119] followed a similar path. The European Directories Group had business in night EU member states, and it used a pre-pack sale of one holding company's share in an intermediate holding company called DH 7. The fact of this case was that DH 6 and DH 7 were companies incorporated in the Netherlands. One intermediate holding company, DH6, owned shares of another intermediate company, DH7, which, in turn, owned shares in the operating subsidiaries in the group. DH6 sold the shares in the intermediate holding company, DH7, that sat below it. As a result, all operating subsidiaries in the insolvent MNC were sold to senior creditors. As the operating subsidiaries were kept intact, the group going concern value was preserved. The inter-creditor allowed the junior claims to be released on enforcement action by senior creditors.[120]

Limitations of market/hybrid solutions

The above practice provides examples of the complex restructuring world in which corporate group going concern value can be preserved by renegotiating debt agreements or a group pre-pack sale. However, it does not mean that every distressed group can find a similar way to avoid group insolvency proceedings or carry out a pre-pack sale. The merits of the restructuring practice should be acknowledged, whereas, on the other hand, their limitation should also be seen.

Limitation of renegotiation of debt agreements at the level of holding companies

Every private debt restructuring case is almost unique due to the different features of different companies and different capital structures. The unique characteristics of one group may make it difficult for other distressed groups of companies to follow the same path.

Though market solutions and hybrid solutions may be able to preserve the going concern value of MCGs through renegotiation of debt agreements at the

---

118 Ibid.; Kon Asimacopoulos and Justin Bickle, *European Debt Restructuring Handbook: Leading Case Studies from the Post-Lehman Cycle* (Globe Law and Business 2013), p. 26.

119 HHY Luxembourg S.A.R.L & Anr v Barclays Bank PLC & Ors [2010] EWHC 2406.

120 Kon Asimacopoulos and Justin Bickle, *European Debt Restructuring Handbook: Leading Case Studies from the Post-Lehman Cycle* (Globe Law and Business 2013), p. 181.

level of holding companies, one cannot expect new agreements to be reached in all cross-border insolvency cases.

One important reason an insolvent MNC can be rescued without triggering the opening of multiple insolvency proceedings in different member states is inter-creditor agreements. If senior creditors of the distressed cross-border corporate groups agree on the terms of the pre-pack sales of the whole corporate group, junior creditors' rights are released by the inter-creditor agreements. The cram-down power of schemes of arrangement or equivalents in other member states may encourage debtors' and the seniors creditors' renegotiation, whereby they can accept a new agreement without the need of approval from all parties. The consequence is that the whole value of the MNC is transferred to the senior creditors as a means of repayment as other creditors' rights in the assets of subsidiaries are released by contracts.[121] Therefore, the full-blown, group-wide insolvency can be avoided using hybrid solutions in the jurisdiction of holding companies; also the going concern value of the MNC is preserved as the relationships among operating subsidiaries are kept intact. An obvious limitation is that in the absence of such inter-creditor agreements, junior creditors' rights cannot be wiped out contractually. This may happen when the profiles of creditors in different subsidiaries are non-identical so that no inter-creditors agreements bind them.

Schemes are well designed to modify long-term contractual obligations in financial contracts at the holding companies level,[122] while they cannot modify employees' rights or tort creditors' rights at the operating subsidiaries level. One reason is that schemes are compromises and arrangements between a company and its shareholders or creditors; therefore, the scheme of the parent company cannot be used to modify other companies' creditors. This is true if the profiles of creditors in parent companies and those in the subsidiaries are different, and creditors are subject to different debt instruments in different companies.[123] Without contracts, such as inter-creditor agreements, to bind all of these creditors regarding who has control and how to distribute loss among senior and junior creditors if the group is wound up, the schemes of the parent company generally cannot modify other subsidiaries' creditors' rights without their consent.

Also, as these rights are non-contractual or mandatory rights shaped by foreign countries' policies, it is difficult for schemes to change them. That is to say, the cram-down power of schemes is ill-equipped to force foreign trade creditors or employees to accept a new deal.

---

121 Chris Howard and Bob Hedge, *Restructuring Law and Practice* (2nd edn, LNUK 2014), pp. 357–359; HHY Luxembourg S.A.R.L & Anr v Barclays Bank PLC & Ors [2010] EWHC 2406.

122 Antony Zacaroli (QC) and Alexander Riddiford, 'Schemes of Arrangement and Chapter 11 of US Bankruptcy Code: A Comparative View' (2015) *South Square Digest*, p. 2.

123 Horst Eidenmüller, 'Comparative Corporate Insolvency Law' (2016) European Corporate Governance Institute (ECGI) – Law Working Paper No. 319, p. 27.

126   *Cross-border insolvency of MCGs in the EU*

Last but not least, UK courts also need to have jurisdiction to sanction schemes. If the foreign subsidiaries have CoMI and registered places in other member states, and the debt agreements are also subject to the law of other member states, it would be almost impossible for the UK courts to sanction the schemes without sufficient connection between the foreign subsidiaries and the UK. To make use of English schemes of arrangement, some foreign creditors may conduct forum shopping. Forum shopping, as discussed in the previous chapter, may give rise to uncertainty to creditors.

The case of Re Magyar Telecom BV.[124] Magyar Telecom BV is a company incorporated in the Netherlands, but the business of the group is centred in Hungary. Its distressed situation may have caused the whole group to fall into fragmented formal insolvency proceedings in different countries as the debts borrowed by the company were secured by the assets of most of the group members.[125] Since the company was registered in the Netherlands and because the notes are governed by New York law, it decided to move the CoMI of the company to the UK in order to use the schemes of arrangement. Ostensibly, the insolvency of corporate groups could be eased with the reorganization of one financing company in the group, while creditors of debt instruments may expect US law or Dutch law to be the appropriate law, rather than English schemes. Such uncertainty is costly as it may cause creditors to be concerned about the risk of uncertainty.

Alternatively, the courts where the foreign subsidiaries are located should initiate their equivalent schemes to deal with the new agreement between those foreign companies and their respective creditors, and meanwhile seek cooperation with other courts. That is to say that a cooperation and coordination framework should be used in this regard.

Problems with a group pre-pack sale

Similar to the limitation of the renegotiation of debt agreements, a group pre-pack sale is subject to similar constraints. The main purpose of group pre-pack sale is to wipe out the out-of-money creditors in the group while supporting the senior creditors to own the main assets of the group-operating subsidiaries. A relatively simple and cheap way to do this is to transfer the shares that are held by one intermediate holding company in the operating subsidiaries to a new company owned by the senior creditors who are in the money. The result is that the debtor group repays the senior creditors by offering them the group going concern value, the operating subsidiaries, while the junior creditors' rights may be left against the holding companies or released according to the inter-creditor agreements.

Similarly, if creditors do not belong to one set of debt instruments, a pre-pack sale at the holding companies' level cannot wipe out other creditors. Even

---

124 Re Magyar Telecom BV [2013] EWHC 3800 (Ch), p. 5.
125 Ibid.

Cross-border insolvency of MCGs in the EU 127

though some senior creditors may obtain the shares of operating subsidiaries, the rights of other categories of creditors of operating subsidiaries have priority over the senior creditors as debts are superior to shares in insolvency. Such a pre-pack sale will carry other creditors' claims to the new company formed by the senior creditors, which makes the sale meaningless. The exception is that the senior creditors also enjoy secured rights and guarantees on the assets of subsidiaries, and have priority over other creditors according to the terms of the inter-creditor agreement. Without help from, for example, an inter-creditor agreement which contractually gives senior creditors power to release the rights of the other creditors, a pre-pack sale cannot leave those other creditors behind. It is also possible that the inter-creditor agreements do not allow certain debts to be released in a way favoured by the senior creditors; in such a case, a pre-pack sale may still be difficult to implement.[126] The alternative solution may be to open more than one insolvency proceeding for different subsidiaries, in different jurisdictions, and sell the assets of subsidiaries to group buyers.

Another limitation of the group pre-pack sale arises from the drawbacks of the pre-pack sale itself. Pre-pack may be conducted for good reasons: no adequate sources of refinancing to support the protracted full administration, preventing damage of goodwill or retaining the key employees who are against insolvency.[127] As one of the tools of hybrid restructurings, it purports to be more efficient than formal proceeding in the sense that it costs less and recovers more for creditors. However, some evidence does not suggest these merits.

The quintessence of a typical pre-pack administration is that the negotiation of sale of almost all businesses or assets of the distressed companies is arranged before the appointment of administrators and the opening of administration proceedings.[128] The later-commenced administration proceedings are used as a tool to provide stay to all the creditors. However, the pre-pack sale is done quickly after the opening of administration proceedings.

Insolvency law grants voting rights to claimants in the creditors' meetings who enjoy residual interests in the insolvent companies. Unsecured creditors are the only creditors allowed to vote on the administrators' plan, but one caveat is that administrators can skip the creditors' meetings if they are sure no value will break down into the unsecured creditors' class.[129]

In the Insolvency Act 1986, Sch. B1 administrators' general power is endowed broadly on behalf of the company's interest: '*The administrator of a company may do anything necessary or expedient for the management of the affairs, business and property of the company*'.[130]

---

126 Re Hellas Telecommunications [2009] EWHC 3199 (Ch).

127 Rebecca Parry *Corporate rescue* (Thomson Sweet & Maxwell 2008), p. 16.

128 Mark Hyde and Iain White, 'Pre-Pack Administrations: Unwrapped' (2009) *Law and Financial Markets Review 3*(2), p. 134.

129 John Armour, 'The Rise of the Pre-Pack, Corporate Restructuring in the UK and Proposal for Reform' (2012), p. 6.

130 Insolvency Act 1986 Sch. B1 para. 59(1).

128 *Cross-border insolvency of MCGs in the EU*

According to Sch. B1 paras. 53–55, administrators are accountable to the creditors' meetings. The creditors' meeting will consider the administrator's plan and approve it with or without modification.[131] Also, the creditors' meeting has the power to dismiss the plan; thereafter, the court may make order where it finds fit.[132] Furthermore, the administrator's request to revise the plan after it has been approved in the last meeting will result in another creditors' meeting.[133] Generally, the administrator of one insolvent company has a duty to invite creditors to join the initial creditors' meeting under para. 51(1) of the Insolvency Act, and the administrator should present his reorganization plan to the creditors' meeting.[134]

However, the administrator believes that all the creditors will be fully compensated due to the adequate assets of the distressed company or the fact that, other than the prescribed part of distribution to unsecured creditors, unsecured creditors have nothing more to receive.[135] If the company cannot be saved as a going concern for the benefit of general creditors,[136] the administrator may not commence the creditors' meeting. This confers administrators the capacity to conduct the business or make decisions without the creditors' meetings.

Para. 68 goes on to state that the administrators should manage business according to the approved or revised proposal; the court only gives instruction to administrators where no proposal is approved or where they think it is appropriate to do so.[137] However, in practice, even if the administrator believes that there may be interests for unsecured creditors in some cases, he can still use his power to sell the assets of the company.[138] This power has been affirmed by the case Re Trans Bus International Ltd.[139]

Such efficiency comes from the fact that the Enterprise act 2002 aims to reduce the courts' involvement in cases where the meetings of creditors are unnecessary; without such new rules, administrators cannot make any decisions in

---

131 Ibid., para. 53(1).
132 Ibid., para. 55(2).
133 Ibid., para. 54(2).
134 Ibid., para. 51(1).
135 See Insolvency Act 1986, 176A, share of assets for unsecured creditors.

> '(2)The liquidator, administrator or receiver —
>
> (a) shall make a prescribed part of the company's net property available for the satisfaction of unsecured debts, and
> (b) shall not distribute that part to the proprietor of a floating charge except in so far as it exceeds the amount required for the satisfaction of unsecured debts.
>
> (3)Subsection (2) shall not apply to a company if—
>
> (a) the company's net property is less than the prescribed minimum, and
> (b) the liquidator, administrator or receiver thinks that the cost of making a distribution to unsecured creditors would be disproportionate to the benefits.'

136 Insolvency Act 1986 B1, para. 52(1).
137 Insolvency Act B1, para. 68.
138 Peter Walton, 'Pre-Packing' in the UK' (2009) *International Insolvency Review* 18 85–108, p. 90.
139 Re Transbus International Ltd [2004] EWHC 932 (Ch) Chancery Division.

the period of administration without the approval of courts.[140] Similar to UK rules, US Bankruptcy Code 363(b) also provides convenience for the application of a pre-pack sale: after a notice and a hearing, the debtor-in-possession has the power to sell all its assets without meeting other requirements of confirmation of a normal Chapter 11 plan.[141] Similar to its counterpart of the UK pre-pack, there is no need to get unsecured creditors' approval.[142]

Therefore, administrators generally have the power to sell the company's assets without the approval of creditors' meetings and orders from courts.[143] As a result, it is difficult for the unsecured creditors to have sufficient information regarding whether their rights are infringed.

In fact, arguably, the unsecured creditors in a given pre-pack sale are most likely to be the victims in that administrators may skip notice to them or approval from them.[144] Where the assets are sold to the existing management team, such pre-pack may be dubious to unsecured creditors as it is very likely that only the senior creditors will be paid off in exchange for further financial support to the Newco established by the existing teams while leaving nothing to unsecured creditors.[145]

The statement of insolvency practice 16 is designed to confer more protection to unsecured creditors by requiring administrators to disclose their background of appointment, to provide explanation to unsecured creditors regarding the justifications of pre-pack sales and to explain why pre-pack sales are the best results for all creditors.[146] However, this design alone cannot thoroughly eliminate all the problems in practice as the administrators are more likely to follow the instructions of senior creditors or directors, not unsecured creditors.

As a result, pre-pack sales may be rigged by the senior creditors, and it may not necessarily maximize the value of the distressed groups of companies. [147]

---

140 Ibid.
141 Elizabeth B. Rose, 'Chocolate, Flowers and § 363(B): The Opportunity for Sweetheart Deals without Chapter 11 Protections' (2006) *Emory Bankruptcy Developments Journal* 23 249, p. 249.
142 Ibid., p. 262.
143 Peter Walton, 'Pre-Packing' in the UK' (2009) *International Insolvency Review* 18 85–108, p. 90.
144 Ibid., p. 87.
145 Gerard McCormack, *Corporate Rescue Law – An Anglo-American Perspective* (Edward Elgar Publishing Limited 2008), p. 72.
146 Bo Xie, 'Protecting the Interests of General Unsecured Creditors in Pre-Packs: The Implication and Implementation of SIP 16' (2010) *Company Lawyer*, p. 6.
147 Empirical research shows that the performance of pre-pack in terms of general recovery rate for creditors only engenders a marginal improvement (22%) vis-à-vis non-pre-pack business sale (21.8%) in administration or administrative receivership. Pre-pack's recovery rate for preferential creditors is only 13%, compared to the non-pre-pack recovery rate of 38%. Pre-pack's recovery rate for unsecured creditors is 1%, which is worse than the non-pre-pack recovery rate of 3%. Sandra Frisby, 'Report to the Association of Business Recovery Professionals a Preliminary Analysis of Pre-Packaged Administrations' (August 2007), p. 50, 56; in an empirical study done by Professor LoPucki, there is only one buyer in more than half of the pre-pack cases. The lucrative bonuses of bankers make them indifferent to achieving as high a price as possible.

130   *Cross-border insolvency of MCGs in the EU*

Even though pre-pack may reduce the cost of long and complex administration fees, the price sold may be significantly lower than the value of a business after reorganization (only the latter's 50%).[148] The unsecured creditors are unlikely to provide their own restructuring plan: for example, they cannot financially afford valuation fees.[149] Delay and cost arising from the challenge of unsecured creditors are something courts try to avoid, which in return increases the difficulty of challenging plans in favour of debtors or senior creditors.[150]

Arguably, one assertion could be made is that at least pre-packs may not significantly increase the overall return to all the creditors, but it is suspected of transferring wealth from the preferential and unsecured creditors to secured creditors.[151] Secured creditors, existing management teams and professional advisors have the inclination to use a pre-pack sale as they can benefit most from it.[152]

To sum up, though the market and hybrid solutions may prevent the insolvency of MCGs or preserve the going concern value of MCGs in some cases, they are not always available. The uncertainty and the abuse from pre-pack mean that market/hybrid solutions are not always reliable solutions to preserve the corporate groups' going concern value.

Cooperation and coordination under protocols

After understanding that it is not always possible to resolve the group insolvency in one jurisdiction, private parties may draft cross-border insolvency agreements to facilitate the group insolvency. The protocol is a typical form of cooperation between courts of different jurisdictions and insolvency practitioners.

Protocols may be used as tools to deal with cross-border insolvency cases. The nature of protocols is ad hoc agreements reached by private parties and supported by courts.[153] The aim of protocols is to build up a framework of cooperation and communication in the context of multiple insolvency proceedings. The provisions of protocols could reflect the international guidelines on

---

They actually may prefer a lower price to the only buyer in exchange for his payback in the future. Lyn M. Lopucki and Joseph. W. Doherty, 'Bankruptcy Fire Sales' (2007) UCLA School of Law & Economics Research Paper Series Research Paper No. 07-07, p. 35.

148 Lopucki found in his study that larger companies only get their 35% book value in a pre-pack sale, while they get 80% of their book value in reorganization. See Lyn M. Lopucki and Joseph. W. Doherty, 'Bankruptcy Fire Sales'' (2007) UCLA School of Law & Economics Research Paper Series Research Paper No. 07-07, p. 3.

149 Ibid., p. 38.

150 Ibid., p. 39.

151 Vanessa Finch, *Corporate Insolvency Law Perspectives and Principles* (2nd edn, Cambridge University Press 2009), p. 463.

152 Gerard McCormack, *Corporate Rescue Law – An Anglo-American Perspective* (Edward Elgar Publishing Limited 2008), p. 73.

153 Paul H. Zumbro, 'Cross Border Insolvencies and International Protocols – An Imperfect But Effective Tool' (2010) *Business Law International* 11 157, p. 158.

cooperation and coordination in cross-border cases. Useful guidelines include the Concordats by the International Bar Association, Guidelines applicable to courts to courts communications in cross-border cases by American Law Institute,[154] ALI's Principles of Cooperation among the NAFTA Countries, Global principles for cooperation in international insolvency cases,[155] the European Communication and Cooperation Guidelines for Cross-border Insolvency by two European professors and UNCITRAL Legislative Guide by UNCITRAL Working Group V.[156]

In the Maxwell case a protocol between the USA and the UK played a ground-breaking role in the history of protocol. Both jurisdictions decided to open the insolvency proceedings. The innovative aspect in this case was that unprecedented cooperation was conducted by means of protocol.[157] This protocol, on the one hand, respected the jurisdiction of the US and the UK courts, and, on the other hand, made the Chapter 11 reorganization and UK administration very coherent and interdependent.

In some cases, the assets and administrative centre of a company are not necessarily in one jurisdiction. Maxwell's CoMI is in the UK, while its principal assets are in the USA.

Due to the sheer size of the assets, the US court also claimed insolvency jurisdiction for Maxwell. The Maxwell case exemplified that a reorganization plan of a group of companies could in fact be enacted through the cooperation of more than one court. What is needed is a framework of coordination among separate reorganization plans, connecting the different insolvency procedures.

The recent Nortel case provides a good example regarding how two national courts can reach an agreement of sale of assets together and of proceeds allocation on the basis of corporate form, irrespective of nationality and the location of certain assets.[158]

The parent company of the Nortel and the Canadian wing of its subsidiaries filed insolvency proceedings in Canada, while the US subsidiaries filed insolvency proceedings in the USA.[159] The head office of the telecom giant Nortel is in Canada. It consists of many subsidiaries globally, but the business relationships among its subsidiaries are said to be integrated, especially with regard to

---

154 Ibid., p. 158.
155 American Law Institute and International Insolvency Institute, 'Transnational insolvency: Global principles for cooperation in international insolvency cases' 2012.
156 See general Ian F. Fletcher, 'Maintaining the Momentum: The Continuing Quest for Global Standards and Principles to Govern Cross Border Insolvency' (2006–2007) *Brooklyn Journal of International Law*' 32 767.
157 Jay Lawrence Westbrook, 'The Lesson of Maxwell Communication' (1996) *Fordham Law Review* 64(6) 2531, p. 2534.
158 In re Nortel Networks, Inc., 532 BR 494 Bankr D Del 2015.
159 (Other companies in other locations do not enter into formal proceedings.) John A.E. Pottow, 'Two Cheers for Universalism: Nortel's Nifty Novelty' (2015) Public law and legal theory research paper series paper No. 487. *Michigan Law Journal*, pp. 335–336.

132 Cross-border insolvency of MCGs in the EU

research and cash management.[160] The Canadian court and the American court prioritized the task of selling the group as a whole while leaving the allocation of proceeds to a later point so that the value of the group could be preserved.[161]

The two national courts agreed to take a universalist view to consider the Nortel group. The courts gave weight to the legal status of each entity but were not concerned so much with the location of one of the most valuable assets – the IP of Nortel located in Canada.[162] The two courts agreed that no company in the group was entitled to the proceeds of the sale of IP asset in full simply because it was fortuitously located in Canada but not somewhere else. The integrated characteristics of the Nortel group provide evidence that all the subsidiaries utilize the IP in their operation and contribute interests to the whole group; therefore, the IP assets should be allocated to group members in a pro rata fashion.[163]

The limitations of protocols arise from their ad hoc contractual nature. Private protocols may not be drafted successfully by various debtors and creditors without their consent. Uncertainty may arise as creditors are not sure what terms will be concluded in the protocol to allocate powers of courts and insolvency practitioners, and procedures of cooperation.[164] Also, some courts may lack the ability to support the ad hoc protocols.[165] It may be more desirable to have a formal legal framework that governs the cooperation and coordination. Also, it may be desirable to have one leading party facilitate the cooperation, lest the otherwise chaotic situation will render the possible group rescue plan dissipated.

The limitations of the market/hybrid solutions and private protocols indicate that it is desirable to have a general framework for procedural coordination among the insolvency courts of different jurisdictions. The next chapter will consider the group coordination proceedings prescribed by EIR recast 2015 and examine whether it fills in this gap.

160 Jay Lawrence Westbrook, 'Nortel: The Cross-border Insolvency Case of the Century' (2015) *Journal of International Banking and Financial Law* 8 498, p. 2.

161 John A.E. Pottow, 'Two Cheers for Universalism: Nortel's Nifty Novelty' (2015) Public law and legal theory research paper series paper No. 487. *Michigan Law Journal*, p. 337.

162 Jay Lawrence Westbrook, 'Nortel: The Cross-Border Insolvency Case of the Century' (2015) *Journal of International Banking and Financial Law* 8 498, p. 3.

163 John A.E. Pottow, 'Two Cheers for Universalism: Nortel's Nifty Novelty' (2015) Public law and legal theory research paper series paper No. 487. *Michigan Law Journal*, pp. 343–345.

164 Bob Wessels, 'Cross-Border Insolvency Agreements: What Are They and Are They Here to Stay?', in Faber *et al.* (eds.) *Insolventie en Overeenkomst* (Nijmegen 2012), p. 11.

165 Ibid., p. 11.

5 Group coordination and planning proceedings

Chapters 3 and 4 reveal that procedural consolidation, market/hybrid legal solutions and private protocols all contain limitations and drawbacks for cross-border insolvency of MCGs. The limitations of procedural consolidation and market solutions suggest that in some cases, cross-border insolvency of MCGs may have to be resolved in more than one jurisdiction. That is to say, in many cases, a general framework for the cooperation and coordination of multiple insolvency proceedings may be required in this aspect.[1]

This chapter examines the third practical solution for the cross-border rescue of multinational corporate groups – group coordination proceedings in EIR recast[2] (new EU regulation on insolvency proceeding 2015) and group planning proceedings under UNCITRAL Model Law. Both pieces of legislation provide cooperative insolvency frameworks for international corporate groups; the former is applicable at the EU level, whereas the latter is at the international level. The main tenet of a group coordination proceeding or planning proceeding is that judges and insolvency practitioners should cooperate with each other to the maximum degree possible. The facilitation of flow of information and a coordinated group-wide rescue plan may help to save the whole group. However, due to the differences of national insolvency laws and a fear of inroad of national judicial sovereignty and national interests, one may expect that national courts are reluctant to offer any support to foreign courts unless local interests are fully protected. The following sections will examine the efficacy of group insolvency proceedings based on the rationale of cross-border cooperation and coordination, with a focus on EIR Group Coordination Proceedings.

---

1 This chapter is partly based on one of my previously published articles in *International Company and Commercial Law Review*, see 'A Recommendation to Improve the Opt-Out Mechanism in the EU Regulation on Insolvency Proceedings Recast' in [2017] I.C.C.L.R, pp. 167–175.

2 Regulation (EU) 2015/848 of the European Parliament and of the Council of 20 May 2015 on insolvency proceedings.

134 *Group coordination & planning proceedings*

EIR group coordination proceedings

Substantive consolidation and procedural consolidation[3] may operate on a general cooperative framework for courts and insolvency practitioners, though these solutions may be applied separately from a general cooperative framework. It is obvious that the efficacy of a pure cooperative framework is limited[4] as one main obstacle of cross-border insolvency of MCGs is that the commencement of too many parallel insolvency proceedings may jeopardize the success of a group rescue. The more member companies enter into insolvency in different jurisdictions, the more difficult it is for insolvency practitioners and courts to cooperate with each other. The European formal group coordination proceeding does not exclude the possibility of using informal rescue options, while it serves as a parallel and general framework for parties to choose. The adoption of procedural cooperation is so far in line with the analysis of this book as both substantive consolidation and procedural consolidation are associated with serious uncertainty.

Group coordination proceedings can be seen as an improvement compared to the previous version of EU regulation, which consisted of nothing in regard to groups of companies.[5] In the new EU regulation on insolvency proceedings, besides previous general requirements for cooperation and communication between insolvency practitioners and courts, Chapter 5 specifically prescribes group coordination proceedings for cross-border insolvency of corporate groups.[6] The ultimate goal of this proceeding is to provide a group reorganization plan for the whole group so that the value of the group can be preserved in a desirable way.

Chapter 5 retains the 'communication and cooperation obligations' of courts and insolvency practitioners.[7] In the group context, it is desirable to connect group members through communication and cooperation. For example, through cooperation, the information of other members can be obtained; it is also a very important precondition to a successful rescue.[8]

What is more, Chapter 5 provides a framework for the coordination of group corporate insolvency. To conduct a group-wide reorganization, a group

---

3 McCormack Gerard, 'Reforming the European Insolvency Regulation: A Legal and Policy Perspective' (2014) *Journal of Private International Law* 10 (1) 41–67, p. 57.

4 Stephan Madaus, 'Insolvency Proceedings for Corporate Groups under the New Insolvency Regulation' (2015), p. 3. At <http://papers.ssrn.com/sol3/papers.cfm?abstract_id=2648850>

5 Reinhard Bork and Renato Mangano, *European Cross-Border Insolvency Law* (Oxford University Press 2016), p. 291.

6 EIR recast 2015 Chapter V.

7 When insolvency practitioners of one group member believe that it would be better to liquidate the assets through a group restructuring plan, they may suggest such a plan to other insolvency practitioners of other member companies under general cooperation and communication basis. See also Art 56 (2) (c) 'Insolvency practitioners shall consider whether possibilities exist for restructuring group members which are subject to insolvency proceedings and, if so, coordinate with regard to the proposal and negotiation of a coordinated restructuring plan'.

8 Chris Howard and Bob Hedger, *Restructuring Law and Practice* (2nd edn, LNUK 2014).

coordination plan[9] can be proposed by a coordinator appointed by any court in which the insolvency proceeding of one group member is opened; insolvency practitioners of different insolvent subsidiaries can also jointly decide an eligible court for the purpose of group coordination proceedings. All these efforts are made to facilitate multiple group insolvency proceedings such that these proceedings of member companies can be coordinated, and a better result can be achieved.[10] The key function of group coordination proceedings is to provide a platform for coordinators to consider recommendations and group coordination plans for the whole group.[11] The group coordination plans are the fulcrum of the group coordination proceedings; one may imagine that relevant group member companies which join in the proceeding may decide to draft a coordinated recovery plan by extending debt maturity or selling group assets to repay debts.[12]

The coordinator[13] has the power to arrange the multiple proceedings. To facilitate the group coordination proceeding, the coordinators also enjoy the power to participate in any foreign hearing and creditors' meetings; to present plans to the relevant creditors; and to make a stay on the insolvency proceedings, which are subject to the group coordination proceedings.[14] Such a stay power may help to deal with the 'the issue of commons'—individual companies with conflict of interest intend to pursue different goals and hinder the group rescue plan.[15] Coordinators therefore enjoy the stay power to resolve this problem in the case of group reorganization.[16]

The group coordination proceedings cannot be employed to extract value from other subsidiaries to the parent companies, or vice versa. A precondition on the court that decides to open group coordination proceedings is that none

---

9 Art 72 (1)(b) 'The coordinator shall propose a group coordination plan that identifies, describes and recommends a comprehensive set of measures appropriate to an integrated approach to the resolution of the group members' insolvencies'.

10 Stephan Madaus, 'Insolvency Proceedings for Corporate Groups under the New Insolvency Regulation' (2015) p. 10 at http://papers.ssrn.com/sol3/papers.cfm?abstract_id=2648850.

11 EIR recast 2015 Art. 70.

12 However, such a plan should not include substantive consolidation as it may fundamentally change the creditors' pre-insolvency rights without justification. Gabriel Moss (QC), Ian Fletcher (QC) and Stuart Isaacs (QC), *The EU Regulation on Insolvency Proceedings* (3rd edn, Oxford University Press Oxford 2016), p. 516.

13 EIR recast Art.72 (2) e.

14 EIR recast Art. 72.

15 Insolvency practitioners under EIR recast enjoy a general stay power which can be used, if certain requirements are met, on other insolvency proceedings. One of the requirements is a reasonable chance of success; another is that such stay benefits the member company on which the stay is imposed. Art 60 (i)(iii) New EU regulation. Coordinator's stay power may be invalid to certain group member companies if certain group members decided not to follow the group plan.

16 By contrast, without the opening of group coordination proceedings, the insolvency practitioner of a member company can only make a stay on other insolvency proceedings if a group-wide sale is possible. See Art.60 (b) EU regulation. See also Gabriel Moss (QC), Ian Fletcher (QC) and Stuart Isaacs (QC), The EU Regulation on insolvency proceedings (Third edition OUP 2016) p. 516.

136 *Group coordination & planning proceedings*

of the subsidiaries which join in the coordination proceeding is likely to be financially disadvantaged.[17] The court should therefore conduct a preliminary cost and benefit analysis to convince it that the benefit is no less than the cost of such proceeding.[18] Therefore, group coordination proceedings provide a more concrete framework where all the relevant insolvency practitioners and courts can reach a group-wide deal.

As a result, group coordination proceedings are a welcome development as they provide a general group insolvency framework which not only has the potential to preserve the group value but can also provide certainty.[19] The voluntary opt-out mechanism provides some certainty and flexibility to the group members. For example, if one subsidiary believes that the group plan is harmful to its creditors, the insolvency practitioners of this subsidiary can choose to opt out of the group plan.

Problems of group coordination proceedings

Group coordination proceedings may have the ability to preserve the group going concern value as they aim to connect the group members via one group coordination proceeding. The flip side is that the desire and effort to rescue the group may be dampened if an important group member which forms valuable relationships with other group member companies could voluntarily choose to opt out of the proceedings without any limitations. The next section will focus on this opt-out mechanism.

Opt-out mechanism of group coordination proceedings

The group coordination proceedings can be objected to by the insolvency practitioners of any member companies, the consequence being that those member companies will be unaffected by the group coordination proceedings.[20] The opt-out mechanism has attracted criticism from some scholars, and it is generally believed that the effectiveness of group coordination proceeding will therefore be negatively affected.[21]

Since the cost of cooperation will be increased due to the incentives for holdout, the cost of group coordination proceedings may outweigh the benefits they

---

17 EIR recast Art 63(b).

18 See EIR recast Recital 58 and see also Reinhard Bork and Renato Mangano, *European Cross-Border Insolvency Law* (Oxford University Press 2016), p. 294.

19 Group coordination proceedings respect entity law; they do not pool the assets and claims of different group members together.

20 EIR recast Art.64.

21 Christoph Thole and Manuel Dueñas, 'Some Observations on the New Group Coordination Procedure of the Reformed European Insolvency Regulation' (2015) *International Insolvency Review* 24 214–227, p. 224; Kristin Van Zwieten, 'An Introduction to the European Insolvency Regulation, as made and as Recast', in R. Bork and K. van Zwieten (eds.), *Commentary on the European Insolvency Regulation* (Oxford University Press 2016), p. 53; Jessica Schmidt, 'Group Insolvency under the EIR Recast' (2015) Eurofenix Autumn.

Group coordination & planning proceedings   137

could bring to creditors.[22] Also, rejection of inclusion has an automatic effect without any restrictions from the court which opens group coordination proceedings.[23] Art 64 (3) also states that such objection of inclusion can obtain the approval from the court where such dissident insolvency practitioners are appointed if it is required under the local insolvency law. In other words, if the local law does not require court approval, the opt-out is in the hands of the insolvency practitioners without the scrutiny of the courts.

The reason group coordination proceedings include an opt-out mechanism for the insolvency practitioners is to avoid the potential coercive inclusion of any group members.[24] The EIR is based on entity law, and therefore, each subsidiary's interests should be protected.[25] That is to say that the goal of preservation of group value should not trump the importance of creditors' protection of subsidiaries.

The above compromise renders the non-binding group coordination proceedings less effective as they should have been as the parties may simply choose not to coordinate.[26] Nonetheless, the concern should not be overestimated. The opt-out itself is a protection to every single subsidiary, especially in the case where the group going concern value is not large enough to cover the cost of cooperation, so the group plan will likely decrease the value of subsidiaries.

Supporting a group plan at the cost of subsidiaries takes issue with the rationale of limited liability which is well established.[27] In the context of group insolvency, respecting each subsidiary is a basic requirement confirmed by the ECJ *Eurofood* case.[28] Also, the directors of the subsidiaries in fact have no obligations to other subsidiaries or the creditors of those subsidiaries; directors only aim to achieve success for their own companies and creditors.[29] Similarly, the office holders, such as administrators, are agents of the companies, and they

---

22 Kristin Van Zwieten, 'An Introduction to the European Insolvency Regulation, as made and as Recast', in R. Bork and K. van Zwieten (eds.), *Commentary on the European Insolvency Regulation* (Oxford University Press 2016), p. 53.

23 Gabriel Moss (QC), Ian Fletcher (QC) and Stuart Isaacs (QC), *The EU Regulation on Insolvency Proceedings* (3rd edn, Oxford University Press Oxford 2016), p. 510.

24 Jessica Schmidt, 'Group Insolvency under the EIR Recast' (2015) Eurofenix Autumn, p. 18.

25 EU regulation on insolvency proceedings recast 2015, Recital 52; cooperation between the insolvency practitioners should not run counter to the interests of the creditors in each of the proceedings, and such cooperation should be aimed at finding a solution that would leverage synergies across the group.

26 Samantha Bewick, 'The EU Insolvency Regulation, Revisited' (2015) *International Insolvency Review* 24 172–191, p. 17; see also Michael Weiss, 'Bridge over Troubled Water: The Revised Insolvency Regulation' (2015) *International Insolvency Review* 24 192–213.

27 Such as reducing risks, encouraging investment, mitigating transaction cost. See F. Easterbrook and D. Fischel, 'Limited Liability and the Corporation' (1985) *University of Chicago Law Review* 52 89; see also Irit Mevorach, 'The Role of Enterprise Principles in Shaping Management Duties at Times of Crisis' (2013) *European Business Organization Law Review* 14(4) 471–496, p. 477.

28 Eurofood [2006] Ch.508.

29 Irit Mevorach, 'The Role of Enterprise Principles in Shaping Management Duties at Times of Crisis' (2013) *European Business Organization Law Review* 14(4) 471–496, p. 480.

138 *Group coordination & planning proceedings*

only owe duties to the companies to which they are appointed; administrators only promote the interests of the creditors of the companies to which they are appointed.[30] All of this supports the opt-out mechanism.

However, a complete free opt-out option may ignore the possibility that in certain cases, such opt-out serves neither the interests of creditors of the hold-out subsidiaries nor the interests of the creditors of the whole group. It is one thing that the insolvency practitioners of some companies would like to stay in the market by means of administration, while the administrators of other group members may prefer to leave the market through a sale of the business;[31] it is another thing that certain senior creditors of subsidiaries who have controlled the companies can choose to opt out of the group plan while enacting strategies that only benefit them. An example could be a pre-pack fire sale of the subsidiary, irrespective of a better group plan which can benefit all the creditors. The latter cases are the main problems, whereby they render the group rescue plan vulnerable to the strategic actions of some creditors or investors. The next section will provide a further discussion on this issue. The discussion of problems of opt-out mechanisms in the context of creditors' control literature forms part of the originality of this book.

Drawbacks of group coordination proceedings

Group coordination proceedings do not necessarily deal with a free fall insolvency of groups of companies where all the group members enter into group proceedings in different member states. As in many group cases financing is arranged at the parent companies' level;[32] group insolvency cases may in fact only involve one or more holding companies.[33] Also, the subsidiaries in one group may have the same creditors, who are bound by one set of loan documents sitting at the level of holding companies. It is possible to argue that in these cases, certain creditors will not be able to take individual action to control one single subsidiary as they are all bound by one inter-creditor agreement.

However, this is not always the case. It is possible that member companies in one group have different profiles of senior creditors[34]; it is also possible that certain investors become creditors of subsidiaries later by buying debts

---

30 Sch. Bl para. 3(2); see also Ian Fletcher, *The Law of Insolvency* (4th edn, Sweet & Maxwell London 2009), p. 568.

31 Burkhard Hess, Paul Oberhammer and Thomas Pfeiffer, *European Insolvency Law Heidelberg-Luxemburg-Vienna Report* (Hart Publishing Oxford 2014), p. 222.

32 Isabel Giancristofano, 'Third Party Securities in the Financial Restructuring of Corporate Groups in Germany' (2016) *International Corporate Rescue* 13(2), p. 111.

33 These holding companies may deal with financial creditors in a package of loan documents and on-lend money to subsidiaries. See Antony Zacaroli (QC) and Alexander Riddiford, 'Schemes of Arrangement and Chapter 11 of US Bankruptcy Code: A Comparative View' (2015) *South Square Digest*, p. 2.

34 Proposals for the revision of the European Insolvency Regulation – a step forward in the rescue culture? Linklaters 2012, p. 4.

Group coordination & planning proceedings 139

at distressed debt market. In the latter cases, creditors or investors may not aim to preserve the group going concern value; rather, they may try to control the valuable subsidiaries simply because their value is underestimated. Allowing these creditors to invoke opt-out mechanism freely will make the goal of preservation of the group going concern value difficult to achieve. Their inconsistent strategies may not only cut off the relationships of group members' companies in the MCGs but also create uncertainty among stakeholders. This section first provides an overview of creditors' control on the debt restructuring practice. Then it moves to discuss the implications on the group coordination proceedings.

Senior creditors' control

Senior creditors or investors could gain control by providing refinancing or buy cheaper debt in the secondary debt market. These senior creditors could therefore, to some extent, influence the debt restructuring plan.[35] It is entirely possible that the senior creditors could expect a sale of business to other buyers or own it by themselves.[36]

Refinancing terms frequently constitute the main provisions of the reorganization plan. As the value of the cash-starved companies can only be kept when the company is operating, refinancing enables it to make payment to employees and trader creditors of operating subsidiaries. The protection of the new money provided after the opening of insolvency proceedings will be granted priority to most pre-insolvency debts or at least enjoy the same priority status with some secured debt.[37] By providing refinancing, the creditors may gain bargaining power over cash-starved companies so that the creditors may in fact force debtors to extract value from other creditors and provide it to the ones who provide new money. Refinancing should be encouraged to the extent that such new money could create new value; it should not be used as a tool to redistribute value.[38]

Certain types of refinancing terms and practice may not bring in value to the debtors' insolvency estate; rather they may lead to value redistribution: roll-up and cross-collateralization. Roll-up describes the situation where certain lenders' pre-insolvency unsecured debts transform into part of the post-insolvency debts so that all the debts of the lenders enjoy priority over other creditors.[39]

---

35 Michelle M. Harner and Jamie Marincic, 'Behind Closed Doors: The Influence of Creditors in Business Reorganizations' (2010–2011) 34 Seattle U. L. Rev. 1155, p. 1158.
36 Ibid., p. 1158.
37 Oscar Couwenberg and Stephen J. Lubben, 'Essential Corporate Bankruptcy Law' (2013) University of Groningen Faculty of Law Research Paper Series No. 04, pp. 8–9, p. 15.
38 George G. Triantis, 'A Theory of the Regulation of Debtor-in-Possession Financing' (1993) Vanderbilt Law Review 46 901, p. 903.
39 Gerard McCormack, 'Super-priority New Financing and Corporate Rescue' (2007) Journal of Business Law 7 701–732, p. 8.

140 *Group coordination & planning proceedings*

Cross-collateralization happens when lenders have pre-insolvency debts which are fully secured. As a result, the lenders require that the post-insolvency assets be used to secure their pre-insolvency debts as well.[40] In other words, the pre-insolvency unsecured debts start to enjoy priority over other creditors due to the cross-collateralization clause. The overall effect of these refinancing methods is to exploit unsecured creditors and preferential creditors who would have ranked higher or *pari passu* with the lenders' unsecured pre-insolvency debts.

Courts and court-appointed monitors need to hold refinancing in check; the purpose is to prevent refinancing from having the power to redistribute value from junior creditors to senior creditors.[41]

Another thing that may happen may be that certain investors have the incentives to control or own the subsidiaries in their own interests.[42] These creditors or investors may achieve this aim by exerting loan-to-own strategies in the debt market. The result will be that certain subsidiaries are pulled out of the group coordination proceeding. This is because the investors may believe that it is the subsidiaries rather than the whole group that they want to purchase. For example, if one foreign subsidiary plays very important R&D functions in the group, the investors or local senior creditors may want to absorb it into their own groups. However, this does not mean that the buyers can use the assets of the subsidiary in a more efficient way than the distressed group. Also, without the subsidiary, other group members in the distressed MCG may lack going concern value as they rely on the relationships with the subsidiary.

Also, it could be the case that some investors who are only interested in short-term profit, like many hedge funds, believe that one subsidiary is undervalued, and they want to buy low and sell high later. They may opt out the group rescue option immediately. As a result, the rescue of the subsidiaries will be arranged following these investors' preferred track.

All these examples show that group coordination proceedings should put a limitation on the use of opt-out mechanisms as creditors of the distressed MCGs may not necessarily be organized by concentrated contracts. Senior creditors may gain control and use the opt-out mechanism to pursue their own interests. The next section will provide more discussion on this issue.

---

40 Charles J. Tabb, 'A Critical Reappraisal of Cross-Collateralization in Bankruptcy' (1986–1987) *Southern California Law Review* 60 109, p. 112.

41 Some countries' refinancing rules may work well to avoid roll-up or cross-collateralization. For example, the UK Insolvency Act 1986 provided that the contract entered into by administrators would enjoy priority to administrators' remuneration and floating charge. Therefore, it is clear that senior creditors who advance post-insolvency financing cannot assert that their pre-insolvency unsecured debts can enjoy any priority as their pre-insolvency loans are simply not the debts incurred by the administrators. See Insolvency Act 1986 Bl 99, Gerard McCormack, 'Super-Priority New Financing and Corporate Rescue' (2007) *Journal of Business Law* 7 701–732, p. 13.

42 Michelle M. Harner, 'Activist Investors, Distressed Companies, and Value Uncertainty' (2014) *American Bankruptcy Institute Law Review* 22 167.

Implication on group coordination proceedings

No matter through which way creditors gain control of the subsidiaries, the most important implication on group coordination proceedings may be that local senior creditors or investors of subsidiaries may have their own reorganization plans which are different from the group plan provided by the coordinator. The group plan and subsidiaries' plans may clash with each other. The key is to decide which one the local insolvency practitioner should pursue.

Senior creditors' control could be a good thing for several reasons. The competition of senior creditors for control can reveal the value of the corporate group.[43] For example, if the corporate group is worth more as a whole than in pieces, senior creditors may try to maintain the integrity of the group assets to achieve maximum recovery.

Also, that competition for control by buying debts may help concentrate the fragmented debts; it reduces the intensity of holdout issues. The creditors who try to exert the loan-to-own strategies will also want to buy debts at the below par price to control the restructuring or insolvency process in the hope of reaping the undervalued asset prices. This debt trading practice will put the fragmented debts into the hands of senior creditors who have informational advantages. The senior creditors are therefore in a better position to make decisions regarding how to rescue the distressed group.

What is equally important is that in the refinancing cases, by injecting money to finance certain members in the group, the insolvency issue could be avoided.[44] Refinancing is therefore a useful method of insolvency planning, and it could decide which companies should be put in insolvency proceedings. Financial creditors can use financing contracts to gain control of the distressed companies when the companies reach the vicinity of insolvency.[45] Such control may bring in the benefit of better decision-making due to certain creditors' information advantages.[46]

After all, whether the group should be rescued or whether the assets should be put together is a commercial judgement which depends on whether or not there is group going concern value. Such a decision is best left to the creditors and the debtors who have the required information.

---

43 The modern financial contracts are very carefully drafted such that the creditors who are in the best position to make decisions obtain power to make business judgement. In the USA, the most likely DIP lenders are the companies' existing lenders as they have the best information regarding the value of the companies. David A. Skeel, Jr., 'The Past, Present and Future of Debtor-in-Possession Financing' (2003–2004) *Cardozo Law Review* 25 1905, p. 1917.

44 Assume that a cross-default will make the whole group enter into fragmented insolvency proceedings. If the group could borrow money at the whole enterprise value, the new money could help the group to preserve the value, and such a solution benefits all the creditors. Steven T. Kargman, 'Financing Company Group Restructurings: Book Review' (2016) Insolvency and Restructuring International Vol 10 (1), p. 37.

45 Douglas G. Baird and Robert K. Rasmussen 'Private Debt and the Missing Lever of Corporate Governance' (2005–2006) *University of Pennsylvania Law Review* 154 1209, p. 1217.

46 Ibid., p. 1219.

142 *Group coordination & planning proceedings*

Nonetheless, problems may arise in that local senior creditors may also choose not to support the beneficial group plan, yet they choose to take advantage of the insolvency laws to enrich themselves. In other words, it is possible that creditors' power to exert control may be abused by senior creditors to extract value from creditors in general. The desirable group plan may not be considered, even if the group plan is to better serve creditors' interest in general. As a result, the group going concern value may be lost.

Since creditors of different subsidiaries may be of various profiles, they may not be bound collectively by one debt instrument. One possibility is that certain senior creditors of the subsidiaries would like to conduct a pre-pack sale of the subsidiaries for a quick return. If so, they may have no incentive to follow the group coordination proceeding, even though such participation will benefit the other creditors of subsidiaries. As one professor in the USA has argued, Chapter 11 of the US bankruptcy law has been a vehicle which is used not so much as a tool for resolving the 'commons' issues as for leaving the junior creditors behind.[47] Debtor-in-possession (DIP) lenders may abuse their power to require debtors to conduct a fire sale of the business as a pre-requisite of financial support.[48] These creditors' power should not be used unscrupulously, and such power requires examination by courts or monitors. Among other things, one important job the courts need to do is to examine whether the refinancing lenders try to inappropriately elevate their unsecured debts to the status of secured debts by exerting their bargaining power.[49]

All these problems are not group-specific issues. They are in fact the short-comings of refinancing mechanisms and pre-pack mechanisms. However, they are part of insolvency law, which, if applied properly, have significant value. For example, refinancing options can resolve the insolvency-specific issue – debt overhang.[50] The distressed companies may be so deeply in debt distress that they cannot invest in efficient investment to trade out of insolvency. In insolvency, the agency issue becomes acute. On the one hand, the shareholders have no incentive to invest new money to facilitate investments which may be efficient.[51] However, debtors may not be able to attract new money invested by the new creditors as they are afraid of most of the proceeds earned from the investment being obtained by the existing senior creditors. Therefore, insolvency law

---

47 Douglas G. Baird and Robert K. Rasmussen, 'Chapter 11 at Twilight' (2003–2004) *Stanford Law Review* 56 673, p. 697.

48 George W. Kuney, 'Hijacking Chapter 11' (2004–2005) *Emory Bankruptcy Developments Journal* 21 19, p. 108.

49 David A. Skeel, Jr., 'Creditors' Ball: The "New" New Corporate Governance in Chapter 11' (2003–2004) *University of Pennsylvania Law Review* 152 917, pp. 941–942.

50 Distressed debtors have difficulties raising money for further investment, which could be profitable because a large part of proceeds will be reaped by existing senior creditors. Kenneth Ayotte and David A. Skeel, Jr., 'Bankruptcy Law as a Liquidity Provider' (2013) *University of Chicago Law Review* 80 1557, p. 1571.

51 George G. Triantis, 'A Theory of the Regulation of Debtor-in-Possession Financing' (1993) *Vanderbilt Law Review* 46 901, pp. 911–912.

Group coordination & planning proceedings   143

provides incentives to attract new money, which allows distressed companies to be kept alive and to engage in efficient investment.

To mitigate the problems caused by some national restructuring tools, one may consider harmonization of insolvency law at the EU level. Harmonization of insolvency law may fix the drawbacks of national insolvency tools and may also make cooperation between courts easier due to the similarity of insolvency laws. Another modest solution is to tolerate the status quo and to consider the possibility of improving the group coordination proceedings under the existing provisions. The next section considers the harmonization first.

Problems of harmonization of insolvency laws

Regulatory competition or harmonization

The regulatory competition and harmonization are different strategies to regulate a specific area of law. In the EU treaties, the word 'harmonization' arguably means a legislative measure whereby the laws of member states can achieve the same purpose.[52] Regulatory competition is especially a phenomenon in US company law, which may either bring in best law and practice or lead to a race to the bottom.[53] In the EU, it may not be possible for regulatory competition of

---

52 Ian Fletcher and Bob Wessels, *Harmonisation of Insolvency Law in Europe* (Kluwer, Deventer 2012), p. 25; see also Walter V Gerven, 'Bringing (Private) Laws Closer to Each Other at the European Level', in F. Cafaggi (ed.), *The Institutional Framework of European Private Law* (Oxford University Press 2006), p. 45.

53 The director may choose states with loose requirements on directors or transactions to incorporate in order to benefit from them; the competition between states may incentives states to be the state with loosest requirements; on the other hand, since the poor behaviour and notorious state company law will impact the company's share value, states will be incentivised to offer shareholders more protection. This hotly debated topic may not provide a clear result regarding whether regulatory competition will be generally beneficial in the USA; see T. Zywicki, 'Is Forum Shopping Corrupting America's Bankruptcy Courts?' (2006) *Georgetown Law Journal* 94 1141, p. 1145. David A. Skeel, 'Bankruptcy Judges and Bankruptcy Venue: Some Thoughts on Delaware' (1998) *Delaware Law Review* 1 1; 'What's So Bad about Delaware' (2001) *Vanderbilt Law Review* 54 309; R. Rasmussen and R. Thomas, 'Chapter 11 Reorganization Cases and the Delaware Myth' (2002) *Vanderbilt Law Review* 55 1987. See also T. Chang and A. Scholar, 'The Effect of Judicial Bias in Chapter 11 Reorganisation' (2006) (available at: www. ssrn.com/). Lynn M. LoPucki, *Courting Failure: How Competition for Big Cases Is Corrupting the Bankruptcy Courts* (Indiana University 2005); T. Eisenberg and L. LoPucki, 'Shopping for Judges: An Empirical Analysis of Venue Choice in Large Chapter 11 Reorganizations" (1999) *Cornell Law Review* 84 967, p. 971; and L. LoPucki and S. Kalin, 'The Failure of Public Company Bankruptcies in Delaware and New York: Empirical Evidence of a "Race to the Bottom"' (2001) *Vanderbilt Law Review* 54 231, p. 264. Robert Daines, 'Does Delaware Law Improve Firm Value?' (2001) *The Journal of Financial Economics* 62 525, 533; Guhan Subramanian, 'The Influence of Antitakeover Statutes on Incorporation Choice: Evidence on the "Race" Debate and Antitakeover Overreaching' (2002) *University of Pennsylvania Law Review* 15 1795 1872. Marcel Kahan and Ehud Kamar, The Myth of State Competition in Corporate Law (2002) *Stanford Law Review* 55 679, p. 748; M. LoPucki, 'Why Are Delaware and New York Bankruptcy Reorganization Failing' (2002) *Vanderbilt Law Review* 55 1933,;

144 *Group coordination & planning proceedings*

insolvency law to appear at the US scale. Companies are not able to freely choose insolvency law by simply moving assets or forming subsidiaries in other member states. Also, the corporate tax directive[54] rules out the possibilities for member states to make profits from franchise tax as Delaware does.[55]

More essentially, Delaware's experience, which is based on competitive federalism, may not necessarily be the model for the future in the EU as the EU aims to preserve the diversity of the laws of member states and discover and learn the good sides of the others.[56] Competition in the EU is compatible with the goal of diversity in the sense that the knowledge and experience are mobilized and learned by member states from the rich diversity of the EU.[57] Member states here do not actively carry out measures to attract business while only defensively reforming their laws to prevent them from becoming unattractive to businesses. The results are positive, as shown by law reforms such as the removal of the administrative burden and simplification of the incorporation process, and reduced minimum capital requirement.[58] Therefore, the concern that that competition would be a race to the bottom in the EU may overstate the danger.

As the internal market is more integrated, the strict binding measures may not be necessary to achieve favourable ends.[59] It would be more desirable to keep the diversity of the European insolvency law in order to obtain the merits of co-evolution of member states' insolvency law. The reason is that maintaining a certain level of diversity not only mitigates the incompatibility between existing national laws and proposed uniform insolvency law but also encourages member states to update their out-of-date insolvency laws, whereby the difficulty of cooperation resulting from varying national insolvency laws in cross-border insolvency of MCGs cases is ameliorated.[60]

Regulatory competition, therefore, is a path to search for efficient and viable law on the basis of diversity and mobilized resources.[61] Insolvency law, as

---

Lucian Bebchuk, Alma Cohen and Allen Ferrell, 'Does the Evidence Favor State Competition in Corporate Law?' (2002) *California Law Review* 1775 1820–1821; Mark J. Roe, 'Delaware's Competition' (2003–2004) *Harvard Law Review* 117 588.

54 Directive 69/335/EEC of 17 July 1969, Art 2, Art 10.

55 Eva-Maria Kieninger, 'The Legal Framework of Regulatory Competition Based on Company Mobility: EU and US Compared' (2005) *German Law Journal* 6 741, p. 767.

56 Simon Deakin, 'Legal Diversity and Regulatory Competition: Which Model for Europe Centre for Business Research' University of Cambridge Working Paper No. 323 (2006), p. 15.

57 Ibid., p. 5.

58 Wolf-George Ringe, 'Corporate Mobility in the European Union – A Flash in the Pan?' (2013) University of Oslo faculty of Law Legal Studies Research Paper Series, p. 31.

59 Walter Van Gerven, 'Harmonization of Private Law: Do We Need It?' (2004) *Common Market Law Review* 41 505, p. 514.

60 Simon Deakin, 'Reflexive Governance and European Company Law' (2009) *European Law Journal*, 15(2) 224–245, p. 229.

61 Paschalis Paschalisdis, *Freedom of Establishment and Private International Law for Corporations* (Oxford University Press 2012), p. 262; Simon Deakin, 'Reflexive Governance and European Company Law' (2009) *European Law Journal*, 15(2) 224–245, p. 229.

Group coordination & planning proceedings 145

part of company law engrained in unique socio-economic culture,[62] reflects one country's political and economic features and needs; it changes along with these factors over the time.[63] The ingenuity of law makers of member states can be tested and spread in the context of competition, with the winning laws being accepted.[64]

With a mild level of competition, in the short term, member states may be able to identify the best practice developed in the EU against the guidelines, benchmark and other indicators,[65] and adjust their suitability to the situation of each member state. In the long run, the mechanism encourages the convergence of relevant policies and laws.[66] By contrast, the harmonized insolvency law may be improved and changed at a sluggish pace which cannot respond to the different needs of each member state quickly.[67] The competition of insolvency laws in the EU is more likely to result in a race to the top.

Competition may lead to forum shopping, which may cause uncertainty.[68] Though the benefit of forum shopping in the area of cross-border insolvency law is doubtful, it cannot be easily prevented. As long as the national insolvency laws are not the same, stakeholders of one company may seek favourable foreign insolvency law for themselves. Also, forum shopping itself reveals that certain member states' insolvency law is outdated or of low effectiveness so that they can take actions to learn from others' merits.[69] One may argue that in cases where the benefits are huge as a result of forum shopping, the ineffective constraint of market forces cannot discourage debtors from forum shopping.[70] Nevertheless,

---

62 Peer Zumbansen, 'Spaces Places: A Systems Theory Approach to Regulatory Competition in European Company Law' (2006) *European Law Journal* 12(4) 534–556, p. 535.

63 Wolf-George Ringe, 'Forum Shopping under the Insolvency Regulation' (2008) *European Business Organization Law Review* 9 579.

64 Gerard McCormack, 'Jurisdictional Competition and Forum Shopping in Insolvency Proceedings' (2009) *The Cambridge Law Journal* 68(01) 169–197, p. 179; see also John Armour, 'Who Should Make Corporate Law? EC Legislation Versus Regulatory Competition' (2005) *Current Legal Problems* 58 369, ECGI working paper.

65 Caroline de la Porte, 'Is the Open Method of Coordination Appropriate for Organising Activities at European Level in Sensitive Policy Areas' (2002) *European Law Journal* 8 38–58, pp. 39–40.

66 Katarzyna Gromek Broc and Rebecca Parry, *Corporate Rescue: An Overview of Recent Developments from Selected Countries in Europe* (Kluwer Law International 2004), p. 6.

67 Ian Fletcher and Bob Wessels, *Harmonisation of Insolvency Law in Europe* (Kluwer Deventerr 2012), p. 50.

68 Paul Omar, 'Modern Prospects for European Insolvency Law Harmonisation' (2015) *Global Law and Practice* (available at: www.globelawandbusiness.com/blog/Detail.aspx?g=6e989a65-610f-4de4-aaac-ad6090c6b9b8).

69 Paul Omar, 'European Insolvency Laws: Convergence or Harmonization?' (2012) *Eurofenix Spring*, p. 22.

70 Bob Wessels, 'Themes of the Future: Rescue Businesses and Cross-Border Cooperation' (2014) *Insolvency Intelligence* 4–9; see also Lucian Arye Bebchuk, 'Federalism and the Corporation: The Desirable Limits on State Competition in Corporate Law' (1991–1992) *Harvard Law Review* 105 1435, pp. 1461–1467.

146   *Group coordination & planning proceedings*

the new anti-forum shopping mechanisms in the EIR recast make such practice more difficult to conduct.[71]

The current attitude of the EU on forum shopping seems to only be against fraudulent forum shopping.[72] If creditors choose English schemes as the governing law for contracts, this implies that parties are sure that the English restructuring law may be the law to reshape the unsustainable capital structure of distressed companies.[73] One thing worth mentioning is that the schemes of arrangement only deal with holding companies without non-adjusted creditors. Moreover, these creditors are generally bound by one package of agreements. Due to financial creditors' ability to adjust their interest rates, to agree ex ante regarding further movement of companies and to vote for the change of governing law of contracts, the uncertainty of forum shopping happening in this type of company may be reduced to the lowest degree.

It is true that English schemes have already become a frequently used mechanism to restructure foreign distressed companies as similar recourses cannot be found under their local laws.[74] Member states may learn from other countries' national laws and improve their own.

Problems of harmonization of insolvency law

Relationship to other laws

Insolvency law is rooted in every country's economic and social policies, though these may be fundamentally different; without unifying the difference of these policies, the task of harmonization of substantive insolvency laws is, if not impossible, intractable.[75] In other words, insolvency law is a node which links many other areas of law, such as employment law and secured credit law, and simply harmonizing the insolvency law in the EU may not be enough without touching other branches of law.[76] Even though rescue culture is generally prevalent in the EU, member states adopt distinct approaches to try to adapt their insolvency law to the other areas of law.[77]

Different countries still have different thoughts on design of insolvency or rescue proceedings to achieve different goals and offer varying levels of protection

---

71 See 3.2.3 Regulatory view on forum shopping.

72 C-339/07 Seagon v. Dekomarty Belgium NV 2009; Jennifer Payne, *Scheme of Arrangement, Theory Structure and Operation* (Cambridge University Press 2014), p. 322.

73 Jennifer Payne, *Scheme of Arrangement, Theory Structure and Operation* (Cambridge University Press 2014), p. 322.

74 Ibid., p. 322.

75 Thomas M. Gaa, 'Harmonization of International Bankruptcy Law and Practice: Is It Necessary? Is It Possible?' (1993) *The International Lawyer* (1993) 27(4) 881–909, p. 893.

76 Christoph G Paulus, 'Global Insolvency Law and the Role of Multinational Institutions' (2006–2007) *Brooklyn Journal of International Law* 32 755, p. 765.

77 Ibid., p. 765.

Group coordination & planning proceedings   147

to stakeholders in an insolvency context.[78] Also, the existing legal structure and rules may become impediments to the new uniform insolvency law.[79]

Since insolvency law is closely related to many other areas of law, it can only be understood with reference to other laws. Law of this kind needs explanation from the meanings of other laws, so it is not enough to harmonize insolvency law alone.[80] Also, law manifests the social norms, so from the perspective of importing countries, it may be difficult to absorb and understand newly created or imported concepts.[81]

Harmonization of insolvency mechanisms, such as refinancing rules or prepack sales rules, may encounter the objection of local lawyers and judges as they are reluctant to accept unfamiliar and untested concepts and doctrines.[82] What is more, insolvency law is developed in a path dependence way; it is better to make existing law adapt to the needs of new demands than to set up completely new regimes.[83]

---

78 Ibid., p. 765.

79 Lucian Arye Bebchuk and Mark J. Roe, 'A Theory of Path Dependence in Corporate Ownership and Governance' Working Paper No. 131 (1999).

80 Katharina Pistor, 'The Standardization of Law and Its Effect on Developing Economies' (2002) *The American Journal of Comparative Law* 50(1), p. 107.

81 For example, insolvency law is closely connected to corporate law. In a country which adopts manager-driven reorganization mechanisms, such as debtor in possession regime in the USA, it usually embraces a dispersed share ownership structure; in the countries embracing manager-displacing reorganization regimes, generally a concentrated share ownership structure will be widely adopted. The reason accounting for this phenomenon is that concentrated shareholders will have strong influence to affect decision-making of the companies at the expense of creditors, which increases the agency cost of creditors, such as monitoring cost. For this reason, to react to the concentrated shareholding, the type of debts is usually concentrated debts, such as bank loans. Therefore, banks can gain more power to obtain information and conduct monitoring. As influential shareholders may affect the managers who lead the company to insolvency, the manage-displacing regime is adopted for reorganization purpose. On the aspect of diffused type of shareholding, it makes individual shareholder difficult to exploit creditors' interests by making risky investments, so that the monitoring cost is lower than concentrated shareholding companies. As a result, companies of this type can borrow public debts at a cheaper price. As managers of the latter type may be in a relatively neutral position without influence of shareholders, it may be beneficial to keep them in the reorganization process due to their knowledge of the business. John Armour, Brian R. Cheffins and David A. Skeel, Jr., 'Corporate Ownership Structure and the Evolution of Bankruptcy Law: Lessons from the United Kingdom' (2002) *Vanderbilt Law Review* 55 1699, pp. 1701–1765; Katharina Pistor, 'The Standardization of Law and Its Effect on Developing Economies' (2002) *The American Journal of Comparative Law* 50(1) 97–130, pp. 111–112.

82 Gerard McCormack, *Secured Credit and the Harmonisation of Law, the UNCITRAL Experience* (Edward Elgar Publishing Limited 2011), p. 49.

83 The existing rules will affect the new development of rules. For example, the new development of corporate rules is built on previous rules. See Lucian Arye Bebchuk and Mark J. Roe, 'A Theory of Path Dependence in Corporate Ownership and Governance' (1999) (available at: http://papers.ssrn.com/paper.taf?abstract_id=192414), p. 23; see Gerard McCormack, *Secured Credit and the Harmonisation of Law, the UNCITRAL Experience* (Edward Elgar Publishing Limited 2011), p. 49.

148　*Group coordination & planning proceedings*

Harmonization of insolvency law may remove obstacles of divergence of laws, and it facilitates business; it also builds up neutral law which is acceptable to member states; the law may fill in the gaps of some member states if they did not have the equivalent before.[84] However, the negotiation of the content of the harmonized law may be prolonged and costly; difficulties exist in which member states may not ratify the new law.[85]

The danger of being captured

Capture theory provides a useful tool to explain why the uniformity of insolvency law is in danger of being captured by interest groups. The theory views regulations as products demanded by the interest groups to act in their own interests rather than in the public interest.[86] Such interest groups enjoy comparable advantages so that they can influence legislation more than the ungrouped individuals.[87]

The existing laws are the products of political bargaining, reflecting the advantageous interest groups' favour. When changes of law are not in the interests of advantageous interest groups, they may object to such changes by using their power to prevent them.[88] The priority of creditors is an example that can hardly be harmonized at the EU level as the unique ranking of priority is the manifestation of the power of each interest group. The preference of senior creditors and managers of member states may share common ground in that they prefer their interests to be enhanced by regimes such as pre-pack administration.

Just as national legislation could be captured by interest groups, legislation process at the international level can also fall victims to interest groups' capture.[89] The redistributive nature of insolvency law creates difficulties with full harmonization of insolvency law. Such radical changes will reshuffle the balance of values that each state prioritizes. Also, full harmonization of insolvency law has the possibility of being captured by the interest groups (senior creditors

---

84 Paul B. Stephan, 'The Futility of Unification and Harmonization in International Commercial Law' (1999) (available at: http://papers.ssrn.com/paper.taf?abstract_id=169209), pp. 2–7; Loukas Mistelis, 'Is Harmonisation a Necessary Evil? The Future of Harmonisation and New Sources of International Trade Law' (2001) (available at: cisgw3.law.pace.edu/ Sweet and Maxwell), p. 19.

85 Loukas Mistelis, 'Is Harmonisation a Necessary Evil? The Future of Harmonisation and New Sources of International Trade Law' (2001) cisgw3.law.pace.edu/ Sweet and Maxwell, p. 21.

86 Richard A. Posner, 'Theories of Economic Regulation', (1974) *The Bell Journal of Economics and Management Science* 5(2) 335–358, pp. 335–336.

87 Sidney A. Shapiro, 'The Complexity of Regulatory Capture: Diagnosis, Causality and Remediation' (2012) *Roger Williams University Law Review* 17 221, p. 225.

88 Lucian Arye Bebchuk and Mark J. Roe, 'A Theory of Path Dependence in Corporate Ownership and Governance' Working Paper No. 131 (1999) (available at: http://papers.ssrn.com/ paper.taf?abstract_id=192414), p. 26.

89 Gerard McCormack, *Secured Credit and the Harmonisation of Law, the UNCITRAL Experience* (Edward Elgar Publishing Limited 2011), p. 35.

and big law firms) who could influence the proposed model of the harmonized insolvency law.[90]

The capture activities are fuelled by the self-interest of interest groups so that they shape the legislation in their own interest, irrespective of the interest of the public.[91] The political power of these interest groups is considered by the legislators as they know that if they deliver on interest groups' demands, they have a better chance of being re-elected.[92] As a result, the regulations may be demanded and shaped in favour of interest groups.[93]

Interest groups usually have significant interests in the legislation results; they are generally small groups of people who can be easily organized.[94] These features not only provide them with the incentive to capture the regulation but also make interest groups suitable to exert their influence. Unlike interest groups, the vast majority of people have very weak incentive and power to influence legislation as each person can only share a tiny percentage of the total benefit but will incur huge costs to do so.[95]

In the cross-border insolvency context, the interest groups may be banks or legal professionals. Senior creditors who hold large claims, such as banks, have strong incentives and the political power needed to shape legislation.[96] Insolvency lawyers also have very strong influence to shape the bankruptcy law legislative process: for example, with regard to the scope and substance of the bankruptcy law.[97] Also it has long been recognized that professionals play important roles in insolvency law reforms.[98] Certain professionals engaged in the legislative processes: for example, drafting the European Economic Council Bankruptcy Convention.[99] Also, it is not surprising to see legal professionals become regulators or regulators become legal professionals; some even do both

---

90 Emilie Ghio, 'European Insolvency Law: Development Harmonisation and Reform, a Case Study on the European Internal Market' (2015) *Trinity College Law Review* 18 154, p. 179.

91 David A. Skeel, Jr., 'Book review: Public Choice and the Future of Public-Choice-Influenced Legal Scholarship' (1997) *Vanderbilt Law Review* 50 647, p. 651.

92 Sidney A. Shapiro, 'The Complexity of Regulatory Capture: Diagnosis, Causality and Remediation' (2012) *Roger Williams University Law Review* 17 221, p. 226.

93 George J. Stigler, 'The Theory of Economic Regulation' (1971) *The Bell Journal of Economics and Management Science* 2(1) 3–21, p. 3.

94 Andrew T. Guzman, 'Choice of Law: New Foundations' (2001–2002) *The Georgetown Law Journal* 90 883, p. 902.

95 Ibid., p. 902.

96 David A. Skeel, Jr., 'Bankruptcy Lawyers and the Shape of American Bankruptcy Law' (1998–1999) *Fordham Law Review* 67 497, p. 508.

97 Ibid. (for example, the article explains how influential the American bankruptcy lawyers are to influence legislative development and to limit other players to provide insolvency law expertise).

98 Law society and the General Council of Bar organized legal professions together. Bruce G. Carruthers and Terence C. Halliday, 'Professionals in Systemic Reform of Bankruptcy Law: The 1978 US Bankruptcy Code and the UK Insolvency Act 1986' (2000) *The American Bankruptcy Institute Law Review* 74 35, p. 61.

99 Bruce G. Carruthers and Terence C. Halliday, 'Professionals in Systemic Reform of Bankruptcy Law: The 1978 US Bankruptcy Code and the UK Insolvency Act 1986' (2000) *The American Bankruptcy Institute Law Review* 74 35, p. 61.

150 *Group coordination & planning proceedings*

at the same time.[100] Regulators sometimes subordinate to the banks as regulators know that they could seek bribes or long-term benefits, such as future job opportunities.[101]

Insolvency law is an area fraught with complexity and technical mechanisms; the uniform process of insolvency restructuring law may be more likely to turn on the interests of experts and sophisticated creditors who have notable interests and knowledge.[102] The capture is more likely to happen where the law contains a redistributive nature, such as in insolvency law and asymmetry of power between interest groups and diffused parties[103]; compared to well-organized interest groups, the public faces a serious collective action problem which makes the people unable even to recognize that the harmonized insolvency law is skewed in favour of interest groups.[104]

There are many NGOs and experts that have the expertise and financial strength to participate in the legislative process.[105] The number of NGOs and experts are much higher than before, and they may be backed up by certain states or interest groups; in many cases, their voices are influential in shaping the law.[106] Professionals, such as judges and lawyers, have a large stake in the law reform and harmonization. The result of harmonization will expand the scope of professionals' activities. The complexity of international cases will provide them with higher income and reputation, and society will rely on them more than before.[107]

To modernize restructuring law of EU member states, the interest groups may be in favour of certain types of rules which can provide them with more power and benefits. One example is a group-wide pre-pack sale. In the pre-pack sale of business, involuntary creditors, such as environmental creditors, may be in danger of losing power that they could have enjoyed in ordinary business reorganization proceedings.[108] Senior creditors are able to exert strong influence in a debt restructuring process and reorganization process using many

---

100 Anita Anand, 'Large Law Firms and Capture: Towards a Nuanced Understanding of Self-regulation' (2013), pp. 492–493 (available at: http://ssrn.com/abstract=2616883).

101 Gerard Caprio, Jr., 'Regulatory Capture: Why It Occurs, How to Minimize It' (2013–2014) *The North Carolina Banking Institute* 18 39, p. 45.

102 Edward J. Janger, 'Predicting when the Uniform Law Process will Fail: Article 9, Capture and the Race to the Bottom' (1998) *Iowa Law Review* 83 569, p. 6.

103 Ibid., p. 19.

104 Ibid., p. 19.

105 Gerard McCormack, *Secured Credit and the Harmonisation of Law, the UNCITRAL Experience* (Edward Elgar Publishing Limited 2011), p. 8.

106 Ibid., p. 8. One example could be 'France's observations on UNCITRAL's working methods' UN Doc A/CN 9/635 2007.

107 Paul B. Stephan, 'The Futility of Unification and Harmonization in International Commercial Law' (1999), pp. 32–33, http://papers.ssrn.com/paper.taf?abstract_id=169209.

108 Stephanie Ben-Ishai and Stephen J. Lubben, 'Involuntary Creditors and Corporate Bankruptcy' (2012) *UBC Law Review* 45 253 (providing evidence that the environmental creditors lose their power to vote against the pre-pack plan, as a result, the senior creditors and the debtors may redistribute their value to secured parties).

Group coordination & planning proceedings 151

methods.[109] One good example is a DIP loan provided by the creditors to debtors. As debtors more often than not desperately need a source of financing, a DIP agreement could significantly increase creditors' bargaining power such that senior creditors could use covenants therein to control almost everything, such as the content of the reorganization plan.[110] DIP loans can also prevent shareholders from changing the control of the board as this will trigger the default the loans.[111]

By the same token, senior creditors may favour the practice of using schemes and pre-pack to prevent junior creditors from competing with them for proceeds of assets. As debtors control the power of determining who should be brought into a proposed scheme,[112] the debtors and senior creditors may use this power to leave junior creditors out of the schemes.[113] One should note that the pre-pack sale may not necessarily increase the value of sale (in some cases, around one fifth of the value may be lost), but it may be applied as a tool to redistribute value.[114]

The above favourable schemes with pre-pack rules can be used to achieve the cross-class cram down; the junior creditors can still be left in the worthless insolvent company, while the assets are transferred to a new company formed by senior creditors.[115] Examples can be shown by the In re Bluebrook Ltd case[116] and the MyTravel case.[117]

The MyTravel case concerned a business transfer from insolvency debtor to new companies. Junior creditors were not offered the chance to participate in the scheme as they were unaffected by the scheme. As a result, these junior creditors were left in the worthless shell company.[118] In the first instance, Mann J applied liquidation value as the basis to measure the value of business since there were no alternative options for the company without schemes. As a result, the junior creditors were completely out of money. Mann J's view may have ignored the fact

---

109 See generally Jonathan C. Lipson, 'The Shadow Bankruptcy System' (2009) *Boston University International Law Journal* 89 1609; see also a study done by Michelle M. Harnert and Jamie Marincic, 'Behind Closed Doors: The Influence of Creditors in Business Reorganizations' (2010–2011) *The Seattle University Law Review* 34 1155.

110 Douglas G. Baird and Robert K. Rasmussen, 'Private Debt and the Missing Lever of Corporate Governance' (2005–2006) *University of Pennsylvania Law Review* 154 1209, p. 1239.

111 Ibid., p. 1240.

112 Unaffected creditors may not be consulted as the proposed schemes do not try to modify their rights.

113 Jennifer Payne, *Scheme of Arrangement, Theory Structure and Operation* (Cambridge University Press 2014), p. 42.

114 Lynn M. LoPucki, *Courting Failure: How Competition for Big Cases Is Corrupting the Bankruptcy Courts* (The University of Michigan Press 2006) p. 109.

115 Jennifer Payne, *Scheme of Arrangement, Theory Structure and Operation* (Cambridge University Press 2014) pp. 44–45.

116 In re Bluebrook [2009] EWHC 2114 (Ch).

117 In re MyTravel Group [2004] EWHC 2741 (Ch).

118 Ibid.

152   *Group coordination & planning proceedings*

that the company was preparing for restructuring. A going concern valuation may therefore be more appropriate.[119]

The re Bluebrook Ltd case involves a similar practice. The senior creditors planned to get rid of junior creditors by way of a business transfer sale. Only the senior creditors were entitled to a debt to equity swap, whereas the junior creditors were not offered anything as the scheme did not seek to change their original rights.[120] When the junior creditors went to court to reject the schemes, the court held that at the basis of going concern valuation, the junior creditors were out of money, so their rejection was not supported.[121]

In the Bluebrook case the court made it clear that going concern valuation should be the proper method to value companies in restructuring process. This decision tempered the inappropriateness of liquidation valuation method in the MyTravel case.[122] However, Mann J in the Bluebrook case also held that to decide whether junior creditors' economic interests were affected, one only needs to consider whether junior creditors have interests in scheme companies; their interests are not measured against the broader backdrop of the restructuring, i.e. one needs not calculate whether they may have interests in the new companies to which the business of the old company was transferred.[123] Therefore, junior creditors may be left in a worthless company if going concern valuation evidence shows that they are unaffected as they have no interest in the insolvent companies.

As a result, it is possible that a group-wide pre-pack may be designed as a result of the harmonization of insolvency law at the EU level, which becomes a tool for senior creditors to exploit junior creditors.

A recommendation

In this section, the book provides a modest recommendation which could be seen as a limit on the invocation of the opt-out mechanism in the group coordination proceedings. The recommendation is that insolvency practitioners of the financially distressed companies in the same group should have an obligation to communicate with each other and consider a group rescue plan along with individual rescue plan at an early stage. This limitation on the opt-out mechanism comes from an interpretation of the Recital 5 and Article 56 of the EIR recast. 'A modest recommendation for group coordination proceeding' will introduce the

---

119 Chi-Ling Seah, 'The Re Tea Corporation Principle and Junior Creditors' Rights to Participate in a Scheme of Arrangement – A View from Singapore' (2011) *International Insolvency Review* 20 161–183, p. 167.

120 Jennifer Payne, *Scheme of Arrangement, Theory Structure and Operation* (Cambridge University Press 2014), p. 42.

121 In re Bluebrook [2009] EWHC 2114 (Ch).

122 Claire Pointing and Adam Rooney, 'IMO Clears up My Travel Issue' (2009) Insolvency Intelligence, p. 50.

123 Ibid., p. 50.

Group coordination & planning proceedings 153

extent and contour of this recommendation, and explain why it can be achieved by interpretation. 'The benefits of the recommendation' will further enunciate the reasons and benefits of this recommendation.

A modest recommendation for group coordination proceedings

The problem of the opt-out mechanism in group coordination proceedings is that if such an opt-out mechanism can be exerted free of restraints, it is likely that local senior creditors who can control certain group member companies will refuse to consider group rescue plan but pursue their own interests.[124] The consequence may be that the group going concern value will dissipate, and creditors of each subsidiary will suffer a loss.

However, it appears that insolvency practitioners should not exert such opt-out power free of any constraint, as Recital 58[125] and Article 56[126] in the EIR recast together require insolvency practitioners to consider group options at an early stage. Two important components can be drawn from Recital 58 and Article 56 of EIR recast: one is that insolvency practitioners should consider group options or communicate to the other insolvency practitioners to discuss the possibilities of group options; another is that they should do so at an early stage.[127] As a result, insolvency practitioners of distressed companies should at least consider the possibilities of group rescue plan before opting for the individual rescue plan. The context that these two provisions operate also supports this view. The EIR recast prescribes that insolvency practitioners in each subsidiary shall exchange information and consider the possibilities of coordination plans and restructuring plans.[128] Also, other insolvency practitioners should be informed at an early stage of the main content of coordination for the purpose of coordination proceedings.[129] At the same time, Article 72(2) gives coordinators the power to request information from other courts and explain their group coordination plan to other courts and creditor meetings. All these provisions could be considered limitations of opt-out mechanisms as insolvency practitioners in each member company of the same group have the obligation to consider the possibilities of a group plan at the time of considering the individual rescue plan. They therefore need to communicate to and inform insolvency practitioners in other member companies regarding the possibilities of group plan at an early stage.

---

124 See 'Problems of group coordination proceedings'.
125 Recital 58 of EIR recast 2015 states, '*in order to allow the insolvency practitioners involved to take an informed decision on participation in the group coordination proceedings, they should be informed at an early stage of the essential elements of the coordination*'.
126 Article 56 of EIR recast 2015 says that insolvency practitioners should '*consider whether possibilities exist for restructuring group members which are subject to insolvency proceedings and, if so, coordinate with regard to the proposal and negotiation of a coordinated restructuring plan*'.
127 See EIR recast 2015 recital 58 and article 56.
128 EIR recast Article 56.
129 EIR recast Recital 56.

154   *Group coordination & planning proceedings*

This obligation can be drawn from a purposive interpretation of Recital 58 and Article 56, even though they are not provisions in the section of group coordination proceedings. A purposive interpretation approach is increasingly endorsed and applied by the UK courts as the primary statutory interpretation approach which aims to explain the meaning of provisions by analysing the underpinning purposes of legislators.[130] This method is also dominantly employed by ECJ as a means of interpretation.[131] In other words, the ECJ will take into account the consequences of the interpretation and the purposes of one given legislation.[132]

The purposes and the underlying objectives of EIR recast allow this interpretation. There are two main objectives in the EIR recast: one is to facilitate effective and efficient administration of insolvency proceedings; another is to avoid fraudulent forum shopping.[133] Effective and efficient administration of insolvency proceeding requires cross-border insolvency proceedings to be able to maximize the return to creditors,[134] while forum shopping prevention, among other things, can be seen as a way of ensuring creditors' protection. In the case where creditors in a given insolvent group agree to cooperate with each other, a well-functioning group coordination framework may reduce the need to conduct procedural consolidation by forum shopping, which, in turn, avoids the drawbacks of it.[135] More importantly, without any constraint on the invocation of opt-out mechanisms, the group going concern value may be torn apart if uncooperative controlling creditors in certain financially distressed subsidiaries refuse to support a group rescue plan without any justification. Since the goal of preservation of going concern value is the value pursued by both EIR recast and corporate rescue law, this interpretation is in line with the purposes behind the legislations. As a result, Recital 58 and Article 56 provide a general obligation that every insolvency practitioner should respect, even without the opening of group coordination proceedings.

---

130 Gary Wilson, *English Legal System* (2nd edn, Pearson Education Limited 2014), p. 56.

131 Nial Fennelly, 'Legal Interpretation at the European Court of Justice' (1996) *Fordham International Law Journal* 20(3) 656, pp. 656, 657.

132 Giulio Itzcovich, 'The Interpretation of Community Law by the European Court of Justice' (2009) *German Law Journal* 10(05) 537–560, p. 555.

133 See Recital 3 and 5 EIR recast 2015.

134 Horst. Eidenmüller, 'Abuse of Law in the Context of European Insolvency Law' (2009) *European Company and Financial Law Review* 6 1–28, p. 14. See also Rolef J. de Weijs, 'Comimigration: Use or Abuse of European Insolvency Law?' (2014) *European Company and Financial Law Review* 11(4), p. 14. Effectiveness and efficiency can be inferred as the ability of the insolvency proceedings to the cost and to preserve the going concern value. See proposal for a Directive of the European Parliament and of the Council on preventive restructuring frameworks, second chance and measures to increase the efficiency of restructuring, insolvency and discharge procedures and amending Directive 2012/30/EU Strasbourg, 22.11.2016 COM(2016) 723 final p. 5.

135 As argued in Chapter 3, procedural consolidation may not only destroy the value of the group, but also impose externality on the creditors who do not expect the whole process.

Group coordination & planning proceedings 155

However, it does not mean that insolvency practitioners should always defer to the group rescue plan. The recitals of the EIR recast have made it clear that the group coordination aims to provide efficient administration for groups of companies, and the opt-out mechanism aims to respect the legal personality of each entity in the same group.[136] In other words, the EIR recast tries to strike a balance between certainty, which requires the law to respect creditors' protection of each member company, and maximization of the group going concern value.

The opt-out mechanism reflects this aim due to its voluntary nature. Creditors of one company in the group know that at the time of advancing credit, their interest will not be mixed with creditors of other group subsidiaries as group coordination proceedings respect each entity in the same group.[137] On the other hand, insolvency practitioners do not need to follow the coordinator's plan as long as they have good reasons for doing it.[138]

Opting out of a group rescue plan is not necessarily an issue, if it can be used correctly. When a subsidiary decides to opt out of the group plan, it may reveal that its share of the group going concern value is not large enough to cover the loss of that subsidiary. Also, the rejection of inclusion may reveal that the subsidiaries are undervalued. An example would be that local creditors or other investors who have better information regarding the assets of the subsidiaries (such as its business networks with local partners or its mandate for research and development head office function) would like to pay a high price to purchase the subsidiary. All this information may not be available to the parent company, which focusses on cash management or other financial tasks.

However, the local rescue plans may not always be in the interests of all the creditors of the subsidiaries. It is in this latter case that one needs to be cautious in that the recovery rate from the local insolvency plan which is abused by the local senior creditors or investors may be lower than that of group plan as the latter could release the group going concern value offered by the coordinator. At the same time that the certainty of the group coordination proceeding is hailed, its efficacy is doubted, especially against the background, when certain creditors can exert strong control over the distressed companies. As the above sections have mentioned, since senior creditors and investors can gain control of distressed companies by refinancing contracts or loan to own debt trading, the result can render a group plan dampened due to their uncooperative and abusive strategies. Particularly, in the groups of companies context, without necessary limitations on the invocation of opt-out mechanisms provided by the group coordination proceedings, the group plan cannot be expected to be respected by certain powerful creditors in subsidiaries, even if the group plan can better serve the creditors in general. The voluntary nature of the opt-out mechanism makes it too easy for subsidiaries to opt out of the group rescue plan without even

---

136 Recital 54–57 of EIR recast 2015.
137 Respecting entity law is also consistent with the corporate rescue law theory discussed in Chapter 2.
138 Article 70 in EIR recast 2015.

156   *Group coordination & planning proceedings*

considering the possibility. Even in the case where the group plan has been proposed, one insolvency practitioner appointed by one subsidiary can still choose to opt out.

On the legislation level, it would be welcome if the problems of certain rules, such as refinancing or pre-pack, could be improved.[139] However, to avoid the abusive usage of opt-out, these are not enough. As long as group members have different views regarding rescue, and the creditors' profiles are varying, the coordination is difficult to achieve.

To achieve the goals of preservation of group going concern value, the opt-out mechanism should not be invoked without any limitations or scrutiny. The aim is not to coerce the subsidiaries to follow the group reorganization plan. In fact, the aim is to make sure the individual plans and the group plan are both considered by insolvency practitioners, so a better option can be selected. The final decision-making power is still vested in the insolvency practitioners of each company in the same group. However, insolvency practitioners of subsidiaries could make a wiser decision based on more information and gain more rescue options by comparing the group plan and individual plans at an early stage. Therefore, the suggested interpretation is consistent with the purposes of EIR recast, and it can strike a good balance between the goal of preservation of going concern value and the protection of creditors of individual company in a group. The next section will consider the main benefits of the recommendation.

The benefits of the recommendation

As the last section has argued, insolvency practitioners of financially distressed subsidiaries should bear an obligation to consider group rescue options at an early stage. Considering group rescue options at an early stage has three benefits.

The first benefit is that such interpretation can reduce information asymmetry so that insolvency practitioners of different companies in the same group can make better decisions regarding what to do, and this is in the best interest of the creditors of the subsidiaries to which they are appointed. More information provides at least two merits. One is that the information relating to the insolvency or financial difficulties of some companies can be passed to other subsidiaries or parent company so that a timely group rescue plan may be considered early. Another merit is that more information can reveal the value of subsidiaries and increase the competition between group bidders and subsidiaries' bidders.

As parent companies may allocate certain head office functions to their subsidiaries, subsidiaries may have better information than parent companies in regard

---

139 Under some countries' insolvency law, courts may play a role in examining the refinancing terms, such as roll-up and cross-collateralization and loan to own strategies, that need to be scrutinized carefully as they can be employed to redistribute assets from junior creditors to senior creditors. Legislators also put in effort to fixing the weakness of pre-pack. See US bankruptcy courts. David A. Skeel, Jr., 'The Past, Present and Future of Debtor-in-Possession Financing' (2003–2004) *Cardozo Law Review* 25 1905, p. 1907.

Group coordination & planning proceedings 157

to how to keep subsidiaries operating in viable ways.[140] It is possible that subsidiaries may have a basic understanding of the value of themselves, such as the valuable employees and relationships with key suppliers.[141] Similarly, coordinators and group bidders may have better information regarding the value of the whole group. The information they possess may allow them to value the subsidiaries against the backdrop of the group going concern value.

The communication of all relevant information between insolvency practitioners of subsidiaries and insolvency practitioners who propose group coordination proceedings is desirable. The information of insolvency practitioners who aim to open a group proceeding may provide clues regarding whether the group going concern value exists and whether it is large enough to cover the cost of coordination. Insolvency practitioners have options including joining in a group plan to benefit from the group going concern value or taking an individual rescue plan to avoid an implausibly costly group plan. Therefore, insolvency practitioners have to compare and assess whether the group plan is a better option to the company in which they are appointed.

The group plan may benefit creditors in the subsidiaries by preservation of group going concern value. If the going concern value is large, the group plan may offer a higher price for the subsidiary than the price of a local reorganization plan. By competition, which offer is better becomes clear. Where the benefit of a group plan is obvious, local senior creditors' opt-out is difficult to justify and support.

Where the deal requires courts' approval, courts should not approve the individual plan if evidence clearly shows that the group plan will offer unsecured creditors of those subsidiaries a better recovery. The local senior creditors may argue that a much higher value should be assigned to one subsidiary. Assuming the group bidders give up purchasing the subsidiary, the higher price that the local senior creditors have claimed from group bidders will make more junior creditors become in-the-money creditors who will share with those hold-out senior creditors.

By considering the group plan, information can be shared with other insolvency practitioners or debtors in possession, and more potential bidders may be identified. This to some extent rectifies the transparency problems of pre-pack as debtors may only disclose information to cherry-picked stakeholders while leaving other creditors with nothing.[142] Considering the group option via communication encourages more information to be exchanged so that the relevant parties and courts can make better options based on more information. Also, it reduces the level of local creditors' control as other insolvency practitioners may provide better offers and challenge the local rescue plan. This, in turn, provides

140 See Chapter 3 regarding the allocation of head office functions in MCGs.
141 See Chapter 2 regarding 'group going concern value'.
142 Horst Eidenmüller and Kristin van Zwieten, 'Restructuring the European Business Enterprise: The EU Commission Recommendation on a New Approach to Business Failure and Insolvency' (2015) ECGI Working Paper 301, p. 13.

158 *Group coordination & planning proceedings*

directors and other stakeholders confidence to enter into insolvency proceedings.[143] More plans and discussions based on the information so disclosed would make the reorganization more transparent.[144] The opinions of representatives of other junior creditors are also critical for the debtors and courts to make sound judgements regarding the option of rescue plans and valuation of the business.[145] Coordinators can be seen as neutral parties[146] who facilitate the group option and monitor the undesirable individual rescue options.

The second benefit is that an early consideration of group rescue option can reduce the strategic opportunism exerted, especially by local bidders. As information asymmetry may be abused by either group bidders or local senior creditors to gain benefit for themselves, this obligation allows creditors or insolvency practitioners to make better decisions. Group bidders may consider the value of a whole group on the basis of a group going concern valuation. The group bidders may want to pay a higher price than the local bidders. Similarly, it is possible that local senior creditors will have access to locally available information, which may indicate that the value of a subsidiary is even larger than the group bidders expected. For the purpose of protection of local interests, the insolvency practitioners or local senior creditors may persuade group bidders to increase the value. If such locally available information is disclosed, it is possible that the group bidders will accept a higher price. Even though the group bidders may still reject the suggested local price, this may be used as a reference price which prevents local senior creditors from deliberately selling the subsidiary at a much lower price in a future pre-pack sale in an individual rescue plan.

Local senior creditors or investors who decide to opt out of the group coordination proceedings may have an incentive to block the flow of information relevant to the true value of the subsidiaries against local junior creditors and other stakeholders. When the negotiation comes to the table of general local creditors, local senior creditors may have an incentive to undervalue the subsidiaries so as to extract value, such as what may happen in a pre-pack. By contrast, when the deal happens between local senior creditors and group bidders, local senior creditors or investors may overestimate the value of subsidiaries with the aim of striking a better deal with the bidders who wish to purchase the whole group.

The difference of the two prices may be remarkable since the local senior creditors may only have incentive to benefit themselves either by extracting value from others or by hold-out. A possible solution is facilitating the exchange of information and communication between relevant group companies so that the true value of an individual subsidiary and the value of the group can be revealed.

---

143 Harvey R. Miller, 'Chapter 11 in Transition – From Boom to Bust and Into the Future' (2007) *American Bankruptcy Law Journal* 81 375, p. 384.

144 Michelle M. Harner and Jamie Marincic, 'Behind Closed Doors: The Influence of Creditors in Business Reorganizations' (2010–2011) *The Seattle University Law Review* 34 1155, p. 1181.

145 Ibid., p. 1182.

146 Similar to ABI commission's idea to appoint a neutral party for the pre-pack deals to monitor the process. See ABI Commission to study the reform of Chapter 11 2014, p. 6.

Group coordination & planning proceedings 159

Therefore, local insolvency practitioners' information may be used to prevent one individual subsidiary from being undervalued by the potential bidders for the whole group. Also, information of coordinators or group bidders can prevent local senior creditors from deliberately selling the subsidiaries that they have controlled at undervalue prices. Whether they decide to join or refuse the group plan, insolvency practitioners should consider it when they consider the individual reorganization plans. After a holistic consideration, they may decide to turn down the group plan or individual plan based on a scrupulous judgement.

The third benefit of considering a group rescue option at an early stage is the requirement of corporate rescue practice, especially the pre-pack sale practice. When the group rescue plan is considered too late, many important stakeholders, such as suppliers of subsidiaries and important employees, may flee.[147] Also, due to the knock-on effect or cross-default covenants, one subsidiary's default may cause other group companies to default. As a result, insolvency practitioners may quickly lose control of the companies in the group, whereas the senior creditors may gain leverage quickly and pursue their interests at the expense of other creditors.[148]

Also, it can prevent a fire sale conducted by pre-pack practice which only benefits senior creditors. In many cases, the parent companies are the first to know the financial difficulties of the group compared to the operating subsidiaries. As parent companies are generally the companies that arrange financing on behalf of the group, they may possess the best financial information. In these cases, the group coordination proceedings may be opened at the court where the parent companies are based. For each subsidiary, the task of the insolvency practitioners is to consider whether the group option offers subsidiaries a better option. It is also possible that the debts of the group are not arranged at the holding companies level so that the parent company has no informational advantages. Therefore, the individual rescue option may be negotiated prior to the group rescue option.

Taking a pre-pack sale case as an example, the creditors of subsidiaries may choose to execute a fast sale of the subsidiaries without considering the group plan. The pre-pack is notorious for a lack of transparency, creditors' protection[149] and limited marketing.[150] When organizing a pre-pack sale for a subsidiary, the insolvency practitioners of other group member companies may not know about it. When the plan has been drafted, the administrator can execute it immediately

---

147 See general Melissa B. Jacoby and Edward J. Janger, 'Ice Cube Bonds: Allocating the Price of Process in Chapter 11 Bankruptcy' (2014) *The Yale Law Journal* 123(4) 862.

148 Chris Howard and Bob Hedge, *Restructuring Law and Practice* (2nd edn, LNUK 2014), Chapter 2, pp. 33–52.

149 Especially in the UK, the pre-pack sale could be done without creditors' and courts' approval. The Netherlands and the USA require the court approval; however, the abuses in pre-pack cases still exist. Ramon Smits, 'Supervision and Efficiency of the Pre-Pack: An Anglo-Dutch Comparison' (2016) *International Corporate Rescue* 13(1) 13–15, p. 35.

150 Tom Astle, 'Pack Up Your Troubles: Addressing the Negative Image of Pre-Packs' (2015) *Insolvency Intelligence* 28 72–74, pp. 1–2.

160   *Group coordination & planning proceedings*

after he is appointed out of court. This leaves other parties with no time to challenge it or offers a group rescue solution.

Such interpretation corresponds to national insolvency law as well. Taking the UK as an example, the third version of the statement of insolvency practice 16[151] requires the administrator to decide whether it is appropriate to conduct a pre-pack sale for the creditors in general rather than for the managers or purchasers.[152] Administrators not only need to carry out broad marketing for the sale of the business but also need to disclose information to the creditors to the extent that informed creditors can judge whether the pre-pack is a good solution for the company.[153] One may therefore argue that without considering the group plan, it is difficult for the administrator of one subsidiary to make the final judgement that saving the subsidiary individually is best in the interest of all the creditors of that subsidiary. The administrators may skip broad marketing which may solicit purchasers who would like to pay a price reflecting the group going concern value. The consequence is that the creditors of that subsidiary will not receive the possible surplus from the group going concern value.

With such interpretation in mind, certain abuses of the opt-out mechanism may be mitigated. Taking the pre-pack of one subsidiary as an example, in a typical UK pre-pack case, the insolvency plan is generally negotiated between certain senior creditors and debtors before the appointment of an administrator. Immediately or shortly after the appointment of the administrator, the administrator is able to sell the assets of the debtor to the purchaser before the creditors' meeting.[154] Assume that such a pre-pack sale plan is negotiated by the senior creditors and directors with the involvement of the would-be administrators. As the administrators have to execute the deal later, they need to provide enough evidence to explain why the pre-pack plan of the subsidiary is the best solution. If they have an obligation to communicate the information to other insolvency practitioners or DIP, and to consider a group restructuring plan at an earlier stage under the EIR recast, their report is not convincing without even considering group rescue plans.

Doubts of such a deal from other parties and courts may arise, especially where the law allows insolvency practitioners to conduct a sale of the whole business without the approval of creditors and courts, as it does in the UK.[155] Together with the fact that administrators could be appointed out of court by holders of floating charge or directors, all these procedures and negotiations may be done in bad faith and in fleeting time. What the rest of the creditors have to face is a

---

151 Statement of practice 16 issued on 01 November 2015 by R3: Association of Business Recovery Professionals.

152 Ibid., p. 2.

153 Ibid., pp. 2, 4.

154 Brief guide to Administration, Linklaters (2008), at <www.linklaters.com/pdfs/Insights/banking/Guidetoadministration.pdf> accessed 17 January 2014, p. 3.

155 Anthony Wijaya, 'Pre-Pack Administration Sale: A Case of Sub Rosa Debt Restructuring' (2016) *International Insolvency Review* 25 119–137, p. 130.

Group coordination & planning proceedings   161

fait accompli conclusion that the sale is in the interests of creditors in general. As a result, administrators may be responsible for the abuse.

In some countries, such as the Netherlands and the USA, a pre-pack deal needs courts' approval.[156] The courts may be good at examining the abuse of law; hence, introducing judicial control to the design of pre-pack may prevent certain abusive uncooperative strategies from being exercised by subsidiaries.[157] Also, the US pre-pack regulation seems to be directed towards a focus on enhanced protection to creditors in general.[158] However, whether the sale is the best solution is a commercial judgement, so the supervisory role of the courts is limited.[159] More importantly, the courts are not the first to hear about the pre-pack deal; relying on court examination will not provide other insolvency practitioners with enough time to prepare the possibilities of an alternative group reorganization plan. A desirable solution in the cross-border insolvency of groups of companies context is to encourage parties to consider the group reorganization plan and the individual group member plan at an earlier stage.

After considering all three benefits that the recommendation could bring, one should notice that the cost of exchange of information throughout a group rescue plan may not be ignored. The recommendation does not suggest that every subsidiary should consider its own version of a group plan. Rather, the key is to exchange information so that the question whether a group rescue plan is desirable can be answered at an early stage. Also, the cost as such does not derive from the recommendation itself; it is a general drawback of procedural cooperation solutions where the cooperation between parties itself will give rise to costs. Nonetheless, it is a workable framework in that it provides certainty to creditors of different subsidiaries in different jurisdictions.

---

156 When considering whether to approve the sale, the court may consider whether it is a de facto reorganization plan while disenfranchising creditor's protection endowed by the confirmation of the chapter 11 plan. The alertness of the US courts highlights that the removal of the creditors' protection is the quid pro quo of the fast speed of pre-packs; the latter may give rise to abuses by senior creditors. Craig A. Sloane, 'The Sub Rosa Plan of Reorganization: Side-Stepping Creditor Protections in chapter 11' (1999–2000) *Emory Bankruptcy Developments Journal* 16 37, p. 61.

157 The court scrutiny could be seen as a form of creditor protection as otherwise insolvency practitioners in a pre-pack sale may go around protective mechanisms offered by meetings of creditors and dispose of debtor's assets without a system of checks and balances. Also, it could be viewed as a solution to the anti-commons issue as otherwise the subsidiaries may strategically choose to hold out by opting out of the group coordination proceeding as long as they receive a not proportionate payment from other member companies.

158 The US Commission to study chapter 11 is of the opinion that since sale of the whole business essentially affects all the stakeholders' interests, the creditors' protection should not be weaker than the general reorganization procedure. Rolef J. de Weijs and Bob Wessels, 'Proposed Recommendations for the Reform of Chapter 11 U.S. Bankruptcy Code', *Amsterdam Law School Legal Studies*, Research Paper No. 2015 (2014), p. 11.

159 For example, the UK courts are more inclined to rely on insolvency practitioners' views. See Bolanle Adebola, 'Proposed Feasibility Oversight for Pre-Pack Administration in England and Wales: Window Dressing or Effective Reform?' (2015) *Journal of Business Law* 8 591–606, p. 3.

162 *Group coordination & planning proceedings*

To sum up, the insolvency practitioners of member companies should consider group rescue options when considering individual rescue options at an early stage. They should do so by disclosing information to other insolvency practitioners in the same group when an individual rescue plan is negotiating; they should also discuss the possibility of group rescue plans. By considering these at an early stage, more information and options are available for the relevant parties and insolvency practitioners. It is easier for them to decide which options may better serve the creditors in general of one member company. As a result, the ability of group coordination proceedings to preserve group going concern value is improved.

UNCITRAL Model Law on cross-border multinational enterprises insolvency

The main purpose of UNCITRAL Model Law is to facilitate the administration of cross-border insolvencies; respect creditors' interests, even though they are spread in many countries; and coordinate multiple insolvency proceedings against the same debtors.[160] Also, the wider that UNCITRAL Model Law can be adopted, the more consistent the terms of Model Law could be in different countries' versions, the more likely that the goals could be achieved.[161]

The Model Law is relevant to our discussion as it also considers the issue of cross-border insolvency of corporate groups. It defines an enterprise group as more than two enterprises, irrespective of their legal forms, that are interconnected by control or significant ownership.[162] This definition is broad as it may include group members, not limited to companies, to the same group.

Compared to the EU insolvency regulation recast, the Model Law provides similar provisions for insolvency practitioners and courts of the same group, and encourages them to cooperate with each other at the international level. The effect is limited as the Model Law is only in the nature of soft law.[163] It has been provided that if countries do not allow universalism, they are free to constrain the power of courts or insolvency practitioners to enter into group solutions.[164] The main suggestion is cooperation and coordination, including that each representative of an insolvency proceeding of a member company in the same group should consider the approval and implementation of a group insolvency

---

160 United Nations Commission on International Trade Law, UNCITRAL Model Law on Cross-Border Insolvency with Guide to Enactment 2014 Preamble and Interpretation.

161 Look Chan Ho 'Overview', in Look Chan Ho (ed.), *Cross-Border Insolvency a Commentary on the UNCITRAL Model Law* (4th edn, volume 1, Global Law and Business 2017), Para. 6.12–6.14.

162 Art 2. United Nations Commission on International Trade Law Working Group V (Insolvency Law) Fifty-third session, Facilitating the cross-border insolvency of enterprise groups: draft legislative provisions A/CN.9/WG.V/WP.158 2018.

163 Art 3 A/CN.9/WG.V/WP.158 2018.

164 Article 9 A/CN.9/WG.V/WP.158 2018.

Group coordination & planning proceedings 163

agreement.[165] Also, joint hearing of a group case by courts in different countries is suggested, even though the independence of each court is respected.[166]

More importantly, it is possible to appoint a single insolvency practitioner to act as the insolvency practitioner for all member companies.[167] This provision may only apply if the certificates of insolvency practitioners can be recognized by other jurisdictions. In the case where directors are still in possession of the control of the companies under restructuring regimes, this may not be a question. However, it is difficult to replace existing directors of different member companies with the appointed directors.

Under Model Law, member companies can choose to join foreign insolvency proceedings with the aim to develop a group solution; however, the member companies do not therefore subject themselves to the foreign court.[168] Group representatives in group planning proceedings may seek various relieves in the foreign courts, not limited to stay of execution of assets, of right to transfer assets, of insolvency proceedings or of individual actions, and administer assets of a member company in the foreign state.[169] More importantly, Model Law largely deals with insolvent companies; it does not aim to deal with preventive restructuring cases. In insolvency proceedings, directors may be replaced by insolvency practitioners, so it is likely to infer that insolvency practitioners will play important roles as far as the Model Law is considered. Another effect may be that relieves may not be available if the target companies against which relieves are sought are solvent companies.

Compared to EU insolvency regulation recast, the UNCITRAL Model Law does not provide an opt-in and opt-out mechanism. Though the existence of an opt-out mechanism may reduce the effectiveness of group coordination proceedings in EU regulation, the Model Law says nothing about such a mechanism at all. Whether participating or not in a group planning proceeding is at the discretion of insolvency practitioners and the relevant regulation of a foreign state. The soft-law nature of Model Law means that countries are free to decide what types of relives are available to a group representative, so one can imagine that varying types of relieves may make it difficult to truly accomplish a group-wide rescue. However, Model Law is a welcome move forward as at least it urges countries with less developed cross-border insolvency law to consider it and gradually harmonize certain concepts, such as COMI and enterprise groups.

One similarity shared by EU regulation and Model Law is that both emphasize the importance of cooperation and coordination between courts and insolvency practitioners. However, when creditors under the Model Law seek relief in foreign courts with regard to the assets of a debtor, foreign courts frequently consider the possible losses of sovereignty and local creditors, even though the

---

165 Art4(d)(f) A/CN.9/WG.V/WP.158 2018.
166 Art6 A/CN.9/WG.V/WP.158 2018.
167 Art 10 A/CN.9/WG.V/WP.158 2018.
168 Article 11 A/CN.9/WG.V/WP.158 2018.
169 Art13(1) A/CN.9/WG.V/WP.158 2018.

164 *Group coordination & planning proceedings*

underlying spirit of the Model Law is modified universalism.[170] EU member states have a stronger trust in each other; one may predict that in the future, the degree of cooperation and coordination will be stronger, and the likelihood of granting relief within the EU will be higher.

One important advantage that Model Law has is its potentially broad scope to include financial corporate groups.[171] That is to say, if the country which adopts Model Law allows financial companies inside the scope of Model Law, the Model Law is equally applicable to financial companies. Nonetheless, in practice, this is unlikely to happen due to the interconnected nature of financial institutions and financial markets, and their potential to cause public interest concerns.[172] It is likely that countries which adopted Model Law will leave financial institutions outside of the Model Law and give them special treatment.

170 For an analysis of model law cases, see Sandeep Gopalan and Michael Guihot, 'Recognition and Enforcement in Cross-Border Insolvency Law a Proposal for Judicial Gap-filing' (2015) *Vanderbilt Journal of Transnational Law* 48 1225, 1269.

171 Irit Mevorach, 'Beyond the Search for Certainty: Addressing the Cross-Border Resolution Gap' (2015) *Brooklyn Journal of Corporate, Financial & Commercial Law* 10 183, p. 213.

172 See Chapter 7.

6 Directors' duties of corporate groups

Directors' duties in general

It is well established that directors owe a series of duties to the companies to which they are appointed. Taking English company law as an example, s.171–177 of Companies Act 2006 prescribes seven general duties that directors owe to their companies, such as duties to promote the success of the company.[1] Insolvency Act 1986 supplements two other duties in the zone of insolvency: fraudulent trading and wrongful trading. Directors include de jure directors, de facto directors and shadow directors.[2] Unless directors are removed, arguably, they may still owe these duties in the vicinity of the insolvency of their companies. Art. 172 of Company Act 2006 makes it clear that directors have a responsibility to consider creditors' interests, even when the companies are not insolvent. Besides their general duties, directors are subject to other duties enshrined in insolvency law, such as fraudulent trading and wrongful trading.[3]

Directors' duties in the vicinity of insolvency and preventive restructuring procedures

EU member states take different strategies to protect creditors in the vicinity of insolvency by imposing varying duties on directors. According to some scholars' observation, most EU countries require directors to file for insolvency proceedings when the companies experience financial difficulties, as defined by law; some countries have wrongful trading; some countries make it clear that in the vicinity of insolvency, the focus of directors should shift to creditors' interests.[4]

---

1 s.171–177 of Company Act 2006. Duties to act within powers; to promote the success of the company; to exercise independent judgement; to exercise reasonable care, skill and diligence; to avoid conflicts of interest; to not accept benefits from third parties; and to declare an interest in a proposed transaction or arrangement.
2 Len Sealy and Sarah Worthington, *Sealy & Worthington's Cases and Materials in Company Law* (10th edn, Oxford University Press 2016), p. 312.
3 For example, see English Insolvency Act 1986 art.213 and 214, respectively.
4 Carsten Gerner-Beuerle and Edmund-Philipp Schuster, 'The Evolving Structure of Directors' Duties in Europe' (2014) *European Business Organization Law Review* 15, p. 224.

166 *Directors' duties of corporate groups*

No matter which approach is adopted, one common thread is that creditors' interests are blended into directors' duties before the commencement of insolvency proceedings. Proposal for a Directive of preventive restructuring proceedings illustrates what directors need to do if there is a likelihood of insolvency:

> *(a) to take immediate steps to minimise the loss for creditors, workers, shareholders and other stakeholders; (b) to have due regard to the interests of creditors and other stakeholders; (c) to take reasonable steps to avoid insolvency; (d) to avoid deliberate or grossly negligent conduct that threatens the viability of the business.*[5]

From the English law perspective, it has been argued that where a company is insolvent, directors' main focus, under s.172 of Company Act 2006, on shareholders in general, convert to the equivalent, i.e. company's creditors as a whole.[6] Common law shows that both subjective test and object test are used to determine whether directors have performed their duties properly; subjectively, directors need to genuinely believe that what they have done is good for the company;[7] more importantly, objectively, an outsider director, with similar skill and knowledge, should conclude that what they have done to the company is justified.[8]

This means that directors are not at liberty to dispose of their company's assets without considering whether such actions will render them unable to repay creditors, even though the company is solvent.[9] On the other hand, the accusation of wrongful trading may loom large if the directors of a company keep trading with third parties, even if they know or ought to have known that there is no prospect for the company to avoid insolvent liquidation in the near future; neither do the directors take every step to minimize the loss of creditors.[10] Some countries, such as Italy, allow the creditors of a solvent company to sue directors for a breach of their duties, while some EU countries do not allow this to happen.[11] When a company enters into insolvency proceedings, the individual actions of creditors or derivative actions of shareholders against directors will be replaced by collective insolvency proceedings.[12] It seems that, in some countries,

---

5 Chapter 5 article 19 European Parliament legislative resolution of 28 March 2019 on the proposal for a Directive of the European Parliament and of the Council on preventive restructuring frameworks, second chance and measures to increase the efficiency of restructuring, insolvency and discharge procedures and amending Directive 2012/30/EU (COM(2016)0723 – C8-0475/2016 – 2016/0359(COD)).

6 Re Pantone 485 Ltd [2002] 1 BCLC 266.

7 Re Southern Countries Fresh Foods Ltd [2008] EWHC 2810 (Ch).

8 Charterbridge Corporation Ltd v Lloyds Bank Ltd [1970] Ch 62 (Ch).

9 Re HLC Environmental Projects Ltd (in liq.) *Hellard v Carvalho* [2014] B.C.C. 337, p. 2.

10 s.214 insolvency act 1986, 246ZB Wrongful trading: administration.

11 Alessandra Zanardo, 'Fiduciary Duties of Directors of Insolvent Corporations: A Comparative Perspective' (2018) *Chicago-Kent Law Review* 93 867, p. 870, 892.

12 11 U.S.C. § 541(a), Alessandra Zanardo, 'Fiduciary Duties of Directors of Insolvent Corporations: A Comparative Perspective' (2018) *Chicago-Kent Law Review* 93 867, p. 883.

Directors' duties of corporate groups 167

such as the UK, creditors have difficulty directly challenging directors' conduct if the directors can show that their companies are not insolvent.

However, it is easy to understand that in the vicinity of insolvency, the value of equity held by shareholders is nearly zero, while the creditors are in the shoes of shareholders as they start to bear the loss if the businesses of companies suffer further deterioration. Therefore, to respond to this hazard, shifting directors' duties to creditors, especially in the vicinity of insolvency, can be seen as offering necessary protection to creditors.[13] It has been recognized that there is no precise test as to when directors' duties should shift, what directors should do to avoid the liabilities and whether creditors' interest should be given more weight than shareholders'.[14]

One classic case is *West Mercia Safetywear Ltd v Dodd*,[15] in which a director of a parent company was also the director of a subsidiary company. The directors transferred some money from subsidiary to parent company in order to pay the debt owed by the subsidiary. However, since the director also personally guaranteed some debts owed by the parent company to a bank, this move is interpreted as not just repayment of debt from subsidiary to parent but a benefit to the director himself as he may reduce his own burden of repayment of the debt of the parent company.[16]

Directors owe duties to companies, whereas an important part of their interests is embodied by shareholders' interests; a shift of directors' duties in the vicinity of insolvency per se does not create any new duties; rather, it is simply a shift of focus onto creditors' interests.[17] In particular, wrongful trading adds another layer of protection for creditors in the vicinity of insolvency of a company. Directors of a nearly insolvent company, at the time that they should have concluded that there is no chance for the company to avoid liquidation or administration proceedings, should stop trading and seek judicial solutions. If the directors do not stop trading, the liquidators or administrators can seek a court declaration that the directors should make a personal contribution to the company.[18] Directors may fear the liability introduced by wrongful trading as, once it has been established that they make the company worse off between the date that they should have stopped trading and the date that they actually stop trading, the net loss can be recovered by liquidators and administrators from the directors.[19]

---

13 Andrew Keay, 'The Shifting of Directors' Duties in the Vicinity of Insolvency' (2015) *International Insolvency Review* 24 140–164, p. 144.

14 Ibid., p. 163.

15 Liquidator of West Mercia Safetywear Ltd v Dodd & Anor. (1988) 4 B.C.C. 30.

16 Ibid., p. 1.

17 Kristin van Zwieten, 'Director Liability in Insolvency and Its Vicinity' (2018) *Oxford Journal of Legal Studies* 38(2) 382–409, p. 383. The author argues that this requirement plays similar functions to the preference rule under section 239 of the Insolvency Act 1986.

18 Sections 214 and 246ZB, Insolvency Act 1986.

19 Re Marini Ltd Liquidator of Marini Ltd v Dickenson & Ors [2004] B.C.C. 172, p. 3.

168 *Directors' duties of corporate groups*

The time to consider the interests of creditors is uncertain. However, in a recent case, the court believed that a test is when the directors of a company believe that it is probable for the company to fail to meet its debts.[20] This test refers to a situation where the insolvency of a company in the near future is a real concern rather than just a remote risk.[21] This corresponds to the general belief that directors need to consider creditors' interests when they believe that there is a *real and not remote risk* that certain transactions and actions of the company may cause it to be unable to repay debts owed to credits when they fall due.[22] In some situations, when directors of member companies require certain subsidiaries to enter into transactions on behalf of the whole group, even if the prospect of the group is bleak, it may still be possible to argue that keeping the group 'alive' is the only way for creditors in the subsidiaries to receive a better recovery.[23]

Generally speaking, a director is able to work for more than one company without the fear of a breach of conflict of interests if it is not limited by the terms of articles of association, if they do not misuse of company's assets and information or if they cause no loss to companies.[24] The Australian Bell case concerned a group of companies where directors of the group granted securities to banks in exchange for further financial support.[25] In the case, directors were in breach of their duties, and banks committed knowing receipt and dishonest assistance as they ought to have known that directors had breached their duties.[26] In 1990, the business interdependent Bell Group entered into liquidation without receiving financial support from banks.[27] The Australian Court believed that it was possible for the directors of each company to conclude a loan with banks as long as the interests received by each company were compatible with the interest of the group.[28] But in the Bell Group case, given that the Group was in the vicinity of insolvency, there was no prospect that it could generate adequate income to repay its debts, and creditors of an individual company may

---

20 Sequana S.A. v Bat Industries Plc, Windward Prospects Limited, Selarl C. Basse [2019] EWCA Civ 112 Para. 220.

21 Ibid., Para. 221.

22 Mark Arnold (QC) and Marcus Haywood, 'Duty to Promote the Success of the Company', in Simon Mortimore (ed.), *Company Directors Duties, Liabilities, and Remedies* (Oxford University Press 2017), p. 307.

23 Facia Footwear Ltd, Wisebird Limited (Both in Administration) v Stephen 1997 WL 1102751; Mark Arnold (QC) and Marcus Haywood, 'Duty to Promote the Success of the Company', in Simon Mortimore (ed.), *Company Directors Duties, Liabilities, and Remedies* (Oxford University Press 2017), p. 309.

24 London and Mashonaland Exploration Co. Ltd v New Mashonaland Exploration Co. Ltd [1891] WN 165; Parker Hood, 'Directors' Duties Under the Companies Act 2006: Clarity or Confusion?' (2013) *Journal of Corporate Law Studies* 13(1) 42.

25 Westpac Banking Corporation v Bell Group Ltd (in liq.) (No. 3] (2012) WASCA 157.

26 K.M. Hayne, 'Directors' Duties and a Company's Creditors' (2014) *The Melbourne University Law Review* 38 795, p. 797.

27 Westpac Banking Corporation v Bell Group Ltd (in liq.) [No. 3] (2012) WASCA 157 Para. 2270.

28 Ibid., Para. 952.

Directors' duties of corporate groups 169

have been prejudiced by this loan.[29] The court opined that directors of group member companies breached their duties by allowing subsidiaries to grant securities to support other members without considering creditors' interests in each subsidiary in the group.[30]

The role of directors in group coordination proceedings and UNCITRAL Model Law

The mainstream view is that directors owe duties to their own companies, not others.[31] This infers that directors of subsidiaries need to consider the welfare of their own companies independently and may not make business decisions solely in the interests of sister companies or parent companies in the group.

s.172 requires directors to promote the success of a company; it by and large, refers to the long-term financial benefits of shareholders' interests.[32] In the setting of corporate group insolvency, this may require directors of solvent subsidiaries to protect themselves. However, one may argue that if the group is business integrated, directors should consider the viability of the solvent companies without the future support of insolvent sister companies. In the case of insolvent subsidiaries, the insolvency practitioners focus on the protection of general creditors. They need to consider how to maximize general creditors' recovery and decide whether or not to join group coordination proceedings.

In MCG cases, if someone is the director of more than one company, they may need to consider the success of those companies separately. However, where the interests of all of these companies can be aligned together, or where the purpose of these companies is more than achieving profits for shareholders,[33] this may provide a basis for the director to consider a group rescue.

Similarly, the UNCITRAL Model Law facilitates the harmonization of cross-border insolvency at the international level. Nevertheless, it needs to be transposed into each country's national law, and all countries enjoy great flexibility in terms of the ultimate provisions that they would like to adopt.[34]

---

29 Ibid., Para. 952.
30 Ibid., Para. 1000.
31 Percival v Wright [1902] Ch 421 (Ch).
32 Section 172(1) the director must have regard (among other matters) to: the likely consequences of any decision in the long term. The interests of the company's employees. The need to foster the company's business relationships with suppliers, customers and others. The impact of the company's operations on the community and the environment. The desirability of the company maintaining a reputation for high standards of business conduct. The need to act fairly as between the members of the company.
33 The concept of success may vary company by company and be defined by companies themselves according to their objectives. Len Sealy and Sarah Worthington, *Sealy & Worthington's Cases and Materials in Company Law* (10th edn, Oxford University Press 2016), p. 339.
34 Reinhard Bork, 'The European Insolvency Regulation and the UNCITRAL Model Law on Cross-Border Insolvency' (2017) *International Insolvency Review* 26 246–269/247–248.

170 *Directors' duties of corporate groups*

The Model Law has identified a situation where a director of one member company is also the director of other member companies; this situation may be particularly relevant with regard to a breach of conflict of interests.[35] The balancing point that every director needs to strike is that in which the individual company's creditors cannot be worse off if the director decides to participate into a group rescue solution that may maximize the value of the whole group.[36] To achieve this, some important factors need to be considered, including the position of the company, the degree of integration of member companies and the possibilities to rescue the group via a group rescue plan; also, the model law recognizes a situation in which, at the beginning of a group-wide cooperation, a single member company may suffer a loss, while later it may prove that it can recover its loss by avoiding a business failure or a group-wide gain.[37] However, without the support of national law, it is unlikely that directors will risk being accused of breaching their duties, unless other member companies provide guarantees or similar protection.

It is a traditional rule that a director cannot be in a situation where his own interest conflicts with, or may possibly conflict with, the interests of his company.[38] UNCITRAL is correct to note that one such situation may be that in which a director is also the director of other member companies in the same group. Arguably, if one director works for two companies with businesses in completely different areas, an issue of conflict of interest will not arise. However, if two member companies form seller-buyer relationships within a group, directors may breach the duty to avoid conflict of interest. Generally speaking, if a director is in a position which may give rise to a conflict of interest concern, they need to inform other directors on both sides and obtain authorization from the board of directors, subject to the terms of articles of association.[39]

In the context of cross-border insolvency of corporate groups, it is possible that the director of an insolvent member company will want to persuade a member company of which he is also a director to save that insolvent company. In this hypothetic case, other directors of the solvent company may need to consider this director's suggestion to see whether it is a reasonable move. Directors straddling different member companies may facilitate corporate group rescue. First, they facilitate the flow of information. Second, they consider the possibility of a group-wide rescue. With the support of other directors and fiduciary duties, it is possible to argue that competing for directorship may bring in an overall positive contribution to the cross-border corporate group rescue.

35 Art 269, A/CN.9/WG.V/WP.153.
36 267(b) A/CN.9/WG.V/WP.153.
37 A/CN.9/WG.V/WP.153, p. 6.
38 Bray v Ford [1896] AC 44 (HL); see also s.175 of Company Act 2006.
39 175(5) of Company Act 2006.

7 Lessons from financial institution resolutions

The main focus of this book so far has been non-financial corporate groups since the financial corporate groups are subject to a special set of laws. EIR recast applies to legal persons and natural persons, while it does not apply to financial institutions.[1] However, financial corporate groups are also important constitutes of corporate groups, and they share some similarities with non-financial ones. In the EU, to solve the insolvency issues of banks and other financial institutions, the bank recovery and resolution directive (BRRD)[2] has been in force since July 2014. In the eurozone, the equivalent is single resolution mechanism (SRM) regulation.[3] Both of these aim to harmonize bank recovery tools and resolution tools in the EU. The purpose of this chapter is not to provide a comprehensive analysis of financial group insolvency or resolution. Rather, the purpose is to consider what lessons non-financial corporate groups can learn from the development of financial institution resolution.

Theories of bank resolution

The raison d'être of bank resolution

Like non-financial companies, banks are not immune from insolvency if their businesses go under. Logically, banks are companies and should be subject to the same corporate insolvency rules of every nation.

However, banks, together with certain financial institutions, are defined as systemically important financial institutions (SIFIs) in that their collapse will

---

1 EIR recast, recital 19.
2 Directive 2014/59/EU of the European Parliament and of the Council of 15 May 2014 establishing a framework for the recovery and resolution of credit institutions and investment firms and amending Council Directive 82/891/EEC, and Directives 2001/24/EC, 2002/47/EC, 2004/25/EC, 2005/56/EC, 2007/36/EC, 2011/35/EU, 2012/30/EU and 2013/36/EU, and Regulations (EU) No. 1093/2010 and (EU) No. 648/2012, of the European Parliament and of the Council Text with EEA relevance.
3 Regulation (EU) No. 806/2014 of the European Parliament and of the Council of 15 July 2014 establishing uniform rules and a uniform procedure for the resolution of credit institutions and certain investment firms in the framework of a single resolution mechanism and a single resolution fund and amending Regulation (EU) No. 1093/2010.

172 *Financial institution resolutions*

have a serious effect on the whole financial system or real economy.[4] As a result, banks, together with other SIFIs, are special; the insolvency of these behemoth institutions deserves more attention than ordinary companies. SIFIs enjoy a privileged position that is coined as 'too-big-to-fail' as the government frequently bails out these institutions when they are crippled in order to avoid financial instability.[5] A bailout will give rise to moral hazard as negligent directors of financial institutions may be encouraged by the availability of bailout and engage in excessive risk-taking activities at the expense of taxpayers.

As discussed above, bailing out banks and other SIFIs will create moral hazard and distort market discipline. After all, managers of SIFIs should be responsible for any conduct that leads to the failure of a financial institution; also, weak companies should be screened out of the market as a result of competition. Nonetheless, bank bailout can be justified by the catastrophic effect that insolvent financial institutions have on the real economy. Without alternative, proper solutions to bailout, the real economy may suffer a huge loss. The interconnected nature of financial products, institutions and market mean that the failure of one bank may lead to the failure of other banks and financial institutions; banks' solvency also connects to the national economy because the role of banks is to provide credit and other forms of financial services to borrowers consisting of a variety of traders and companies, and other financial institutions.[6] The issue is whether there are any alternative solutions to bailout. One default rule is corporate insolvency law, which is available in almost every country. The limitation of insolvency law is that it is a prolonged procedure for creditors to reach a new bargain, and it does not consider systemic risks which may threaten payment and lending systems.[7]

It seems that we need something more than corporate insolvency law. Bank resolution is designed to be such an alternative. It should allow banks to fail without heavily relying on public funds; it also allows banks to fail safely without causing systemic risks. It is worth noting that if the goal of avoiding systemic risk is given paramount position in a bank resolution context, given that national or international resolution funds may not be adequate in every case, bailout can still have a role in exceptional cases.[8] In the next section, we will consider the difference between traditional corporate law theory and bank resolution theory.

---

4 Key Attributes Assessment Methodology for the Banking Sector 2016 <www.fsb.org/wp-content/uploads/Key-Attributes-Assessment-Methodology-for-the-Banking-Sector.pdf>. accessed on 03 Feb 2017

5 Steven L. Schwarcz, 'Too Big to Fool: Moral Hazard, Bailouts, and Corporate Responsibility' (2017) *Minnesota Law Review* 102 761 (as a result, moral hazard is created).

6 Gabriel Moss (QC), Bob Wessels and Matthias Haentjens, 'The EU Financial Institution Insolvency Law Framework', in Gabriel Moss (QC), Bob Wessels and Matthias Haentjens (eds), *EU Banking and Insurance Insolvency* (2nd edn, Oxford University Press 2017), pp. 6–7.

7 Marco Bodellini, 'To Bail-In, or to Bail-Out, That Is the Question' (2018) *European Business Organization Law Review* 19 381–388, p. 368.

8 The issue is how to provide a structured and legitimate framework for bail-outs. See Michael Anderson Schillig, 'The (Il-)Legitimacy of the EU Post-Crisis Bailout System' <https://ssrn.com/abstract=3202118>, p. 2; Marco Bodellini (2018) pp. 387–388.

A comparison of corporate insolvency theory and bank resolution theory

This section aims to provide an analysis of the limitations and benefits of corporate insolvency law in coping with insolvent financial institutions; it also examines the relationship between corporate insolvency theory and bank resolution theory.

The purposes of insolvency law and bank resolution are different. When considering bank resolution, the main goals are to preserve the functioning of payment and settlement systems, protection of deposit and key credit intermediation functions.[9] Bank resolution tools not only deal with liquidation or rescue of an individual financial institution but also focus on the issue of public interest protection.[10] That is to say, bank resolution envisions a larger picture, including the protection of financial markets and infrastructures, as the failure of market or infrastructure may cause more SIFIs to collapse. In 2007, for example, the default of sub-prime borrowers may have given rise to the downgrading of mortgage-backed securities held by financial institutions, such as Lehman Brothers, which used those securities as collateral to borrow money; the plummeting of securities assets, together with runaway counterparties, indicates that the failure of a financial market can lead to the collapse of other SIFIs.[11]

However, this does not mean that judges of bankruptcy courts never consider the externalities of a failed company; neither does it mean that bank resolution is always desirable, compared to insolvency rules. Insolvency law considers systemic risks by giving derivatives and repo contracts privilege, by releasing them from the control of stay and avoidance mechanisms under insolvency proceedings.[12] This is because many derivative and repo contracts play the role of quasi-money, whereby the holders take them as a cash management tool and expect a timely and undisruptive access to such quasi-money.[13] Staying the actions of holders is likely to give rise to collapse of other financial institutions.[14] In other words, the stay power of insolvency law may help to preserve the value of one financial institution; however, it exponentially destroys the value of other financial institutions. The existence of safe harbour provision in insolvency law sits uneasily with

---

9 International Monetary Fund and the World Bank, 'An Overview of the Legal, Institutional, and Regulatory Framework for Bank Insolvency' 2009 <www.imf.org/external/np/pp/eng/2009/041709.pdf>(accessed on 1 February 2019), p. 16.

10 Steven L. Schwarcz, 'Beyond Bankruptcy: Resolution as a Macroprudential Regulatory Tool', (2018) *Notre Dame Law Review* 94 709, p. 729.

11 Ibid., pp. 730–731.

12 U.S. Code: Title 11. BANKRUPTCY, § 507 and § 726. Mark J. Roe, 'The Derivatives Market's Payment Priorities as Financial Crisis Accelerator' (2011) *Stanford Law Review* 63 539, p. 548 (it is argued that in AIG's bankruptcy case, the counterparties of financial contracts were allowed to grab and realize AIG's collaterals, which may otherwise constitute a preference, had the contracts not been financial contracts).

13 Chrystin Ondersma, 'Shadow Banking and Financial Distress: The Treatment of Money-Claims in Bankruptcy' (2013) *Columbia Business Law Review* 79.

14 Ibid., p. 107.

174 *Financial institution resolutions*

other traditional insolvency law provisions, such as stay. A classic understanding of insolvency law is that it is designed to solve a tragedy of the commons issue. Therefore, stay mechanism may be the most obvious characteristic of insolvency law. As an exception safe harbour provisions make certain financial contracts free from the control of such stay mechanism under insolvency law, which may destabilize its effectiveness. There must be a reason for that. In fact, many financial contracts are derivatives and money market instruments, such as repos; they are very liquid and stable, and similar to money.[15] These counterparties of a debtor care less about how much the debtor can pay them after a prolonged insolvency proceeding; what they care about is whether they can access these instruments immediately as, otherwise, counterparties have to suddenly decrease their investment due to a shortage of money[16] and suffer a huge loss from disruption of services and opportunity costs.[17]

In spite of that, corporate insolvency law may be used to deal with bank resolution. However, it is criticized for being too slow to provide a timely response to a financial crisis. Neither can the court find a buyer for a failed SIFI within a short period of time due to the huge size of its assets and liabilities, and its complex businesses. Bank resolution rules, such as bail-in, writing down bail-inable debts without[18] creditor negotiation and court supervision,[19] can provide a fast track for a failed bank. In this respect, bank resolution is similar to a pre-pack deal, where the participation of creditors and court monitoring is reduced to the minimum level. It may be said that bank resolution achieves the desirable speed of rescue at the expense of creditor protection.

It has been submitted that corporate insolvency law also has many benefits over bank resolution rules. For example, bank resolution is typically an administrative procedure controlled by resolution authorities; therefore, one may argue that the values of transparency and rule of law may be sacrificed.[20] Since governmental officials are not judges, they may not understand basic principles of law, such as no-creditor-worse-off principles of bank resolution or the *pari passu* principle of insolvency law. Another important aspect is that creditors in insolvency proceedings understand that they will not be protected by taxpayers' money, so they have stronger incentive to exercise market discipline, i.e. bargain with each other, monitor the behaviour of debtors and exchange information.[21]

---

15 Morgan Ricks, 'Regulating Money Creation after the Crisis' (2011) *Harvard Business Law Review* 1 75, p. 92.
16 Ibid., p. 108.
17 Ibid., p. 124.
18 Stephen J. Lubben, 'A Functional Analysis of SIFI Insolvency' (2018) *Texas Law Review* 96 1377, p. 1392.
19 Ibid., p. 1396.
20 Thomas H. Jackson and David A. Skeel, Jr., 'Dynamic Resolution of Large Financial Institutions' (2012) *Harvard Business Law Review* 2 435 (the US resolution authority FDIC enjoys very broad discretion with regard to which assets and liabilities will be saved), p. 443.
21 Thomas H. Jackson and David A. Skeel, Jr., 'Dynamic Resolution of Large Financial Institutions' (2012) *Harvard Business Law Review* 2 435, pp. 447–448.

Financial institution resolutions 175

However, regulators may have access to some information that private parties do not have access to: examples are the financial conditions of financial institutions, submitted to authorities to meet legal compliance requirements. It is not obvious that insolvency law may help to provide more information to all relevant parties.

It is important to be aware that bank resolution is an area which is not completely different from insolvency law since both share important principles and tools to deal with insolvent companies, not limited to liquidation and rescue dichotomy, transfer of assets and liabilities free of secured interests, the *pari passu* principle or the use of avoidance power to claim back company's assets.[22] The only obvious difference is that bank resolution has a unique macro-level task to fulfil.[23] It seems that bank resolution theory is built on the basis of insolvency law theory by striking a balance between fair treatment of creditors and financial stability. In a non-financial company setting, the externalities of a failed company are almost negligible, so insolvency law may give priority to the consideration of value maximization and the predictability of insolvency rules. In the case of financial companies, given that the externalities are too large to ignore, it makes sense for the government to intervene so as to constrain external losses.

Financial companies also have something in common with business-integrated non-financial corporate groups. First, they all, to some degree, exist in an integrated network, whereby one member bank not only connects to members within the same group but also connects to financial institutions outside of the group in a broader financial market or by some common financial products.[24] Second, SIFIs are melting ice cubes whose value will be lost immediately upon insolvency. A loss of confidence in a financial market will quickly cause a run on the banks, which will dissipate their deposits. This means that solutions to SIFIs, such as banks, must be very swift so as to prevent a bank run or contagion effect. Third, SIFIs' value lies in their network, and the operation of subsidiaries needs to be kept intact. This may necessitate similar early entry mechanisms and preventive restructuring tools that are available to ordinary companies.

Therefore, large parts of insolvency law and bank resolution rules, in fact, overlap with each other. It seems the only obvious difference is that bank resolution theory should also take systemic risks into consideration. For example, in the USA, the Federal Deposit Insurance Corporation (FDIC) may save a bank if it is likely to cause systemic risks.[25] The FDIC was established as a traditional bank resolution authority under the Federal Deposit Insurance Act (FDIA)

---

22 Douglas G. Baird and Edward R. Morrison, 'Dodd-Frank for Bankruptcy Lawyers' (2011) *American Bankruptcy Institute Law Review* 19 287.

23 Mark J. Roe, 'The Derivatives Market's Payment Priorities as Financial Crisis Accelerator' (2011) *Stanford Law Review* 63 539, p. 548, pp. 550–551.

24 Rosa M. Lastra, 'System Risk and Macro-prudential Supervision', in Niamh Moloney, Elilis Ferran and Jennifer Payne (eds), *The Oxford Handbook of Financial Regulation* (Oxford University Press 2015), p. 312.

25 Michael S. Barr, Howell E. Jackson and Margaret E. Tahyar, *Financial Regulation Law and Policy* (2nd edn, Foundation Press 2018), p. 983.

176 *Financial institution resolutions*

1950; its main mandate was to maintain the soundness of the banking system and the safety of insured depositors.[26]

As long as the relationship between insolvency law and bank resolution is clear, it is free for member states to design their own version of bank resolution rules and consider their structural positioning in the area of insolvency law. It has been argued that, in the context of large financial institution bankruptcy, EU countries may be more likely to choose bank resolution as a solution, given that the public interest test is easily met, while the US authorities may have a preference for bankruptcy law; different tastes for different tools may give rise to cooperative issues.[27]

Bank resolution may be a separate set of rules from insolvency law or part of insolvency, controlled by either judicial proceedings or administrative proceedings. Some countries take the approach that one single set of insolvency rules will apply to both bank and non-financial company insolvency, while other countries may provide a special set of insolvency rules used by resolution authorities.[28] In the EU, the BRRD harmonized bank resolution tools. It was inspired by the Banking Act 2009 in the UK, which provides a special resolution regime[29] for banks; also, similar to the BRRD, the scope of the Banking Act 2009 is extended to systemically important investment firms and parent financial companies, and central counterparty clearing by the Financial Services Act 2012.[30] In the USA, the Dodd-Frank Act provides a new procedure termed Orderly Liquidation Authority (OLA) for financial institutions. An affiliating strategy called single point of entry (SPOE) is also suggested to be used with OLA, whereby the resolution of a financial corporate group only needs to happen at the parent company level, as long as the parent company can absorb all the losses through its equities and some long-term debts.[31] SPOE provides two benefits. First, it is particularly useful in an environment where an international cooperation framework is not available; second, it preserves the key operating subsidiaries whose businesses, not limited to payment system and custody services, form the foundational basis of a country's economy.[32] This SPOE strategy can be seen as a method to preserve value for all creditors in a given financial group as its successful operation will help to keep all subsidiaries' businesses intact.

---

26 Ibid., p. 961.

27 Costanza A. Russo, 'Resolution Plans and Resolution Strategies: Do They Make G-SIBs Resolvable and Avoid Ring Fence?' (2019) *European Business Organization Law Review,* pp. 4–5.

28 Rosa Maria Lastra, *International Financial and Monetary Law* (2nd edn, Oxford University Press 2015), p. 165.

29 Part 1 of the Banking Act 2009.

30 Part 3 of the Banking Act 2009.

31 John Crawford, 'Single Point of Entry: The Promise and Limits of the Latest Cure for Bailouts' (2014–2015) *Northwestern University Law Review* Online 109 107–108 (103).

32 Michael S. Barr, Howell E. Jackson and Margaret E. Tahyar, *Financial Regulation Law and Policy* (2nd edn, Foundation Press 2018), p. 1000.

The BRRD covers most of the SIFIs. In the UK, implementation of the BRRD means that banks, building societies and largest investment firms[33] whose initial capital reach 730,000 euros are all captured by this Directive.[34] Some scholars have identified that the scope of BRRD in the EU may not necessarily cover all SIFIs, so systemic risks may exist in regulatory gaps, and issues such as regulatory arbitrage may be created.[35] More flexibility can be had by following the approach taken by OLA: the relevant resolution authorities may determine whether certain financial institutions amount to SIFIs.[36]

In a cross-border bank resolution context, at least in the EU, universalism is the underlying theory. Generally speaking, BRRD, Credit Institutions Reorganisation and Winding Up Directive,[37] and the Solvency II Directive for insurance companies[38] all advocate universalism.[39] The Credit Institutions Reorganisation and Winding Up Directive makes it clear that the home country of a credit institution has the jurisdiction to deal with winding-up or reorganization measures with regard to that institution, including its branches in other member states.[40] The law of the home country will apply.[41] The judicial or administrative jurisdiction of reorganization and winding-up of a bank lies with the authority of the bank's home member state;[42] this, in turn, refers to the member state which authorizes the bank.[43] This indicates that in the area of bank insolvency, the theory is likely to be universalism as the jurisdiction is allocated to one member state rather than the member states which are in possession of the bank's assets.

Since the winding-up or reorganization of a bank is an issue beyond just creditor protection, the COMI test for non-financial companies is replaced by home

---

33 'The term "investment firm" includes financial institutions whose activities require them to be authorised under the MiFID II Directive (2014/65/EU). The definition covers a broad variety of entities including asset managers, securities brokers, firms that operate certain trading venues and some financial advisers'. https://uk.practicallaw.thomsonreuters.com/4-625-3739?originationContext=document&transitionType=DocumentItem&contextData=%28sc.Default%29&comp=pluk.
34 Art 28(2) of the CRD IV Directive (2013/36/EU) https://uk.practicallaw.thomsonreuters.com/1-576-2705?originationContext=document&transitionType=DocumentItem&contextData=%28sc.Default%29&comp=pluk#co_anchor_a996304.
35 Danny Busch and Mirik B. J. van Rijn, 'Towards Single Supervision and Resolution of Systemically Important Non-Bank Financial Institutions in the European Union' (2018) *European Business Organization Law Review* 19 356.
36 Ibid., p. 356.
37 Credit Institutions Reorganisation and Winding Up Directive (2001/24/EC).
38 The Solvency II Directive (2009/138/EC).
39 Matthias Haentjens and M. Haentjens, 'Financial Institutions', in Gabriel Moss Ian Flectcher and Stuart Isaacs (eds.), *Moss, Fletcher and Isaacs on the EU Regulation on Insolvency Proceedings* (3rd edn, Oxford University Press 2016), p. 222.
40 Winding-Up Directive, art 3(2).
41 Matthias Lehmann, 'Bail-In and Private International Law: How to Make Bank Resolution Measures Effective Across Borders' January (2017) ICLQ 66, p. 117.
42 Directive 2001/24/EC of the European Parliament and of the Council of 4 April 2001 on the reorganization and winding up of credit institutions Article 3(1).
43 Directive 2000/12/EC of the European Parliament and of the Council of 20 March 2000, relating to the taking up and pursuit of the business of credit institutions Article 1(6).

178 *Financial institution resolutions*

country as the test of jurisdiction.[44] The Credit Institutions Reorganisation and Winding Up Directive therefore gives the home country which authorized one bank exclusive jurisdiction to open its insolvency proceedings, no matter where the creditors and assets are located, without interruption from other host countries in the EU.[45] The approach taken by the EU is universalism.

Clearly, it is possible to argue that financial MCGs also have synergies in their group structures. For example, holding companies may decide to centralize certain functions to take advantage of economy of scope while locating some functions at the subsidiary level to reduce agency costs.[46] The purposes of forming a corporate network may be multiple, including seeking research and development opportunities from outside partners, due to limited international resources spent on the advancement of knowledge and technologies,[47] or adapting to a fast response to the ever-changing business environment where consumers' demand may change swiftly.[48] Financial MCGs may also form a network internally or externally. Furthermore, one may argue that, due to the interconnectedness of financial institutions, such linkage is likely to be very strong. The failure of one bank may cause other financial institutions to fail. This calls for a stronger cooperative regime to deal with bank resolution issues and an effective preventive insolvency scheme for this purpose.

However, the main job of bank resolution is not solely to release the group going concern value for creditors. Rather, the tenet is to avoid systemic risk. Different from non-financial companies, financial institutions outside the financial MCGs may have a strong influence on the fate of financial companies inside the group due to the interconnectedness of financial products and markets. One of the findings of business network theory is that parties outside the group may also exert significant control over member companies. This is especially true in a financial MCG context. For example, a non-member financial institution may cause significant counterparty risk to a member financial company.[49] The network through which systemic risk can pass from one to another may be different from the international group network.[50] However, it is the former which defines

---

44 Matthias Lehmann, 'Bail-In and Private International Law: How to Make Bank Resolution Measures Effective Across Borders' January (2017) *ICLQ* 66, p. 119.

45 Charles Proctor, *The Law and Practice of International Banking* (Oxford University Press 2015), p. 266; Thomas C. Baxter, Jr., Joyce M. Hansen and Joseph H. Sommer, 'Two Cheers for Territoriality: An Essay on International Bank Insolvency Law' (2004) *American Bankruptcy Law Journal* 78 57, p. 58.

46 Ozlem Yidrim, 'Theoretical Driver of Diversification', in G. de Laurendis (ed.), *Strategy and Organisation of Corporate Banking* (Springer 2005), p. 23.

47 Christian A. Witting, *Liability of Corporate Groups and Networks* (Cambridge University Press 2018), p. 40.

48 Ibid., p. 42.

49 Wolf-Georg Ringe and Jatine Patel, 'The Dark Side of Bank Resolution: Counterparty Risk through Bail-In' (available at: https://ssrn.com/abstract=3314103) accessed on 10 March 2019.

50 Federico Lupo-Pasini and Ross P. Buckley, 'Global Systemic Risk and International Regulatory Coordination: Squaring Sovereignty and Financial Stability' (2015) *American University International Law Review* 30 665.

the features of bank resolution regimes. For this reason, even though the same concept group CoMI is adopted, it is far-fetched to argue that the CoMI of a member financial company lies in the location of its holding company.

Another important factor that should be considered when discussing the jurisdictional rule of bank resolution is the alignment between bank resolution, bank supervision and provision of funding for resolution.[51] It is desirable for the prudential authorities and resolution authorities to cooperate with each other as the need of resolution comes from the failure of supervision.[52] Also, similar to DIP financing, the operation of bank resolution entails an injection of funds to support it. As a result, it is desirable to allocate the resolution jurisdiction of a bank to the location where it was licensed, insured and supervised. However, this may not be the approach outside of the EU. For example, it is still possible for a third country that is outside of the EU to assert that foreign bank branches in its territory will be controlled by its own jurisdiction. Therefore, without treaties and harmonization of bank resolution rules, the future international bank resolution cooperation is difficult.

To sum up, insolvency law and bank resolution share many similarities in theory. Since depositors are the creditors of banks, nothing in bank resolution rules denies the importance of the value of creditor protection and predictable insolvency rules. Both financial creditors and ordinary creditors of banks need to have a certain degree of predictability with regard to what would happen to their credits should banks enter into insolvent status. So in this sense, insolvency law and bank resolution rules overlap. However, bank insolvency law considers another important value – financial stability. As banks are so important to the economy of any state, the collapse of a bank is likely to cause significant losses to other financial institutions and other non-financial businesses. This may extend beyond the borders of countries and cause global issues. One important question is how to balance the goals of creditor protection and financial stability. In reality, financial stability is given priority over other goals under ordinary insolvency law. This indicates that the externalities of a bank failure outweigh the losses of creditors of banks. The remaining issue is the appropriate level of discretion that bank resolution authorities should display when infringing creditors' expectations and entitlements. The ideal balance seems to be that resolution authorities should respect the basic rules of insolvency law as much as possible while they protect financial stability.

A comparison of corporate preventive insolvency mechanisms and bank recovery and resolution plans

In the case of non-financial corporate groups, the development of preventive restructuring mechanisms shows that there is also a trend for early intervention in

---

51 Jay Lawrence Westbrook, 'SIFIs and States' (2014) *Texas International Law Journal* 49 329, 336–342.
52 Ibid.

180   *Financial institution resolutions*

corporate insolvency law. To rescue a corporate group which may contain group going concern value, it may be too late to take actions if the whole group is already insolvent. A similar development has taken place in the context of financial MCGs. The so-called living wills, i.e. bank recovery and resolution plans, which are pre-commitments, are also made by competent authorities and resolution authorities for banks and other important financial institutions.[53] Avoiding the insolvency of financial MCGs is desirable, perhaps not only due to the preservation of group going concern value. Rather, systemic risks may be another strong reason to justify an early intervention.

Preventive restructuring procedures, on the one hand, aim to send signals to non-financial companies and corporate groups so that they can take some early actions before the commencement of a group-wide insolvency proceeding. On the other hand, preventive restructuring procedures provide necessary tools for corporate groups to plan for debt restructurings and insolvency in order to avoid a group-wide cross-border collapse. The BRRD also equips resolution authorities in the EU with resolution tools, such as bail-in. One subtle difference is that it adds an extra layer of care: in the area of bank and financial institution resolution, the BRRD has harmonized preventive methods by (a) requiring financial institutions to prepare recovery plans and (b) requiring resolution authorize to prepare resolution plans. Since the collapse of a financial corporate group will lead to systemic risks to the real economy, it makes sense for financial groups to prepare for their resolution at an early stage. The purpose of bank recovery and resolution plans is to facilitate orderly resolution of financial institutions in the future.[54]

Preparation of recovery plans becomes a duty that is embedded in each financial institution's corporate governance system.[55] Banks and other SIFIs' financial institutions in the EU need to prepare their own recovery plans for their respective supervisory authorities every year.[56] A recovery plan provides a conduit for a financial institution to explain how it can restore its financial healthiness without public financial support and what actions it decides to take either when the financial condition deteriorates or the early intervention is initiated.[57] The recovery plan of a financial firm will be reviewed by a national prudential

---

53 Dalvinder Singh, 'Recovery and Resolution Planning: Reconfiguring Financial Regulation and Supervision', in Jens-Hinrich Binder and Dalvinder Singh (eds.), *Bank Resolution: The European Regime* (Oxford University Press 2016); Adam Feibelman, 'Living Wills and Pre-Commitment', (2011) *American University Business Law Review* 1 93.

54 Dalvinder Singh, 'Recovery and Resolution Planning: Reconfiguring Financial Regulation and Supervision', in Jens-Hinrich Binder and Dalvinder Singh (eds.), *Bank Resolution: The European Regime* (Oxford University Press 2016), para. 1.02. The main purpose of recovery plans is to encourage financial institutions to provide information, including its own organizational structure, financial healthiness and areas of businesses, to the relevant authorities and prepare for any possible financial distress in the future. Art. 5(2) of the BRRD.

55 Art.5(1) of the BRRD.

56 Art. 5(4) of the BRRD.

57 Art.5(3)(5) of the BRRD.

Financial institution resolutions 181

authority, which will, in turn, communicate with other foreign prudential supervisory authorities if the firm has branches in other member states.[58] Resolution authorities, based on the available information provided by financial institutions, need to prepare resolution plans. The resolution plans need to assure that by using resolution tools in a financial crisis, the financial institutions will be resolvable. Resolvability is defined as imposing costs of resolution on shareholders and creditors without tapping into taxpayers' money; the critical functions of financial institutions can be preserved and continued without giving rise to systemic risks.[59] However, in practice, whether the failed financial groups receive timely financing may directly affect the effectiveness of bank recovery and resolution activities. Since resolution aims to rely less on public financial support, intra-group financing, by means of transferring loans upstream or downstream, may be desirable, subject to the constraints of each national law.[60] It seems that a well-functioning mechanism for recovery and resolution plans requires member states to relax some requirements on directors' duties, and it is also desirable for member companies to discuss the terms and methods of such an arrangement with relevant authorities in their recovery and resolution plans.

As with non-financial corporate groups which operate in more than one country, banks have subsidiaries around the world. If more than one member is insolvent, cross-border cooperation between supervision and resolution authorities is desirable. Due to the contagion effect of the failure of a bank, banks are not only supervised on a solo basis but also supervised on a consolidated basis; depositors and creditors in the market may not be knowledgeable about the complex legal structure of a banking group and they may want to withdraw money from a subsidiary bank, even though it is another bank in the same group that meets with financial difficulties.[61]

To respond to financial corporate groups, Article 7 of BRRD also requests that the parent financial company draft a group recovery plan, which will be reviewed by authorities of both the parent companies and the subsidiaries.[62] This may be supported by the fact that in terms of bank supervision in the EU, a single supervisor may be chosen to supervise a group of banks, even though this leading supervisor has no particular power over banks outside its home country.[63] This leading supervisor is frequently the competent authority of the parent company in a banking group and will supervise the group on a consolidated

---

58 Art. 6 of the BRRD.
59 Financial Stability Board (2014) Key Attributes of Effective Resolution Regimes for Financial Institutions, 15 October 2014.
60 Dalvinder Singh, 'Recovery and Resolution Planning: Reconfiguring Financial Regulation and Supervision', in Jens-Hinrich Binder and Dalvinder Singh (eds.), *Bank Resolution: The European Regime* (Oxford University Press 2016), para. 1.44–1.45.
61 Simon Gleeson, *International Regulation of Banking-Capital and Risk Requirements* (2nd edn, Oxford University Press 2012), pp. 393–394.
62 Art 7 and 8 of the BRRD.
63 Simon Gleeson, *Gleeson on the International Regulation of Banking* (3rd edn, Oxford University Press 2018), p. 492.

182 *Financial institution resolutions*

basis.[64] Similar rules apply for resolution plans. In this case, it is the resolution authorities that draft them, with a focus on the resolvability of a given financial institution or group, based on the information provided by financial institutions.[65] Resolution authorities also need to cooperate in order to draft a group resolution plan.

Arguably, the group recovery and resolution plans are very useful as they provide a full picture with regard to the structure and other financial conditions of a financial group; also this practice invites all relevant authorities to review the plans and identify the deficiencies of the effectiveness of this group recovery or resolution plan. The communication facilitates the exchange of information and fosters mutual trust. It is possible for the competent authority to suggest certain financial institutions to change their capital and operational structures, and business line, critical functions if they are impediments to recovery or resolution.[66] One may argue that in a bad economic era, the relevant authorities can cooperate with each other more effectively.

By analogy, the practice of preparation of recovery and resolution plans means that, in the non-financial corporate group context, all directors of the group must sit together and work out what a possible group rescue plan is. Important questions may include which part is business-integrated and which part is not, which part of the group should enter into group insolvency proceedings or co-ordinating proceedings together and which part does not need to do it. Courts of different countries are requested to work together and examine whether they may have some cooperative difficulties based on the group rescue plan. However, preparation of bank recovery and resolution plans will give rise to costs which may not be bearable by some corporate groups. Therefore, it may be justified for non-financial corporate groups to prepare their own living wills. Even though the Directive on preventive restructuring framework makes it possible to consider corporate group rescue at an early age, it may not be feasible to enforce their preparing recovery plans.

The BBRD also allows competent authorities to take certain early intervention measures if they have identified a deterioration of the financial condition of an institution subject to the BRRD.[67] The relevant authorities can direct managers of the financial institutions to restore financial conditions by exercising activities in the recovery plans of the institutions, such as convening a shareholder meeting or considering a restructuring plan with creditors.[68]

Another power enjoyed by the authorities is removing the managers of a financial institution, changing that institution's business plans and legal and operational structure, and conducting an on-site inspection.[69] Similar to the

---

64 Ibid.
65 Art. 10(2) of the BRRD.
66 Art. 6(6)(c)(d)(e) of the BRRD.
67 Article 27 of the BRRD.
68 Article 27(1)(a)(c)(e) of the BRRD.
69 Article 27(1)(d)(f)(g)(h) of the BRRD.

Financial institution resolutions 183

effect of opening an insolvency proceeding in many states, the managers may be replaced by temporary administrators when necessary as part of the early intervention measures.[70] However, even though the temporary administrators have the knowledge and skills to operate the business of the financial institutions, one question is whether they can quickly familiarize themselves with the business strategies of the financial institutions. An important aspect worth mentioning is that during the early intervention stage, relevant supervisory and resolution authorities have already cooperated with each other, coordinated by the supervisor college and EBA.[71] When one national authority would like to appoint a temporary administrator for a member financial company in a given group, either a parent company or a subsidiary, the BRRD encourages resolution authorities to communicate with the consolidating supervisor, who may, in turn, contact other national resolution authorities. When making decisions, all authorities need to consider the opinion of other member states and the impact on other member state's financial stability.

Finally, it is clear that preventive methods are different in non-financial corporate groups and financial groups. Due to the fear of systemic risks, certain SIFIs and resolution authorities are required to prepare for their respective recovery and resolution plans. The purpose of these plans is to make large financial institutions resolution-ready should any financial crisis happen. This stage can be said to be a transitional stage between bank supervision and resolution. It is also part of corporate governance in the sense that a resolution-ready financial group may not have efficient capital and operational structures without the help of those plans. There are no equivalent requirements for non-financial corporate groups as these requirements will impose too much of a burden on them without justification. However, one may argue that if non-financial corporate groups may consider their recovery plans as part of their corporate governance practices, it may help to elevate the reputation of the groups and reduce the costs of borrowing, even though this suggestion may only be introduced as a soft law recommendation.

A comparison between corporate debt restructuring tools and bank resolution tools

Bank resolution tools can only be used when the public interest is met. That is to say, insolvency law is still the first line of recourse for a failed bank or other financial institutions. This is especially true if they are not SIFIs or are unable to cause systemic risks to the real economy. The wide discretion enjoyed by resolution authorities, together with no participation of creditors or shareholders in the resolution plans, means that the commencement of bank resolution may infringe stakeholders' proprietary interests without adequate compensation or

---

70 Article 29 of the BRRD.
71 Article 30 of the BRRD.

184 *Financial institution resolutions*

justification. This indicates that resolution tools should not be used imprudently. Both the Financial Stability Board and the Basel Committee believe that countries should be equipped with effective resolution tools to deal with banking crises.[72]

Resolution tools

From the BRRD article 39 to article 43, four resolution tools are provided: the sale of business tool, the bridge institution tool, the asset separation tool and the bail-in tool.[73] In practice, it is possible to combine these tools in order to achieve a better result. Generally speaking, the sale of business tool aims to give resolution authorities the power to transfer assets and liabilities to other buyers or bridge banks.[74] The bridge bank tool is designed to receive a failed bank's critical functions and protected creditors, and wait for an opportunity to merge with another buyer bank.[75] The asset separation tool is used where bad assets of a failed bank are transferred to a publicly owned asset management company whose task is to orderly liquidate those assets.[76] The most important tool in the BRRD is the bail-in tool.[77] It is interesting to observe that there are two types of bail-ins: direct bail-in, which is used in the EU, whereby the terms of debts can be changed directly through bail-in power, and indirect bail-in, which is used widely in other regions of the world, such as the USA, whereby bad assets and non-performing loans will be left in a failed bank, while good assets will be transferred to a bridge bank.[78] Direct bail-in preserves the failed bank itself, while indirect bail-in preserves the critical business of that failed bank.[79]

Financial Stability Board (FSB) provides that the purpose of bail-in is to recapitalize a failed bank or capitalize a bridge bank which undertakes the critical function of that failed bank.[80] Therefore, the quintessential feature of bail-in is to write down the equity and debts of a failed financial institution or convert them into equities of a newly formed bank, according to the ladder of priority of creditors under national solvency proceedings, subject to certain exceptions.[81]

---

72 Recommendation 1 of Basel Committee on Banking Supervision Report and Recommendations of the Cross-Border Bank Resolution Group (2010). National authorities should have appropriate tools to deal with all types of financial institutions in difficulties so that an orderly resolution can be achieved that helps maintain financial stability, minimize systemic risk, protect consumers, limit moral hazard and promote market efficiency; FSB Key Attributes of Effective Resolution Regimes for Financial Institutions (2014), para. 3.2–3.6.

73 Art.39–43 of the BRRD.

74 Rodrigo Olivares-Caminal and others, *Debt Restructuring* (2nd edn, Oxford University Press 2016), p. 615.

75 Ibid., p. 616.

76 Ibid., p. 617.

77 Art. 43 of the BRRD,

78 Simon Gleeson and Randall Guynn, *Bank Resolution and Crisis Management: Law and Practice* (Oxford University Press 2016), p. 187.

79 Ibid., p. 191.

80 Financial Stability Board (2014) Key Attributes of Effective Resolution Regimes for Financial Institutions, p. 7.

81 Ibid., p. 9.

Financial institution resolutions 185

The bail-in tool can be considered a bank reorganization tool as it maintains the main functions of a bank or keeps a financial group operating.[82]

Banks resolution in the USA is traditionally dealt with by the FDIC under a special receivership regime, while bank holding companies and other financial institutions may be subject to the Bankruptcy Code. After the Dodd-Frank Act, another procedure, OLA, is designed for bank holding companies and non-bank financial institutions, including broker-dealers and insurers.[83] OLA aims to avoid systemic risks caused by those non-bank financial institutions, should they enter into the chapter bankruptcy proceedings. The name liquidation indicates that failed financial institutions will not be bailed out; rather, they will be liquidated after preserving and transferring the healthy parts of the businesses to a bridge company or a private party. FDIC is the receiver for failed banks and most financial institutions. It enjoys the power to sell assets together with liabilities to a third party, either a bridge bank or a buyer, with the residual assets and liabilities liquidated by FDIC.[84] As observed, the junior unsecured debt and unsecured intercompany loans will be sacrificed and turned into equity, followed by a transfer of assets and protected debts to a bridge bank, which will be sold to the public or a new holding company when recovered.[85] This is the standard approach to resolving a bank in the USA, termed as purchase and assumptions, whereby another bank buys the assets and liabilities of a failed bank.[86] Both buyers and bridge banks should have relevant charters, such as a bank charter, to conduct this transaction.[87]

Now it is possible to compare those resolution tools with non-financial corporate group restructuring practices. In a non-financial corporate group scenario, the purpose of the restructuring is to preserve the value of the whole group. Cram-down schemes of arrangement and pre-pack schemes of arrangement are popular in that a group-wide insolvency can be avoided, and the group value can be preserved. By the same token, a sale of a business tool or a bail-in tool under the BRRD or SRM regulation in the form of either a sale of shares or a sale of assets aims to transfer the systemically important part of the businesses to a third party.[88] The purpose of doing that, besides preservation of financial group value, is to avoid systemic risks caused by an uncontrolled collapse of the group.

---

82 Wolf-Georg Ringe, 'Bank Bail-In between Liquidity and Solvency' (2018) *American Bankruptcy Law Journal* 92 299, p. 304.

83 Hal S. Scott and Anna Gelpern, *International Finance Transactions, Policy and Regulation* (21st edn, Foundation Press 2016), p. 314.

84 Simon Glesson and Randall Guynn, *Bank Resolution and Crisis Management: Law and Practice* (Oxford University Press 2016), p. 96.

85 Ibid., pp. 97–98.

86 Michael S. Barr, Howell E. Jackson and Margaret E. Tahyar, *Financial Regulation Law and Policy* (2nd edn, Foundation Press 2018), p. 966.

87 FDIA 11(n)(1)(A).

88 Article 38(1) BRRD, article 24(1) SRM Regulation; Jens-Hinrich Binder, 'Resolution: Concepts, Requirements, and Tools', in Jens-Hinrich Binder and Dalvinder Singh (eds.), *Bank Resolution: The European Regime* (Oxford University Press 2016), para. 2.48.

186 *Financial institution resolutions*

Different from schemes of arrangement, which provide a structured framework for affected creditors to vote for a proposed restructuring plan, bail-in is compulsory so that debt write-down will be initiated without creditors' consent; it is a good way to quickly solve the collective issues of creditors' bargain and dangerous market conditions.[89] Since bank resolution does not need to seek creditors' approval, it can progress very swiftly compared to insolvency law. It is generally believed that a simple transfer tool is suitable for small banks, while bail-in by means of bridge banks has the potential to be used for large banks due to the fact that bridge banks can temporarily keep the critical function of a failed bank and buy time for seeking a potential buyer.[90] In non-financial corporate group settings, transfer tools or bridge bank tools are similar to the effect of a pre-pack scheme. In a pre-pack scheme, out-of-money unsecured creditors and shareholders will be left in a failed corporate group, whereas money creditors will be transferred to a bridge company, which will hold all shares of operating subsidiaries. This private practice does not rely on public financial support since non-financial groups generally are not too-big-to-fail. Similarly authorities have the power to transfer assets and liabilities without the consent of creditors; pre-pack schemes do not need to seek out-of-money creditors' consent.

Under the BRRD, a direct bail-in is similar to a cram-down scheme, whereby certain creditors' claims are directly modified. Without the concern of systemic risk, schemes of arrangement have to respect dissident creditors' votes and cannot ignore them if they vote to reject a restructuring plan. The only way to leave them behind is to use a pre-pack scheme to leave them in the failed company. By contrast, bail-in tools are public law in nature whereby resolution authorities do not need to seek the consent of bail-inable debt-holders. The question of who will be transferred to a bridge bank and who will be left behind is at the discretion of resolution authorities with reference to a prescribed list of bail-inable debts. To some degree, direct bail-in reduces the need for good/bad assets separation within a short time frame, and it is particularly advantageous over the bridge bank approach as the latter may need to deal with a transfer of foreign assets in foreign branches and subsidiaries subject to foreign law.[91] Similarly, pre-pack schemes are not always available as their usage is limited by the possibility to transfer senior creditors' claims and the main assets of the failed group to a newly set up holding company free of any claims of previous unsecured creditors and shareholders. This may require a series of complicated steps at the level of subsidiaries, which will encounter foreign laws.

---

89 Federico Lupo-Pasini and Ross P. Buckley, 'International Coordination in Cross-Border Bank Bailins: Problems and Prospects' (2015) *European Business Organization Law Review* 16 214, p. 209.

90 Jens-Hinrich Binder, 'Resolution: Concepts, Requirements, and Tools', in Jens-Hinrich Binder and Dalvinder Singh (eds.), *Bank Resolution: The European Regime* (Oxford University Press 2016), para. 2.48, para. 2.49.

91 Simon Gleeson and Randall Guynn, *Bank Resolution and Crisis Management: Law and Practice* (Oxford University Press 2016), p. 199.

Financial institution resolutions 187

In a large international financial institution insolvency case, bail-in may step in and offer an alternative solution by writing down certain equity and unsecured debts.[92] However, even though bail-in is a great innovation for bank resolution, it does not create liquidity for failed banks.[93] The cash flow issue is still unsolved simply by exercising a bail-in. It has been reported that in the recent Italian bank bankruptcy and resolution cases, the Italian resolution fund provided more money than shareholders and junior creditors' debt write-down as the latter was not enough.[94]

It is right to point out the limitations of sale and bridge institution tools under BRRD, considering the daunting task of transferring a group of financial institutions with international operation to a buyer within a short time, varying goals of resolution regimes and different substantive and procedural rules in different member states.[95] Similarly, a transfer creditor scheme for an ordinary non-financial corporate group could be extremely difficult to achieve as, in some cases, it entails pushing debts upwards to the parent company's level through the novation of contracts among subsidiaries, parent company and creditors. Some scholars have argued that had Lehman Bros used bail-in to preserve its huge amount of derivative books rather than relied on Chapter 11, its negative effect on the world might have been reduced as its counterparties did not need to rush to find new counterparties.[96] In some cases, the fear of systemic risks makes governments choose bailout as a safe option. For example, AIG, which is one of largest insurance companies in the world, had been bailed out by the US Fed Reserve; as it held a large amount of CDS affecting counterparties' value of debts, it was said to be able to cause a domino effect on other financial institutions.[97]

A transfer scheme is functionally similar to a bridge bank, where the assets and/or shares of operating subsidiaries will be transferred to a newly set up company.[98] Senior creditors' debts will be transferred to the new company or exchanged for shares issued by the company. By contrast, the unsecured creditors

92 Jens-Hinrich Binder, 'Resolution: Concepts, Requirements, and Tools', in Jens-Hinrich Binder and Dalvinder Singh (eds.), *Bank Resolution: The European Regime* (Oxford University Press 2016), para. 2.48, para. 2.54.
93 Marco Bodellini, 'To Bail-In, or to Bail-Out, That Is the Question' (2018) *European Business Organization Law Review* 19 381–388, p. 376.
94 Banca delle Marche, Cassa di Risparmio di Ferrara, Banca Popolare dell'Etruria e del Lazio and Cassa di Risparmio della Provincia di Chieti still needed the Italian Resolution Fund to provide 3.7 billion euros after shareholders and subordinated creditors paid 870 million euros. Marco Bodellini, 'To Bail-In, or to Bail-Out, That Is the Question' (2018) *European Business Organization Law Review* 19 381–388, p. 381.
95 Jens-Hinrich Binder, 'Resolution: Concepts, Requirements, and Tools', in Jens-Hinrich Binder and Dalvinder Singh (eds.), *Bank Resolution: The European Regime* (Oxford University Press 2016), para. 2.50.
96 Douglas G. Baird and Edward R. Morrison, 'Dodd-Frank for Bankruptcy Lawyers' (2011) *American Bankruptcy Institute Law Review* 19 287, p. 316.
97 William K. Sjostrom, Jr., 'The AIG Bailout' (2009) *Washington and Lee Law Review* 66 943, p. 978.
98 Christian Pilkinton, *Schemes of Arrangement in Corporate Restructuring* (2nd edn, Sweet & Maxwell 2017), p. 16.

188 *Financial institution resolutions*

will not join the scheme as they are out of money. However, it is possible that some junior creditors also have secured interests or guarantees in one or a few subsidiaries; this makes it difficult for the transfer scheme to completely abandon them.[99] Therefore, this approach may heavily rely on inter-creditor agreement, where, according to the agreement, the junior creditors' debts could be released. Without an effective inter-creditor agreement to tame junior creditors, it seems that the only way is to give them something in the newly set up company.[100] A cram-down scheme is similar to a direct bail-in as there is no need to transfer a group of subsidiaries to a bridge company, and the original identity of a failed company is preserved by debt for equity swap or simply debt write-down.[101] The problem is that senior creditors may need to share a slice of pie with potentially out-of-money junior creditors; also, more parties in the scheme will increase the difficulty of achieving a result.[102]

All in all, the value of resolution tools and the value of preventive restructuring tools should be appreciated. Not only can they save the business of an individual company: they can also be applied to save a group of companies.

MREL and no-creditor-worse-off principle

Since bank resolution respects the priorities of secured and preferential creditors, it exempts some debts from the scope of bail-in; along with debt with priority, some debts that will give rise to systemic risks will also be exempted.[103] For example, covered bonds of creditors and employees' salaries, as the representatives of secured interests and preferential interests, are exempt from the scope of bail-in.[104] On the other hand, short-term liabilities whose maturity was within seven days, owed to the insolvent financial institutions, were exempted as well.[105]

One potential issue of the bail-in mechanism is that it allows resolution authorities, including SRB and national equivalents, to have discretion with regard to which creditors, in exceptional circumstances, can be excluded from a bail-in. The circumstances include:

> (a) it is not possible to bail-in that liability within a reasonable time notwithstanding the good faith efforts of the resolution authority; (b) the exclusion is strictly necessary and is proportionate to achieve the continuity of critical functions and core business lines in a manner that maintains the ability of the institution under resolution to continue key operations, services and transactions; (c) the exclusion is strictly necessary and proportionate to avoid giving rise to widespread contagion, in particular as regards eligible

99 Ibid.
100 Ibid.
101 Ibid., p. 23.
102 Ibid., p. 25.
103 Art. 44 of the BRRD.
104 Art. 44 of the BRRD.
105 Art. 44 of the BRRD.

Financial institution resolutions 189

deposits held by natural persons and micro, small and medium sized enterprises, which would severely disrupt the functioning of financial markets, including of financial market infrastructures, in a manner that could cause a serious disturbance to the economy of a Member State or of the Union; or (d) the application of the bail-in tool to those liabilities would cause a destruction in value such that the losses borne by other creditors would be higher than if those liabilities were excluded from bail-in.[106]

The exemption of bail-in scope at least touches on two issues. The first issue is whether an entity still has enough bail-inable debts to absorb a financial crisis. This is particularly important if the parent company would like to absorb loss at the subsidiary level so as to avoid a group-wide collapse. To guarantee that a financial institution is resolvable using bail-in tools, the institution has to maintain a minimum level of bail-inable debts, termed minimum requirements for own funds and eligible liabilities (MREL).[107] At the international level, FSB also suggested a similar concept, referred to as total loss absorbing capacity (TLAC). In the UK, the bail-inable debts (MREL) are encouraged to be issued at the parent company level, and later they are moved down to subsidiaries so that MREL debts are structurally junior to liabilities of subsidiaries.[108] Since it has been recognized that financial institutions are interwoven together by financial markets, payment system and counterparties relations,[109] having MREL at the parent company level will facilitate a bail-in and rescue of the whole financial group.

Another important issue is whether the principle of *pari passu* of insolvency law can be respected during a bail-in procedure. After all, creditors who are situated in the same class should receive the same treatment in a pro rata fashion.[110] Similarly, the BRRD provides basic insolvency law protection to all creditors by adopting a no-creditor-worse-off principle whereby every creditor should receive at least the liquidation value of its claims.[111] The no-creditor-worse-off principle draws a line of minimum protection for creditors who are subject to a bail-in; they are entitled to their apportioned share of the liquidation value of a failed financial institution. In the USA, given that OLA is close to a liquidation proceeding, the FDIC, when applying OLA to a financial institution, has to consider the no-creditor-worse-off principle.[112]

---

106 BRRD, Art. 44(3). SRM Regulation, Art. 27(5).
107 BRRD Art. 45.
108 Peter G. Brierley, Ending Too-Big-To-Fail: Progress since the Crisis, the Importance of Loss-Absorbing Capacity and the UK Approach to Resolution' (2017) *European Business Organization Law Review* 18 471.
109 Michael S. Barr, Howell E. Jackson and Margaret E. Tahyar, *Financial Regulation Law and Policy* (2nd edn, Foundation Press 2018), p. 987.
110 Recital 77 of the BRRD.
111 Article 74 of the BRRD, Federico Lupo-Pasini and Ross P. Buckley, 'International Coordination in Cross-Border Bank Bail-Ins: Problems and Prospects' (2015) *European Business Organization Law Review* 16 214.
112 Michael S. Barr, Howell E. Jackson and Margaret E. Tahyar, *Financial regulation Law and Policy* (2nd edn, Foundation Press 2018), p. 995.

190 *Financial institution resolutions*

However, in previous practices, it seems that bank resolution involves too much discretion and political influence with regard to the scope of bail-inable debts and the discretion to use different resolution tools.[113] As a result, the no-creditor-worse-off principle and the *pari passu* principle were not respected.

Examples of a breach of the *pari passu* principle and the no-creditor-worse-off principle can be found in the case of Cypriot bank resolution.[114] In 2013, the failure of two large Cypriot banks – the Bank of Cyprus and Cyprus Popular Bank (Laiki) – after a decision made by the European Commission (EC), the European Central Bank (ECB) and the International Monetary Fund (IMF), resulted in their selling their foreign operations to Greek banks and imposing a bail-in on all depositors, including insured ones, in exchange for bailout financing.[115] Part of the deal was to sell Laiki Bank to Piraeus Bank. Laiki Bank was separated into a good bank and a bad bank, with shareholders, junior creditors and a significant amount of value of deposits in the bad bank subject to a debt write-off,[116] while the creditor, such as the University of Cyprus and[117] Greece-based depositors, were largely exempted. Some evidence showed that Greek depositors of foreign branches of these two Cypriot banks, due to the deal with Piraeus Bank, were almost untouched by the resolution, whereas Cypriot uninsured creditors had not been treated fairly and proportionately.[118] Cypriot depositors would have been better off if depositors in foreign branches also bore some losses.[119] The final compensation that Cypriot depositors had received might be less than the liquidation value of their claims,[120] so neither the *pari passu* principle or the no-creditor-worse-off principle were observed.

Political elements might also play a role in Cypriot banks' resolution and bailout. A large percentage of depositors were foreign depositors but not local ones,

---

113 Pierre de Gioia Carabellese and Daoning Zhang, 'Bail-In Tool and Bank Insolvency: Theoretical and Empirical Discourses around a New Legal (or Illegal) Concept' (2019) *European Business Law Review* 30(3) 14–16 (forthcoming), pp. 14–16.

114 Mikaella Yiatrou, 'The Myth of Cypriot Bank Resolution "Success": A Plea for a More Holistic and Less Costly Supervision & Resolution Approach' (2017) *European Business Organization Law Review* 18 503–533, pp. 526–527. (It is reported that even though the deposit guarantee scheme is not used, uninsured depositors are treated less favourably than insured depositors.)

115 Costas Xiouros, 'Handling of the Laiki Bank ELA and the Cyprus Bail-In Package', in Alexander Michaelides and Athanasios Orphanides (eds), *The Cyprus Bail-In Policy: Lessons from the Cyprus Economic Crisis*, 33 (Imperial College Press 2016). John Theodore and Jonathan Theodore, *Cyprus and the Financial Crisis – The Controversial Bailout and What It Means for the Eurozone*, para. 14.23 (Palgrave Macmillan 2015).

116 Thomas Philippon and Aude Salord, 'Bail-Ins and Bank Resolution in Europe: A Progress Report' (2017) *Geneva Reports on the World Economy Special Report* 4 32.

117 Pamela Lintner and Johanna Lincoln, 'Bank Resolution and "Bail-In" in the EU: Selected Case Studies Pre and Post BRRD' (2016).

118 John Theodore and Jonathan Theodore, *Cyprus and the Financial Crisis – The Controversial Bailout and What It Means for the Eurozone* (Palgrave Macmillan 2015), para. 14.102.

119 Costas Xiouros, 'Handling of the Laiki Bank ELA and the Cyprus Bail-In Package', in Alexander Michaelides and Athanasios Orphanides (eds.), *The Cyprus Bail-In Policy: Lessons from the Cyprus Economic Crisis*, 33 (Imperial College Press 2016).

120 Ibid., p. 84.

Financial institution resolutions 191

and this might explain part of the story. However, what is important is how much certainty bank resolution should provide to creditors and how much protection creditors are entitled to in a bail-in. One possible improvement is to define the categories of bail-inable debts as clearly as possible, and another is to constrain the discretion of resolution authorities that can be made based on clearly established principles and precedents. It is clear that the discretion enjoyed by authorities may affect creditors' prediction and give rise to an unfair reallocation of assets among creditors of different classes. Therefore, the principles of insolvency law should be respected by the bank resolution regimes as much as possible to achieve a fairer result.

SPOE approach

As mentioned, under BRRD, bank resolution advocates a universalist approach in that the jurisdiction of bank resolution is conferred to the country which authorizes that bank. Nonetheless, considering the interconnectedness of banks and other financial institutions, and the number of members in a financial corporate group, it is still different for courts in various jurisdictions to cooperate with each other. Taking the Bank of America as an example, the group has more than 2000 subsidiaries in 97 different jurisdictions.[121] Interestingly, even in the USA alone, different parts of the group are subject to different sets of law: banks are subject to FDIC receivership, insurance companies are subject to state-court receivership, broker-dealers are subject to the Securities Investor Protection Act (SIPA) liquidation procedures[122] and holding companies and other companies are subject to OLA or Chapter 11.[123] At the international level, different bank resolution laws and different priorities of values may stymie any possibilities of cooperation.

Due to this undesirable situation, a seemingly promising option is SPOE based on a 'super universalist' approach as opposed to an ordinary universalist approach, i.e. multiple point of entry (MOPE). One characteristic of OLA is that it employs the SPOE type of strategy whereby OLA will target the holding companies of a financial group; creditors and shareholders of holding companies will bear the risks, while creditors of subsidiaries will not be protected.[124] The success of this strategy depends on the fact that the holding companies should issue enough subordinate bonds which are large enough to absorb all the loss of the group. Under the SPOE approach, bank resolution can be solved only at the parent company and only by one resolution authority; by contrast, under MOPE,

---

121 Stephen J. Lubben, 'Resolution, Orderly and Otherwise: B of A in OLA' (2012) *University of Cincinnati Law Review* 81 485, p. 491.
122 The Securities Investor Protection Act.
123 Stephen J. Lubben, 'Resolution, Orderly and Otherwise: B of A in OLA' (2012) *University of Cincinnati Law Review* 81 485, p. 513.
124 Hal S. Scott and Anna Gelpern, *International Finance Transactions, Policy and Regulation* (21st edn, Foundation Press 2016), p. 315.

192 *Financial institution resolutions*

more than one resolution authority will participate in the group resolution, and the group may be sliced into different parts.[125] If the financial corporate groups are not very interconnected, one may argue that MOPE may be a good option. There is no one-size-fits-all option for cross-border bank resolution.

For example, the parent company does not operate any business except holding shares and borrowing money from the securities market or from other third parties; then it lends the money to subsidiaries. The benefits of doing this are that whenever a subsidiary in a group is insolvent and may implicate other members the parent company will recapitalize that subsidiary by writing down its debts or purchasing new shares issued by that company.[126] As a result, a group-wide crisis is avoided at the expense of shareholders and debt-holders of the parent company without opening multiple bank resolution procedures. Since the parent company issues long-term debts which cannot run before reaching maturity, the debt-holders will become 'voluntary victims' of such bank rescue.[127]

SPOE clearly provides many benefits to cross-border bank resolution. It has been submitted that long-term debts issued at the parent company level increase transparency and market discipline. SPOE concentrates control into one jurisdiction; therefore, it avoids difficulties of cross-border cooperation; it also preserves the critical functions and values of subsidiaries in the group.[128]

However, its application is subject to some limitations. The US version of the SPOE may not be viable in jurisdictions where the banking groups do not adopt a holding company structure. Therefore, cross-border cooperation and coordination of resolution authorities are necessary to deal with the collapse of a large bank group. Generally, parent companies may only take a passive role with limited businesses.[129] Also, will the jurisdiction of the parent company be happy to save subsidiaries all in its own country by using its own resources? In practice, the financial distress may affect parent companies' ability to receive further sources of financing since it decreases the value of assets in subsidiaries; also on the part of parent companies, their reduced ability to generate income may cause them struggle to pay interests of either the existing or further debts.[130]

Another question is will the jurisdictions of subsidiaries have any trust in the parent jurisdiction so that they do not need to take actions to save the

---

125 Costanza A. Russo, 'Resolution Plans and Resolution Strategies: Do They Make G-SIBs Resolvable and Avoid Ring Fence?' (2019) *European Business Organization Law Review*, pp. 4–5, p. 30.

126 John Crawford, 'Single Point of Entry: The Promise and Limits of the Latest Cure for Bailouts' (2014–2015) *Northwestern University Law Review* Online 109 107–108 (103), pp. 107–108.

127 Ibid. (Long-term debt-holders are expert investors who have charged an adjusted interest rate for the debts. Therefore, it is fair for them to be the 'victims' as they have chosen to be them.)

128 Wolf-Georg Ringe, 'Bank Bail-In between Liquidity and Solvency' (2018) *American Bankruptcy Law Journal* 92 299, p. 30.

129 Michael S. Barr, Howell E. Jackson and Margaret E. Tahyar, *Financial Regulation Law and Policy* (2nd edn, Foundation Press) 2018, p. 1001.

130 Stephen J. Lubben and Arthur E. Wilmarth, Jr., 'Too Big and Unable to Fail' (2017) *Florida Law Review* 69 1205, p. 1228, p. 1234.

subsidiaries?[131] Without trust and recognition of bail-in taking place in a foreign country, it is almost impossible to expect any international cooperation.[132] European Banking Union, in the future, may have an important role to play as a facilitator for both the home countries and the host countries of banks in the EU with regard to cooperation and information sharing.[133] Under the Single Resolution Board, supervisory and resolution powers are centralized into ECB so that it can address the resolution of international banks more effectively in the EU. However, the abuse of power issue may plague the benefits yielded from such centralization.[134] Also, it is important to note that at the international level outside of the scope BRRD, host countries may open local bank resolution procedures for the branches or subsidiaries of foreign banks due to a lack of confidence with regard to the financial strength of a holding company in a banking group or the availability of deposit insurance funds and resolution funds from home countries.

Even though SPOE may have some limitations in practice, its particular benefits for restructuring large financial corporate groups should not be underestimated. As previously mentioned, both non-financial and financial corporate groups face the same issues, arising from separate corporate personality, varying national insolvency law and impossibility of cooperation among many jurisdictions. Under multiple points of entry, different jurisdictions may feel it challenging to align their conflicting goals within a short time frame; they may also have no obligation to communicate with foreign jurisdictions with regard to a bank resolution case.[135] This is especially true when national interest and local creditors' interests are affected. As a result, it seems that the best way is to avoid those issues by cooperating on solving the problem within one jurisdiction.

Lessons for multinational corporate groups

One interesting convergent development in non-financial MCGs insolvency law and financial MCG resolution rules is the SPOE idea. Arguably, preventive restructuring frameworks and bail-in tools can be used to avoid a group-wide insolvency or limit the number of jurisdictions involved.

---

131 Federico Lupo-Pasini and Ross P. Buckley, 'International Coordination in Cross-Border Bank Bail-Ins: Problems and Prospects' (2015) *European Business Organization Law Review* 16 214, p. 221.
132 Ibid., p. 216.
133 Alexander Michaelides, 'Cyprus: From Boom to Bail-In' (2014) *Economic Policy* 29 678.
134 Jens-Hinrich Binder, 'Proportionality at the Resolution Stage: Calibration of Resolution Measures and the Public Interest Test' (available at: https://papers.ssrn.com/sol3/papers.cfm?abstract_id=2990379p23), p. 23.
135 Federico Lupo-Pasini and Ross P. Buckley, 'International Coordination in Cross-Border Bank Bail-Ins: Problems and Prospects' (2015) *European Business Organization Law Review* 16 214, p. 222. (This article states that the Federal Reserve may not be placed under an obligation to consult foreign jurisdictions about starting bank resolution procedures for foreign companies.)

194 *Financial institution resolutions*

It is important to note the limitations of the SPOE approach. The home country where the financial institutions are authorized is the one which has jurisdiction to resolve near-collapsed institutions. However, different countries advocate different degree of territorialism in the sense that some countries may treat foreign banks or branches of foreign banks differently from local banks. Some countries may require local depositors or creditors to be paid before extending support to the resolution authorities of home countries.[136] However, the SPOE approach, corresponding to the Directive on preventive restructuring frameworks, is a desirable direction of development.

Another convergent area is directors' duties. It has been argued that directors of a subsidiary that is not subject to the OLA have recognized that supporting another bank in the same group may help to avoid the bankruptcy of the whole bank group; the directors need to make sure that doing so is also in the interest of that subsidiary.[137] One justification of supporting a group resolution may be that all financial subsidiaries in a given group are reputationally connected, so it is almost impossible for any of them to be unaffected by the collapse of parent companies.[138] Similarly, as Chapter 5 discussed, insolvency practitioners of a non-financial member company also have duties to consider a group plan before considering using an opt-out mechanism.

Also, it is better for a non-financial corporate group to examine their corporate group structure and check whether the whole group or some parts of it form a business integrated economic unit that contains significant synergies. If so, it may be desirable to design a brief corporate organization plan and consider obstacles to implementing this plan. Where the costs to adapt to it are not high, the group or parts of it may change relevant capital and corporate group structure in order to make a group or parts of it ready for a group-wide transfer.

Furthermore, non-financial MCGs can learn from the design of recovery and resolution plans, and cooperative framework for financial institutions. First, banking groups are subject to the so-called ring-fencing rule, where the investment banks should be separated from retail banks, and each separated group should have its own prudential requirement and liquidity requirement.[139] In article 17 of BRRD, national resolution authorities shall have the power to remove obstacles in the way of the operation of resolution proceedings; among others, article17(g) points out that the legal and operational structure of a bank group may need to be changed in order to separate banks with deposit-taking functions

---

136 For example, the USA takes a territorial approach. Jacopo Carmassi and Richard Herring, 'The Cross-Border Challenge in Resolving Global Systemically Important Banks', in Thomas Jackson, Kenneth Scott and John Taylor (eds.), *Making Failure Feasible: How Bankruptcy Reform Can End Too Big to Fail* (Hoover Institution Press 2015), p. 259.

137 Stephen J. Lubben and Arthur E. Wilmarth, Jr., 'Too Big and Unable to Fail'(2017) *Florida Law Review* 69 1205, p. 1228.

138 Ibid., p. 1229.

139 Thom Wetzer, 'In Two Minds: The Governance of Ring-Fenced Banks' (available at: https://ssrn.com/abstract=3325292), accessed on 12 February, p. 9.

Financial institution resolutions 195

and banks with investment functions.[140] Given the importance of banks to the overall economics and financial stability, such a requirement for separateness can be justified in that reduction of complexity of bank structure will contribute, to some degree, to the chances of success of bank resolution.

By contrast, it is difficult to apply the same requirement to non-financial companies by requiring an ordinary group to separate certain functions from others. This is because, on the one hand, the business of non-financial companies may rarely amount to the status of 'systemically important financial institutions'. One may expect that some auto companies or utilities companies' businesses may be important to the local communities; however, the interconnectedness of businesses and contagion caused by the failure of one member in a group may not justify such separateness. Any corporate group owner should enjoy the freedom to design their own legal and capital structure. Such structure may fall into their own business judgement and should not be restrained. On the other hand, it may make some sense for a corporate group to reduce the complexity of legal structure for the part of the group where the businesses of members are integrated. The group may want to make sure that the assets and structure of the integrated subgroup do not interweave into the assets or structure of other parts of the group. This will help to reduce the complexity of subgroup structure and make it rescue-ready. However, to do this, the group may need to consider whether the costs of adjusting the structure will outweigh the benefits of the rescue. I imagine that if the group structure is too complex to be adjusted, and the group is financially healthy, the incentive to change group structure, without the pressure from regulation, will be limited.

Next, the Basel Committee suggested a supervisory college whereby national supervisory authorities may cooperate and coordinate together with regard to recovery and resolution plans, exchange information and promote the harmonization of the relevant substantive financial institution resolution rules.[141] FSB also recommends the formation of a crisis management group at the international level. In the EU, Resolution College was established for the purpose of bank resolution. Resolution College can work together to design a resolution strategy for a bank group. The College groups EU countries as a unit and facilitates cooperation with resolution authorities in a third country.[142] The cooperative framework under BRRD is similar to the group coordination proceedings under EIR recast in that both aim to facilitate cooperation among the main players in the context of group insolvency or resolution. Supervisory and resolution authorities can exchange information before the insolvency of banks; the directive on preventive restructuring frameworks also provides early cooperation and communication mechanisms for MCGs. The experience gained from one

---

140 BRRD article 17.
141 Iris H-Y Chiu and Joanna Wilson, *Banking Law and Regulation* (Oxford University Press 2019), p. 674.
142 Ibid., p. 675.

196 *Financial institution resolutions*

regime, in terms of methods of cooperation, may be useful for another to learn in the future.

Finally, the rationale of the bail-in tool bears some resemblance to pre-pack schemes, in respect to group rescue. Both of them need to strike a balance between efficiency and fairness. Bail-in tools and pre-pack schemes, by transferring control to a single authority or group of senior creditors, sell the business of a company or bank to a third party in order to preserve the group value or avoid systemic risk. However, both of these regimes need to prevent an abuse of power of sale and too much discretion, given that powers are centralized. Considering the catastrophic consequence of a failure of SIFIs, it seems the drawbacks of bail-ins and SPOE are tolerable. Nevertheless, since no effective mechanism exists for creditors to solve their compensation and debt valuation issues, it is desirable to make the bail-in tool as predictable as possible.[143] On the part of pre-pack schemes, the future debate point is how to strike a balance between a speedy group-wide solution and fair protection for junior creditors.

---

143 Jens-Hinrich Binder, Bank Bail-In and Disputed Claims: Can It Cope? The Case for and against a vis Attractiva Resolutionis (2019) (available at: https://ssrn.com/abstract=3325882).

8 A way forward

The interaction of all relevant regimes

This book examines theories and solutions for cross-border insolvencies of non-financial and financial MCGs, with a focus on non-financial MCGs. Since many businesses are conducted in the form of multinational companies, the issue of cross-border insolvency of MCGs is important. Given the complex legal and operational structures of MCGs and the multiple and varying values that insolvency law and resolution regimes aim to protect, it is safe to say that there is no one size fits all solution or theory. At least, from a theoretical perspective, cross-border insolvency law area is a battlefield where insolvency law theories, cross-border insolvency law theories, multinational enterprise group theories and bank resolution theories try to reach a compromise.

Corporate insolvency law theories can reveal what fundamental goals we aim to achieve;[1] a good understanding of multinational enterprise theories can help to draw a fuller picture of the characteristics of multinational enterprises and direct us as to how to achieve these goals in the context of MCG insolvencies. The fact that there is value in rescuing MCGs as a group may conflict with the certainty requirement of insolvency law and cross-border insolvency law. MCG theories, such as business network theory, reveal that a group CoMI, which underpins the procedural consolation theory, may be too elusive to determine.[2] That is not to say that procedural consolidation should be completely denied. In cases where evidence clearly shows that the CoMIs of all subsidiaries are in the jurisdiction of the parent company, procedural consolidation is still an option.

---

1 Preservation of going concern value and certainty are the main values which corporate rescue law aims to achieve. Gerard McCormack, *Corporate Rescue Law – An Anglo-American Perspective* (Edward Elgar Publishing Limited 2008), p. 4; Douglas G. Baird and Thomas H. Jackson, 'Corporate Reorganizations and the Treatment of Diverse Ownership Interests: A Comment on Adequate Protection of Secured Creditors in Bankruptcy' (1984) *University of Chicago Law Review* 51, 109.
2 The head office functions of MCGs may be spread across subsidiaries in different countries in order to increase group value. Therefore, it is difficult to create a group CoMI concept whereby all the foreign subsidiaries are centrally controlled by a parent company.

198 *A way forward*

The difficulties caused by unharmonized national insolvency law and out-dated debt restructuring rules, together with bank resolution regimes, lead to the enactment of new legislation at the EU and international level, not limited to the EIR recast, Directive on preventive restructuring frameworks,[3] BRRD and UNCITRAL Model Law.

In line with the recent Directive on preventive restructuring frameworks, some private or hybrid ad hoc solutions are able to avoid group-wide insolvencies by either writing down debts or selling a MCG as a going concern at the parent company's level. These solutions may preserve the group going concern value and provide some degree of certainty; they are especially useful in situations where financial creditors are collectively subject to concentrated loan agreements. However, the book also identified the limitations of informal/hybrid legal solutions.

Next, group coordination proceedings under EIR recast and group planning proceedings under UNCITRAL Model Law are modest cooperative frameworks. It is plausible to predict that member states in the EU will achieve more under group coordination proceedings, given that the mutual trust among EU member states facilitates the cooperation and coordination of insolvency proceedings. It is generally believed that the opt-out mechanism in the group coordination proceedings will significantly reduce utility of the mechanism in practice. It has been pointed out that the opt-out mechanism may take issue with the goal of preservation of group going concern value as it allows local senior creditors or investors of subsidiaries to benefit themselves at the expense of local creditors and group interest. Though harmonization of insolvency law may help to redress certain drawbacks of national insolvency law and facilitate cooperation, it is unlikely for member states to reach consensus, given that the policies underpinning insolvency law values are different from country to country. To address this issue, this book provides a modest recommendation. It argues that EIR recast in fact prevents member companies from completely ignoring the group restructuring option as directors and insolvency practitioners have duties to consider it. On the other hand, it is important to note that the cost of international cooperation may be high. Future research may be conducted with a focus on clear and concrete conditions of invocation of opt-out mechanisms in the context of cross-border insolvency of MCGs.

On the part of financial corporate group resolution, similar developments can be observed: bank recovery and resolution plans are similar to pre-insolvency proceedings for non-financial companies; resolution tools, such as bail-in and the usage of bridge banks, are similar to cram-down and pre-pack schemes of arrangement. SPOE functionally would like to achieve the goals of financial MCG

---

3 European Parliament legislative resolution of 28 March 2019 on the proposal for a directive of the European Parliament and of the Council on preventive restructuring frameworks, second chance and measures to increase the efficiency of restructuring, insolvency and discharge procedures and amending Directive 2012/30/EU (COM(2016)0723 – C8-0475/2016 – 2016/0359(COD)).

rescue without triggering multiple resolution regimes in different jurisdictions. Corporate rescue law and bank resolution regimes are different. Whereas corporate insolvency law focusses on the goals of maximization of creditors' value and predictable insolvency rules, bank resolution adds another value: avoiding systemic risk. For this reason, the latter relies on administrative authorities' procedures which can swiftly control and solve insolvency issue with financial stability in mind.

However, in many respects, important similarities between these two regimes can be found. For example, both corporate group insolvency regimes and bank resolution regimes have developed preventive restructuring frameworks or tools which allow insolvency practitioners or resolution authorities to take necessary precautions and actions to either avoid insolvency or solve the issue at an early stage. Also, the modernization of restructuring tools and resolution tools means that a certain level of harmonization has been achieved in the area of both cross-border insolvency law and bank resolution. These developments pave the grounds for further harmonization, and they have proven to be very useful.[4] More importantly, preventive restructuring tools and bank resolution tools can sometimes be used innovatively to avoid a group-wide insolvency. Examples are pre-pack schemes and single point of entry strategies. The rationale is obvious: due to the complex corporate structures of corporate groups and financial institutions, and unharmonized insolvency and resolution rules, it is impossible to achieve the goals of preservation of value for creditors or to avoid systemic risks by relying on weak or clumsy international cooperation if multiple insolvency proceedings are opened all over the world.

One caveat is that the international cooperation framework is useful to the extent that only a small number of insolvency proceedings are opened. If one financial corporate group has 2,000 subsidiaries in 100 jurisdictions, it seems that preventive restructuring frameworks and single point of entry regimes are more useful in that they may be able to solve the problem in a single jurisdiction. However, where SPOE is not available, for example, due to the fact that parent companies do not have adequate bail-inable debts to absorb all the losses incurred by foreign subsidiaries, or due to the fact that the host country has no confidence in the home country's conduct of SPOE,[5] cooperative frameworks and MPOE will be in order.

Also, restructuring law and bank resolution can work together to deal with the insolvency of a financial corporate group. In a financial conglomerate, part of the group may not be financial institutions or at least not systemically important financial companies. In that case, insolvency law will be used to deal with those

---

4 The recovery and resolution plans in fact give national competent and resolution authorities an opportunity to consider further harmonization of bank resolution rules. Emilios Avgouleas *et al.*, 'Bank Resolution Plans as a Catalyst for Global Financial Reform' (2013) *Journal of Financial Stability* 9 210–218.

5 Jay Lawrence Westbrook, 'SIFIs and States' (2014) *Texas International Law Journal* 49 329 341–353.

200 *A way forward*

companies' financial distress; resolution tools will be used when the collapse of an SIFI will lead to systemic risks.

Another important development is directors' duties in the vicinity of the insolvency of companies as they are the people who control their companies using first-hand information on financial healthiness. Their duties to take early actions or to cooperate with other directors or insolvency practitioners in drafting a group rescue plan are welcome and necessary. The development of directors' duties in a cross-border insolvency area with a focus on the duty of international cooperation, the development of cross-border insolvency law theories and the harmonization of cross-border insolvency law in international private law, and the modernization of restructuring and resolution tools all contribute to achieving the goals of insolvency law and bank resolution. Directors and insolvency practitioners, together with resolution authorities, will be alerted if they realize that part of a corporate group is experiencing financial difficulties.

In the context of financial organizations, the supervisory authorities, resolution authorities and financial organization themselves need to work together to achieve the same goal. Restructuring and resolution tools allow them to plan how to 'save' the group and how to save the group within one jurisdiction; cooperation duties and frameworks allow different directors, insolvency practitioners, courts and authorities to cooperate with each other.

Theoretically, it is clear that universalism has gained widespread support in the areas of cross-border insolvency and cross-border resolution. Since the sheer number of member companies in a group often creates a significant challenge for international cooperation, universalism helps to reduce the number of insolvency or resolution proceedings. Universalism theory can help to reduce the numbers of jurisdictions. The equivalent of EIR recast in the area of financial institutions, the Credit Institutions Winding Up Directive, facilitates recognition of other member state's bank liquidation and reorganization decisions.[6] Now the effect of the application of resolution tools can be recognized under the BRRD.[7] All of this legal development completes a full picture that cross-border insolvency and resolution may be more effective than they were in the past. The existence of bank resolution tools to a large extent avoids the necessity of bailout. One may predict that in the future, government bailouts will only be used in large-scale financial crises affecting the majority of financial institutions, after losses have been taken by shareholders and junior creditors.[8]

To conclude, with a good understanding of the interaction of the above relevant theories in cross-border insolvency/resolution of MCGs, we can identify what goals need to be achieved and analyse whether the existing tools are adequate to achieve them. None of the existing solutions can solve all the problems,

---

6 Directive 2001/24/EC of the European Parliament and of the Council of 4 April 2001 on the reorganization and winding up of credit institutions.

7 BRRD art.66.

8 Anthony J. Casey and Eric A. Posner, 'A Framework for Bailout Regulation' (2015) *Notre Dame Law Review* 91 479, p. 529.

A way forward   201

so it is desirable to use the whole armoury in practice. The similarities and differences between corporate insolvency law and bank resolution regimes allow us to learn from each other's experiences and consider the direction for further development.

A prediction of future development

It has been accepted that insolvency law is the default rule for all insolvent companies, with the exception of large financial institutions whose collapse may give rise to systemic risks. Nevertheless, it is worth noting that avoiding systemic risk does not mean that resolution authorities can do whatever they want without any legal constraints or consideration of basic insolvency law principles. Quite the contrary is true: bank resolution tools need to be exercised within the framework of the no-creditor-worse-off principle and the *pari passu* principle. Bank resolution regimes need to respect the ladder of priority under insolvency law as much as possible in order to avoid jeopardizing creditors' legitimate expectation.

The current mainstream cross-border insolvency theory is modified universalism for non-financial companies; in the field of bank resolution, arguably, the jurisdictional rule is even closer to universalism. For corporate insolvency and financial institution resolution, universalism may be the main direction of future development. The modified universalism has gained wide support both at the EU level and at the international level, and it has been argued as customary international law in the area of cross-border insolvency.[9] However, courts and resolution authorities may fear that universalism will lead to a loss of sovereignty, so they may, on some occasions, step back to territorialism. Bias against universalism, short-termism and bounded self-interests all lead to an unnecessary universalism-averse.[10] Due to the need to avoid systemic risks and the impossibility of dismantling a bank across jurisdictional lines, universalism seems to be a better option compared to territorialism.

Both cross-border insolvency of ordinary companies and resolution of SIFIs entail a significant level of international cooperation. Harmonization of insolvency law and resolution rules may also be helpful in removing the difficulties arising from the varying treatment of creditors' interests and their priority. There is a stronger case to call for harmonization of resolution tools as the losses from systemic risks are remarkable.

The fact that most businesses are operated by means of MCGs infers that simply relying on the cooperation of courts or resolution authorities in different countries is unlikely to preserve group value or avoid systemic risks. A better strategy may be one in which the necessary tools are available to private parties or resolution authorities and are used to deal with insolvency or resolution

---

9 Irit Mevorach, *The Future of Cross-Border Insolvency-Overcoming Biases and Closing Gaps* (Oxford University Press 2018), p. 81.

10 Irit Mevorach, *The Future of Cross-Border Insolvency-Overcoming Biases and Closing Gaps* (Oxford University Press 2018), pp. 58–74.

proceedings in a small number of jurisdictions. The recent application of pre-pack schemes for corporate groups and SPOE schemes shows that, even though they are not perfect, they are the best way to move forward. The challenge from the complex structures of corporate groups and the different cultures and values embraced by different countries mean that it is difficult to save an insolvent MCG at the international level. The good news is that newly enacted legislation, including EIR recast, BRRD and Directive on preventive restructuring frameworks and directors' duties, can work together to provide solutions. It can be expected that they together pave the grounds for future development.

Bibliography

Official documents

ABI Commission to Study the Reform of Chapter 11.

American Law Institute and International Insolvency Institute, 'Transnational insolvency: Global principles for cooperation in international insolvency cases' 2012.

Commission staff working document executive summary of the impact assessment – accompanying the document-commission recommendation on a new approach to business failure and insolvency SWD(2014) 61 final.

Commission staff working document executive summary of the impact assessment – accompanying the document-commission recommendation on a new approach to business failure and insolvency SWD(2014) 62 final.

Commission staff working document, impact assessment, accompanying the document Revision of Regulation (EC) No. 1346/2000 on insolvency proceedings SWD(2012) 416 final <available at: ec.europa.eu/justice/civil/files/insolvency-ia_en.pdf>.

Commission staff working document impact assessment. Revision of Regulation (EC) No. 1346/2000 on insolvency proceedings Strasbourg, 12.12.2012.

Commission staff working document executive summary of the impact assessment – accompanying the document-commission recommendation on a new approach to business failure and insolvency SWD(2014) 61 final.

External Evaluation of Regulation No. 1346/2000/EC on insolvency proceedings.

European Added Value Assessment EAVA 3/2012, Directive on the cross-border transfer of a company's registered office 14th Company Law Directive, European Parliament resolution of 2 February 2012 with recommendations to the Commission on a 14th company law directive on the cross-border transfer of company seats (2011/2046(INI)).

Financial Stability Board (2014) Key Attributes of Effective Resolution Regimes for Financial Institutions, 15 October.

'France's Observations on UNCITRAL's Working Methods' UN Doc A/CN 9/635 2007.

International Monetary Fund and the World Bank 'An Overview of the Legal, Institutional, and Regulatory Framework for Bank Insolvency' 2009, p. 16 <www.imf.org/external/np/pp/eng/2009/041709.pdf> accessed on 01 February 2019.

Impact Assessment on the Directive on the Cross Border Transfer of Registered Office Brussels, 12.12.2007.

IMF Orderly & Effective Insolvency Procedures 2000 <available at: www.imf.org/external/pubs/ft/orderly/index.htm>.

204 *Bibliography*

Key Attributes Assessment Methodology for the Banking Sector 2016 <www.fsb.org/wp-content/uploads/Key-Attributes-Assessment-Methodology-for-the-Banking-Sector.pdf>.

OECD Model Convention with respect to taxes on income and on capital.

Proposal for a regulation of the European Parliament and of the Council amending Council Regulation (EC) No. 1346/2000 on insolvency proceedings 2012/0360 (COD).

Proposals for the revision of the European Insolvency Regulation – a step forward in the rescue culture? Linklaters 2012.

Proposal by INSOL Europe revision of EU Regulation.

Proposal for a Directive of the European Parliament and of the Council on preventive restructuring frameworks, second chance and measures to increase the efficiency of restructuring, insolvency and discharge procedures and amending Directive 2012/30 – confirmation of the final compromise text with a view to agreement 15556/18.

Proposal for a Directive of the European Parliament and of the Council on preventive restructuring frameworks, second chance and measures to increase the efficiency of restructuring, insolvency and discharge procedures and amending Directive 2012/30/E 2016/0359 (COD).

Report of the Review Committee on Insolvency Law and Practice (1982) Cmnd 8558.

Report from the Commission to the European Parliament, the Council and the European economic and social committee on the application of Council Regulation (EC) No. 1346/2000 of 29 May 2000 on insolvency proceedings COM(2012) 743 final.

Report from the Commission to the European Parliament, the Council and the European Economic and Social Committee on the application of Council Regulation (EC) No. 1346/2000 of 29 May 2000 on insolvency proceedings.

Revision of the European Insolvency Regulation Proposals by INSOL Europe 2012.

The Third King Report on corporate governance in South Africa.

The proposal for 14th Company Directive.

UNCITRAL Legislative Guide on Insolvency Law – Part three.

Virgos-Schmit Report on the Convention on Insolvency Proceedings 6500/96 1996.

Books

Ambos, B. and Schlegelmilch, B., *The New Role of Regional Management* (Palgrave McMillan 2010).

Arnold, M. (QC) and Haywood, M., 'Duty to Promote the Success of the Company', in Simon Mortimore (ed.), *Company Directors Duties, Liabilities, and Remedies* (Oxford University Press 2017), p. 309.

Asimacopoulos, K. and Bickle, J., *European Debt Restructuring Handbook: Leading Case Studies from the Post-Lehman Cycle* (Globe Law and Business 2013).

Barr, M.S., Jackson, H.E. and Tahyar, M.E., *Financial Regulation Law and Policy* (2nd edn, Foundation Press 2018).

Bartlett, C.A. and Ghoshal, S., *Managing Across Borders: The Transnational Solution* (Harvard Business School Press 1989).

Belcher, A., *Corporate Rescue* (Sweet & Maxwell 1997).

Binder, J.H. and Singh, D., *Bank Resolution: The European Regime* (Oxford University Press 2016).

Bork, R. and Mangano, R., *European Cross-Border Insolvency Law* (Oxford University Press 2016).

Bibliography 205

Chiu, I.H.Y. and Wilson, J., *Banking Law and Regulation* (Oxford University Press 2019).

Donaldson, L., *The Contingency Theory of Organizations* (Sage Publications 2001).

Ferran, E., Payne, J. and Moloney, N., *The Oxford Handbook of Financial Regulation* (Oxford University Press 2015).

Finch, V., *Corporate Insolvency Law Perspectives and Principles* (2nd edn, Cambridge University Press 2009).

Fletcher, I., *Insolvency in Private International Law* (2nd edn, Oxford University Press 2005).

——— *The Law of Insolvency* (4th edn, Sweet & Maxwell London 2009).

Fletcher, I. and Wessels, B., *Harmonisation of Insolvency Law in Europe* (Kluwer Deventer 2012).

Forsgren, M. *Theories of the Multinational Firm* (2nd edn, Edward Elgar 2013).

Forsgren, M. *et al.*, *Managing the Embedded Multinational – A Business Network View* (Edward Elgar 2006).

Gerven, W.V., 'Bringing (Private) Laws Closer to Each Other at the European Level', in F. Cafaggi (ed.), *The Institutional Framework of European Private Law* (Oxford University Press 2006).

Gleeson, S., *International Regulation of Banking-Capital and Risk Requirements* (2nd edn, Oxford University Press 2012).

——— *Gleeson on the International Regulation of Banking* (3rd edn, Oxford University Press 2018).

Gleeson, S. and Guynn, R., *Bank Resolution and Crisis Management: Law and Practice* (Oxford University Press 2016).

Goode, R., *Principle of Corporate Insolvency Law* (4th edn, Sweet Maxwell London 2011).

Hakansson, H., *International Marketing and Purchasing of Industrial Goods – An Interaction Approach* (John Wiley & Sons 1982).

Håkansson, H. and Snehota, I., *Developing Relationships in Business Networks* (Routledge 1995).

Hess, B., Oberhammer, P. and Pfeiffer, T., *European Insolvency Law Heidelberg-Luxemburg-Vienna Report* (Hart Publishing Oxford 2014).

Ho, L.C., *Cross-Border Insolvency a Commentary on the UNCITRAL Model Law* (4th edn, volume 1, Global Law and Business 2017).

Howard, C. and Hedge, B., *Restructuring Law and Practice* (2nd edn, LNUK 2014).

Ireland, R.D. *et al.*, *The Management of Strategies Concept and Cases* (9th International Edition, South-Western Cengage Learning 2012).

Jackson, T.H., *The Logic and Limits of Bankruptcy Law* (Harvard University Press 1986).

Lastra, R.M., *International Financial and Monetary Law* (2nd edn, Oxford University Press 2015).

Lopucki, L., *Courting Failure: How Competition for Big Cases Is Corrupting the Bankruptcy Courts* (University of Michigan Press 2006).

Mall, C.A., *Corporate Governance* (4th edn, Oxford University Press 2012).

McCormack, G., *Corporate Rescue Law – An Anglo-American Perspective,* (Edward Elgar Publishing Limited 2008).

——— *Secured Credit and the Harmonisation of Law, the UNCITRAL Experience* (Edward Elgar Publishing Limited 2011).

Mevorach, I., *Insolvency within Multinational Enterprise Groups* (Oxford University Press 2009).

206   Bibliography

—— *The Future of Cross-Border Insolvency-overcoming Biases and Closing Gaps* (Oxford University Press 2018).

Miles, J.A., *Management and Organization Theory* (Jossey-Bass 2012).

Moss, G., Fletcher, I. and Isaacs, S., *The EU Regulation on Insolvency Proceedings* (3rd edn, Oxford University Press Oxford 2016).

Muchlinski, P.T., *Multinational Enterprise and the Law* (2nd edn, Oxford University Press 2007).

Nohria, N. and Ghoshal, S., *The Differentiated Network* (Jossey-Bass Inc. 1997).

O'dea Geoff Long, J. and Smyth, A., *Schemes of Arrangement Law and Practice*, (Oxford University Press 2012).

Olivares-Caminal, R. *et al.*, *Debt Restructuring* (Oxford University Press 2011).

—— *Debt Restructuring* (2nd edn, Oxford University Press 2016).

Parry, R., *Corporate Rescue* (Thomson Sweet & Maxwell 2008).

Paschalisdis, P., *Freedom of Establishment and Private International Law for Corporations'* (Oxford University Press 2012).

Payne, J., *Scheme of Arrangement, Theory Structure and Operation* (Cambridge University Press 2014).

Pfeffer, J. and Salancik, G., *The External Control of Organizations: A Resource Dependence Perspective* (Harper & Row 1978).

Pilkington, C., *Schemes of Arrangement in Corporate Restructuring* (Sweet & Maxwell 2013).

—— *Schemes of Arrangement in Corporate Restructuring* (2nd edn, Sweet & Maxwell 2017).

Proctor, C., *The Law and Practice of International Banking* (Oxford University Press 2015).

Sealy, L. and Worthington, S., *Sealy & Worthington's Cases and Materials in Company Law* (10th edn, Oxford University Press 2016).

Solomon, J., *Corporate Governance and Accountability* (4th edn, John Wiley & Sons Ltd. 2013).

Theodore, J. and Theodore, J., *Cyprus and the Financial Crisis – The Controversial Bailout and What It Means for the Eurozone* (Palgrave Macmillan 2015), para. 14.23.

Thompson, J.D., *Organizations in Action* (McGraw-Hill 1967).

Tricker, B., *Corporate Governance Principles, Policies, and Practices* (Oxford University Press 2009).

Wessels, B., *International Insolvency Law* (Kluwer 2006).

Wilson, G., *English Legal System* (2nd edn, Pearson Education Limited 2014).

Witting, C.A., *Liability of Corporate Groups and Networks* (Cambridge University Press 2018).

Zwieten, K.V., 'An Introduction to the European Insolvency Regulation, as Made and as Recast', in R. Bork and K. van Zwieten (eds.), *Commentary on the European Insolvency Regulation* (Oxford University Press 2016).

Articles

Adams, C.W., 'An Economic Justification for Corporate Reorganisation' (1991–1992) *Hofstra Law Review* 20 117.

Adams, E. and Fincke, J.K., 'Coordinating Cross-Border Bankruptcy: How Territorialism Saves Universalism' (2008–2009) *Columbia Journal of European Law* 15 43.

Bibliography 207

Adebola, B., 'A Few Shades of Rescue: Towards an Understanding of the Corporate Rescue Concept in England and Wales' (2014) <available at: http://ssrn.com/abstract=2524488> accessed on 22 May 2015.

—— 'Proposed Feasibility Oversight for Pre-Pack Administration in England and Wales: Window Dressing or Effective Reform?' (2015) *Journal of Business Law* 8 591–606.

Adler, B.E., 'Bankruptcy and Risk Allocation' (1992) *Cornell Law Review* 77 439–489.

Alfoldi, E.A. *et al.*, 'Coordination at the Edge of the Empire: The Delegation of Headquarters Functions through Regional Management Mandates' (2012) *Journal of International Management* 18 276–292.

Ambos, B. and Mahnke, V., 'How Do MNC Headquarters Add Value?' (2010) *Management International Review* 50(4) 403–412.

Ambos, T.C., 'Learning from Foreign Subsidiaries: An Empirical Investigation of Headquarters' Benefits from Reverse Knowledge Transfers' (2006) *International Business Review* 15 294–312.

Anand, A., 'Large Law Firms and Capture: Towards a Nuanced Understanding of Self-regulation' (2013) <available at: http://ssrn.com/abstract=2616883> accessed on 17 February 2014.

Anderson, H., 'Ebbs and Flows of Universalism' (2015) *Recovery*. R3, the Association of Business Recovery Professionals <available at: https://www.r3.org.uk/media/documents/publications/recovery/Summer15.pdf>

Andersson, U. and Forsgren, M., 'Subsidiary Embeddedness and Control in the Multinational Corporation' (1996) *International Business Review* 5(5) 487–508.

—— 'In Search of Centre of Excellence: Network Embeddedness and Subsidiary Roles in Multinational Corporations' (2000) *Management International Review* 40(4) 329–350.

Andersson, U. *et al.*, 'Balancing Subsidiary Influence in the Federative MNC: A Business Network View' (2007) *Journal of International Business Studies* 38(5) 802–818.

—— 'The Contribution of Local Environments to Competence Creation in Multinational Enterprises' (2014) *Long Range Planning* 47 87–99.

Armour, J., 'The Law and Economics of Corporate Insolvency: A Review' (2001) ESRC Center for Business Research University of Cambridge, Working Paper No. 197.

—— 'Who Should Make Corporate Law? EC Legislation versus Regulatory Competition' (2005) *Current Legal Problems* 58 369.

—— 'The Rise of the Pre-Pack, Corporate Restructuring in the UK and Proposal for Reform' (2012) <available at: http://ssrn.com/abstract=2093134> accessed on 6 June 2016.

Armour, J. and Deakin, S., 'Norms in Private Insolvency: The "London Approach" to the Resolution of Financial Distress' (2001) *Journal of Corporate Law Studies* 1(1) 21–51.

Armour, J. *et al.*, 'Corporate Ownership Structure and the Evolution of Bankruptcy Law: Lessons from the United Kingdom' (2002) *Vanderbilt Law Review* 55 1699.

Arnold, M., 'The Insolvency Regulation: A Service or an Overhaul' (2013) *South Square Digest* February.

—— 'Truth or Illusion? COMI Migration and Forum Shopping under the EU Insolvency Regulation' (2013) *Business Law International* 14 245.

Arnold, M. (QC) and Haywood, M., 'Duty to Promote the Success of the Company', in Simon Mortimore (QC) (ed.), *Company Directors Duties, Liabilities, and Remedies* (Oxford University Press 2017), p. 309.

Asakawa, K., 'Organizational Tension in International R&D Management: The Case of Japanese Firms' (2001) *Research Policy* 30(5) 735–757.

208 *Bibliography*

Asher, C.C. *et al.*, 'Towards a Property Rights Foundation for a Stakeholder Theory of the Firm' (2005) *Journal of Management and Governance* 9 5–32.

Astle, T., 'Pack Up Your Troubles: Addressing the Negative Image of Pre-Packs' (2015) *Insolvency Intelligence* 28 72–74.

Avgouleas, E. *et al.*, 'Bank Resolution Plans as a Catalyst for Global Financial Reform' (2013) *Journal of Financial Stability* 9 210–218.

Ayotte, K. and Skeel, D.A., 'Bankruptcy Law as a Liquidity Provider' (2013) *University of Chicago Law Review* 80 1557.

Baaij, M.G. *et al.*, 'Why Do Multinational Corporations Relocate Core Parts of their Corporate Headquarters Abroad?' (2015) *Long Range Planning* 48 46–58.

Baird, D.G., 'The Uneasy Case for Corporate Reorganizations' (1986) *The Journal of Legal Studies* 15 127.

——— 'Loss Distribution, Forum Shopping, and Bankruptcy: A Reply to Warren' (1987) *University of Chicago Law Review* 54 815.

——— 'The Hidden Virtues of Chapter 11: An Overview of the Law and Economics of Financially Distressed Firms' (1997) Coase-Sandor Institute for Law & Economics, Working Paper No. 43 <available at: https://chicagounbound.uchicago.edu/cgi/viewcontent.cgi?article=1526&context=law_and_economics> accessed on 1 February 2014.

——— 'Bankruptcy's Uncontested Axioms' (1998–1999) *The Yale Law Journal* 108 573.

——— 'Substantive Consolidation Today' (2005–2006) *Boston College Law Review* 47 5.

Baird, D.G. and Jackson, T.H., 'Corporate Reorganizations and the Treatment of Diverse Ownership Interests: A Comment on Adequate Protection of Secured Creditors in Bankruptcy' (1984) *University of Chicago Law Review* 51 97.

Baird, D.G. and Morrison, E.R., 'Dodd-Frank for Bankruptcy Lawyers' (2011) *American Bankruptcy Institute Law Review* 19 287.

Baird, D.J. and Rasmussen, R.K., 'The End of Bankruptcy' (2002) *Stanford Law Review* 55 751.

——— 'Chapter 11 at Twilight' (2003) *Stanford Law Review* 56.

——— 'Private Debt and the Missing Lever of Corporate Governance' (2005–2006) *University of Pennsylvania Law Review* 154 1209.

——— 'Anti-Bankruptcy' (2010) *The Yale Law Journal* 119(4) 648.

Bang-Pederse, U.R., 'Assets Distribution in Transnational Insolvencies, Combining Predictability and Protection of Local Interests' (1999) *American Bankruptcy Law Journal* 73 385.

Barney, J.B., 'Firm Resources and Sustained Competitive Advantage' (1991) *Journal of Management* 17 99–120.

Baxte, T.C., Hansen, J.M. and Sommer, J.H., 'Two Cheers for Territoriality: An Essay on International Bank Insolvency Law' (2004) *American Bankruptcy Law Journal* 78 57.

Bebchuk, L.A. 'Federalism and the Corporation: The Desirable Limits on State Competition in Corporate Law' (1991–1992) *Harvard Law Review* 105 1435.

——— 'A New Approach to Corporate Reorganizations' (1988) *Harvard Law Review* 101 775–804.

——— 'Using Options to Divide Value in Corporate Bankruptcy' (2000) *European Economic Review* 44 829.

Bebchuk, L.A. and Guzman, A.T., 'An Economic Analysis of Transnational Bankruptcies' (1999) *The Journal of Law and Economics* 42 775.

Bebchuk, L.A. and Roe, M.J. 'A Theory of Path Dependence in Corporate Ownership and Governance' (1999) Working Paper No. 131.

Bibliography 209

Bebchuk, L.A. *et al.*, 'Does the Evidence Favor State Competition in Corporate Law?' (2002) *California Law Review* 1775 1820–1821.

Belohlavek, A.J., 'Center of Main Interest (COMI) and Jurisdiction of National Courts in Insolvency Matters (Insolvency Status)' (2008) *International Journal of Law and Management* 50(2) 53–86.

Ben-Ishai, S. and Lubben, S.J., 'Involuntary Creditors and Corporate Bankruptcy' (2012) *UBC Law Review* 45 253.

Berends A.J., 'The Eurofood Case: One Company, Two Main Insolvency Proceedings: Which One Is the Real One' (2006) *Netherlands International Law Review* 53(2) 331–361.

Bewick, S., 'Schefenacker plc: A Successful Debt-for-Equity Swap' (2008) *International Corporate Rescue* 5(2).

——— 'The EU Insolvency Regulation, Revisited' (2015) *International Insolvency Review* 24 172–191.

Biermeyer, T., 'Case C-396/09 Interedil Sri, Judgment of the Court of 20 October 2011, Court Guidance as to the COMI Concept in Cross-Border Insolvency Proceedings' (2011) *Maastricht Journal of European and Comparative Law* 18 581.

Binder, J.H. 'Proportionality at the Resolution Stage: Calibration of Resolution Measures and the Public Interest Test' <available at: https://papers.ssrn.com/sol3/papers.cfm?abstract_id=2990379> p. 23.

——— 'Resolution: Concepts, Requirements, and Tools' in Jens-Hinrich Binder and Dalvinder Singh (eds.), *Bank Resolution: The European Regime* (Oxford University Press 2016), para. 2.48.

——— 'Bank Bail-In and Disputed Claims: Can It Cope? The Case for and against a vis Attractiva Resolutionis' (2019) <available at: https://ssrn.com/abstract=3325882>

Birkinshaw, J.M. and Fry, N., 'Subsidiary Initiatives to Develop New Markets' (1998) *Sloan Management Review* 39(3) 51–61.

Birkinshaw, J.M. and Morrison, A.J., 'Configurations of Strategy and Structure in Subsidiaries of Multinational Corporations' (1995) *Journal of International Business Studies* 26(4) 729–754.

Blumberg, P.I., 'The Corporate Entity in an Era of Multinational Corporations' (1990) *Delaware Journal of Corporate Law* 15(2) 283–374.

Bodellini, M. 'To Bail-In, or to Bail-Out, That Is the Question' (2018) *European Business Organization Law Review* 19 381–388.

Bork, R., 'The European Insolvency Regulation and the UNCITRAL Model Law on Cross-Border Insolvency' (2017) *International Insolvency Review* 26 246–269/ 247–248.

Bowmer, S., 'To Pierce or Not to Pierce the Corporate Veil – Why Substantive Consolidation Is Not an Issue under English Law' (2000) *Journal of International Banking Law* 15 193–197.

Bradley, M. and Rosenzweig, M., 'The Untenable Case for Chapter' 11' (1992) *The Yale Law Journal* 101 1043.

Brierley, P.G. 'Ending Too-Big-To-Fail: Progress since the Crisis, the Importance of Loss-Absorbing Capacity and the UK Approach to Resolution' (2017) *European Business Organization Law Review* 18 471.

Broc, K.G. and Parry, R., *Corporate Rescue: An Overview of Recent Developments from Selected Countries in Europe* (Kluwer Law International 2004).

Brouwer, M., 'Reorganization in US and European Bankruptcy Law' *European Journal of Law and Economics* (2006) 22 5–20. Springer Science Business Media, LLC.

210 Bibliography

Brunstad, G.E., 'Bankruptcy and Problems of Economic Futility: A Theory on the Unique Role of Bankruptcy Law' (1999–2000) *Business Law* 55 499.

Buckley, K., 'Wind Hellas: Pre-Packs and COMI Shift; Abuse or Innovation?' (2010) *Journal of International Banking & Financial Law* 6 342.

Buckley, P.J. and Casson, M.C., 'The Internalization Theory of the Multinational Enterprise: A Review of Progress of a Research Agenda after 30 years' (2009) *Journal of International Business Studies* 40 1563–1580.

Buckley, P.J. and Strange, R., 'The Governance of the Multinational Enterprise: Insights from Internalization Theory' (2011) *Journal of Management Studies* 48(2) 460–470.

Bufford, S.L. 'International Insolvency Case Venue in the European Union: The Parmalat and Daisytek controversies' (2005–2006) *Columbia Journal of European Law* 12 429.

———— 'Center of Main Interests, International Insolvency Case Venue, and Equality of Arms: The Eurofood Decision of the European Court of justice' (2006–2007) *Northwestern Journal of International Law & Business* 27 351.

———— 'Coordination of Insolvency Cases for International Enterprise Groups: A Proposal' (2012) *American Bankruptcy Law Journal* 86 685.

Busch, D. and Van Rijn, M.B.J. 'Towards Single Supervision and Resolution of Systemically Important Non-Bank Financial Institutions in the European Union' (2018) *European Business Organization Law Review* 19 356.

Butler, R.V. and Gilpatric, S.M., 'A Re-Examination of the Purposes and Goals of Bankruptcy' (1994) *The American* Bankruptcy Institute Law Review 2 269.

Buxbaum, H.L., 'Rethinking International Insolvency: The Neglected Role of Choice of Law Rules and Theory' (2000) *Stanford Journal of International Law* 36 23.

Cantwell, J. and Mudambi, R., 'MNE Competence-Creating Subsidiary Mandates' (2005) *Strategic Management Journal* 26(12) 1109–1128.

Caprio, G., 'Regulatory Capture: Why It Occurs, How to Minimize It' (2013–2014) *The North Carolina Banking Institute* 18 39.

Carmassi, J. and Herring, R. 'The Cross-Border Challenge in Resolving Global Systemically Important Banks', in Thomas Jackson, Kenneth Scott, and John Taylor (eds.), *Making Failure Feasible: How Bankruptcy Reform Can End Too Big to Fail* (Hoover Institution Press 2015), p. 259.

Carruthers, B.G. and Halliday, T.C., 'Professionals in Systemic Reform of Bankruptcy Law: The 1978 US Bankruptcy Code and the UK Insolvency Act 1986' (2000) *The American Bankruptcy Institute Law Review* 74 35.

Casey, A.J. and Posner, E.A., 'A Framework for Bailout Regulation' (2015) *Notre Dame Law Review* 91 479.

Chang, T. and Scholar, A., 'The Effect of Judicial Bias in Chapter 11 Reorganisation'" (October 2006) <available at: www.ssrn.com/>.

Chung, J.J., 'The New Chapter 15 of the Bankruptcy Code: A Step Toward Erosion of National Sovereignty' (2007) *North-Western Journal of International Law & Business* 27 89.

Ciabuschi, F. 'The Role of Headquarters in the Contemporary MNC' (2012) *Journal of International Management* 18 213–223.

Ciabuschi, F. *et al.*, 'Dual Embeddedness, Influence and Performance of Innovating Subsidiaries in the Multinational Corporation' (2014) *International Business Review* 23 897–909.

Coase, R.H., 'The Nature of the Firm' (1937) *Economica*, New Series 4(16) 368–405.

Bibliography 211

Cohen, A., 'Eurofood for Thought: Additional Guidance on COMI' (2012) *Journal of International Banking and Financial Law* 1 52.

Conner, K.R. and Prahalad, C.K., 'A Resource-Based Theory of the Firm: Knowledge versus Opportunism' (1996) *Organization Science* 7 477–501.

Couwenberg, O. and Lubben, S.J., 'Essential Corporate Bankruptcy Law' (2013) University of Groningen Faculty of Law Research Paper Series 4.

Crawford, J. 'Single Point of Entry: The Promise and Limits of the Latest Cure for Bailouts' (2014–2015) *Northwestern University Law Review* Online 109 107–108 (103).

Crespo, C.F., 'The Performance Effects of Vertical and Horizontal Subsidiary Knowledge Outflows in Multinational Corporations' (2014) *International Business Review* 23 993–1007.

Cyert, R.M. *et al.*, 'Information, Market Imperfections and Strategy' (1993) *Strategic Management Journal* 14 (Winter Special Issue) 47–58.

Dahlin, P. *et al.*, 'Netquakes – Describing Effects of Ending Business Relationships on Business Networks' (2005) Working Paper to be presented at IMP in Rotterdam.

Daines, R., 'Does Delaware Law Improve Firm Value?' (2001) *The Journal of Financial Economics* 62 525, 533.

Davies, S., 'Pre-Pack-He Who Pays the Piper Calls the Tune' (2006, Summer) *Recovery* 16.

Dawson, A.B., 'Offshore Bankruptcies' (2009) *Nebraska Law Review* 88(2).

Deakin, S., 'Legal Diversity and Regulatory Competition: Which Model for Europe Centre for Business Research' (2006) University of Cambridge, Working Paper No. 323.

——— 'Reflexive Governance and European Company Law' (2009) *European Law Journal* 15(2) 224–245.

Dellestrand, H., 'Subsidiary Embeddedness as a Determinant of Divisional Headquarters Involvement in Innovation Transfer Processes' (2011) *Journal of International Management* 17 229–242.

De Gioia Carabellese, P. and Zhang, D., 'Bail-In Tool and Bank Insolvency: Theoretical and Empirical Discourses around a New Legal (or Illegal) Concept' (2019) *European Business Law Review* 30(3) 14–16 (forthcoming).

De Weijs, R.J. *et al.* 'The Imminent Distortion of European Insolvency Law: How the European Union Erodes the Basic Fabric of Private Law by Allowing "Relative Priority" (RPR)' (2019) Centre for the Study of European Contract Law <available at: https://ssrn.com/abstract=3350375>

Diamantis, M.E., 'Arbitral Contractualism in Transnational Bankruptcies' (2005–2007) *Southwestern University Law Review* 35 327.

Doz, Y. and Santos, JFPS, 'On the Management of Knowledge: From the Transparency of Collocation and Co-Setting to the Quandary of Dispersion and Differentiation' (1997) INSEAD, Fontainebleau, France.

Dunning, J.H., 'The Eclectic Paradigm as an Envelope for Economic and Business Theories of MNE Activity' (2000) *International Business Review* 9 163–190.

Dyer, J.H. and Singh, H., 'The Relational View: Cooperative Strategy and Sources of Inter-Organisational Competitive Advantage' (1998) *The Academy of Management Review* 23(4) 660–679.

Easterbrook, F.H., 'Is Corporate Bankruptcy Efficient' (1990) *Journal of Financial Economics* 27(2).

Easterbrook, F.H. and Fischel, D., 'Limited Liability and the Corporation' (1985) *University of Chicago Law Review* 52 89.

212   Bibliography

Eidenmüller, H. 'Abuse of Law in the Context of European Insolvency Law' (2009) *European Company and Financial Law Review* 6 1–28.

—— 'Comparative Corporate Insolvency Law' (2016) European Corporate Governance Institute (ECGI) – Law Working Paper No. 319.

Eidenmüller, H. and van Zwieten, K., 'Restructuring the European Business Enterprise: The EU Commission Recommendation on a New Approach to Business Failure and Insolvency' (2015) ECGI Working Paper 301.

Eisenberg, T. and LoPucki, L., 'Shopping for Judges: An Empirical Analysis of Venue Choice in Large Chapter 11 Reorganizations' (1999) *Cornell Law Review* 84 967.

Feibelman, A., 'Living Wills and Pre-Commitment' (2011) *American University Business Law Review* 1 93.

Fennelly, N., 'Legal Interpretation at the European Court of Justice' (1996) *Fordham International Law Journal* 20(3) 656.

Finch, V., 'Control and Co-Ordination Incorporate Rescue' (2005) *Legal Studies* 25 374.

—— 'Corporate Rescue in a World of Debt' (2008) *Journal of Business Law* 8 756–777.

—— 'Corporate Rescue: A Game of Three Halves' (2012) *Legal Studies* 32(2) 302.

Fletcher, I.F., 'Maintaining the Momentum: The Continuing Quest for Global Standards and Principles to Govern Cross Border Insolvency' (2006–2007) *Brooklyn Journal of International Law* 32 767.

Foss, K. and Foss, N.J., 'Resources and Transaction Costs: How Property Rights Economics Furthers the Resource Based View' (2005) *Strategic Management Journal* 26 541–553.

Foss, K. *et al.*, 'MNC Organisational Form and Subsidiary Motivation Problems: Controlling Intervention Hazards in the Network of MNC' (2011) <available at: http://ssrn.com/abstract=1969402>

Franken, S.M., 'Three Principles of Transnational Corporate Bankruptcy Law: A Review' (2005) *European Law Journal* 11(2) 233–258.

Frisby, S., 'In Search of a Rescue Regime: The Enterprise Act 2002' (2004) *MLR* 67(2) 247–272.

—— 'Report to the Association of Business Recovery Professionals a Preliminary Analysis of Pre-Packaged Administrations' (2007).

Gaa, T.M., 'Harmonization of International Bankruptcy Law and Practice: Is It Necessary? Is It Possible?' *The International Lawyer* (1993) 27(4) 881–909.

Galanis, M., 'Vicious Spirals in Corporate Governance: Mandatory Rules for Systemic (Re)balance?' (2011) *Oxford Journal of Legal Studies* 31(2) 327–363.

Galen, R.V., 'The European Insolvency Regulation and Groups of Companies' INSOL Europe Annual Congress, Cork, Ireland, October (2003).

—— 'Insolvent Groups of Companies in Cross Border Cases and Rescue Plan' Report to the Netherlands Association for Comparative and International Insolvency Law (2012).

Galunic, D.C. and Eisenhardt, K.M., 'The Evolution of Intra-Corporate Domains: Divisional Charter Losses in High Technology, Multidivisional Corporations' (1996) *Organization Science* 7(3) 255–282.

Gant, R.M., 'Toward a Knowledge-based Theory of the Firm' (1996) *Strategic Management Journal* 17 109–122.

Garrido, J.M., 'No Two Snowflakes the Same: The Distributional Question in International Bankruptcies' (2010–2011) *Texas International Law Journal* 46 459.

Gates, S.R. and Egelhoff, W.G., 'Centralization in Headquarters-Subsidiary Relationships' (1986) *Journal of International Business Studies* 17(2) 71–92.

Bibliography 213

Georgakopoulos, N.L., 'Bankruptcy Law for Productivity' (2002) *Wake Forest Law Review* 37 51.

Gerard, M., 'Super-priority New Financing and Corporate Rescue' (2007) *Journal of Business Law* 7 701–732.

―――― 'Jurisdictional Competition and Forum Shopping in Insolvency Proceedings' (2009) *The Cambridge Law Journal* 68(01) 169–197.

―――― 'Reconstructing European Insolvency Law-Putting in Place a New Paradigm' (2010) *Legal Studies* 30(1) 126–146.

―――― 'COMI and Comity in UK and US Insolvency Law' (2012) *Law Quarterly Review* 140.

―――― 'Bankruptcy Forum Shopping, the UK and US as Venues of Choice for Foreign Companies' (2014) *International and Comparative Law Quarterly* 04 63.

―――― 'Reforming the European Insolvency Regulation: A Legal and Policy Perspective' (2014) *Journal of Private International Law* 10(1) 41–67.

―――― 'Something Old, Something New: Recasting the European Insolvency Regulation' (2016) *The Modern Law Review* 79(1) 102–146.

Gerner-Beuerle, C. and Schillig, M., 'The Mysteries of Freedom of Establishment after Cartesio' (2010) *International and Comparative Law Quarterly* 59(2) 303–323.

Gerner-Beuerle, C. and Schuster, E.P., 'The Evolving Structure of Directors' Duties in Europe' (2014) *European Business Organization Law Review* 15 224.

Gerven, W.V., 'Harmonization of Private Law: Do We Need It?' (2004) *Common Market Law Review* 41 505.

Geva, E.Z., 'National Policy Objectives from an EU Perspective: UK Corporate Rescue and the European Insolvency Regulation' (2007) *European Business Organization Law Review* 8(4) 605–619.

Ghio, E., 'European Insolvency Law: Development Harmonisation and Reform, a Case Study on the European Internal Market' (2015) *Trinity College Law Review* 18 154.

Giancristofano, I., 'Third Party Securities in the Financial Restructuring of Corporate Groups in Germany' (2016) *International Corporate Rescue* 13(2).

Goldschmid, P.M., 'More Phoenix than Vulture: The Case for Distressed Investor Presence in the Bankruptcy Reorganization Process' (2005) *Columbia Business Law Review* 191.

Gopalan, S. and Guihot, M. 'Recognition and Enforcement in Cross-Border Insolvency Law a Proposal for Judicial Gap-filing' (2015) *Vanderbilt Journal of Transnational Law* 48 1225, 1269.

Grant, R.M., 'Toward a Knowledge-Based Theory of the Firm' (1996) *Strategic Management Journal,* 17(Winter Special Issue) 109–122.

Gropper, A.L., 'The Payment of Priority Claims in Cross-Border Insolvency Cases' (2010–2011) *Texas International Law Journal* 46 559.

Gross, K., 'Taking Community Interests into Account in Bankruptcy: An Essay' (1994) *Washington University Law Quarterly* 72 1031.

Gulati, R., 'Alliances and Networks' (1998) *Strategic Management Journal* 19 293–317.

Gulati, R. *et al.*, 'Strategic Networks' (2000) *Strategic Management Journal* 21 203–215.

Guzman, A.T., 'International Bankruptcy: In Defence of Universalism' (1999–2000) *Michigan Law Review* 98 2177.

―――― 'Choice of Law: New Foundations' (2001–2002) *The Georgetown Law Journal* 90 883.

Haentjens, M., 'Financial Institutions' in Gabriel Moss Ian Flectcher and Stuart Isaacs (eds.), *Moss, Fletcher and Isaacs on the EU Regulation on Insolvency Proceedings* (3rd edn, Oxford University Press 2016).

214 *Bibliography*

Håkansson, H. and Snehota, I., *Developing Relationships in Business Networks* (Routledge 1995).

Hanrahan, L. and Mehta, S., 'A Comparative Overview of Transatlantic Inter-creditor Agreement', in *The International Comparative Legal Guide To: Lending & Secured Finance* (2nd edn, GLG 2014).

Harner, M.M., 'Activist Investors, Distressed Companies, and Value Uncertainty' (2014) *American Bankruptcy Institute Law Review* 22 167.

——— 'The Value of Soft Variables in Corporate Reorganizations' (2015) *University of Illinois Law Review* 2015 509.

Harner, M.M. and Marincic, J., 'Behind Closed Doors: The Influence of Creditors in Business Reorganizations' (2010–2011) *The Seattle University Law Review* 34 1155.

Hayne, K.M., 'Directors' Duties and a Company's Creditors' (2014) *The Melbourne University Law Review* 38 795, p. 797.

Hennart, J.F., 'Theories of the Multinational Enterprise', in A.M. Rugman (ed.), *The Oxford Handbook of International Business* (2nd edn, Oxford University Press 2009).

Hirte, H., 'Towards a Framework for the Regulation of Corporate Groups' Insolvencies' (2008) *European Council on Foreign Relations* 5 213.

Ho, V.H., 'Theories of Corporate Groups: Corporate Identity Reconceived' (2012) *Seton Hall Law Review* 42(3).

Höher, G., 'ESUG: German for 'Modernising Bankruptcy Law' (2012) *Eurofenix Spring*.

Hood, P. 'Directors' Duties Under the Companies Act 2006: Clarity or Confusion?' (2013) *Journal of Corporate Law Studies* 13(1) 42.

Hooley, R., 'Release Provisions in Intercreditor Agreements' (2012) *Journal of Business Law* 3 213–233.

Hopt, K.J., 'Groups of Companies – A Comparative Study on the Economics, Law and Regulation of Corporate Groups' (2015) <http://ssrn.com/abstract=2560935>

Howcroft, N.J., 'Universal versus Territorial Models for Cross Border Insolvency: The Theory, the Practice and the Reality that Universalism Prevails' (2007–2008) *UC Davis School of Law – Business Law Journal* 8 366.

Howell, B.J., 'Hedge Funds: A New Dimension in Chapter 11 Bankruptcy Proceedings' (2008–2009) *The DePaul Business and Commercial Law Journal* 7 35.

Hyde, M. and White, I., 'Pre-pack Administrations: Unwrapped' (2009) *Law and Financial Markets Review* 3(2) 134–138.

Itzcovich, G., 'The Interpretation of Community Law by the European Court of Justice' (2009) *German Law Journal* 10(05) 537–560.

Jackson, T.H., 'Bankruptcy, Non-Bankruptcy Entitlements and the Creditors' (1982) Bargain', *Yale Law Journal* 91 857.

——— 'Avoiding Powers in Bankruptcy' (1984) *Stanford Law Review* 36 725.

——— 'Of Liquidation, Continuation, and Delay: An Analysis of Bankruptcy Policy and Non-bankruptcy Rules' (1986) *American Bankruptcy Law Journal* 60 399.

Jackson, T.H. and Scott, R.E., 'On the Nature of Bankruptcy: An Essay on Bankruptcy Sharing and the Creditors' Bargain' (1989) *Virginia Law Review* 75 155.

Jackson, T.H. and Skeel, D.A., 'Dynamic Resolution of Large Financial Institutions' (2012) *Harvard Business Law Review* 2 435.

Jacoby, M.B. and Janger, J.E., 'Ice Cube Bonds: Allocating the Price of Process in Chapter 11 Bankruptcy' (2014) *The Yale Law Journal* 123(4) 865.

James, S.D., 'Strategic Bankruptcy: A Stakeholder Management Perspective' (2016) *Journal of Business Research* 69 492–499.

Janger, E.J., 'Predicting when the Uniform Law Process will Fail: Article 9, Capture and the Race to the Bottom' (1998) *Iowa Law Review* 83 569.
—— 'Universal Proceduralism' (2006–2007) *Brooklyn Journal of International Law* 32 819.
—— 'Virtual Territoriality' (2009–2010) *Columbia Journal of Transnational Law* 48 401.
—— 'Reciprocal Comity' (2010–2011) *Texas International Law Journal* 46 441.
—— 'Silos, Establishing the Distributional Baseline in Cross Border Bankruptcies' (2014–2015) *Brooklyn Journal of Corporate, Financial & Commercial Law* 9 85.
Janger, T., 'Crystals and Mud in Bankruptcy Law: Judicial Competence and Statutory Design' (2001) *Arizona Law Review* 43 559, 566.
Jensen, M.C., 'Value Maximization, Stakeholder Theory, and the Corporate Objective Function' October (2001) *Business Ethics Quarterly* 12(2) 235–256.
Johnston, J.B., 'The Bankruptcy Bargain' (1991) *American Bankruptcy Law Journal* 65 213.
Kahan, M. and Kamar, E., 'The Myth of State Competition in Corporate Law' (2002) *Stanford Law Review* 55 679.
Kargman, ST, 'Financing Company Group Restructurings: Book Review' (Gregor Baer and Karen O'Flynn, Editors) (2016) *Insolvency and Restructuring International* 10(1) 37–39.
Kaufman, A.M., 'The European Union Goes CoMI-Tose: Hazards of Harmonizing Corporate Insolvency Laws in the Global Economy' (2006–2007) *The Houston Journal of International Law* 29 625.
Keay, A. 'The Shifting of Directors' Duties in the Vicinity of Insolvency' (2015) *International Insolvency Review* 24 140–164, p. 144.
Kieninger, E.M., 'The Legal Framework of Regulatory Competition Based on Company Mobility: EU and US Compared' (2005) *German Law Journal* 6 741.
Kipnis, A.M., 'Beyond UNCITRAL: Alternatives to Universality in Transnational Insolvency' (2007–2008) *Denver Journal of International Law and Policy* 36 155.
Klee, Kenneth N., 'Cram Down II' (1990) *American Bankruptcy Law Journal* 64 229.
Kogut, B., *Multinational Corporations* (International Encyclopaedia of the Social & Behavioural Sciences Elsevier Science Ltd 2001).
Kogut, B. and Zander, U., 'Knowledge of the Firm and the Evolutionary Theory of the Multinational Corporation' (1993) *Journal of International Business Studies*, Fourth Quarter 24 625–645.
Korobkin, D.R., 'Rehabilitating Values: A Jurisprudence of Bankruptcy' (1991) *Columbia Law Review* 91(4) 717–789.
—— 'Contractarianism and the Normative Foundations of Bankruptcy Law' (1992–1993) *Texas Law Review* 71 541.
—— 'Employee Interests in Bankruptcy' (1996) *The American Bankruptcy Institute Law Review* 4 5.
Kuney, G.W., 'Hijacking Chapter 11' (2004–2005) *Emory Bankruptcy Developments Journal* 21 19.
Labovitz, M.N. and Basil, J.I., 'How Will New Chapter 15 Affect Multinational Restructurings?' (2005) *New York Law Journal Law and Financial Markets Review* 3(2).
Lastra, R.M., 'System Risk and Macro-prudential Supervision', in Niamh Moloney, Elilis Ferran and Jennifer Payne (eds.), *The Oxford Handbook of Financial Regulation* (Oxford University Press 2015), p. 312.

216 *Bibliography*

Latella, D., 'The "COMI" Concept in the Revision of the European Insolvency Regulation' (2014) *European Company and Financial Law Review* 11(4) 479–494.

Lavie, D., 'The Competitive Advantage of Interconnected Firms: An Extension of the Resource-Based View' (2006) *The Academy of Management Review* 31(3) 638–658.

Lehmann, M., 'Bail-In and Private International Law: How to Make Bank Resolution Measures Effective Across Borders' January (2017) *ICLQ* 66.

Lintner, P. and Lincoln, J., 'Bank Resolution and "Bail-In" in the EU: Selected Case Studies Pre and Post BRRD' (2016).

Lipson, J.C., 'The Shadow Bankruptcy System' (2009) *Boston University International Law Journal* 89 1609.

LoPucki, L.M., 'Strange Visions in a Strange World: A Reply to Professors Bradley and Rosenzweig' (1992–1993) *Michigan Law Review* 91 79.

—— 'The Trouble with Chapter 11' (1993) *Wisconsin Law Review* 729.

—— 'Cooperation in International Bankruptcy: A Post Universalist Approach' (1998–1999) *Cornell Law Review* 84 696.

—— 'The Case for Cooperative Territoriality in International Bankruptcy' (1999–2000) *Michigan Law Review* 98 2216.

—— 'Why Are Delaware and New York Bankruptcy Reorganization Failing' (2002) *Vanderbilt Law Review* 55 1933.

—— 'The Nature of the Bankrupt Firm: A Response to Baird and Rasmussen's "The End of Bankruptcy' (2003) *Stanford Law Review* 56(3) 645–671.

—— 'Global and Out of Control' (2005) *American Bankruptcy Law Journal* 79 79–104.

—— 'Universalism Unravels' (2005) *American Bankruptcy Law Journal* 79 143.

LoPucki, L.M. and Doherty, J.W., 'Bankruptcy Fire Sales' (2007) UCLA School of Law & Economics Research Paper Series Research Paper No. 07-07.

LoPucki, L.M. and Kalin, S., 'The Failure of Public Company Bankruptcies in Delaware and New York: Empirical Evidence of a "Race to the Bottom"' (2001) *Vanderbilt Law Review* 54 231.

Lubben, S.J., 'Some Realism about Reorganization: Explaining the Failure of Chapter 11 Theory' (2001–2002) *Dickinson Law Review* 106 267.

—— 'Credit Derivatives and the Future of Chapter 11' (2007) *The American Bankruptcy Law Journal* 81(4) 409–412.

—— 'Resolution, Orderly and Otherwise: B of A in OLA' (2012) *University of Cincinnati Law Review* 81 485, p. 491.

—— 'The Overstated Absolute Priority Rule' (2016) *The Fordham Journal of Corporate & Financial Law* 21 581.

—— 'A Functional Analysis of SIFI Insolvency' (2018) Texas Law Review 96 1377, p. 1392.

Lubben, S.J. and Wilmarth, A.E. Jr., 'Too Big and Unable to Fail' (2017) *Florida Law Review* 69 1205, p. 1228.

Luca, N., 'Cross Border Insolvency: New Trends' (2015) *European Insolvency Law.*

Luna, J., 'Thinking Globally, Filing Locally, the Effect of the New Chapter 15 on Business Entity Cross Border Insolvency Cases' (2007) *Florida Journal of International Law* 19 671.

Lupo-Pasini, F. and Buckley, R.P., 'Global Systemic Risk and International Regulatory Coordination: Squaring Sovereignty and Financial Stability' (2015) *American University International Law Review* 30 665.

Bibliography 217

——— 'International Coordination in Cross-Border Bank Bail-Ins: Problems and Prospects' (2015) *European Business Organization Law Review* 16 214.

Mabey, R.R. and Johnston, S.P., 'Coordination among Insolvency Courts in the Rescue of Multi-National Enterprises' (2008) *34th Lawrence P. King & Charles Seligson Workshop on Bankruptcy and Business Reorganization*, New York. University School of Law.

Madaus, S., 'Insolvency Proceedings for Corporate Groups under the New Insolvency Regulation' (2015) <available at: http://papers.ssrn.com/sol3/papers.cfm?abstract_id=2648850>

Makadok, R., 'Toward a Synthesis of the Resource-based and Dynamic-capability Views of Rent Creation' (2001) *Strategic Management Journal* 22 387–401.

Markusen, J.R., 'The Boundaries of Multinational Enterprises and the Theory of International Trade' (1995) *The Journal of Economic Perspectives* 9(2) 169–189.

Martin, C., 'Eurofood Fight: Forum Shopping Under the E.U. Regs' (2005) *ABIJ* 24.

McNabb, R., 'Olympic Airlines: A First Step to Tighter Controls in Secondary Proceedings?' (2013) *Corporate Rescue and Insolvency* 5 129.

Menjucq, M., 'EC-Regulation No. 1346/2000 on Insolvency Proceedings and Groups of Companies' (2008) ECFR.

Menjucq, M. and Damman, R., 'Regulation No. 1346/2000 on Insolvency Proceedings: Facing the Companies Group Phenomenon' (2008) *Boston University International Law Journal* 9 145.

Mevorach, I., 'The Road to a Suitable and Comprehensive Global Approach to Insolvencies within Multinational Corporate Groups' (2006) *Norton Journal of Bankruptcy Law & Practice* 15(5) 455–564.

——— 'Appropriate Treatment of Corporate Groups in Insolvency: A Universal View' (2007) *European Business Organization Law Review* 8 179–194.

——— 'The "Home Country" of a Multinational Enterprise Group Facing Insolvency' (2008) *International & Comparative Law Quarterly* 57 427–448.

——— 'The Role of Enterprise Principles in Shaping Management Duties at Times of Crisis' (2013) *European Business Organization Law Review* 14(4) 471–496.

——— 'Cross Border Insolvency Law of Enterprise Groups: The Choice of Law Challenge' (2014) *Brooklyn Journal of Corporate, Financial & Commercial Law* 9 107.

——— 'Beyond the Search for Certainty: Addressing the Cross-Border Resolution Gap' (2015) *Brooklyn Journal of Corporate, Financial & Commercial Law* 10 183.

Michaelides, A, 'Cyprus: From Boom to Bail-In' (2014) *Economic Policy* 29 678.

Miller, H.R., 'Chapter 11 in Transition – From Boom to Bust and Into the Future' (2007) *American Bankruptcy Law Journal* 81 375.

Miller, R.W., 'Economic Integration: An American Solution to the Multinational Enterprise Group Conundrum' (2011–2012) *Richmond Journal of Global Law and Business* 11 185.

Milman, D., 'Schemes of Arrangement and Other Restructuring Regimes under UK Company Law in Context' (2011) *Company Law Newsletter* 301.

Mistelis, L., 'Is Harmonisation a Necessary Evil? The Future of Harmonisation and New Sources of International Trade Law' (2001) cisgw3.law.pace.edu/ Sweet and Maxwell.

Mitchell-Fry, L. and Lawson, S., 'Defining CoMI, Where Are We Now?' (2012) *Corporate Rescue and Insolvency*.

Møller C, 'COMI and Get It: International Approaches to Cross-Border Insolvencies' (2015) *Corporate Rescue and Insolvency Journal* 6 223.

Mooney, C.W. Jr., 'A Normative Theory of Bankruptcy Law: Bankruptcy as (Is) Civil Procedure' (2004) *Washington and Lee Law Review* 61 931.

―――― 'Harmonisation Choice of Law Rules for International Insolvency Cases: Virtual Territoriality and Virtual Universalism and the Problem of Local Interests' (2014) *Brooklyn Journal of Corporate, Financial and Commercial Law* 9 120.

Moss, G., 'Group Insolvency-Choice of Forum and Law: The European Experience under the Influence of English Pragmatism' (2006–2007) *Brooklyn Journal of International Law* 32 1005.

―――― 'Group Insolvency-Forum-EC Regulation and Model Law under the Influence of English Pragmatism Revisited' (2014–2015) *Brooklyn Journal of Corporate, Financial & Commercial* 9 179.

Moss, G. and Paulus, C.G., 'The European Insolvency Regulation – The Case for Urgent Reform' (2006) *Insolvency Intelligence* 19(1) 1–5.

Moss, G. (QC), Wessels, B. and Haentjens, M., 'The EU Financial Institution Insolvency Law Framework', in Gabriel Moss (QC), Bob Wessels and Matthias Haentjens (eds.), *EU Banking and Insurance Insolvency* (2nd edn, Oxford University Press 2017), pp. 6–7.

Moulton, W.N. and Thomas, H., 'Bankruptcy as a Deliberate Strategy: Theoretical Considerations and Empirical Evidence' (1993) *Strategic Management Journal* 14(2) 125–135.

Mucciarelli, F.M., 'The Hidden Voyage of a Dying Italian Company, from the Mediterranean Sea to Albion' (2012) *European Company and Financial Law Review* 9(4) 571.

―――― 'Private International Law Rules in the Insolvency Regulation Recast: A Reform or a Restatement of the Status Quo?' (2015) <available at: http://ssrn.com/abstract=2650414>

Mudambi, R. and Navarra, P., 'Is Knowledge Power? Knowledge Flows, Subsidiary Power and Rent-Seeking within MNCs' (2004) *Journal of International Business Studies* 35(5) 385–406.

Mudambi, R. *et al.*, 'How Subsidiaries Gain Power in Multinational Corporations' (2014) *Journal of World Business* 49 101–113.

Muñiz, B., 'New Restructuring Regime in Spain' (2012) *Eurofenix Spring*.

Nohria, N. and Ghoshal, S., 'Differentiated Fit and Shared Values: Alternatives for Managing Headquarters-Subsidiary Relations' (1994) *Strategic Management Journal* 15(6) 491–502.

O'Donnell, W.S., 'Managing Foreign Subsidiaries: Agents of Headquarters, or an Interdependent Network' (2000) *Strategic Management Journal*, 21 525–548.

Oliver, C., 'Sustainable Competitive Advantage: Combining Institutional and Resource-Based Views' (1997) *Strategic Management Journal* 18(9) 697–713.

Omar, P.J., 'European Insolvency Laws: Convergence or Harmonization?' (2012) *Eurofenix Spring*.

―――― 'Modern Prospects for European Insolvency Law Harmonisation' *Global Law and Practice* (2015) <available at: www.globelawandbusiness.com/blog/Detail.aspx?g=6e989a65-610f-4de4-aaac-ad6090c6b9b8> accessed on 10 January 2016.

―――― 'The Inevitability of "Insolvency Tourism"' (2015) *Netherlands International Law Review* 62 429–444.

Ondersma, C. 'Shadow Banking and Financial Distress: The Treatment of Money-Claims in Bankruptcy' (2013) *Columbia Business Law Review* 79.

Pachulski, I.M. 'The Cram Down and Valuation under Chapter 11 of the Bankruptcy Code' (1980) *The North Carolina Law Review* 58 925.

Partnoy, F. and Skeel, D.A., 'The Promises and Perils of Credits Derivatives' (2006–2007) *The University of Cincinnati Law Review* 75 1019.

Bibliography 219

Paterson, S., 'COMI: The Elephant in the Room' (2012) *Corporate Rescue and Insolvency Journal* 4 135.

—— 'Rethinking the Role of the Law of Corporate Distress in the Twenty-First Century' (2014) *LSE Law, Society and Economy Working Papers* 27.

Paulus, C.G., 'Global Insolvency Law and the Role of Multinational Institutions' (2006–2007) *Brooklyn Journal of International Law* 32 755.

—— 'Group Insolvencies – Some Thoughts about New Approaches' (2007) *Texas International Law Journal* 42 819.

Payne, J, 'Cross-Border Schemes of Arrangement and Forum Shopping' (2013) *European Business Organization Law Review* 14(04) 563.

Philippon, T. and Salord, A., 'Bail-Ins and Bank Resolution in Europe: A Progress Report' (2017) *Geneva Reports on the World Economy Special Report* 4 32.

Phillips, M. and Goldring, J., 'Rescue and Reconstruction' (2002) *Insolvency Intelligence* 15 75, 76.

Pilkington, C. *et al.*, *Wind Hellas a Complex Restructuring in Global Recession* (Practical Law Publishing Limited 2011).

Pistor, K., 'The Standardization of Law and Its Effect on Developing Economies' (2002) *American Journal of Comparative Law* 50(1) 97–130.

Pointing, C. and Rooney, A., 'IMO Clears Up My Travel Issue' (2009) *International Financial Law Review* 28(8) 50.

Porte, C., 'Is the Open Method of Coordination Appropriate for Organising Activities at European Level in Sensitive Policy Areas' (2002) *European Law Journal* 8 38–58.

Posner, R.A., 'Theories of Economic Regulation' (1974) *The Bell Journal of Economics and Management Science* 5(2) 335–358.

Pottow, J.A.E., 'Procedural Incrementalism: A Model for International Bankruptcy' (2004–2005) *Virginia Journal of International Law* 45 935.

—— 'Greed and Pride in International Bankruptcy: The Problems of and Proposed Solutions to Local Interests' (2005–2006) *Michigan Law Review* 104 1899.

—— 'A New Role for Secondary Proceedings in International Bankruptcies' (2010–2011) *Texas International Law Journal* 46 579.

—— 'Beyond Carve-Outs and Toward Reliance: A Normative Framework for Cross-Border Insolvency Choice of Law' (2014) *Brooklyn Journal of Corporate, Financial & Commercial Law* 9 202.

—— 'Two Cheers for Universalism: Nortel's Nifty Novelty' (2015) Public law and legal theory research paper series paper No. 487. *Michigan Law Journal.*

Prentice, D.D., 'Some Aspects of the Law Relating to Corporate Groups in the United Kingdom' (1998–1999) *Connecticut Journal of International Law* 13 305.

Rabbiosi, L, 'Subsidiary Roles and Reverse Knowledge Transfer: An Investigation of the Effects of Coordination Mechanisms' (2011) *Journal of International Management* 17 97–113.

Ragan, A.C.C., 'CoMI Strikes a Discordant Note, Why US Court Are Not in Complete Harmony Despite Chapter 15 Directives' (2010–2011) *Emory Bankruptcy Developments Journal* 27 117.

Rajak, H., 'Corporate Group and Cross Border Bankruptcy' (2009) *Texas International Law Journal* 44 521.

Rasmussen, R.K., 'The Efficiency of Chapter 11' (1991) *Emory Bankruptcy Developments Journal* 8 319.

—— 'A New Approach to Transnational Insolvency' (1997–1998) *Michigan Journal of International Law* 19 1.

220 *Bibliography*

—— 'Resolving Transnational Insolvency through Private Ordering' (1999–2000) *Michigan Law Review* 98 2252.

—— 'Where Are All the Transnational Bankruptcies, the Puzzling Case for Universalism' (2006–2007) *Brooklyn Journal of International Law* 32 983.

Rasmussen, R.K. and Skeel, D.A., 'The Economic Analysis of Corporate Bankruptcy Law' (1995) American Bankruptcy Institute Law Review 3 85.

Rasmussen, R.K. and Thomas, R., 'Chapter 11 Reorganization Cases and the Delaware Myth' (2002) *Vanderbilt Law Review* 55.

Rickford, J., 'Current Developments in European Law on the Restructuring of Companies: An Introduction' (2004) *European Business Law Review* 15 1225.

Ricks, M. 'Regulating Money Creation after the Crisis' (2011) *Harvard Business Law Review* 1 75, p. 92.

Ringe, W.G., 'No Freedom of Emigration for Companies?' (2005) *European Business Law Review* 16 621.

—— 'Forum Shopping under the EU Insolvency Regulation' (2008) *European Business Organization Law Review* 9 579.

—— 'Corporate Mobility in the European Union – A Flash in the Pan?' (2013) University of Oslo faculty of Law Legal Studies Research Paper Series.

—— 'Bank Bail-In Between Liquidity and Solvency' (2018) *American Bankruptcy Law Journal* 92 299.

Ringe, W.G. and Patel, J., 'The Dark Side of Bank Resolution: Counterparty Risk through Bail-In' <available at: https://ssrn.com/abstract=3314103> accessed on 10 March 2019.

Roe, M.J., 'Delaware's Competition' (2003–2004) *Harvard Law Review* 117 588.

—— 'The Derivatives Market's Payment Priorities as Financial Crisis Accelerator' (2011) *Stanford Law Review* 63 539, p. 548.

Roe, M.J. and Tung F., 'Breaking Bankruptcy Priority: How Rent-Seeking Upends the Creditors' (2013) Bargain *Virginia Law Review* 99 1236.

Rose, E.B., 'Chocolate, Flowers and § 363(B): The Opportunity for Sweetheart Deals without Chapter 11 Protections' (2006) *Emory Bankruptcy Developments Journal* 23 249.

Rosenberg, R.J. and Riela, M.J., 'Hedge Funds, the New Masters of the Bankruptcy Universe' (2008) International Insolvency Institute Eighth Annual International Insolvency Conference.

Rotem, Y., 'Pursuing Preservation of Pre-Bankruptcy Entitlements: Corporate Bankruptcy Law's Self-Executing Mechanisms' (2008) *Berkeley Business Law Journal* 5 79.

Roth, W.H., 'From Centros to Ueberseering: Free Movement of Companies, Private International Law, and Community Law' (2003) *International and Comparative Law Quarterly* 52 177.

Rugman, A.M., 'New Theories of the Multinational Enterprise: An Assessment of Internalization Theory' (1986) *Bulletin of Economic Research* 38(2) 101–118.

—— 'Reconciling Internalization Theory and the Eclectic Paradigm' (2009) *The Multinational Business Review* 18(1) 1–12.

Rugman, A.M. and Verbeke, A., 'Subsidiary-Specific Advantages in Multinational Enterprises' (2001) *Strategic Management Journal* 22(3) 237–250.

Russo, C.A. 'Resolution Plans and Resolution Strategies: Do They Make G-SIBs Resolvable and Avoid Ring Fence?' (2019) *European Business Organization Law Review* 4–5.

Rustein, M. and Bloomberg, L., 'A Wind Blow through an English Brothel' (2010) *Corporate Rescue and Insolvency Journal*.

Sano, S.D., 'COMI: The Sun Around Which Cross-Border Insolvency Proceedings Revolve' (2009) *Journal of International Banking Law* 24(2) 88.

Schillig, M.A. 'The (Il-)Legitimacy of the EU Post-Crisis Bailout System', p. 2 <available at: https://ssrn.com/abstract=3202118>.

Schmidt, J., 'Group Insolvency under the EIR Recast' (2015) *Eurofenix Autumn*.

Schön, W., 'The Mobility of Companies in Europe and the Organizational Freedom of Company Founders' (2006) *European Company and Financial Law Review* 3 122.

Schwarcz, S.L., 'Too Big to Fool: Moral Hazard, Bailouts, and Corporate Responsibility' (2017) *Minnesota Law Review* 102 761.

———— 'Beyond Bankruptcy: Resolution as a Macroprudential Regulatory Tool' (2018) *Notre Dame Law Review* 94 709, p. 729.

Schwartz, A., 'A Normative Theory of Business Bankruptcy' (2005) Faculty Scholarship Series Paper 303 <http://digitalcommons.law.yale.edu/fss_papers/303> accessed on 12 June 2014.

Scott, H.S. and Gelpern, A., *International Finance Transactions, Policy and Regulation* (21st edn, Foundation Press 2016).

Scott, R.E., 'Through Bankruptcy with the Creditors' Bargain Heuristic' (1986) *University of Chicago Law Review* 53 690.

Seah, C.L., 'The Re Tea Corporation Principle and Junior Creditors' Rights to Participating a Scheme of Arrangement, A View from Singapore' (2011) *International Insolvency Review* 20 161–183.

Shapiro, S.A., 'The Complexity of Regulatory Capture: Diagnosis, Causality and Remediation' (2012) *Roger Williams University Law Review* 17 221.

Siems, M.M., 'SEVIC: Beyond Cross-Border Mergers' (2007) *European Business Organization Law Review* 8 307.

Singh, D., 'Recovery and Resolution Planning: Reconfiguring Financial Regulation and Supervision', in Jens-Hinrich Binder and Dalvinder Singh (eds.), *Bank Resolution: The European Regime* (Oxford University Press 2016).

Sjostrom, W.K., 'The AIG Bailout' (2009) *Washington and Lee Law Review* 66 943.

Skeel, D.A., 'Markets, Courts, and the Brave New World of Bankruptcy Theory' (1993) *Wisconsin Law Review* 2 465.

———— 'Public Choice and the Future of Public-Choice-Influenced Legal Scholarship' (1997) *Vanderbilt Law Review* 50 647.

———— 'Bankruptcy Judges and Bankruptcy Venue: Some Thoughts on Delaware' (1998) *Delaware Law Review* 1.

———— 'Bankruptcy Lawyers and the Shape of American Bankruptcy Law' (1998–1999) *Fordham Law Review* 67 497.

———— 'What's So Bad about Delaware' (2001) *Vanderbilt Law Review* 54 309.

———— 'Creditors' Ball: The "New" New Corporate Governance in Chapter 11' (2003–2004) *University of Pennsylvania Law Review* 152 917.

———— 'The Past, Present and Future of Debtor-in-Possession Financing' (2003–2004) *Cardozo Law Review* 25 1905.

———— 'European Implications of Bankruptcy Venue Shopping in the US' (2006–2007) *Buffalo Law Review* 54 439.

Sloane, C.A., 'The Sub Rosa Plan of Reorganization: Side-Stepping Creditor Protections in Chapter 11' (1999–2000) *Emory Bankruptcy Developments Journal* 16 37.

Smits, R., 'Supervision and Efficiency of the Pre-Pack: An Anglo-Dutch Comparison' (2016) *International Corporate Rescue* 13(1) 13–15.

Stephan, P.B., 'The Futility of Unification and Harmonization in International Commercial Law' (1999) <http://papers.ssrn.com/paper.taf?abstract_id=169209>

Stigler, G.J., 'The Theory of Economic Regulation' (1971) *The Bell Journal of Economics and Management Science* 2(1) 3–21.

Stones, K., 'UK Schemes and Forum Shopping' (2014) *Corporate Rescue and Insolvency Journal* 4 161.

Story, S.E., 'Cross Border Insolvency: A Comparative Analysis' (2015) *Arizona Journal of International and Comparative Law* 32 431.

Subramanian, G., 'The Influence of Antitakeover Statutes on Incorporation Choice: Evidence on the "Race" Debate and Antitakeover Overreaching' (2002) *University of Pennsylvania Law Review* 15 1795 1872.

Subramaniam, M. and Watson, S., 'How Interdependence Affects Subsidiary Performance' (2006) *Journal of Business Research* 59 916–924.

Surlemont, B., 'A Typology of Centres within Multinational Corporations: An Empirical Investigation', in J. Birkinshaw and N. Hood (eds.), *Multinational Corporate Evolution and Subsidiary Development* (Macmillan Press 1998).

Szydlo, M., 'The Notion of Comi in European Insolvency Law' (2009) *European Business Law Review* 20 747.

Tabb, C.J., 'A Critical Reappraisal of Cross-Collateralization in Bankruptcy' (1986–1987) *Southern California Law Review* 60 109.

Teece, D.J., 'Transactions Cost Economics and the Multinational Enterprise: An Assessment' (1986) *Journal of Economic Behavior and Organization* 7 21–45.

Teece, D.J., et al., *Firm Capabilities, Resources, and the Concept of Strategy* (Mimeo, University of California at Berkeley, Haas School of Business 1990).

Teichmann, C., 'Corporate Groups within the Legal Framework of the European Union: The Group-Related Aspects of the SUP Proposal and the EU Freedom of Establishment' (2015) *European Company and Financial Law Review* 12(2) 202–229.

Thole, C. and Dueñas, M., 'Some Observations on the New Group Coordination Procedure of the Reformed European Insolvency Regulation' (2015) *International Insolvency Review* 24 214–227.

Triantis, G.G., 'A Theory of the Regulation of Debtor-in-Possession Financing' (1993) *Vanderbilt Law Review* 46 901.

Tung, F., 'Is International Bankruptcy Possible?' (2001–2002) *Michigan Journal of International Law* 23 31.

Vallens, J.C., 'Reforms Planned in France' (2014) *Eurofenix Spring*.

Van Zwieten, K., 'Director Liability in Insolvency and Its Vicinity' (2018) *Oxford Journal of Legal Studies* 38(2) 382–409.

Vette, E.M.F., 'Multinational Enterprise Groups in Insolvency: How Should the European Union Act?' (2011) *Utrechtlawreview.org* 7(1) 216.

Walton, P., 'Pre-Packing' in the UK' (2009) *International Insolvency Review* 18 85–108.

Warren, E., 'Bankruptcy Policy' (1987) *University of Chicago Law Review* 54 775.

——— 'Bankruptcy Policymaking in an Imperfect World' (1993) *Michigan Law Review* 92(2) 336–387.

Warren, E. and Westbrook, J., 'Contracting Out of Bankruptcy: An Empirical Intervention' (2004–2005) *Harvard Law Review* 118 1197.

Weijs, R., 'Comi-Migration: Use or Abuse of European Insolvency Law?' (2014) *European Company and Financial Law Review* 11(4).

Weijs, R. and Wessels, B., 'Proposed Recommendations for the Reform of Chapter 11 U.S. Bankruptcy Code' (2015) *Amsterdam Law School Legal Studies Research Paper No.*

Weiss, M., 'Bridge Over Troubled Water: The Revised Insolvency Regulation' (2015) *International Insolvency Review* 24 192–213

Wessels, B., 'Cross Border Insolvency Agreements: What Are They and Are They Here to Stay?' in Faber *et al.* (eds.) *Insolventie en Overeenkomst* (Nijmegen 2012).

———— 'Themes of the Future: Rescue Businesses and Cross-Border Cooperation' (2014) *Insolvency Intelligence* 4–9.

Westbrook, J., 'Theory and Pragmatism in Global Insolvencies: Choice of Law and Choice of Forum' (1991) *American Bankruptcy Law Journal* 65 457.

———— 'The Lesson of Maxwell Communication' (1996) *Fordham Law Review* 64(6) 2531.

———— 'Universal Priority' (1998) *Texas International Law Journal* 33 27.

———— 'Globalisation of Insolvency Reform' (1999) *New Zealand Law Review* 401.

———— 'A Global Solution to Multinational Default' (1999–2000) *Michigan Law Review* 98 2276.

———— 'Multinational Enterprises in General Default: Chapter 15, the ALI Principles, and the EU Insolvency Regulation' (2002) *American Bankruptcy Law Journal* 76 1.

———— 'Universalism and Choice of Law' (2004–2005) *Penn State International Law Review* 23 625.

———— 'Multinational Financial Distress: The Last Hurrah of Territorialism' (2006) *Texas International Law Journal* 41 321.

———— 'Locating the Eye of the Financial Storm' (2007) *Brooklyn Journal of International Law* 32 1019.

———— 'Priority Conflicts as a Barrier to Cooperation in Multinational Insolvencies' (2008–2009) *Penn State International Law Review* 27 869.

———— 'Comments on Universal Proceduralism' (2009–2010) *Columbia Journal of Transnational Law* 48 503.

———— 'Breaking Away, Local Priorities and Global Assets' (2010–2011) *Texas International Law Journal* 46 601.

———— 'SIFIs and States' (2014) *Texas International Law Journal* 49 329, 336–342.

———— 'Nortel: The Cross-Border Insolvency Case of the Century' (2015) *Journal of International Banking and Financial Law* 8 498.

Wetzer, T. 'In Two Minds: The Governance of Ring-Fenced Banks' <available at: https://ssrn.com/abstract=3325292> accessed on 12 February.

Wheeler, D. *et al.*, 'Focusing on Value: Reconciling Corporate Social Responsibility, Sustainability and a Stakeholder Approach in a Network World' (2003) *Journal of General Management* 28(3) 1–28.

White, M.J., 'Does Chapter 11 Save Economically Inefficient Firms' (1994) *Wash. U. L. Q.* 72 1319.

Wijaya, A., 'Pre-Pack Administration Sale: A Case of Sub Rosa Debt Restructuring' (2016) *International Insolvency Review* 25 119–137.

Winkler, M.M., 'From Whipped Cream to Multibillion Euro Financial Collapse: The European Regulation on Transnational Insolvency in Action' (2008) *Berkeley Journal of International Law* 26 352.

Winter, S.G., 'On Coase, Competence, and the Corporation' (1988) *Journal of Law, Economics, and Organization* 4 163.

Xie, B., 'Protecting the Interests of General Unsecured Creditors in Pre-Packs: The Implication and Implementation of SIP 16' (2010) *Company Lawyer.*

Xiouros, C. 'Handling of the Laiki Bank ELA and the Cyprus Bail-In Package', in Alexander Michaelides and Athanasios Orphanides (eds.), *The Cyprus Bail-In Policy: Lessons from the Cyprus Economic Crisis*, 33 (Imperial College Press 2016).

224 Bibliography

Yamin, M. and Andersson, U., 'Subsidiary Importance in the MNC: What Role Does Internal Embeddedness Play?' (2011) *International Business Review* 20 151–162.

Yiatrou, M. 'The Myth of Cypriot Bank Resolution 'Success': A Plea for a More Holistic and Less Costly Supervision & Resolution Approach' (2017) *European Business Organization Law Review* 18 503–533.

Yidrim, O., 'Theoretical Driver of Diversification', in G. de Laurendis (ed.), *Strategy and Organisation of Corporate Banking* (Springer 2005).

Zacaroli, A. and Riddiford, A., 'Schemes of Arrangement and Chapter 11 of US Bankruptcy Code: A Comparative View' (2015) *South Square Digest.*

Zanardo, A., 'Fiduciary Duties of Directors of Insolvent Corporations: A Comparative Perspective' (2018) *Chicago-Kent Law Review* 93 867.

Zhang, D., 'A Recommendation to Improve the Opt-Out Mechanism in the EU Regulation on Insolvency Proceedings Recast' (2017) *International Company and Commercial Law Review* 5 167–175.

——— 'Reconsidering Procedural Consolidation for Multinational Corporate Groups in the Context of the Recast European Insolvency Regulation' (2017) *International Insolvency Review* 26(3) 241–357.

——— 'Preventive Restructuring Frameworks: A Possible Solution for Financially Distressed Multinational Corporate Groups in the EU' (2019) *European Business Organization Law Review.* https://doi.org/10.1007/s40804-018-0125-3; T.M.C. Asser Press.

Zumbansen, P., 'Spaces and Places: A Systems Theory Approach to Regulatory Competition in European Company Law' (2006) *European Law Journal* 12(4) 534–556.

Zumbro, P.H., 'Cross Border Insolvencies and International Protocols – An Imperfect but Effective Tool' (2010) *Business Law International* 11 157.

Zywicki, T., "Is Forum Shopping Corrupting America's Bankruptcy Courts?" (2006) *Georgetown Law Journal* 94 1141.

Websites

Art 28(2) of the CRD IV Directive (2013/36/EU) <available at: https://uk.practicallaw. thomsonreuters.com/1-576-2705?originationContext=document&transitionType= DocumentItem&contextData=%28sc.Default%29&comp=pluk#co_anchor_a996304>.

Birch, C. and Procter, V., 'Brexit – Implications for the UK Restructuring and Insolvency Market' (2016) <available at: www.eversheds.com/documents/services/commercial/ Brexit-implications-for-UK-restructuring-and-insolvency-market.pdf> accessed on 22 May 2016.

Brief guide to Administration, Linklaters (2008) <available at: www.linklaters.com/ pdfs/Insights/banking/Guidetoadministration.pdf> accessed on 19 November 2015.

DIP financing <available at: www.investopedia.com/terms/d/debtorinpossession financing.asp>

Forum Shopping and COMI Shifting – Overview, Lexis PSL <https://www.lexisnexis. com/uk/lexispsl/restructuringandinsolvency/document/393781/55KG-P041-F18C-C001-00000-00/Forum_shopping_and_COMI_shifting_overview> accessed on 22 June 2014.

Going Concern Concept Definition <available at: www.investopedia.com/terms/g/ going_concern_value.asp> accessed on 1 June 2015.

Group relief visited 21/09/2014 <available at: www.out-law.com/en/topics/tax/ corporate-tax-/group-relief/> accessed on 12 June 2015.

ISDA Credit Event definition <available at: http://credit-deriv.com/isdadefinitions.htm>

Ken Baird *et al.*, 'Brexit: What Does It Mean for Restructuring and Insolvency?' (2016) <available at: www.law.ox.ac.uk/business-law-blog/blog/2016/07/brexit-what-does-it-mean-restructuring-and-insolvency> accessed on 12 August 2016.

The MiFID II Directive (2014/65/EU). The Definition Covers a Broad Variety of Entities Including Asset Managers, Securities Brokers, Firms that Operate Certain Trading Venues and Some Financial Advisers' https://uk.practicallaw.thomsonreuters.com/4-625-3739?originationContext=document&transitionType=DocumentItem&contextData=%28sc.Default%29&comp=pluk.

Index

Note: Page numbers followed by "n" denote footnotes

Adler, B. E. 107
administrators 160–161; temporary 183
aims of this book 5–7
alternative approaches to insolvency law: contract approaches, theoretical limitations of 107–109; and hold-out 109–112; London approach 113–115
anti-forum shopping covenant 59
asset separation tool 184
Australia, HIH case 52–53
autonomy, of subsidiaries 37–38, 89

bail-in 186, 187, 188, 189; Cypriot bank resolution 190–191; minimum requirements for own funds and eligible liabilities (MREL) 189–191; *pari passu* principle 189–190
bail-in tool 184–185, 196
bailouts 172
Bank Recovery and Resolution Directive (BRRD) 171, 176, 177, 180, 186, 193, 200; Article 7 181–182; Article 17 194–195; bank resolution 191; bridge institution tool 187; resolution tools in 184
bank resolution 5, 11, 171–172, 198–199, 201; bail-in 184–187, 188, 189; comparison of corporate restructuring tools and bank resolution tools 183–184; comparison with corporate preventive insolvency mechanisms 179–183; and corporate law theory 173–179; harmonization of rules 179; minimum requirements for own funds and eligible liabilities (MREL) 189–191; resolution plans 181; resolvability 181; SPOE approach 191–193; *see also* Cypriot bank resolution

Banking Act (2009) 176
bankruptcy 19n51, 25, 25–26; chapter 11 161n158; cost of 54–55n60; modified universalism 51–54; non-insolvency mechanisms 26; territorialism 48–49; traditionalist approaches 20, 21; universalism 49–54; *see also* forum shopping
banks: bail-in 184; bridge 186; Credit Institutions Reorganisation and Winding Up Directive 178; insolvency 176–178; subsidiaries 181; *see also* systemically important financial institutions (SIFIs)
Barclays Bank Plc v HHY Luxembourg Sàrl case 123
Basel Committee 2, 184n72, 195
Bell Group case 168–169
breaches of conflict of interest in directors' duties 168–169, 170
Brexit 3–4, 4n19
bridge banks 186
bridge institution tool 184, 187
BRRD (Bank Recovery and Resolution Directive) 2, 5
business networks 6, 9, 88, 90, 178; interdependent relationships 36, 36n161; and MCGs 33–36
business rescue 15–16, 17; Cork Report 2; *see also* corporate rescue

Cambridge Gas Transportation Corpn v Official Committee of Unsecured Creditors of Navigator Holdings plc and others 54
capture theory, and uniformity of insolvency law 148–152
Cartesio case 61

Index

cases: *Barclays Bank Plc v HHY Luxembourg Sàrl* 123; *Bell Group* 168–169; *Cambridge Gas Transportation Corpn v Official Committee of Unsecured Creditors of Navigator Holdings plc and others* 54; *Cartesio* 61; *Collins and Aikman* 98; *Daisytek* 71–72, 101; *Eurofood* 72–75, 137–138; *European Directories* 124; *HBH* 64–65; *HIH* 52; *IMO car wash* 123–124; *Interedil* 76–78; *La Seda* 121; *Maxwell* 131; *MPOTEK case* 75; *MyTravel* 151–152; *Primacom Holding GmbH* 121; *Public Prosecutor v Segard* 84; *re Bluebrook Ltd* 151–152; *Re MG Rover Espana SA* 81; *Re Nortel Networks SA* 52; *Re Standford International Bank Ltd* 75–76; *Re Zlomrex International Finance SA* 58; *Schefenacker* 57–58, 57n80; *West Mercia Safetywear Ltd v Dodd* 167; *Wind Hellas* 102–103
centralization of control 39
centre of main interest (CoMI) 6, 8, 9, 44, 45, 46, 48, 49, 52–53, 54, 56, 59, 60, 64, 65, 66, 68–69n141, 82, 179; certainty of 78–79; choice of law theory 78n195; Daisytek case 71–72; Eurofood case 72–75; *ex post* approach to procedural consolidation 100–101; HIH case 53; Interedil case 76–78; MPOTEK case 75; *Re Standford International Bank Ltd* 75–76; statutory definition of 67–70; synthetic secondary proceedings 98–99; theoretical underpinnings of 66–67; transfer of registered place 60–61; unclear group rule 99–100; universalism versus territorialism 67; Virgós-Schmit Report 67–68; *see also* forum shopping; group CoMI
certainty 6, 8, 27, 41, 44; of CoMI 78–79; forum shopping 58–59; of insolvency law 21–27
chameleon equity 107
change of subsidiaries' roles 88–90
chapter 11 161n158, 191
circular holding in a chain structure 28–29
collective insolvency procedures 23, 25–26, 27
Collins and Aikman case 98
comparison of corporate law theory and bank resolution theory 173–179
competition 145–146
contingency theory, and MCGs 33–36
contracts 29, 30, 141n43; as alternative approach to insolvency law, limitations of 107–109; hold-out 109–112; majority voting clause 58n85; narrow protection 112–113
contractualism 47–48, 48n13, 91–94
control 27, 88; centralization of 39; circular holding in a chain structure 28–29; by contracts 29; and corporate groups 28; *de jure* 28; in EU competition law 29; by ownership 28; of senior creditors in group coordination proceedings 139–140; by shareholding 29–30
cooperative territorialism 9, 48–49, 85
coordinators, of group coordination proceedings 135
Cork Report 2
corporate groups 28; and control 28, 29; group CoMI 85–87; insolvency of 3; restructuring 185–186; subsidiaries 87
corporate law theory, comparison with bank resolution theory 173–179
corporate rescue 5, 7–8, 12, 15–16, 17, 41, 44, 198–199; benefits of 1n4; certainty 41; certainty of insolvency law 21–27; comparison with bank recovery and resolution plans 179–183; goals of 27; going concern value 13–17; London approach 113–115; preservation of going concern value 17–21; theoretical views of 12–13; *see also* formal rescue; hybrid rescue procedures; informal rescue
cram-down mechanisms 120–122, 121n101, 188
credit default swaps (CDS) 109–110
Credit Institutions Reorganisation and Winding Up Directive 177, 178
creditors 7, 17, 24–25, 108; adjusting 80n208; anti-forum shopping covenant 59; challenges to insolvency proceedings 65; corporate rescue 15–16; economic distress 14–15; exclusion from bail-in 188–189; financially distressed companies 15; forum shopping 55–58; going concern value 13; hold-out 109–112; insolvency law 45; junior 188; loan contracts 17; local 96n310; modified universalism 51–54; pre-pack sale 7; priority rankings 42–43, 46; schemes of arrangement 186; transfer schemes 122–123; unsecured 13, 22, 130, 188; *see also* forum shopping

cross-border cooperation 4, 133, 181; 'group coordination proceeding' 3
cross-border insolvency 5, 8, 9, 9–10, 29, 44; certainty requirement 43; dangers posed by interest groups to insolvency law 148–152; forum shopping 54–55, 56–59; of MCGs 4–5; procedural consolidation 8, 43, 45; protocols 130–132; substantive consolidation 42–43; theoretical underpinnings of CoMI 66–67; treatment of MCGs in 40–43; universalism 200
cross-class cram-down mechanism 118
cross-collateralization 140
cross-filling 49n22
Cypriot bank resolution 190–191

Daisytek case 101; centre of main interest (CoMI) 71–72
de jure control 28
debt: corporate rescue 15–16; economic distress 14–15; financially distressed companies 15; and going concern value 17–18; renegotiation 6, 10; roll-up 139–140
debt to equity swaps 58
debtor-in-possession (DIP) financing 112, 112n42, 142, 151, 179
Delaware, regulatory competition in 144
diffused shareholding 147n81
direct bail-in 184, 188
Directive on preventive restructuring frameworks 115, 116–119, 198; confirmation of restructuring plans 18–119; cross-class cram-down mechanism 118; early warning tools 116–117; group pre-pack sale 122–124; renegotiation of debt agreements at holding companies level 119–122; schemes of arrangement 120–122; stay power 117; viability test 117
directors' duties: breaches of conflict of interest 168–169; in group coordination proceedings and UNCITRAL Model Law 169–170; in insolvency and preventive restructuring procedures 165–169, 200; in MCGs 194
Dodd-Frank Act 176, 185
drawbacks: of contract and market approaches 108–109; of group coordination proceedings 138–139; of pre-pack sale 127; of procedural universalism 97

early consideration of group coordination proceedings, benefits of 156–162
early warning tools 116–117
economic account of insolvency law 17–18, 21–22, 26
economic distress 14–15, 22–23; DIP financing 112; and freedom of establishment 60–61; going concern value 20; *see also* insolvency
efficiency 14n16, 21n61
efficient companies, going concern value 13–14
EIR group coordination proceedings 134–136
EIR Recast 1, 3, 3n17, 4, 5, 8, 29–30, 44, 46, 47, 56–57, 62, 66, 135n15, 137, 195, 200; Article 3 63, 69; Article 4 64; Article 24 63; Article 25 63; Article 28 64; Article 56 7, 153, 154; Article 72 153; and forum shopping 56–57; group coordination proceedings 7; and Model Law 163–164; opt-out mechanism of group coordination proceedings 7; purposive interpretation approach 154; Recital 28 69–70, 69n144; Recital 30 70, 70n145; Recital 58 7, 153, 154; statutory definition of CoMI 67–70; *see also* group coordination proceedings
embeddedness 34n147
Enterprise Act (2002) 2, 16, 128
EU Commission 1
Eurofood case 72–75, 137–138
Europe: insolvency of large corporate groups in 3; MCGs 38–39; substantive consolidation 42
Europe 2020 strategies 1
European Banking Union 193
European Commission, definition of CoMI 69
European Court of Justice (ECJ) 61–62, 154; *Eurofood* case 137–138
European Directories case 124
European Union (EU): Accounting Directive 2013/34/EU 29; Bank Recovery and Resolution Directive (BRRD) 2, 171, 176, 177, 180, 186; corporate rescue law in Member states 41; Directive on preventive restructuring frameworks 115, 198; directors' duties in member states 165–167; freedom of establishment 59–62; reformed insolvency law of member states 1, 2; regulatory competition 143–144; Resolution College 195; Single

230 Index

Resolution Mechanism Regulation 2; unharmonized insolvency law 5, 11; *see also* Directive on preventive restructuring frameworks

ex ante solutions for cross-border insolvency: contractualism 91–94; group main proceeding 94–95; universal proceduralism 95–100

ex post approaches of procedural consolidation: by CoMI interpretation 100–101; by forum shopping 102–104

Federal Deposit Insurance Act (FDIA) 175
Federal Deposit Insurance Corporation (FDIC) 175, 185
financial groups: insolvency of 3; resolution 11; resolution rules 4–5
Financial Stability Board (FSB) 2, 184–185
financially distressed companies 8, 15; bailouts 172; *see also* going concern value
fire sales 159
formal rescue 106, 115
forum shopping 54–55, 100, 145–146; and certainty 58–59, 82–84; creditors' challenges 65; *ex post* approach to procedural consolidation 102–104; and freedom of establishment 59–62; jurisdictional examination 64–65; maximization of value 55–58; moving registered place 61n102; Re Zlomrex International Finance SA case 58; regulatory view on 62–63; Schefenacker case 57–58; secondary proceedings 65–66; suspect period 63; theoretical views on 55; transfer of registered place 60–61; transparency 63–64
freedom of establishment 59–62

Gebhard test 61–62
global financial crisis of 2007–2008 2
goals, of corporate rescue law 27
going concern value 8, 13–17, 13n3, 18n40, 23, 27, 36; debate on the preservation of 17–21; economic distress 14–15; of efficient companies 13–14; financially distressed companies 15; of inefficient companies 14–15; in knowledge-based theory 13–14; and non-contractual parties 24–25; in resource-based theory 13–14; *see also* group going concern value; preservation of going concern value

group CoMI 85–87, 97, 197; location uncertainty 105
group coordination plans 135
group coordination proceedings 3, 7, 10, 133, 134–136, 135n16, 198; benefits of the recommendation 156–162; considering at an early stage 156–162; coordinators 135; directors' duties 169–170; drawbacks 138–139; implication on 141–143; opt-out mechanism 7, 136, 136–138, 153, 155–156; preliminary cost and benefit analysis 136; recommendation for 153–156; senior creditors' control 139–140, 141–143
group cross-border insolvency theories: contractualism 91–94; group main proceeding 94–95; universal proceduralism 95–100
group going concern value 27, 44; and head office functions in MCGs 37–40
group main proceeding 94–95
group pre-pack sale 122–124, 150, 152; problems with in hybrid rescue procedures 126–130
group procedural consolidation 90
group rescue 181–182
group-wide insolvency 6–7; market/hybrid legal solutions 10
group-wide reorganizations 134–135

harmonization of insolvency law 198, 201; danger of being captured 148–152; in the EU 11; and regulatory competition 143–146; relationship to other laws 146–148
HBH case 64–65
head offices 35n151, 197n2; business network perspective 88; CoMI 6, 68, 79, 87–88; of MCGs 37–40
hedge funds 110
hierarchically centralized groups 34n144
HIH case 52–53
holding companies 7
hold-out 109–112; cross-class cram-down mechanism 118
hybrid rescue procedures 6–7, 106, 115; limitation of renegotiation of debt agreements at the level of holding companies 124–126; London approach 113–115; problems with group pre-pack sale 126–130; protocols 130–132; *see also* Directive on preventive restructuring frameworks

Index

IMO car wash case 123–124
indirect bail-in 184
inefficient companies, going concern value 14–15
informal rescue 106; hold-out 109–112; London approach 113–115; narrow protection 112–113; negotiation stage 110
innovations 33
insolvency: collective insolvency procedures 23; of corporate groups 3, 28; corporate rescue 15–16; economic distress 14–15; of KPNQwest N.V. 3; liquidation 18; of MCGs 4–5; and national law 4–5; protection of stakeholders 23–25; unharmonized law of EU member states 5; universalism 8, 45; *see also* group-wide insolvency
Insolvency Act (1986) 119, 128n135; Sch. B1 127–128
insolvency law 17, 26n90, 201; collective insolvency procedures 25–26; collective nature of 46; comparison with bank resolution 173–179; creditors 24–25; debate on certainty of 21–27; economic account of 17–18, 21–22, 26; forum shopping 55–59; Model Law 162–164; modified universalism 51–54; and non-contractual parties 23–25; *pari passu* principle 174, 175, 189–190; preservation of going concern value 18; rehabilitation function 24n81; stay mechanism 174; strategic behaviours 22; territorialism 48–49; traditionalist approaches 18–19, 20–21, 21–22; universalism 49–54; unsecured creditors 22; *see also* forum shopping; insolvency proceedings
insolvency proceedings: directors' duties 165–169; group CoMI 85–87; strategic behaviours 22–23; transparency 63–64
inter-creditor agreements 123
interdependent relationships 36n161
Interedil case 76–78
interest groups, dangers of posed to insolvency law 148–152
interest rates 23
internalization theories of MCGs 30–31, 33

Janger, J. E. 86, 98
junior creditors 188; inter-creditor agreements 123
jurisdictional examination 64–65

jurisdictional rule 46; cross-border insolvency law theories on 46–48; forum shopping 55–58, 58–59; modified universalism 51–54; territorialism 48–49, 67; universalism 49–54, 67; *see also* forum shopping

knowledge transfer 30
knowledge-based theory 35–36; going concern value 13–14; of MCGs 31–33
KPNQwest N.V., insolvency of 3

La Seda case 121
legal definition of MCGs 27–30
legislation, dangers posed by interest groups to insolvency law 148–152
Lehman Brothers 2, 173, 187
lex concursus 50
lex fori concursus 67
lexi fori concursus 47
licenses 30–31
limitations of alternative approaches to insolvency law: contracts 107–109; hold-out 109–112; narrow protection 112–113
limited liability companies, corporate groups 28
liquidation 12n1, 18, 19, 21, 26n93; financially distressed companies 15; Orderly Liquidation Authority (OLA) 185; Securities Investor Protection Act (SIPA) 191
loan contracts: cross-collateralization 140; uncertainty in 17; *see also* bail-in
local rescue plans 155
London approach 113–115
Lopucki, L. M. 48, 65

market/hybrid legal solutions to cross-border insolvency 10, 105
maximization of value 55–58
Maxwell case 131
MCGs 4n20, 5, 5n23, 6, 7–8, 9, 10, 12, 29, 197, 201; business network theory 33–36; contingency theory 33–36; and control 27, 28–30; directors' duties 194; European 38–39; 'group coordination proceeding' 3; group going concern value 37–40; group members 32; head office functions 37–40, 197n2; internalization theories of 30–31; issues and difficulties of insolvency 4–5; knowledge-based theories 31–33; legal definition of 27–30; resource-based

232 *Index*

theories 31–33; single point of entry (SPOE) 193–194; transaction costs 30–31; treatment of in cross-border insolvency context 40–43; universal proceduralism 95–100

mezzanine inter- creditor agreements 123–124

minimum requirements for own funds and eligible liabilities (MREL) 189–191

MNCs 28

Model Law 162–164; directors' duties 169–170

modified universalism 9, 51–54, 81, 84, 99

moving registered place 60n97, 61n102

MPOTEK case 75

multilateralism 78n195

multinational businesses 27–28

multinational enterprise theories 5, 8, 12

multiple point of entry (MPOE) 199; and bank resolution 191–193

MyTravel case 151–152

narrow protection of informal restructuring 112–113

national insolvency law regimes 4–5; protocols 130–132; unharmonized law 5

networks 35–36, 90; *see also* business networks

no-creditor-worse-off principle 189–190, 201; Cypriot bank resolution 190–191

non-contractual relationships 23–25

non-financial corporate groups: comparison of corporate preventive insolvency mechanisms and bank recovery and resolution plans 179–183; cross-border insolvency and rescue 4–5; preventive methods 181–183

non-governmental organizations (NGOs) 150

Northern Rock 2

opt-out mechanism 7; of group coordination proceedings 136, 136–138, 153, 155–156

Orderly Liquidation Authority (OLA) 176, 177, 185, 189–190, 191

ownership 28

parent companies 28; control of subsidiaries 38, 88; head office functions 39–40; transfer of knowledge to subsidiaries 36

pari passu principle 174, 175, 189–190, 201; Cypriot bank resolution 190–191

planning proceedings 133

pre-insolvency procedures 106

pre-insolvency rights 23

pre-pack sale 6, 7, 56, 102n344, 103, 106, 158, 159–160, 161n157; administrators 160–161; court approval 161; drawbacks of 127; group 122–124, 126–130, 152; recovery rate 129–130n147

pre-pack scheme 186, 196

preparation of recovery and resolution plans 181–182

preservation of going concern value 17–21, 23, 27, 44; economic account of 17–18; territorialism versus universalism 80–82; traditionalist approaches 18–21

preventive restructuring procedures 199; comparison with bank recovery and resolution plans 179–183; directors' duties 165–169

Primacom Holding GmbH case 121

priority ranking of creditors 46

private restructuring 4n21, 111–112, 113

problems of harmonization of insolvency law: danger of being captured 148–152; regulatory competition 143–146; relationship to other laws 146–148

procedural consolidation 8, 9, 43, 44, 45, 46, 86, 133; *ex post* approach by CoMI interpretation 100–101; *ex post* approach by forum shopping 102–104; implications of MCG theories on 87–90

protocols 10, 130–132

Public Prosecutor v Segard case 84

purposive interpretation approach 154

re Bluebrook Ltd case 151–152

Re MG Rover Espana SA case 81

Re Nortel Networks SA case 52

Re Standford International Bank Ltd case 75–76

Re Zlomrex International Finance SA case 58

recommendation for group coordination proceedings 153–156

redistribution 17; non-insolvency mechanisms 26

refinancing, cross-collateralization 140

regulatory competition 142–143n53; and harmonization of insolvency law 143–146

regulatory view on forum shopping 62–63
rehabilitation function of insolvency law 24n81
renegotiation of debt agreements 6, 124–126
reorganization 17–18; of banks 177–178; group-wide 134–135; non-insolvency mechanisms 26; strategic behaviours 22–23
rescue 17, 106; company 16; corporate 15–16; informal 106
resolution 11, 198–199, 201; bail-in 184–187, 188, 189; of MCG insolvency 4–5; minimum requirements for own funds and eligible liabilities (MREL) 189–191; SPOE approach 191–193; tools 184–188; *see also* Cypriot bank resolution
Resolution College 195
resolution plans 181
resolution rules 4–5
resolvability 181
resource dependence theory 37
resource-based theory 32n133; going concern value 13–14; of MCGs 31–33
restructuring law 58, 111n35; comparison of corporate restructuring tools and bank resolution tools 183–184; *see also* Directive on preventive restructuring frameworks
roll-up 139–140

sale of business tool 184
Schefenacker case 57–58, 57n80
schemes of arrangement 115n62, 120–122, 120n93, 125–126, 186
secondary proceedings 65–66, 82, 97n319, 101
Securities Investor Protection Act (SIPA) 191
senior creditors 158; in group coordination proceedings 139–140, 141–143; inter-creditor agreements 123
shadow directors *see* directors' duties
shareholding 147n81
single point of entry (SPOE) 176, 199; and bank resolution 191–193
Single Resolution Board 193
Single Resolution Mechanism Regulation 2
single resolution mechanism (SRM) 171
single-point-of-entry mechanism 5

stakeholders 19; protection of during insolvency proceedings 23–25; and strategic behaviours 22
statutory definition of CoMI 67–70
stay power 174
strategic behaviours 22; uncertainty of 22–23; value-decreasing 22n66
subsidiaries 6–7, 28, 31–32, 87; autonomy of 37–38, 89; of banks 181; business network perspective 9, 34–36, 88; centre of main interest (CoMI) 9, 87–88, 89–90; change of roles 88–90; circular holding in a chain structure 28–29; embeddedness 34n147; opt-out mechanism of group coordination proceedings 7; parent companies 28; pre-pack sale 160–161; transfer of knowledge 35–36; transfer schemes 187–188; value creation 38–39
substantive consolidation 42–43, 44
suspect period 63
synthetic secondary proceedings 98–99
systemic risks 188
systemically important financial institutions (SIFIs) 171, 173, 174, 175, 177, 180, 195, 196; bailouts 172

temporary administrators 183
territorialism 8, 46, 47, 48–49, 48n14, 67, 81n216, 201; ability to preserve value 80–82; certainty-forum shopping 82–84; cooperative 9; drawbacks 85
theoretical views of corporate rescue 12–13; debate on certainty of insolvency law 21–27; debate on the preservation of going concern value 17–21; going concern value 13–17; knowledge-based theory 13–14; resource-based theory 13–14
theoretical views on forum shopping 55
tort law 26n89
total loss absorbing capacity (TLAC) 189
traditionalist approaches 18–19, 20, 21–22, 24n81
transaction costs 30–31
transfer of knowledge, between subsidiaries 35–36
transfer of registered place 60–61, 79
transfer schemes 122–123, 187–188
transfer tools 186
transparency, of insolvency proceedings 63–64
treaties 48n15

234 *Index*

Treaty on the Functioning of the European Union, freedom of establishment 60

unbounded rationality 30
uncertainty 30; of loan contracts 17; of strategic behaviours 22–23
UNCITRAL Model Law 5; on cross-border multinational enterprises insolvency 162–164; directors' duties 169–170
unclear group CoMI rule 99–100
unharmonized insolvency law 5, 198
uniformity of insolvency law, and capture theory 148–152
United Kingdom: Bank Recovery and Resolution Directive (BRRD) 177; Banking Act (2009) 176; Brexit 3–4; Cork Report 2; cost of bankruptcy proceedings 54–55n60; directors' duties in 166–167; EIR Recast, applicability of 4; HIH case 52–53; Insolvency Act (1986) 119, 127–128, 140n41; jurisdictional examination 64–65;

schemes of arrangement 115n65, 120–122; substantive consolidation 42
United States: bank resolution 185; chapter 11 16; Dodd-Frank Act 176, 185; regulatory competition 143–144; substantive consolidation 42
universal proceduralism 47–48, 95–100
universalism 8, 45, 47, 49–54, 67, 177, 200, 201; ability to preserve value 80–82; and bank resolution 191; certainty-forum shopping 82–84; modified 9, 51–54, 81, 84; protection of foreign creditors 51n36
unsecured creditors 13, 22, 130, 188

value creation 32n133; in subsidiaries 38–39
value-decreasing strategic behaviors 22n66
Virgós-Schmit Report 67–68
virtual territoriality 86, 98

West Mercia Safetywear Ltd v Dodd 167
Wind Hellas case 102–103

Zlomrex International Finance SA 58